# JOSEPHINE
# HERBST

# JOSEPHINE HERBST

*by*
Elinor Langer

**MECHANICS' INSTITUTE**

*An Atlantic Monthly Press Book*
LITTLE, BROWN AND COMPANY · BOSTON · TORONTO

FIRST EDITION

Portions of this book appeared in *Grand Street* and *Ms.*
Excerpts from *An Ethnic at Large* by Jerre Mangione. Reprinted
by permission of G. P. Putnam's Sons. Copyright © 1978 by
Jerre Mangione.

The Maxwell Anderson poems: Copyright © 1983 by Gilda Anderson, Alan Anderson, Terence Anderson, Quentin Anderson
and Hesper Anderson. ALL RIGHTS RESERVED: All inquiries
for the use of the poems, "Evening" and "Grief Castle," in any
manner whatsoever should be addressed to the author's agent,
Harold Freedman Brandt & Brandt Dramatic Department, Inc.
at 1501 Broadway, suite 2310, New York, New York 10036.

LIBRARY OF CONGRESS CATALOGING IN PUBLICATION DATA
Langer, Elinor,
  Josephine Herbst.

  "An Atlantic Monthly Press Book."
  Includes bibliographical references and index.
  1. Herbst, Josephine, 1892–1969—Biography.
  2. Authors, American—20th century—Biography.
  3. Radicals—United States—Biography.  I. Title.
PS3515.E596Z75  1984      813'.52  [B]      84–2910
ISBN 0-316-51399-7

ATLANTIC-LITTLE, BROWN BOOKS
ARE PUBLISHED BY
LITTLE, BROWN AND COMPANY
IN ASSOCIATION WITH
THE ATLANTIC MONTHLY PRESS

MV

*Designed by Patricia Girvin Dunbar*

*Published simultaneously in Canada
by Little, Brown & Company (Canada) Limited*

PRINTED IN THE UNITED STATES OF AMERICA

For Josie's Friends

# Contents

CONTENTS

# A Letter from
# Josephine Herbst

Dear Mary & Neal,

*... I went to see the Madrid movie alone. ... I am afraid that I wept most of the time during the picture and couldn't stop. I found it almost unbearable and yet I would not have missed it for anything. There was a brief shot of my friend Gustav Regler, now dead, who was political commissar of the XI Brigade. One of Hans Kahle, the commander of the XI whose signed photo I have, but in general it was the subject and the incidents which counted. Separate individuals were not featured except those wonderful photographs of Lorca and Unamuno. They also showed scenes of the men in the line learning to write which is one of my impressive memories for they were hard at it, in front line bunks, and showed me proudly their efforts. They wrote in little blue books of the kind we used to use in college for exams. One of their lines was "The cause of the proletariat shall triumph." They were also proud of being able at last to write their names. The scenes from the Jarama & the Guadarrama where I had often gone were the real thing all right. The Guernica scenes — the farewell to the children — and at the end it IS the International Brigade going off with the population running alongside and the flowers, but then also the Spanish women and children hurrying over the mountains to escape Franco's revenge.*

*I wouldn't have wanted anyone I knew to be seated near me, not unless they too had gone through the same experience. I not only felt as if I were dying but that I had died. And afterward, I sat in the lobby for a good while, trying to pull myself together, smoking, and the whole scene outside, and on the street when I got there, seemed completely unreal. I couldn't connect with anything or feel that it meant anything, somewhat in the same way that I had felt when I got down from the plane in Toulouse after I flew out of Barcelona and had expected to enjoy ordering a real lunch for a change and instead sat sobbing over an omelet — all I could bear to try to eat — and wine — and looking at people calmly passing by as if I had entered into a nightmare where the "real" world had suddenly been wiped off with a sponge and vanished forever. And actually, sitting in the lobby, smoking, it came to me that in the most real sense my most vital life did indeed end with Spain. Nothing so vital, either in my personal life or in the life of the world, has ever come again. And in a deep sense, it has all been a shadow picture for years and years. In Toulouse, though the war had not yet ended, I knew it would end and with defeat. And that nothing was going to stop World War II. Nothing. And most of the time since then has been lived on buried treasure of earlier years, on a kind of bounty I could still take nourishment from, and I suspect that the kind of dwindling I have come to feel is due to the lack of enough vital elements streaming in events and circumstances. It is all too repetitive, and too terrible, with no lessons ever learned. Yet, grim as my view has come to be, I think it absolutely necessary, to continue on any line available, the harassment and the protest. . . .*

*Thursday, Erwinna, Pa., February 17, 1966.*

# PART ONE

# INTRODUCTION

# "If in Fact I Have
# Found a Heroine . . ."

JOSEPHINE HERBST was dead four years before I heard of her, a handful of ash in an Iowa cemetery, her grave not yet marked. Her exit was noted by *The New York Times* and *The New York Review of Books,* which is more than you could say about her existence much of the time, but blaming the reviewers would be too simple, for if she was not among the saved in the literary sense, she was in the personal, and there they were by her bedside, the cast of characters of several disastrous decades, distinguished critics of culture and art, writers great and small, radicals and former radicals of every degree of hope and despair, as awed by the spirit of her dying as they had been by the spirit of her life. Toward the end she wasn't writing very much. She kept her memoirs with her at all times, and even as late as the last few days she liked to think she would finish them at last, but by then it was as much the memories for their own sakes as it was the achievement she was after, and there were readier avenues to memory than the exhausting struggle with art. Her past drifted across her consciousness and occasionally across her lips. She had spent the last few weeks even physically surrounded by the past, preparing her personal papers for the university archives that now seemed her likeliest guarantor of posterity and settling a number of old scores via marginal comment as she did so. Every now and then an opinion or two escaped her. Frightened as she was by the ordeal of her body, from the outside she looked almost as impressive as ever. Propped up in bed, hair combed by a friend, a nineteenth-century novel resting heavily on her frail chest, she dictated a letter to a distant relation who had sent his final greetings to the hospital. "I cannot pretend any of this is easy, nor that I know the outcome," she began, in the tone of apparent confession she had brought to perfection in her later writings, but the outcome was as certain as nature. It was 1969, she was seventy-seven years old, and she had seen very many people die before her. I was much younger than that, I had seen very little, and I knew nothing whatever about it at the time.

In 1973, when I first heard of Josephine Herbst, I was living by myself in a small town in Vermont and teaching at a small college — ordinary enough situations as far as the eye could see — yet what I appeared to be doing and what I was doing were two different things because, like so many people I knew then, I was in retreat from the radical movement of the 1960s, and in reality I was spending most of my time mulling over what had happened to the movement, and to myself, and why. I knew, of course, that mine was not the first radical generation to rise and founder, as I hoped it would not be the last, at least to rise, and to the extent that it was possible in my immediate circumstances I included in my brooding and my browsing as much of the literature of the 1930s as I was able to find — something I had always done, more or less, because the 1930s had felt like family history to me even before the "New Left" was born, but which I now pursued with a greater urgency than ever before. On a visit to Chicago, in a secondhand bookstore, on a shelf labeled "Marxism," I found a collection of essays by participants in the events of the 1930s called *As We Saw the Thirties*, and I bought it as a matter of course. The essay on literature had been written by Granville Hicks, and in it, along with praise for other neglected fiction of the period, was a small, inviting reference to a trilogy by Josephine Herbst. Not much — "three excellent titles and three excellent books" depicting the decline of the middle class was all he said — but it was enough to send me to the university library the following morning and home with the novels that very day.

My notes from my first reading of the trilogy are a cross between a sigh of relief and a shout of joy: as if I were a traveler who had somehow gotten detached from my party, and Josephine Herbst were the rescuer sent out to bring me home. They look like one extended quotation: as if I were so taken with what I was reading I had to copy it in my own hand to prove to myself it wasn't going to go away. The decades between when the trilogy was written and when I was reading it simply fell away from me as I held it in my hands and I felt as if a conversation brusquely terminated with the turn of the 1970s had suddenly been renewed, for it was a radical reenactment of American history from the Reconstruction era almost to the outbreak of World War II, and it took place within a political and intellectual framework I then completely shared. Of my lit-

4

erary reactions I was far less certain. I felt that if Herbst were forgotten there had to be a reason for it, and the reason was no doubt some literary defect beyond my aesthetic powers to comprehend. In my judgments, therefore, I attempted to be reserved, searching for the lapses that would have put her beyond the literary pale, but, though she wrote in a political spirit which I understood was unfashionable, it never diminished her emotional power. For sheer absorption, for identification, I felt as I had at no other time in my life except when I read *The Golden Notebook*, and the closest time before that was probably reading *Little Women*. A mysterious kinship linked me with this female stranger as if not only our blood but the cells of our marrow were somehow matched. In the cyclone cellar of the wood frame house where the heroine, Anne Wendel, recounted her family's epic, there were not four wide-eyed little girls, her daughters, but five. When the cottonwood trees bent double in the author's stories I heard the wind racing across the Iowa prairie, and when the Great Depression bent the backs of the farmers as the wind bent the trees, I called out with her to them, Rise, Rise. From the briefest appearance of a marginal character I knew that character's heart as well as I knew my own, and as for the major characters, the Wendel sisters, they could well have been — I felt they were — my friends. That the trilogy was autobiographical I did not doubt from the beginning. That it left things out I did not understand until closer to the end. But who was the woman who was its author? How could it be that I, who wished my father had stalked the barricades of Spain so that I could attend reunions of the Abraham Lincoln Brigade: who envied my red-diaper-baby friends the warmth and security of their extended families: who claimed the radicals of the 1930s as my rightful ancestors and for years had pored over their histories as faithfully as any daughter of the other revolution had ever studied her family tree: How could it be that I had never heard of Josephine Herbst?

Over the next weeks, as I followed the question further, the intensity of my interest did not lessen but increased, for I quickly discovered that far from having been only a minor figure whose trilogy was one of those singular emanations of the 1930s, Josephine Herbst was a substantial writer with a productive career spanning half a century, from the little magazines of Europe and New York in the 1920s to the international literary quarterlies of the 1950s and '60s, with more than a hundred pieces of fiction, criticism, journalism and memoirs — as well as several other novels and a biography — in between. Of the work which I was able to locate immediately, the fiction was remarkable particularly for its modern representations of women; the journalism was breathtaking in the daring and skill it had taken to get it and in the vividness of the human images it evoked; the criticism had obviously been written by a great student and lover of literature; and as for the memoirs, they were as

5

graceful in prose and as rich in substance as any I had ever encountered. That as a person she had had considerable standing I learned from a tantalizing obituary in *The New York Times* which included her acquaintances as part of her achievements. "JOSEPHINE HERBST, NOVELIST AND SOCIAL-POLITICAL REPORTER, DEAD," announced the five-column headline.*

> Josephine Herbst, the novelist and critic, died yesterday of cancer at New York Hospital. She was 71 years old.
>
> Although best known for the novels she published in the nineteen-thirties, Miss Herbst enjoyed a long and highly diverse literary career. In recent years, she was active as a critic and memoirist. In the thirties, in addition to her fiction she published a great deal of social and political reportage; and in the twenties, she had been part of the expatriate circle in Germany and France that contributed to Transition and other avant-garde journals of the period.
>
> Radical politics and modern literature were the dominant interests of Miss Herbst's career, but she also had a passionate concern for natural history, and her last published book was "New Green World" (1954), a study of John and William Bartram, the 18th-century American naturalists.
>
> Miss Herbst was born in Sioux City, Iowa, on March 5, 1897. She received an A.B. degree at the University of California at Berkeley in 1919 and the next year moved to New York.
>
> Her first literary job was as a reader for a group of magazines, including the Smart Set, supervised by H. L. Mencken and George Jean Nathan. From this point onward, Miss Herbst was in the thick of the literary and political travails of the next two decades.
>
> She went to Europe for the first time in 1921, living in Germany during the political and cultural turmoil of the Weimar Republic. Three years later, in Paris, she met the American writers associated with Transition — Ernest Hemingway, who remained a close friend for many years; Robert McAlmon, Nathan Asch, and the novelist John Herrmann, to whom Miss Herbst was married in 1925. (They were later divorced.)
>
> Her first novel, "Nothing Is Sacred," was published in 1928, and her second, "Money for Love," a year later.
>
> In the decade after the Wall Street crash, Miss Herbst divided her time between periods of travel and political journalism and periods of sustained writing at her country home in Erwinna, Pa. In 1930, she attended the Second World Conference of the International Union of Revolutionary Writers in Kharkov, the Soviet

* See Notes.

Union, and the next year covered the Scottsboro case for the New Masses.

Thereafter she reported on Iowa farm strikes for Scribner's magazine, and joined a committee of writers (including Theodore Dreiser and John Dos Passos) investigating terrorism in the Kentucky coal fields.

But Miss Herbst's most spectacular journalistic feats of the period were her reports from abroad. In Cuba during the 1935 general strike, she visited Oriente and Realengo 18, said to be the first "soviet" in America. In 1935 she returned to Germany and wrote extensively about Hitler's regime for The New York Post and The Nation. In 1937, she went to Spain, one of the few women correspondents allowed to report from the frontline villages.

As Harvey Swados observed in his study "The American Writer and the Great Depression," published in 1966, "She had the knack of being in the significant place at the crucial moment, and of being on a footing of comradely equality with many of the most important figures of the day."

Meanwhile, Miss Herbst continued to publish fiction. Her trilogy of novels, "Pity Is Not Enough," was frequently compared to Dos Passos's "U.S.A." by critics of the period. . . .

In recent years, Miss Herbst had been at work on a volume of memoirs, which had become eagerly sought after in the New York publishing world. Her friendships with many of the most important American writers from the twenties to the present led to an immense correspondence. A few months ago she established an archive of her voluminous personal papers at Yale University.

Miss Herbst received a grant from the National Institute of Arts and Letters in 1966 and last year served on the fiction jury of the National Book Award.

She is survived by a sister, Mrs. Alice Hansen of Vienna, Va.

The funeral will be private.

Yet her literary reputation was nonexistent. She was not mentioned by Edmund Wilson, she was not mentioned by Maxwell Geismar, she was not mentioned by Matthew Josephson, she was not mentioned by Malcolm Cowley. As far as the classics of American criticism were concerned, she had never lived. Alfred Kazin, author of an eloquent and loving eulogy to her published in *The New York Review of Books* in 1969, in his famous 1942 study of American writing, *On Native Grounds*, had dismissed her with two words: "desperate pedestrianism." She was in a number of anthologies of radical writers, and I found her — sometimes under the heading "Mrs. John Herrmann" — in a handful of other literary and political memoirs, but these references were usually anecdotal, focusing on the color of her eyes or her presence in the vicinity of others more famous, and, with a single scholarly exception, I did not find any serious discussion of her work anywhere. As for the work itself, essentially it had not survived her. Though it was retrievable here and there through various research devices, for all practical purposes it was out of print.

It is not as if I could not explain this. On the contrary, I could explain it far too readily. Josephine Herbst was not only an innate feminist whose strong female characters consistently had a central place in her writing, leading male critics, to whom they were therefore invisible, to conclude that her writing was about nothing. She was also, it appeared, an unshakable leftist, which would have tainted her politically as well. She was thus a victim not only of the patriarchal literary establishment but also of the cultural anti-Comintern pact whose adherents had governed American letters since the end of World War II, and — now that I was thinking about it — weren't those groups pretty much the same? Even the contradiction between her personal reputation and her professional obscurity could have a political interpretation, for what more classic an illustration of the dilemma of the feminine eminence could there be than her friendships with all the distinguished literati who came to call at her house in the country, yet did not discuss her work? Certain that there was no problem in interpretation, for I had solved the puzzle already, I arranged to write an article about her for a feminist magazine, but something was unsettling about it, right from the beginning. The very people to whom from a distance I attributed her extinction were surprisingly friendly on the telephone. Critics, editors, publishers, and writers from whom I felt myself divided by all the suspicions of a recently polarized era unburdened themselves to me with real feeling when I asked about Josephine Herbst and kept me on the telephone, sometimes for hours, pouring out detail after detail they knew about her life, as if she had been an enormous traveling camera and it was her eyes they were using to scan the surface of the earth backward and forward through time. What it was like in Berlin during the 1920s . . . The Hemingway circle in Paris . . . the farm strikes in Iowa during the Depression . . . even her personal tragedies: they seemed to know it all. "There was the time when . . ." and out would follow a long intimate story. "There was the story that . . ." It seemed to go on and on. The people who had cast themselves at her feet, by their own telling — it was hard for me to believe even while hearing it, while my questions about her work brought forth not so much criticism as a strangely uncomfortable silence. Whether it was because the woman was so poor and isolated and had no plumbing in her old stone farmhouse — a fact I was told with peculiar frequency — and they were uneasy about the degree of human assistance they had given or not given her; whether it was because she was publicly neglected and they did not sincerely respect her as a writer, much as they enjoyed her company; whether politics had torn them asunder and now they regretted it — this I could not tell: but that the friends of Josephine Herbst were far from finished with her — of that I was already sure. Far from being supercilious or indifferent, they appeared to be deeply involved. If the elements of the story were aligned as I had supposed them with the literary establishment the victimizers, Herbst the vanquished, and myself the avenger, what accounted for my sense of being initiated into an inner circle where the connections had carried such feeling that, years after her dying, they were still producing real pain? Between my assumptions and their emotions there was clearly some sort of disjunction, and I did not know quite what it was.

Undeterred by these intuitions, and intending to limit my effort, within a short time after I began, I completed an article on her work and its vicissitudes which explained in a largely political context how it was possible that the work, though not the woman herself, had become obscure. Not long afterward, I received the following reply:

> A number of editors have now read your article and there's a general consensus that she's a fascinating woman, that her politics and her writing merit our attention, but that she's not brought to life in the article. I think that would not be a difficult thing for you to do, if you wish to. And I hope you wish to, because I'd very much like to publish you and Herbst. Let me know how you feel about some rewrite.

"Her politics and her writing merit our attention." Nothing could have offended me more. So much more substance had Herbst's politics and writing than the politics and writing of the journal in question that when I imagined them weighing whether she merited their attention, I felt that the tables ought to have been turned. I knew what the editors meant by "life." A superficial combination of personal description and social gossip. That's what they meant by "life." It was not my style. Even the "cornflower blue eyes" that had appeared in my manuscript was a concession to their taste for externals I had anticipated in advance. It was her work I was writing about, I had said it was her work, and her work was all it legitimately could be about. It was republication, not resurrection, I was after. I could not raise her ghost. Dashing off a private proclamation asserting as an elementary tenet of feminism the validity of discussing a woman in terms of her work alone, I withdrew the article from consideration and sent it next to a liberal magazine with whose editors I had also been in contact during the course of my research.

"[Your article] leaves out a lot about [her] that it is important for the uninstructed reader to know," they responded.

9

Who were her friends (Katherine Anne Porter? Maxwell Anderson?) Who did she run with? What was her life like? The piece as written seems to be light on this kind of thing and there is no reason why the reader should know if you don't tell him.

In principle [we are] most interested in a piece on Herbst and would be glad to work with you in shaping this piece to [our] desire. . . . But [we] think you should know that all of us . . . think you put a bit too much weight on the political side of the scales. The Josephine Herbst case is worth opening up; but we're not persuaded that ideological concerns were *primarily* responsible for her eclipse. [We] think it is worth venturing the suggestion that the political issue interests *you* more than it did *her.*

If I had been trying to capture in a phrase the shallowness that I believed lay at the heart of the literary community, I could hardly have bettered that "Who did she run with?" "The political issue interests *you* more than it did *her.*" That was simply wrong. It misunderstood not only Herbst but the entire generation of writers of which she was a part. "Shaping this piece to their desire." I would be no copywriter for their tepid entertainments. I was indignant. But, then, I was frequently indignant. Indignation, in fact, had been one of the principal sources of my work. No bottomless well, I was beginning to see, a surface spring in increasing danger of running dry, not a profound source, but a source. I was also intellectually intrigued. The objections of the two sets of editors seemed similar, and both seemed roughly in accord with what appeared to be the verdict of history. Since both raised issues I thought I had successfully argued in the article, I had to conclude that my case for Josephine Herbst had failed to make its points. But why? When I tried to fathom what was wrong with it exactly, I found myself at an impasse.

The more I thought about it, the more it appeared to me that the aspect of my writing about Josephine Herbst the editors found lacking was related to whatever it was in her writing that they and others also found lacking, but that I admired. It had to do with the relationship suggested between the individual and society. One possibility, therefore, was that Josephine Herbst and I were right and everyone else was wrong. Common to her critics and mine was the absence of an understanding of life that included politics. "The present phase that tends to the compulsive presentation of people as isolated moral atoms without any sensible relation to society or the ideas of their times ought to have departed before this," she had written in *The Nation* in the 1950s, but here it was, so many years later, and the same situation was still upon us. As a radical it had been her ambition to understand people in relation to the social forces that affected them — as it had been my ambition in relation to her — but it was a transient sensibility, in or out according to conditions of the moment, and ever since the beginning of the Cold War it had been largely out. It was precisely as she had so frequently argued. The belief in society as a nexus between the individual and eternity which had characterized her own generation, characterized, indeed, all writers who were not mystics since the dawn of literacy in the West, which was far deeper than the partisan expedience to which it was often attributed, and which tended to recur, was simply gone, vanished, wiped away in the recoil against the radical '30s which had accompanied the end of World War II. In its place was a new consensus so insistent that our true dilemmas were either existential or private that to emphasize cultural over individual factors in the explanation of anything had become subversive. If society was out, personality was in. Idiosyncrasy was the order of the day. To revive the reputation of Josephine Herbst in a period so hostile to her convictions was beyond my powers, and I should relax about it. Another turn of the wheel of history and it would be another story.

Possibility two was the opposite. They were right and we were wrong. It was true I was annoyed by the cloying question "What was her life like?", but I had to admit to myself that I thought I had told them what her life was like simply by describing her career. What we disagreed about was life. I said life was about history and politics. They said it wasn't. But mine was, or at least I had wanted it to be — and so, evidently, had Josephine Herbst. What was the stuff of life to us was only business as far as others were concerned. Beyond history, beyond politics, was a flesh and blood woman whose life attracted friends and strangers alike, and I was contented with a facsimile. The force of being of the woman herself, her interplay with circumstances, her own contributions to the making and unmaking of her destiny — all this I barely acknowledged. The implications of the argument were not so much ideological as they were personal. Beneath the criticism of my article was a criticism of myself which might be useful for me. It was time to open myself up to complexities of existence beyond what I had previously imagined. I was the one who was missing something.

I put the manuscript away with no further interest in publishing it and returned to my teaching, but a substantial correspondence followed, and if my thoughts continued to dwell on her, it appeared I was not alone. "I found your account of [her] novels quite fine (to the extent that it *was* an account of her novels), but the account of her life and personality, while not exactly wrong, was — well, pious," wrote one of her friends in a frank three-page letter so filled with information about matters ranging from her most personal relationships to her most intellectual tastes that I found myself longing for more. "Everything is more complicated than your piece makes it out to be," he maintained. "Without putting her work down in the least, I did love *her* — and if I never re-read the novels it was to avoid any embarrassment between us," declared another gently, adding that whatever his differences with my article, he would urge, would even implore me, to go on. My errors, my insinuations, my politics, my naiveté — it seemed nothing would drive them away. There appeared to be a Herbst Committee of Elders actively guarding her memory, and I was mysteriously welcome to join. Out of the exchanges and counterexchanges with the people who knew her in her later years, the idea of writing her biography gradually emerged. It was not at first an inviting prospect. Originally a journalist with an instinctive preference for impersonal subjects, I was not exactly a natural for the form. As a reader, I did not even like biography. The typical biographical sentence in my mind was something like "So and so was born in such and such, the eighth child of a remarkably felicitous union, and her birth was the source of much joy in the household because of the seven siblings six were male and the only daughter, Bernardine, then eighteen, had not been quite right since she had fallen from her horse Poky gamboling in the meadow a few years before." The next sentence either toted up the number of miscarriages, stillbirths, and infant burials borne cheerfully by the happy family, in which case the characters in question seemed so unlikely that not even the most thorough documentation could persuade me that they had actually lived, or else it consisted of a musty portrait gallery in which each of the ancestors appeared to have the same name and title as every other, and I was left with the feeling that everything would have been the same in the world if they hadn't — a feeling which extended to the biographer. Politically, too, I was dubious about it. It was such a bourgeois conception. In a biography, at least by convention, the character took center stage. There was no way in which historical events like wars, revolutions, or depressions could be treated with anything like the true impact they had on individual lives. If they were present at all, social forces were only also-rans, winds-of-change sweeping through every chapter while the heroine, or more often the hero, grew up, went to school, got married, whatever, as if all of his or her energy were coming from within. It must be true, as I was beginning to gather, that Josephine Herbst was something more than just a creature of the zeitgeist, but where would I find the balance? To write a biography with a heroine for whom those winds of change were the breath of life could only be a contradiction.

I am writing these words at a geographical place, at a moment in time, at a point in my own history so far removed from the time I first read the trilogy that it has gotten harder and harder of late for me to recapture the person I was when I began. To declare my present departures from my initial misapprehensions is not my intention. Protestations of newfound maturity are scarcely to be trusted, for one thing, and it would anticipate the pages that follow. Nor will I "summarize" Josephine Herbst. Biography is not taxonomy with the specimen to be re-classified according to the latest findings — it is the story of one life as seen by another, with both always growing and changing. The reader, like the writer, is entitled to discovery. A life is not an idea. But if I am not the young woman I once was, neither was Josephine Herbst the woman I first imagined her to be, and if in fact I have found a heroine, it is far from the one I expected when I started out. I am grateful to the earlier self who forged my link with Josephine Herbst in the first place, for I am not sure it would have happened later, but I am glad to have left her behind. To come to terms with what really happened to this woman in her lifetime, more than politics was required.

I am sitting at a long oak table in an old shingled house on the Oregon coast not far along the beach from Neskowin where Josephine Herbst first saw the ocean on a visit to her mother's brother at the age of six. The beach is wide and flat here and the ocean is calm, though the day is gray; the house is high on a cliff so that even the occasional walker who wanders by is far away. In front of the window is a wind-blown beach pine posing for my word photograph, its needled top in the backward position of a hand pointing, suddenly paralyzed, to the chair where I sit, staring out. The grasses are blowing, and occasionally there is a bird. I have a fire going in the fireplace. It is picturesque and lonely but I have come here for it to be picturesque and lonely because the unimpeded self-indulgence clears my thoughts. I think of Josie in her old stone house, night after night, as the snow piled higher. She lit herself a fire, but hers was for heat. She fixed herself dinner and served it up with a flourish on the old trestle table that John had made when things were still all right between them, and she looked around at the other possessions of their life together. She smoked one cigarette, she smoked another, she smoked a third, repopulating her empty chamber in the haze of the past. *"There became here and now was then"* she was writing in her memoir of the time on this very beach when her mother and uncle recounted their own histories by the light of the fire. It was just as true for her. The memories in her head and the memoirs on the table — they both offered company of sorts. When her meal was finished, she mixed up and baked some cookies and set them out to crisp for she was hoping for visitors on the weekend and she kept the jars filled when she could. The telephone was harder to hear lately, and anyway it was too expensive to use. She went outdoors to the outhouse and stood outside awhile, looking at the stars. The night was clear, but it was cold. It was still too early to go to sleep. She climbed the tiny stairway and as she did on most of these solitary nights sat leafing through her file drawers and making notes on the cardboard covers and the backs of envelopes. In Erwinna that day the calendar said March 5. "Your little Fifth of March." How often had she written home on her birthday, toting up the remembrances she had gotten and throwing in an extra package or two when the actual receipts had been too slim. How much Muddie loved her holiday letters. And Papa's peppermints. He never forgot. John remembered once. When was that? She got up from the floor, which was cold, and sat down at the typewriter to begin writing a letter. A consolation? An exegesis? A diatribe? Which would it be? When was it, exactly, that I became a biographer? I realize that of all the distances I have traveled since I began this work, the geographical distances are the ones that matter least.

# PART TWO

# THE LITTLE STRANDS
# AND TREES

# Magicians and
# Their Apprentices

SHE WAS BORN in Sioux City, Iowa, on March 5, 1892, in a tiny two-family house a few steps down the hill from the high clay bluffs below which the Missouri River runs its wide flat way across to Nebraska. Her parents, Mary Frey and William Benton Herbst, were strangers in town, Easterners, Pennsylvanians to be exact, American stock as old as it came at that time, respectable, but poor. William and Mary were distant cousins. William's people were small farmers and storekeepers in the rolling Pennsylvania countryside in the vicinity of Harrisburg, Mary's more prosperous landowners in the territory closer to Allentown. At least they had been prosperous, cultivators of a claim said to have been granted around 1700 by William Penn himself, but when her father had died, in debt, in the early years of Mary's childhood, leaving his wife to support their six young children on her own, there had been a dramatic fall. Mary's father, Joshua Frey, was a man who had earned the respect of his neighbors. Legislator, farmer, scrivener, and finder of water, he was also a surveyor who led parties of Swiss immigrants across the country to establish new homes, and it was on one such trip, in 1859, that he caught the typhoid that brought him down. His wife, Mary Ann Wieand, Josie's grandmother, had been an indentured servant when Joshua rescued her, bought her, in fact, or so goes the family story, carried her off to freedom on a white horse, and she was as tough as they come. Small, fiery, and headstrong, she knew English perfectly, but an idiosyncratic Pennsylvania Dutch German dialect was her language of command. When her husband died she took her children to Philadelphia where she set up shop with a borrowed sewing machine on the second story of a rented house, stitching uniforms for the Union Army, and she kept the family together. Photographs taken of her over the years reveal her shrinking in size but growing in determination. She outlived her husband by forty years, traveled back and forth across the country many times, speculated in property, and eventually took to painting landscapes. From her husband's death to hers, in 1900, she was never seen in public except in black.

With all the upheavals affecting her family, Mary did not have a conventional childhood. A romantic girl, strongly drawn to culture and books, between the interstices of the family's demands on her, she largely educated herself. She was always reading, Tolstoy, Shakespeare, Emerson, always quoting philosophy, always using her perceptions of the past or future to put a better light on the difficult present, and she was inclined to believe all she read. Nor was she only intellectually romantic. Mary's husband, William, always called "Bent," was not her first love. That place was held by a mysterious Englishman, John Gason, whom she had met while working as a telegrapher in Philadelphia to help keep the family going, and, incidentally, to gain a little freedom. Gason had charmed her, flattered her, wooed her, given her presents, and Mary believed she was engaged, but then he had vanished, it appeared to Australia, and she never heard from him again. For seven years she waited, thinking she would never marry, first at a Philadelphia boardinghouse, then at a new home in Vineland, New Jersey, where the family had moved without her. Hard times they were for her, too, longing to be on her own, yet sharing a household with her mother, sitting around helplessly lost in her own brooding while her youth passed her by. Mary's were not the only troubles in the family. Indeed, of the remaining offspring, it was hard to decide who was faring worst. Among the sisters, the oldest, Priscilla, had fallen ill and died of "brain fever" in 1873, and the youngest, Alice, was so consumed with wanting to marry she was practically ill herself. Among the brothers, Marcus, the oldest, had fallen in love with a married actress, the youngest, Daniel, was threatening to go on the stage, and the middle, Joseph, the one to whom Mary was closest, was in serious trouble with the law. "Poor Joe" was the family refrain in Mary's lifetime and "Poor Joe" it would be again, in her daughter's novels. He had gone South after the Civil War when he was only nineteen and had made a fortune, showering his family with expensive gifts, including, at one point, a Philadelphia town house, but how he made the money was a matter of some uncertainty, and in the general cleanup that followed the Reconstruction period he had had to go on the lam. He had joined them for a time in Vineland, disguised as a "hired man," but the authorities had become suspicious and he had had to sneak away. Now he was a fugitive again, pursuing the dollar in a mining claim in South Dakota under the name of "Victor Dorne." He had also suffered the loss of an eye. Mary had seen him last at a secret meeting in Canada, where she had brought him money and clothes. She thought about him often as she sat, sad and idle, on her mother's front porch, old before her time.

In the spring of 1882, stirring for the first time, she left Vineland and returned to Pennsylvania to visit the cousins in another branch of the family. While she was there, illness came over the household. First one, and then another, of the daughters died of typhoid. Mary was much taken with the brother, "Bent," on whom, along with her, the survivors were depending for comfort and understanding, and the emotion she felt surprised her with its seriousness and reality. It was not the grand passion she had felt for Gason, but she trusted it. Bent was a quiet, kind, unaggressive man with a thin face that narrowed at the chin and a drooping handlebar moustache that accentuated the narrows rather than concealed them. His hair, which was thin and brown, was slipping back to a point well behind a decent hairline already, at thirty-three. He had little money and less ambition. His idea of a satisfactory life, then and later, was a good smoke and a good newspaper and a comfortable chair set somewhere on the fringes of the family circle where the intensity could be avoided but the comedy could be observed. Mary, at twenty-seven, was beautiful and fresh. She had a headful of fine, coppery hair that glinted with the light, fair skin, and eyes so blue they were almost violet, flecked with yellow, like a cat's. She had emphatic features, a strong voice, a slender body, and a muscular hand. "If anyone had been sent to select a husband for me they most likely would never have chosen this one, you will think so too when you see him, but if I had had my choice out of the whole world I could not be better satisfied as regards his qualities," she wrote to a friend. As for Bent, he was more than satisfied, he was astonished that such a woman wanted to be his wife, but in not very long he had come to trust her, too. Appearances notwithstanding, it was more than Mary's last chance. She was attracted to him, and he to her. In the private understanding that constituted one of their married secrets, she was the sail and he was the anchor, she was the grasshopper and he was the ant, she was the flame and he would be the candle. Their relationship was sensual, durable, and profound. When they married, in 1883, they mated securely, and neither one of them ever had cause to doubt it.

Bent was "in the farm implement business": that is to say, he was a salesman. He traveled a large territory in western New York and eastern Ohio selling machinery to individual farmers on a commission basis, and he did not like his work. He was constantly on the road, upholding the interests of the manufacturers over the interests of his customers, whose company he preferred, and, now that he was a married man with a place to come home to, he wanted to see more of his wife. They lived at first in an apartment in Pittsburgh, so that Mary would be closer to his route, but when she became pregnant, in 1884, they agreed she ought to return to Vineland. Bent got there when he could, which was not often. "I find that it is quite possible to be happy & contented even if much that we longed & hoped for is denied us," Mary wrote to her brother Daniel, who had moved to Oregon, and she quoted Thackeray on the dissatisfaction that follows even the satisfaction of desire, but despite her philosophy, she was not very happy. Between the domination of her mother, the absence of her husband, and a struggle for money that had been part of her life for as long as she could remember, she was hardly living the life of her dreams. In the early years of the Herbsts' marriage, the talk was all of the West. Pamphlets, flyers, leaflets, ads, subsidized by the states and the railroads, were on every cracker barrel, every saloon counter, every empty railroad seat, implying that even an honest fellow could make a killing on the prairie. The late 1880s was the golden era of Iowa in general, Sioux City in particular. The town was in a phase of extravagant growth, self-glorification, and hope based on the defeat of a twenty-five-year grasshopper plague in the surrounding farmlands, the development of the packing industry, and an explosion of transportation including railroads, streetcars, cablecars, and the foundations of a permanent bridge across the Missouri River. And land. Always land. The sale and resale of land. The population grew from 600 in 1860 to 3,500 in 1870 to 7,500 in 1880 and to 38,000 in 1890, an exuberant, half-crazed boom population which every year from the late '80s on raised exotic, almost ritual harvest structures, palaces made of corn elaborated into the shapes of Arab mosques or Russian churches, to give thanks for the season's bounty — and attract the attention of eastern capital. The money to gain a foothold in this rising empire was not easy to come by, nor was a move without many risks, but such was the spirit of the moment that not to take a chance on the possibility of success seemed instead to be betting on the certainty of failure. In 1886 Bent visited Sioux City to survey the opportunities. "I'm greatly pleased with your [account], for I know that even if you were 'dead gone' on the place I could depend on your description being accurate. . . . You are not the kind to run wild with enthusiasm," Mary responded to one of his letters. But whatever their reservations, they decided to make the move. In 1888, Bent went out alone. He clerked for a while in an implement shop owned by someone else and then, with an acquaintance from the East, established a small farm equipment store of his own, Herbst & Hannam, in Sioux City's teeming commercial flats. He bought himself a ten-gallon hat. Mary came the next year, bringing their two daughters, Frances, who was five, and Alice, four.

Mary knew at once that she did not like Sioux City. The unpaved

streets caked not just her boots but her spirits, and the endless prairie did
not strike her as an invitation to a better life but as an offense against the
one she had known. If the town was crude, so were the neighbors: she
preferred not to go out among them. For a woman who had spent her
spare time reading the classics, it was not a very noble existence. She had
not yet made her peace with the dismal landscape or the crowded quarters or the aching unfamiliarity of being so far away when word came
which further absorbed her in family worry. It was about her brother Joe.
Now he was not only a pauper and nearly blind, he was also losing his
mind, and his heartless wife had had him committed to an institution. He
was an inmate in a state asylum in Yankton, South Dakota, communing
only with Jesus. Sioux City was not so far from Yankton, and in the fall of
1891 Mary went up on the train and brought her brother home. She was
pregnant at the time and the trip was difficult as well as sad. Her mother
came from Oregon where she had been visiting brother Daniel to take
her "Poor Joe" home to New Jersey and try to nurse him back to health.
Joe was shipped away around Thanksgiving, 1891, and died in Vineland
in January, 1892, after a fitful decline, a lot of which was spent arguing
with his mother over Jesus. Mary and Bent's third daughter was born six
weeks later looking unaccountably Iowan, a broad-faced healthy baby
with cornflower blue eyes and hair the color of an autumn hayfield who
her parents wished briefly, but only that, had been a boy. Josephine Frey
Herbst was the name she was given. She was named, of course, for Joe.

One of the first things she noticed was the smell of bread, and
throughout her life in foreign cities or alone in domestic ones its aroma
would fill her senses the way flowers draw bees and make her think of
Mary, but then again what wouldn't? Mary inhabited her daughter's life
as if both were characters in a single story, which in a way they were.
Josie was always thinking about her mother. In Erwinna, when she and
John Herrmann first moved there, it was her mother's lost Pennsylvania
household she was reestablishing. In Cuba, when she was lonely, she was
glad her mother wasn't there to see her sad. She rarely had a pleasant experience like walking through an olive grove in the country north of San
Francisco or visiting a village in the heart of the German forest without
wishing her mother could have it with her. In Spain, when she was hungry, she dreamed about the bread.

The Herbsts were tenants and they moved at the convenience of
their landlords but the houses of Josie's childhood were the same in their
essentials — small wooden structures with two to four rooms set onto
grassy plots barely big enough for the chickens, the outhouse, and the
woodpile. It was the kind of house — all their cottages were — where
doors creaked against handmade doorjambs as the children banged in
and out, the perfume of lilac mingled with the odor of food and sweet-

ened the air at the oddest moments, and the Guernsey cow, unpastured, rolled her neck freely with a clang as she walked to and fro on the yellow dirt road. It was a house of smells: the bread every day and jam in season, meat pies during the week and chicken on Sunday. It was a house of routine. It was a house of sounds and voices but it was Mary's voice mainly that Josie heard when she was young, a quiet, constant murmuring repeating to herself and her babe her sorrows for the past and her wishes for the future and all of her memories of the wonderful "East." For the first years of her life, Josie lived almost as an only child. Frances and Alice were already in school, Bent was always at work. She was alone with her mother for hours at a time, she clung to Mary's neck while Mary made the bread or jam or collected the eggs or dusted or swept or, when she could, just sat and rocked, suckling the little one and thinking about the East. It was a strong beginning to life, but from Josie's point of view, it must have seemed much too short. In June, 1895, when she was three, there was a new baby, Helen, who took over her spot in her mother's arms. Helen was the prettier of the two, prettier even than most children, wide-eyed, wide-browed, trusting and irresistible, a flirt from birth. Strangers stopped on the street to pass their fingers through her golden hair and turned their eyes upward murmuring "Angel," staring at Mary as at a Madonna, as she wheeled the carriage along its rutted way. Uncle Daniel, who should have known better, said, "The more children Mary has, the prettier they get, that little one is a daisy," when meeting both Josie and Helen for the first time, and Frances, who did know better and was doing it on purpose, said, "How pretty — wouldn't it look sweet on Helen," whenever Josie exhibited a sweater or ribbon to show off her own appearance, right through their teenage years. "Mother never called me precious names — used to hear her calling H. lamb — my precious lamb my baby — but never me. . . . I longed for words too. I said to H. You are my baby and I am mama's," reads a note Josie wrote when she was already grown, but if her heart burned with a childish rage at the presence of her sister in the place that had so recently been hers it was not something she was aware of then, for she converted her rage to love and she adored her beautiful sister, made her her "Pet" as she had been her mother's, cherished and protected and encouraged and supported her all her life. And Helen loved her back. The two were indispensable to one another. If Josie was the ideal big sister, always offering advice, Helen was the ideal little sister, always wanting it. Of all the members of the family, only Helen treated Josie with the respect she knew she deserved. Twinlike, the sisters shared the experience of childhood. They slept in the same bed, sat beside one another in the two-seated outhouse, concocted out of their shreds of experience in the world a shared version of what life was like so unified it was indivisible, so that Mary wrote Josie after Helen died, "You were like *one being* in so many things. *You and she knew.*" She might almost have included herself, because her youngest daughters wore their mother like an inner skin, and she them, and in the struggles that came to characterize the little household it was never a matter of two against two with the mother in the middle but of three against two with the mother on the side of the young ones. When night fell and her husband returned from work, Mary would quiet her quarreling daughters, and there was often quarreling to hush. It was a house where privacy was impossible and tensions among the children created drama as fascinating and significant as theater.

The older versus the younger. The two born in the East versus the two born in the West, with the pairs going opposite directions. Frances and Alice, uprooted in the move, rooting themselves in Sioux City. Josie and Helen, so rooted they were more or less trapped, scornful of Iowa's ways. Within the war of the teams was a war of the captains, Frances and Josie, in which Josie was always the loser because Frances was so much older. Dominating and difficult, Frances was a master of the small pains of childhood, spilling ink on the tablecloth before one of Josie's birthday parties, ruining her favorite blouse, and accidentally pressing down on her fingers with a rock when they were out in the garden one day looking for frogs. Frances' preference for her less competitive sisters was an open secret. What were the anxieties that led to Frances' behavior no one knew, but Mary had written Bent when Frances was very small, "she cannot help being born with a never ceasing & ever increasing unrest in her" and she grew more and more troubled throughout her girlhood. At the time of her graduation from high school she suffered a nervous collapse so serious that she lay prostrate in the living room for a period of some months, and everyone but Mary believed she would die. It was a frightening episode. Josie, guilty and scared, read to her every day. It was not until the transformation of Frances' personality that seemed to accompany her recovery and subsequent marriage that the warring sisters finally became friends. In the meantime, between Alice supporting Frances and Helen defending Josie, there was frequently something of a scene. . . .

The way I picture it (thanks largely to a draft of an unpublished memoir), an evening in the Herbst household, say around 1900, say on Center Street, might have looked something like this. Downstairs, in the living room, a group of teenagers is standing around the piano singing fervid Methodist hymns, only it isn't called the living room anymore, it is now "the parlor," for Frances and Alice have taken to reading Victorian literature and they have rechristened every room in the house. The piano is covered with photographs of their beaux and a heavy English plant-stand sits awkwardly and inappropriately in the tiny window. In the "butler's pantry," née kitchen, every pan is sticky with fudge, because fudge is the substance of communion in Sioux City, a holy food, and when Frances' boyfriend moved out of town she wrote in her diary "Today Robert Fliegel moved to Kansas City and on the anniversary of this day ever after I will make a pan of fudge and consecrate it to his memory" — meaning she would eat it all by herself. Josie and Helen are banished from the living room and then from the kitchen but their tiny bedroom is off the kitchen and it is hard for them to go to sleep. They think their sisters are absurd. They sneak upstairs in their flannel night-gowns in search of attention. Bent is dozing in a chair, which is all that he usually does do, and Mary is sewing or reading. Mary scolds them and welcomes them at the same time but secretly she is glad to see them, for she is just as estranged as they are from the scene downstairs and all she can get from Bent is his cheerful, mundane, "Don't worry, they'll out-grow it." Junior boosters, Mary thinks to herself. Social butterflies. Evan-gelicals. How did *she* get daughters like *that?* It was the preachers, she suspected, and not the preachings. Forbearance is all she can muster to her older daughters' insistent religion and not even that when they de-nounce their father and claim he will roast in hell for his one-night-a-week at the Royal Arcanum Lodge. They demand that he repent. Of what shall he repent? Mary asks. Of Adam's Fall. Papa is guilty of origi-nal sin. Then and only then Mary loses her temper, shaking with rage at their stupidity and asking don't they know a good man when they see one? "That his own daughters should quibble about the simple pleasure of a lodge evening for such a man was *ridiculous.*" Why their father was a man "whose honor was so much a habit he did not even know he pos-sessed it," and as far as she was concerned their Mr. Gladway, the rich deacon, was a perfect hypocrite, "passing the collection plate on Sunday and adulterating butter on Monday." Bring them in, bring them in, bring them in from the fields of sin, croon the singers downstairs. Mary and Bent were Unitarians, at heart agnostics. Why did she let Josie and Helen go to Sunday School? What if . . . ? It was not going to happen. Four Methodist daughters would be too many. Mary was a loving mother to all her girls and on many of the nights Josie and Helen came to her door she was up sewing for Frances and Alice who had an endless need for outfits. And there in her bedroom surrounded by snips of basting papers that re-minded Josie of worms, she indulged with the little ones in a feast of mu-tual cultivation, laughing at the narrow horizons of the teenagers downstairs, pressing the pedal down and up as she unveiled story after story for them from the Frey epic, always stressing independence, always asking the question "And what would have happened to us then and there if my mother hadn't been able to support us when Joshua died?" Down and up, down and up. There was tragedy in life: the story of Joe. Adventure and maybe even a little evil: the story of Jacob, her father's brother, who seduced the housemaids under the nose of his family, and died an "unrepentant drunkard, pouring liquor down his throat as long as he could swallow." Josie liked that one best. There was romance: the story of Gason, suitably transformed to end for the best in the present happy marriage. It is impossible to exaggerate the influence of Mary or her stories. In 1927, when Josie's husband visited Sioux City for the first time, Frances wrote Josie that all through their childhoods whenever there was a knock on the door she never opened it without the feeling it might be Gason returned from Australia, and she was so startled by the resemblance between John Herrmann and the Gason miniature that her first thought was that he had finally arrived. Josie's earliest published story was "The Elegant Mr. Gason." So closely were her life and work bound to her mother's stories that she appears almost to have experienced the two lives as one. When she titled her memoir of childhood "Magicians and Their Apprentices," it was her apprenticeship to her mother's magic that she had in mind. Compared to Mary the silent Bent was recessive in the extreme.

Night after night the stories continued, down and up, down and up. "Maybe you'll be a lawyer," Mary would say, pushing Josie's bangs back from her forehead and looking down at her intently, blue eyes into blue. "Or a legislator. Like my father." She criticized the neighboring women, who, she said, had marriage on the brain, and she spoke approvingly of the town's woman physician and of its women preachers. She was not excluding marriage. No. Marriage was a blessing, love was an opportunity, and children were the point of it all. She would glance significantly at her sleeping mate. That having everything would be difficult for her girls, Mary never seemed to realize, then or later. You could not call Mary impractical. She ran the house on very little money, she made everything her children wore, she invented gadgets — none of which ever sold — she "invested in real estate" — none of which ever made any money — and she did all she could to contribute to the accumulation of "capital" she was convinced would give the girls a start, though in this she did not succeed. Certainly she was not unintelligent. She kept up with her reading, as the children grew older she participated more and more in the cultural affairs of Sioux City, which she had not done in the years right after she arrived, and she always wrote interesting letters. But Mary was unrealistic and she drew her conclusions not from her experience, which was limited, but from her imagination, which was not. With Mary, although she did not know it, excitement always came first. Her typical letter is an affirmation of the emotional truth or pleasure at the heart of some experience coupled with a pallid and unconvincing moral injunction against it. When Josie wrote her from college that she had gone on a night picnic with a young man in a ravine, Mary replied, "Do you go *alone* with a young man on moonlight picnics in deep ravines? That sounds nice but surely it is not the thing to do." She would never deny that it was nice. Even a mere postmark could set her off. Once after a long letter to Helen filled with pieties about relations between the sexes and *"keeping the heart pure,"* she noticed that a letter she was forwarding was postmarked Spearfish, South Dakota. Suddenly she was writing, yes, there is a school there. She knew the spot. "It is in the Black Hills. Uncle Joe's country. How I have often longed to go there. Some day I shall get reckless and do all the things I have been debarred from doing all my life almost. Lovingly, Mother." The force of her attention was always on the side of the immediate. In a speech to the Sioux City Woman's Club left among her papers she began with a rational discourse on the position of women and ended up via internal logic at a different destination entirely, just as she would leave the dishes dirty or a pot bubbling on the stove to pick roses while the dew was fresh on them or watch rainbows form and fade across the river. Josie and Helen were both their mother's daughters and she was not a bad mother to be the daughters of. The legacy of her mother's belief in her was the greatest resource that Josie had. The worst you can say of Mary is that she was too large a character in a setting a little narrow for her talents. She tended to minimize circumstances. She implied too much was possible and she was not really worldly enough to understand the obstacles. When she told the family stories, she left the bad parts out.

# Shakespeare Avenue

TUCKED AWAY in the archives of the Sioux City Public Museum is a portrait of the entire first grade class of the Edith Everett Elementary School in 1898 and a grim sight it is, too — two dozen children in sober-looking outfits that must have weighed five pounds apiece, the girls draped in layers of generally dark material in almost military designs, black stockings, and boots, the boys in knickers, boots, and jackets, with only a rare dress or shirt appearing even tolerably bright. Josie is among the grimmest of the lot. She is a pretty enough child, despite the family comparisons, with an evenly proportioned face, bangs, and tenderly home-made curls, but she is standing near the center of the front row looking stolidly ahead as if she is determined to hold back tears, and her chin is thrust slightly forward and tensed. It was the same year that Mary took her brood on the train trip across the country to visit her family in Oregon that stood out for Josie later as the heart of the romance of childhood. From Salem the families of Mary and her brother Daniel crossed the mountains in an open wagon to spend the summer camping by the sea and many snapshots were taken as reminders. In most of them Josie's expression is much the same. Dangling on a fence in the middle of the forest, bending over a stream for a glimpse of a speckled trout, listening to the roar of her beloved ocean with her bloomers filled with sand, or simply standing with the others in an ordinary family group, she is wide-eyed but miserable-faced, her head often at a peculiar angle, her mouth set into a sickly smile or literally cast downturned. What is striking about all these photographs is the effort involved in the poses. Instead of looking like a little girl, she looks like a little girl trying to look like a little girl, which is to say, insincere. The distance between the virtuous child she was attempting to portray and the actual emotions she was struggling to contain reflected a schism in Josie's nature she never overcame, though her performances improved with time. The first act of Josie's lifetime was the play "A Happy Childhood." Aged six, she was on a stage.

If there was a division in Josie's nature, Sioux City was a mirror, if not the cause. It, too, was interested in appearances. Barely past the frontier era during the years Josie was growing up there, it was a community that put on airs. Like the false faces of its flimsy storefronts, its culture was largely facade. It is as if by their refined tones and elaborate dress the citizens hoped to call forth the blessings of the gods of civilization, as the Indians by their costumes and rituals had hoped to win the favor of the gods of rain, sun, and war. The Indians and the buffalo were not long gone from the prairie, nor the outlaws from the streets of town. When the Herbsts arrived there were more saloons than churches, more whorehouses than schools, more breweries than anything. Life in the flatland alleys called "the Soudan," after African seamen, and "Hell's half acre," was vicious, and business was good. The minister brought in to clean it up died in a pool of his own blood, shot down from behind as he was unhitching his horse. Nature was vicious as well. There were periodic catastrophes: blizzards and fires and cyclones and floods. Against all this the "better element" which eventually triumphed set up a constrained unnatural life. It is as if the men and women of the second generation were denying the pioneer days, denying the blood of the Indians, denying the bones of the 100-foot-long plesiosaurus dug up close to the surface of the land just across the river in Ponca, Nebraska. Their building styles came from everywhere, Constantinople to Oz: there is something poignant in the very bluff and variety of their eclectic mansions and fantastic monuments: the gallantly concealed insecurity of people who had been uprooted so many times, chased so many dreams, that they no longer knew where they were. Their manners came from the cultivated eastern seaboard. Their governing commandment was "Thou Shalt Be Refined." It was a town of boosters and joiners. Everyone belonged within the pattern of clubs, lodges and churches that platted community life as the maps had platted the prairie. With the passing of the frontier, the economic depression of the early 1890s, and the swelling of foreign immigration, social pressures steadily increased. The Sioux City of Josie's girlhood was not a good place to be different.

The schools were where the crooked were to be made straight and the rough places plain. Given the fact that one of the principal purposes of education was to instill obedience, it is perhaps not surprising that most of the little pupils, Josie included, did not enjoy it very much. Nor is there much to be said about it. In her memoirs she tells a story or two, but these lack the force of her recollections about her family, and there is no other record. What evidence there is points in one direction: she wanted to be like the others and, for the most part, she succeeded. In one of the anecdotes she tells how, having been singled out to help demonstrate a new method of teaching arithmetic, she collaborated for a while, accepting the bags of gumdrops that came with the distinction, but then she rebelled, refusing to recite one day in front of a visitor from Omaha, which embarrassed the principal. Exasperated, this female Caesar brought her pointer down violently so close to Josie's cheek she was nearly struck, and she ran home to Mary, crying. It was not until Mary sent a note chastising the principal, and forbidding her further use of Josie in demonstrations, that Josie secured her popular standing with her fellow pupils once more. Another time a classmate tormented her by pulling her braids very hard, and again she burst into tears. Mary sent a note to the teacher and all the male suspects were hauled into the principal's office for a confrontation. When it was the turn of the culprit, he and Josie stared at one another intensely. "That's not the boy," she said at last. At recess the playground buzzed with the admiring "She didn't snitch on Charles." A week later he gave her a celluloid comb. Identification with the underdog? Possibly. Dependence on her mother? No doubt. But everyone was an underdog in relation to the tyrannical principal, and all the children in Sioux City were just as dependent on their mothers. If anything in these incidents distinguished Josie from her contemporaries, it is not apparent from the way she recalled them what it was.

In high school the pattern continued. By the time Josie was ready for it, the town's great fortress had been completed. Medieval on the outside, with immense red masonry turrets, it sat ponderously upon a hill which made it difficult to approach without humility. It was as classical within as feudal without. Bas-reliefs from the Parthenon and "Cicero's Denunciation of Catiline" decorated its corridors. The ideal student was cultured as an Athenian, patriotic as a Spartan, and righteous as Jesus Christ. In the middle of the sunburnt prairie, Hellenism and Christianity baked in a pious cake. Josie was not an exception. She was interested in her classes, in which she did consistently well, and she received a foundation, particularly in literature, which in later years she had many reasons to respect, but usually her heart was elsewhere. She was a class officer, on the staff of the yearbook, a member of the Committee for Pins. She was an actress — she played the cook in an antifeminist farce called *The Champion of Her Sex* — and, with even more zeal, a debater. When she was a junior she won a statewide debating contest held in Fort Dodge, defending the affirmative in a political-theoretical discussion of "commission government." Other debate topics were more far-fetched. "Resolved, that the Czarina's position is more to be desired than that of the Queen of England." "Resolved, that if a Russian had had the Advantages of an American he would have been Equal in Rank." Outside of school her life was dominated by relationships with "The Eight," a select intense little sisterhood of slumber parties, multi-course luncheons whose menus were reported in the Sioux City society columns, and afternoon teas. Their traces are left mainly in an autograph book filled with the eternal verities of American adolescence. "Yours till Niagara falls." "You with your husband will organize a college fraternity — the Kappa Kap Pajama." "Don't smoke ladies' cigarettes — use opium." Only one of the dozens suggests the presence among her intimates of a spirit in the slightest akin to what was emerging in herself and Helen. "When I the kitchen floor did scrub and rinsed the dishrag in the tub, I softly swore a word or two that this again I wouldn't do." Don't smoke ladies' cigarettes — use opium. So absent is the self she became from the public traces of a conventional adolescence one looks for it in vain. It is only in Josie's own little diaries given to her every year by Mary as soon as she could write, and kept irregularly the rest of her life, and in scattered unpublished jottings, that the private character who developed alongside the public one has any voice.

[From the diaries.] Grade school. *1901*. February 1. "Today I fell in a mud puddle. No I did not. It was Gussie not me. I fell in a well. I do believe I would have drowned if it had not been for my friend Gussie Andrewson. She pulled me out. I did not no I would go down for there was board there." *1902*. "Am ten years old. Am sick. Have sore throat. Can't go to school. Am sorry. Ain't sorry." It was as if the very use to which she would put language, put writing, put truth, was in doubt, uncertainty, for her. *1903*. Josie was 11 when she got her period. [From an unpublished memoir.] She was out climbing a tree and when she came in she found blood on her pants. She went to the kitchen to find Mary. Her mother took her into a room apart. Didn't you ever notice anything? Your big sisters? Numbly the child shook her head, she had not, though how she had not in the tiny house is a question in itself and must have involved desire as well as chance. Three to five days every month, Mary said. The days are special. "Be a little careful those days, don't go jumping around, you always leap from high places like a squirrel. Keep your feet dry." Now they were facing each other, mother and daughter, and Josie wanted more. Mary was tender. "You're too early for this. Fourteen is the commoner age. But then you got your first tooth sooner than most." Then romantic. "This [is] the first signal of the body's ripening for love, for children." Then indignant. "But you're only a child yourself, it's too soon." Josie was subdued, astonished, scared. She still wanted more. Dr. Pierce, author of the household *Golden Medical Discoveries,* discursive on "catarrh," was silent on "menstruation." The librarian offered *What Every Boy Should Know.* Pulling a hint from this book, a line from that, sniffing around for the scent of life, she contrived her own understanding, a more or less literary metaphor of a great chain of female being linking herself — her mother — her sisters — her teachers — the Brontë girls! — George Sand!! — the Queen of England!!! — into a "vast company" of sisters who were "regularly reminded in language of the blood what they were." It was far from being a welcome revelation. The facts of life and the fear of death were closely related. All her life she would be nervous about bodily symptoms. She noted her period every month in her little diaries with this word: "Sick."

*1906.* Recovering from a case of scarlet fever, which affected her heart, Josie suddenly grew, so she was weak and spindly at the same time. When she entered high school she was taller than the others. There are many dance programs among her souvenirs, but these mislead. In her heart she felt she was not a favorite of the boys. She goes through a slovenly phase in the house. [From the diaries.] July 12. "Mama has promised me a new dress (the nicest I ever had) if I am straight by my 16 birth." July 20. "I've tried but it don't work. The more I try — I've given up. Whenever I dust M. or someone looks at me, when I neglect for one day to get dinner a heap of abuse is piled on me." *1907,* a year of compulsive cleaning. Eleven pages of her diary list nothing but household tasks performed. For instance: "Swept with a broom thoroughly parlor, sitting room then dusted same wiped woodwork with damp cloth swept my room back room bath room stairs also a little in mama's room dusted in my room and mama's and made bed did night's dishes." Or, Monday, June 17. "Swept with sweeper sitting room parlor dusted same made my bed made mama's helped with washing helped get supper set table did night's dishes cleaned sink." This goes on for more than a week until Tuesday, June 25. "Did nothing, was sick." *1908,* her sixteenth year, exists only as a summary. Uncle Daniel came to visit that year and took Mary with him to the Democratic convention in Denver nominating William Jennings Bryan. Alice married John Hansen in October. "The house was beautiful as was everyone." *1909,* the year of her debating victory in Fort Dodge. It is a happier year. Josie feels pretty, popular, smart. But sitting on the front porch, June 9, euphoric about her own nature, she writes, "How pretty the world is. People wouldn't be so sad if they came out into it more often. They wouldn't be so bad either, for there is something so mystical and lovely in nature which brings forth one's better self and covers all the wickedness." What wickedness? What is bothering her about herself so much? Can the compulsive cleaning possibly cover it up? Of the days the following June filled with graduation activities she scrawls across two pages, "How hard these days are to pull through. I graduated so many years ago." To this moment I am not certain what she means.

Throughout Josie's childhood the financial footing of the household was very precarious. The boom that had brought Mary and Bent to Sioux City had been brief and the town had actually lost population in the years they had been there. Between adverse conditions in general, increasing competition, and his own uncompetitive nature, Bent was not a success in business. Struggling for the money that would enable them to stay ahead Mary turned at times to her successful brother Daniel, who had money to spare, but he usually refused. For two years after her graduation from high school in 1910 Josie continued to live at home, for there was no possibility of schooling out of town. She went to Morningside College, a church-sponsored school newly established at the edge of Sioux City which was probably inferior, in both breadth and quality, to the high school, and she worked in her father's store. She continued to be absorbed in her high school friendships. From the summer of 1912, when she joined her friends for a vacation at a nearby camp, she saved a packet of lovely photographs. There is a lush sensuality to this company of girls. They are all about twenty now. One picture shows them sitting on wooden chairs on the porch of an old cabin, their lake-soaked hair hanging glistening far below their waists. In another they are lying on camp cots set side by side, curled around each other or reading books under soft faded quilts while the sun streaks through the screening. In a third they are on the porch, affectionately clowning, heads on one another's shoulders, hands around one another's waists. When three of them, Josie included, stand in front of a cabin in their cotton ginghams with their small curved waists exquisitely displayed, their heads at coquettish tilts just this side of affectation, their arms filled with bouquets, they look as fresh as their flowers. They also look exactly alike. The flowers are all daisies, all cut in a measured distance from top to stem as if they were intended for a vase on a table. Even knowing the photographs as well as I do, I still have to look twice to tell Josephine Herbst from Mabel Pecaut or Tena Crum. If it seems hard to find her it is because these are the years before she has found herself. She is entwined with the others in a wreath of undifferentiated young girlhood. Within this wreath, every rustle of a twig, every turning of a leaf, is felt with all the painful exquisite sensitivity that will later be reserved for the relationship of marriage. For Josie the winds blow hardest around her relationship with "Das," another student at Morningside, and she speaks of her frequently, but elusively, in her journals. "Das" is a brown-haired, round-cheeked, serious-looking young woman with rimless pince-nez glasses and an expression peculiarly like Trotsky's. There is an emotional intensity, an instability, in Josie's notations about her. "What's the use," on May 9, 1911. "Das left,"

June 13. One day there is "nice mail from Denver"; on the next "why try to write?" She does not try very often. Most of the pages are blank. Of the passing of 1911 she muses, "Let the old year slip off unmolested." She will not comment on it in her diary. Occasionally there is a reference to being "sick." Once she remarks as if significantly, *"Had to leave tea at Pieria early today."* On June 15, 1912, Frances married Ben Wells, an event from which Josie later dated the beginning of her real friendship with her oldest sister. But it is not only the pages that are blank. The fact is that Josie is bored. She is beginning to feel stuck. It was all very well to dwell in platitudinous innocence — "My hope is that whatever happens I meet [the New Year] bravely and with good cheer, with a courage that mitigates trouble, with a sportsmanship that laughs at any pain," she wrote in 1912 — but that "rank highstepping idealism" she described as "laudable and necessary" later, she felt was smothering her at the time. All at once she was eager to leave. She saved ten cents every day on her trips to and from Morningside by walking several miles instead of transferring to another car line but even after two years such thrift did not add up. Instead of heading for Smith or Oberlin which she had hoped to be able to manage, in the fall of 1912 she enrolled at the University of Iowa in Iowa City where her expenses would be under $200 for the year.

In 1912 the University of Iowa was an all-American paradise. It was the first state-supported coeducational university in the country — more than half its 2,000 students were women — and in theory it offered as many educational opportunities as could be found anywhere at the time. But Greek letter life was fastened onto the community like a tick on a dog and it was in the parasite, not the host, that the real vitality of the organism seemed to lie. Josie was disillusioned. "I feel a million years wiser than I did a week ago," she wrote to her family in the fall.

> I do not like Iowa. It has been stripped of all the pretty dreams I wove around it. It isn't fairyland nor even happiness. It is merely Iowa. I am almost sick with disappointment. . . . You see, I thought it would be a wonderful thing to be a sorority girl. I thought they stood for all that was best in college life and I find instead that here . . . at least they stand for snobbery and money. . . . They think of parties and men and that is about all. . . . I still think that in coming to Iowa I did the only thing possible but it taught me a lesson. . . . Now I am ready for genuine work and I know that I can do more now than I could ever have been capable of before. . . .

But if joining a sorority did not guarantee happiness, not joining one guaranteed isolation and Josie pledged Delta Delta Delta and tried to follow the crowd. Ignoring her own misgivings, she wrote home empty sentimental letters about banquets and dances, ohing and ahing in such imitative ecstasy over the table decorations and the floral displays that she sounded like nothing so much as the Sioux City society columns. Once she told Helen that outside her window before a football game with Wisconsin she could hear all Iowa City singing "We're rambling, we're rambling, we're rambling down the line." Another time she actually signed a letter "ta-ta." But what she was writing was false. One of her earliest stories for which any fragments exist is about a coed named Elsie who writes lying letters home about her popularity and a young man named Carl who guards the campus museum at night tormented by sexual longings. In the description of outsiders who watch from the shadows while the heads of dancing couples bob gaily in the lighted windows there is more of Josie's real feeling than in any of her letters. She had occasional dates, but outside of her exaggerated communications home, the boys seemed to get relatively little of her attention. Nor did she much like the girls. However much she wavered in her own sense of being, her opinion of her sorority sisters did not improve. There was an exception, the "Das" of the year, another dark-haired young woman also from Sioux City, this one named Bernice. "I am very happy. Bernice and I took each other home tonight. I have something worthwhile," she wrote in her diary in April. Almost certainly it was just an ordinary girlish "best-friendship" that she meant. "May 12. Bernie's birthday. We walked in the eve. I had to tell her something that hurt so. Lilies of the Valley." She frequently notes that they spent the night together. In June, on the day she was leaving Iowa City, she wrote, "Left Bernie in bed. Beautiful day. When will I see Iowa City again?" The answer was, she would not, for by the end of the academic year, her father's business had completely failed. To forestall becoming a clerk again, at the mercy of another owner, and to forestall losing his dream, Bent traveled to Oregon to see brother Daniel and investigate whether to risk a further westward move, but Daniel was not willing to help. Bent returned to Sioux City to a job as a watchman in a warehouse and he worked for others, for low pay, for the rest of his life. With Frances and Alice out of the house and struggling to establish families of their own, both Josie and Helen now felt an obligation not only to support themselves but to help their parents. "No use writing these days," Josie remarked in her diary at home. "I wouldn't dare write what I feel, and nothing happens." Helen went straight from her high school graduation to teach in an ungraded country school in a small town near Sioux City. Josie, with three years of college behind her, got a job teaching seventh and eighth grades in the larger town of Stratford, in the north-central part of the state, between Ames and Fort Dodge.

"Isn't it strange that a town that expects to educate its young and imports teachers for the purpose seems to be totally unconcerned about the welfare of those teachers?" she wrote to her parents shortly after her arrival. The dissection of provincial piety that popped out spontaneously is the earliest moment in Josie's correspondence she sounds like her later self.

> Nobody wants to room or board anybody else except for the most ridiculous skinflint prices. The *one* modern house in town refuses me a room for less than $10. She wanted 2 girls to take the room & pay $10 for it or $5 apiece. But I would so much rather room alone and I offered her $7 but she held out — the brute! Her husband's wealthy and on the school board and you would think it would have been a pleasure to do such a *little* favor to a poor teacher, but she held fast to her $10 and wouldn't budge. She and her tight husband have had me trotting up to their place three times to see what their decisions were, after "they thought it over once more." But their thoughts revolve in one circle with a dollar for an axis. Not even the minister's plea softened them. I went to church this morning and saw the pious skinflint in the first pew. He seemed touched by the sermon, which was a plea to help others without thought of gain, and he sang loudly & with great gusto the hymn about sacrifice for others, but after the sermon he crept into his old shell and reiterated his '$10' with as much emphasis as before.

"Why do people in little towns have one of two expressions . . . either sluggish, ambitionless countenances or else eager, stingy, calculating ones?" she wanted to know. Why did the men sit on a ledge without even talking? "They aren't living, they are vegetating," she said. Why were they all so *blonde?* With its squat unadorned buildings and its sober unadorned population, in 1913 Stratford was in many ways the essence of rural Iowa and it was here that Josie realized that its essence and hers were not the same. Apart from naming its main street "Shakespeare Avenue" — others were named Dryden, Milton, Tennyson and Pope — even its aspirations to culture did not run very deep. "The ignorance of my children in regard to things that mean the most to me — namely books, and appreciation of out-of-door things, is appalling," she complained in an early letter. "It is a sad shock to find my children's minds are more like cabbages than brains," she exploded another time. More to her liking than contending with the cabbages was the work she was starting to do herself. She kept a journal, not a childish diary but a deliberate exercise in observation, and she began writing stories. When she took them to a professor she had had at Iowa and he encouraged her to send them out for consideration, she was elated by his response. "Bless you, I expect *hundreds* of failures to *one* success but that isn't discouraging. I'd rather *fail* in story writing than succeed in anything else," she wrote to Helen.

Alone for the first time, she suddenly seemed to know who she was. Yet for all the sense of direction that was building up in her writing, it was a year of frustration and strain. Between the demands of her teaching, her social isolation, and her worries about the future, she found herself often in despair. "I am wondering if there may not be many such moods ahead of me — much unhappiness, even tho it do not last," she wrote to herself in her journal. "I must train myself better — be more flinty to these things." To reach what was becoming her ambition to be a writer, she would have to be "flinty" indeed.

## CHAPTER FOUR

# "I Fairly Writhe . . ."

IF IOWA WAS confining, at least it was a confinement from which it was possible to escape. The same was not true for sex: for gender: and Josie was beginning to realize it. "I fairly writhe to think of how fine it would be if I had been a boy," she wrote to Mary from Stratford. "That was a huge mistake — I feel sure. Don't see how it happened yet. As it is I'm a girl with the ambitions and aspirations of a boy. I ought to be delighted with needlework & it's time I began to dream of wedded bliss. I do neither. A vast mistake, Snowdrop. You must see it." Frequently she would sign her letters "Jo," instead of "Josie," and occasionally she would even write it "Joe." Once she sent a telegram, "Your wandering boy is anxious . . ." A "Rover Boy," a "gent," and a "good man" were some of the other ways she referred to herself as the years passed. It was not only men who thought the universal pronoun was male.

The core of Josie's impatience had more to do with adventure than with sex. Morally, she was still very conventional. Her letters to Helen are filled with the most pious invocations to chastity, and she had every expectation of becoming a wife and mother. Still, there was something in her restlessness that was made infinitely more complicated by the fact of being a woman, and increasingly, there were beginning to be temptations. By the summer of 1914, when Josie returned to Sioux City, she found it somewhat different from when she had left. Europe was already at war, and as far away as it was from the worldly turbulence that would make the prewar era look like an idyll that had never happened, even in Iowa there were currents of thought and action never possible before. Having forsworn teaching, Josie took courses in shorthand, got a job in a law office, and started to look around. Tucked away next to "Tolstoy" on the shelf of the new library she found a novel by a more obscure Russian, Michael Artzibasheff. Called *Sanine*, it was a celebration of sensuality, an assault on inhibition, and she read it with rising feeling. On another shelf she found D. H. Lawrence. The Wobblies had come to town, organizing seasonal workers on the ice harvest, and for a time two or three men were dropping off every passing freight to add their bodies to the war of labor against capital. In the streets there was marching and singing. In the library *The Masses* and *The Little Review*. To take dictation in a dreary office while politics and literature were bursting out in new directions was hardly a cure for "writhing." Living at home, she saved money for both herself and Helen, who was staking her entire earnings on one year of college at the University of Wisconsin. In September, 1915, when she decided she had saved enough, Josie headed for Seattle where she hoped to get a job and finish college at the same time.

Why she chose Seattle is not apparent from her papers except that a high school friend named Ethel Collier had decided to go there too, but if Josie had any illusions about the consequences to her life of being female rather than male, it was in Seattle that its implications were first fully revealed. She and Ethel had scarcely found an apartment and taken jobs when they were plunged into a mutual nightmare that was the result of nothing other than the best contemporary understanding of what constituted proper female medicine. "It all started with Ethel," Josie wrote home to her mother.

> She has been having so much back-ache, dragged down feeling etc and so she went to a very fine surgeon here, who had done so much for a girl in the Extension Dept. He examined her and told her that her womb had become misplaced — instead of being upright as it should be it had fallen backward and was pressing against the spine where there was a nerve center: — this caused the backaches also headaches and pains in the back of the head and neck (which Ethel did not have). Well — this girl at the University had had the same trouble, only hers was worse, the womb had been misplaced so long that it had grown there and the tissues were fixed, also her ovaries had become affected. She had an operation, and had parts of her ovaries removed and her muscles holding the womb tightened and now she is in splendid shape. Ethel went to the same doctor and he said she would not have to have an operation, only treatments, as she had not let it go so long, but had discovered it before it had advanced so far. Well, when she

38

told me how she had felt and what the doctor had said about letting a thing go so long until other organs were affected, I decided to have an examination too. I had been having backaches for so long I almost ceased to know when I had one, but I have felt lately that there must be something wrong with me. So I went too. And he said I was just exactly like Ethel, only much worse, for my womb had fallen back so long it had become fastened there, also I was so run down that all the pelvic organs were very weak and he said I certainly needed attention badly. . . .

Now what he intended to do — that is the treatment of our case, was to insert a small rubber thing which would hold the womb in place. But this could not be inserted without a small operation. So we both had the operation . . . We had to take chloroform. Ethel had no trouble, but because I was so run down it took two hours for me to come out from the chloroform and when I did I was sick. . . . But now we will have no pain at all at our sick times and Ethel came sick last night and is usually in great agony and this time she had not one pain. The doctor said he expected to have more trouble with me, but so far I have done finely, although for several days after the operation I was in constant pain because of adhesions — the womb having grown fast was tearing away in an effort to right itself. . . .

About six weeks later both Josie and Ethel had major surgery. "Ethel had more done to her than I did — several things the doctor did not know about until he operated," Josie reported.

He took out her appendix, tightened the cords of the womb to replace it in position, and removed a small tumor on the womb. He tightened the cords of my womb & removed my appendix which was in a very bad condition he said. I had had some pain in my side lately but did not think of that. He said my ovaries were not in a good condition but now that my womb was straightened that would very probably be better & become entirely normal, — also the varicose veins of the Fallopian tubes — which he could do nothing for, not wishing, of course to operate at my age for that. He said I might have to have another operation in 20 years or so. . . .

From diagnosis to recuperation nothing was prescribed for one which was not prescribed for the other right down to the details of the ether administered during the surgery and the "hypodermics" afterward to ease the pain. Josie does not seem to have found any of this unusual. Indeed, she was grateful for the experience. "I have learned so much about myself since I have talked with this doctor," she wrote home. "Ah — it's all wrong not to teach girls more about themselves — not to tell them more of their own bodies — and the school physiologies — oh the farce of it to ignore the very organs that mean most to a girl's happiness. . . . What I should have had was specific information — Nothing else counts. Well, thank the merciful heavens it isn't too late and I can still be husky and happy. . . ." Even during the darkest hours of her postoperative suffering her principal emotion was relief. "I feel new bubbling life & vitality and things come fresh to me as they haven't come for two years. I feel as if the days of goading myself on were over," she confided. Yet far from recovering vitality, she became increasingly ill. Her year was completely ruined. Despite the fact that she had made a good beginning at the University of Washington both in classes and in a job she was too tired most of the year to maintain her level of effort, and as for all the things she had expected to be able to do in Seattle, between her doctor's orders and her own exhaustion, they were out of the question. She and Ethel were forbidden to walk much, forbidden to dance, and night after night sat at home in their boardinghouse, practicing the doctor's "positions." Her savings were wasted and her energies drained — all as a result of surgery I think it is nearly certain she should never have had to begin with. If Josie and Ethel had anything at all it is possible that what they had were uterine "retroversions" or tilts, conditions reported much more frequently in the past than they are now when less attention is given to the idea of a uterine "norm." In addition to being a catchall for a variety of physical symptoms a woman might present or even, like the "pains in the back of the head and neck (which Ethel did not have)," the ones she didn't, a wide range of psychological symptoms from crankiness to depression were also attributed to the supposed displacement. In the early years of this century it gradually became understood that corrective surgery was being performed much too often. "It should not be deemed presumptuous on the part of the gynecologist if, failing to find definite pelvic pathology, he ventures [a different] diagnosis," editorialized the *American Journal of Surgery* in 1916. But it was too late for Josie and Ethel. Their doctor was not a quack. The medicine he offered was the accepted practice of the moment. Personally he seems to have been a decent man. It was the practice of the moment with its ignorance of women that was at fault. Josie thought that the operation had saved her from a lifetime of pain and sterility. I think she was lucky to have escaped with her sexual organs intact.

It was not only the anatomy of her sexual organs with which Josie was unfamiliar — it was also their power. For Josie at twenty-four the "sexual revolution" was purely a theoretical matter. It was true that something was happening in Greenwich Village that with every issue of *The Masses* was coming to seem more real, but the personal implications — for example, of its crusade for birth control — were still remote. As far as Josie was concerned, the most problematic outlet for any sexual feeling was a man. It was much too dangerous. Men meant marriage and marriage meant settling down and whatever it was that she wanted out of life she knew that for the moment at least it wasn't that. "I have no other idea for your future than marriage," she wrote to Helen from Seattle in January, 1916. "Not that it will be the end, but for you it can only be the proper beginning. With me, I think of it as neither end nor beginning — but rather hope it will be a *part*. With you there must be a husband and a home to live. With me there must be *life*, abundant life — before I will ever reach a husband and a home." Yet she was increasingly physically restless. Recuperating from her exhaustion at her Uncle Daniel's in Salem, Oregon, she embarked with her cousin Jennie Fry* on a course of mutual exploration that was as close as she had yet come to the reality of sex. With its nineteenth-century girlish context and twentieth-century womanish content, whether Josie's relationship with her cousin was closer to her earlier romantic friendships or her later sexual affairs is difficult to tell. In recounting her emotional history, even at her most candid, she herself always left it out. But that sex was at the heart of it in some fashion — that much is certain. The overwhelming sense that arises from the evidence is one of great physical and intellectual hunger. "We knew so little then," said cousin Jennie, when I met her in 1974 when she was in her eighties. "Sex. Contraceptives. How we wanted to know." Several of her letters to Josie had been filled with discussions of pessaries, and even little drawings. What she did not say was how alarming was a little knowledge. Shortly after Josie left Jennie was reading *The Sexual Question*, by August Forel, which had been advertised in *The Masses*, and was distressed by a reference to love between two women. "It repulsed me and made me think," she confided. Now it was Josie's turn to be unhappy. Her full reply is not available but from notes she made on the back of Jennie's envelope it is possible to glimpse her reaction. "It isn't perverted & even if it were — it is beautiful," she wrote. With the letters back and forth producing such histrionics that the families on both sides began urging a truce, cousinly harmony was quickly restored but the innocence of their special connection was forever broken. As an introduction to the risks of love, Josie's relationship with her cousin was far more instructive than it was satisfactory.

What Josie concluded from her experience with Jennie was less about sexual attraction than it was about emotional involvement: that its price was high. The feelings unleashed by the episode had been so upsetting that a year after it was over she was still nursing her wounds. "I've been haunted all week and have had to thresh things out all over again,"

* Daniel evidently adopted the "Fry" spelling when he moved to Oregon. For her middle name, Josie always retained the original "Frey."

she wrote to Helen around the time of her cousin's marriage. "I really cared so much — you wouldn't understand." It was not an experience she was anxious to repeat. She had returned to Sioux City and had taken another stenographic position, trying to save the money for another start, and she wanted nothing to stand in her way. If that meant a dull year with no relationships that would raise the possibility of attachment, she was willing to wait it out. Helen was back too, teaching in another country schoolhouse, and the differences between the sisters were becoming more obvious. Helen, too, had decided to become a writer, and Helen, too, had won the praise of her professors for her stories, but similar as they were in talents and ambitions, their temperaments were coming more and more to diverge. Where Josie would hold back, Helen would press forward; where Josie was cautious, Helen was bold. "You are in a tremendous hurry to live. You want life thick and fast," Josie had written to her sister at Madison, and it seemed to be true. At college she had had several affairs, including one with a Jewish soldier — daring on both counts — and at one point she had even feared she might be pregnant. Now she was dating a Sioux City farm boy named Andrew Bernhard who lived across the road from the schoolhouse, and their relationship was serious. With the entire family except for Josie hounding her about her not-very-secret activities, there was pressure on her to marry, which was what Andrew wanted, but Helen did not want to decide. *For* Andrew were intelligence, ambition, and an uninhibited devotion; *against* were his Sioux City origins, as well as the finality of choice. Nonetheless, their attraction was solid. At the end of her year of teaching Helen took a job as a society reporter for the Sioux City *Tribune* with the hope that she might be able to stay in Sioux City and advance herself professionally at the same time. Josie would not be sidetracked. By the summer she had saved enough money for another attempt to escape. This time she would take herself to Berkeley. And this time she would finish college: or else.

# Preamble

WHEN JOSIE got to Berkeley in the summer of 1917 she still had about her a trace of the coed. She was met at the boat by a woman from her Iowa sorority and for a time she lived at the sorority house and took her meals there, but she was irritated by the atmosphere of girlish socializing and she soon moved to a house in the hills, on her own. "I guess I have seen too much of reality to swallow the stick candy side of college life," she wrote to Helen shortly after her arrival. "I can't stand around on one foot and pull off sweet nothings . . . I can't hang around and coo like a young dove when some sliver of a male deigns to draw near . . . I thought I could, but I can't. . . . I want the dances but not so badly I have to turn monkey to get them." The University was another disappointment. "The student body is smug and comfortable. . . . They are very proud of their contented state and attribute it to student government. Why student government should shrivel up their capacity for thinking, I can't see, but they don't put it that way, of course. . . . They are a healthy, patriotic bunch. The girls knit, knit, knit and the men enlist, enlist, enlist," she complained. Her classes were not much consolation. Large formal lectures where the students "gulped down" all their teachers gave them without criticism or challenge, they were a far cry from the fiery exchanges of ideas which existed in her mind, and she soon dropped traditional courses in English and economics for the more exotic pursuits of forestry and beekeeping which could substitute at least the possibility of profit for the mockery of enlightenment. But there was one exception: a class that made all the others worthwhile: an English composition class taught by a young man not long out of Yale, Harold Bruce. Bruce saw not only Josie's ability but her maturity and he treated her with respect. He read her stories aloud to his classes, praised her and encouraged her to continue, and even invited her to lecture to the other students about her ideas on modern writing. It was he who introduced her to the radical community in Oakland and San Francisco: to the first group of men and women she was proud to call her friends.

The story of Josie's first immersion in radicalism has a special air to it because it is all future and no past. "Do not look too hard for the 'origins' of her radicalism," her brother-in-law Andrew Bernhard advised me, of the personality that seems to have emerged full-blown with her first crossing of San Francisco Bay. "She simply *was* radical. She was the same in 1917 as she was in 1967." The evidence bears him out. When she met Max Stern, an editor of the *San Francisco Bulletin*, Carl Hoffman, another editor, and many of the other radical and Socialist newspapermen, poets, writers, and artists who lived in the Bay area during the war, she met them not as mentors but as equals and she felt relief that she was no longer going to be alone. "I always knew that somewhere in the world were people who could talk about the things I wanted to talk about and do the things I wanted to do and in some measure at least I have found them," she told her mother. With their opposition to the war, their enthusiasm for the revolution in Russia, and their desire for exciting lives very unlike the lives of most of their parents she already, instinctively, agreed. The characteristic which underlay what Josie and her new friends had in common had something to do with a refusal of passivity. The radicals of 1917 were people who protested the large part of life which is simply governed by convention. They believed it was possible to make things happen differently if they chose. By the time she got to California, Josie knew what it was to be frustrated by circumstances. It was in that year, in fact, that she first got the idea for a trilogy of novels that would be largely about economic and generational traps. But she also knew what it was to resist circumstances, and so did most of the others. Originally, they were all outsiders. The men and women like Josie who had been out of place at home had as great a longing for the ordinary joys of life as did the brothers and sisters they left behind. Their radicalism had in it a health, a delight, an optimistic conviction that they would no longer have to stand with their noses pressed against the panes of other people's lives, that they could have all the joys the others had, and more besides. Things could be done in this world. Change was possible. A small town, with its social rigidities, was not the universe. When they came together in San Francisco or New York they were not consciously trying to start movements or parties. They were simply trying to find places where it was possible to be themselves.

Nothing Josie did with her friends in San Francisco seems very remarkable now. They listened to speeches and climbed Mount Tamalpais and shared festive bohemian dinners where the men did the cooking and sometimes even the washing up or just sat around at the old house in Oakland belonging to Max Stern's parents arguing about the war and capitalism and wondering what was going to happen next. Along with Genevieve Taggard, a rare kindred spirit who was also a student, a writer, and a radical, Josie was usually one of few women present at these gatherings and it was all right. For the first time in her life she was comfortable with men. "Don't show your brains," was the sorority's wisdom. "They don't like it." But they did. "It woke them up, excited them" to have conversation with a woman about these subjects, especially a woman with flashing eyes. What was important to Josie in this circle had little to do with sex or marriage. It was something bigger, more exciting. With Max Stern she began a friendship which he would have liked to convert to romance, but it was more the atmosphere of his life than it was the man she was attracted to and despite some passionate entwinings in the hills of Berkeley, they never really altered the terms. "Oh pitiful preamble, so tiresome, so wasteful" reads a note that she wrote about her relationship with him years later. "I'm going to waste. Hurry hurry for life is fleeting." But it was "not the season, not the man," and for the moment there would be no other. If anything, her experience with Max solidified her determination to wait for the real thing. "Poor Muddie," she wrote to Mary who was starting to find her absence of traditional inclinations alarming. "Most of your talk of love is quite beside the mark as far as I'm concerned. No one is demanding 'intellect' or anything else but just what do you mean by 'love'? That is the split — and you talk just like books or the talk of everybody else [and] I can't take that. Of course, 'any woman's heart would leap at the man who could inspire her with love' — that's the whole point. But suppose her heart doesn't leap?" It was her whole being that was leaping. It wasn't her heart.

Helen's heart, on the other hand, was leaping freely, only in her case Mary would have preferred that it didn't. Andrew had been drafted and was in training in Kansas and Helen had begun an affair with a married newspaperman she had met at her office in Sioux City. Mary had found out about it by reading through the letters in which Josie and Helen discussed it with one another and insisted unabashedly on having her say. All Mary's life she had been a snooper and her daughters knew about it and forgave her, taking the attitude that if anything she learned that way displeased her, it was up to her to make her own peace with it. But this time the situation was different. With Mary upset not only by the affair itself but by Helen's disregard for the man's wife and children, Helen worried not only by having to sneak around but by the implications of her "erotic nature" for her relationship with Andrew, and even Frances in the act strongly supporting her mother on the importance of moral order, the atmosphere in the family reached a point of unaccustomed tension, and both sides turned to the distant Josie for help in setting things right. In a burst of correspondence, Josie told her mother her methods were too hysterical to be effective, she told Helen she should think more about love than about sex, and she told them all she resented being dragged into their quarrels when she was trying so hard to establish herself on her own, but she was distressed by the little drama despite herself and she urged Helen to join her in California to give it a chance to settle down. When Helen arrived she was listless and unhappy. She was not interested in Josie's friends or in the University, she was not impressed by the scenery, she could respond only barely to the pressure of necessity by taking a job. She sat around in the small Berkeley bungalow thinking over her recent experiences and looking into her heart, and what she found there when she looked hard enough was a desire to marry Andrew, who was about to be shipped overseas. " 'I'm going to wire him I'm coming,' she said, powdering her face lightly, rubbing a slight bit of rouge on her cheeks that were so like the Blessed Damozel of Dante Rossetti": Josie: recreating the moment in her trilogy. Mary was overjoyed. "I truly feel you will be happier and more contented married to him before he goes & I know he will," she wrote. "The years may be long & many without [him], but . . . do . . . as your heart dictates. . . . I would do nothing to rob you of one day one hour even of the unutterable happiness I feel in my heart would be his & yours if you *belonged to one another*. . . . These are not ordinary times & we cannot be considering the expediency of this or that." After only a short visit Helen turned around and left California to go to Andrew in Kansas. They were married at the home of a local preacher near Camp Funston on May 27, 1918, only a few days before his troop train was scheduled to leave.

Josie graduated from the University of California at Berkeley on May 15, 1918, at twenty-six, eight years after she had begun college for the first time, with a number of honors and distinctions it was too late for her to treat as anything but a joke, a handful of pieces that had appeared in campus publications and with which she was genuinely pleased, and a strong literary voice, emerging chiefly in her letters, of which she seems to have been largely unaware. Her credentials did not change her basic dilemma: how to position herself so she could make a good start. She got a stenographic job in a law office in Oakland and, tiring of that, at another one in Seattle. Helen, alone and restless, came west to join her again; Frances was there too, with her husband, Ben Wells, who was considering a permanent move; and they were all living together in a Seattle boardinghouse when the end of the war was announced. For Josie the Seattle stay was brief but vivid for with the security of her family around her and an undemanding job she was free to observe the public ferment, and between the flu epidemic and the general strike there was plenty of ferment to observe. A letter she wrote her mother at the time of the Armistice is perhaps its own best summary of the mixture of politics, sentiment, and natural power that was in both her writing and her life at that moment — as well as a description of the occasion that it is hard to imagine could have been bettered. "I wish you could have been here when Seattle heard that the war was over," she wrote on November 13.

The news reached here about 12:30 at night. I was . . . asleep but heard whistles blowing over and over. It roused me and I thought at once that the war must be over. After several long blasts the city began to wake up. First other whistles blew — some shrill and others deep and booming. Then sounds from around our neighborhood broke forth — people's voices and the sound of tin pans and shooting. The University chimes began to play — just the solemn doxology but it sounded full of meaning in the middle of the night. It kept on playing — it played America, Battle Hymn of the Republic and lots of war songs. Beneath it one could hear the roar of the sailors over at camp — they had wakened and were out marching. Their band played "Keep the Home Fires Burning" — I could hear their shouts over and over. I wanted to get up but it was late and no one in our house stirred. Afterwards I found out that there was a parade and people flocked down town and the sailors broke all quarantine rules and came out of camp and marched on the streets with their band at the head, shouting and almost crying for joy. . . . If I had known so many people would turn out I too would have gotten up. In a sense though it was better right in bed. I had such a sense of detachment there — and could be conscious of *all* the many noises, not just of the few at hand. It was a very solemn sort of sensation to lie there in bed and know that the war was really over — and that the boys could come pouring back home again — come back to just simple ways of living — to golden roads and sunlight and happy family picnics by some quiet river, to raising turnips and tending bees, to having babies and making little homes. And not only in this country but in all the countries —

The next day was better yet — in the morning I went down to the office. My office is up on the 7th floor and I could look down in the streets and see the ship yard workers coming up from the ship yards. Everybody was taking a holiday. Soon great dark throngs of ship yard workers began to pulse through the street — They went along shouting and waving their handkerchiefs. Girls in thin bright colored waists ran out of office buildings and were dragged along in the impromptu parade of the ship yard workers. . . . The streets soon were crowded. People went mad. In the

47

office building across the street the offices were little ferments of
excitement. One fat old codger that I have seen bully his stenogra-
pher many a time, forgot his gruffness and patted her affectionately on the arm. He got real gay and lowered a tin bucket tied
with a little string out of his window, bumping it hilariously
against the window ledge of the floor below. On the street women
and men and boys and girls waved to each other. Trucks began to
roll by and anyone who wanted to clambered on and helped make
noise. Confetti began to color the pavement. One could hardly
hear for the noise. All the offices shut up. I walked up and down
the street just smiling and wanting to cry. It was really splendid —
the show of feeling. I kept thinking of Paris and how mad the people there must be. I thought of old Germany and the socialists who
were about to have their day — of the red flag waving in that land
where the black flag has been paramount for so long — of Karl
Liebknecht out of prison and being cheered by the mobs in Berlin — of the people in London thronging through Downing St. and
calling for Lloyd George — of the really miraculous ending of it
all — Germany awakened and asserting its rights against its own
autocracy — the only thing that really counts.

If only things are allowed to go and not be muddled and spoiled
like the Russian revolution. That was a crime the allies will always
have to bear — intervention in Russia when the Reds should have
been given assistance and not have been regarded as enemies and
fought against. If the Reds in Germany have a chance reconstruction will come about normally there, but the trouble is we all
want to spread our own little propaganda. The Russians want to
make Bolsheviks out of the Germans and we want to make Americans out of the Bolsheviks. . . .

Still, Seattle was only an interlude and both Josie and Helen were
looking for opportunities to move along. Helen's came first. Her newspaperman was now an editor in Detroit and he offered her a job. In early
1919 she left once more to take up residence there and wait for Andrew's
return. Josie intended to go farther than Detroit. Schemes for getting to
South America, to France, to Russia, to Armenia: schemes for working in
a gold mine, doing relief work, entering the Red Cross: schemes of a
thousand kinds crossed her mind that year, but none of the possibilities
ever managed to become real. She returned to San Francisco where,
along with the usual office work, she obtained a few free-lance editing
assignments, but nothing so promising it could tempt her to stay. All of
her thoughts were turning east. If she could not get to Europe, at least
she could get to New York. Most of her life was still ahead of her when
she left San Francisco and she could not have said what it was going to

be. Its relationship to all that had gone before is not really so obvious as a biography may make it seem. She wondered about it herself. Toward the end of her life, jotting notes for her eternal memoirs, she asked herself questions with the genuine curiosity we each reserve in all its intensity only for ourselves when we realize how little our explanations explain. "The little strands and trees, the imprints of a design, had they been there from the beginning? What was the inventive spark? What really happened? And that all that really mattered was secret and concealed and worked its obstinate way in the dark. Toward what?"

# PART THREE

# UNMARRIED

# Love — and Revolution

WHEN JOSIE arrived in New York in October, 1919, there were two things she was interested in. The first was her writing — not so much any particular writing as the life of a writer she had come to the city to lead. The second was politics — particularly the question of revolution. Nineteen-nineteen was one of the most turbulent years in American history. From the shipyard workers of Seattle to the policemen of Boston, workers in industry after industry rose up in protest against the combination of high prices, low wages, and long hours which had followed the war, and a struggle began between strikes and strikebreaking which led conservatives and radicals alike to suspect that the class warfare which had emerged in Russia might also be emerging here. The raids on radicals by which the government hoped to deport not only individual aliens but their ideas were just getting underway. Apart from a woman in the labor movement with whom she briefly shared a Chelsea apartment, Josie's sole New York acquaintance was Genevieve Taggard, who had come to New York from California at about the same time, found a job with a publisher, and was already publishing poetry in *The Liberator* and *The Nation.* Taggard, usually called Jed, was living in a large basement apartment at 12 St. Luke's Place in Greenwich Village with a shifting population of independent young women including Helen Black, who worked for *The Nation,* Jessica Smith, a Quaker working for Russian relief, and an assortment of other artists, actresses and radicals who attracted into their bohemian quarters an equally shifting population of some of the most engaging men in America, including almost the entire mastheads of *The Masses* and *The Liberator* — Mike Gold, who was having an affair with Helen Black; Max Eastman, who was having an affair with everyone; Joseph Freeman; Floyd Dell — men who liked women who took themselves seriously. Every day after work the apartment was open for flirtation and conversation and between the politics, the poetry, and the overwhelming awareness of sexual possibility, the mood was always intense. Another gathering spot was the Union Square apartment of Frankie and Alex Gumberg. Gumberg was a Russian-born American socialist who was a semiofficial representative of the Bolshevik government; his wife, Frankie, had the added distinction of having been born an Adams. Here the mood was international, cosmopolitan, with workers and intellectuals mingling freely as if the revolution had already happened, drinking tea sweetened with raspberry jam from clear glasses while someone with brooding eyes played melancholy folk tunes on the piano and accented foreigners passed each other significantly on the rickety staircase with their collars turned up. It was exactly the world Josie was looking for and she was ushered into it warmly, for in 1919, year of the founding of the American Communist Party, the American radical community was open and diverse, and one was a member of it as much by having read its magazines and argued for its ideas in a thousand towns across the nation as by having written the articles or published the journals in New York. The authors who milled around, drinks in hand, were not leaders to be followed, only the articulators of ideas widely shared. Luckily for Josie, it was not even necessary to be sycophantic. In circles where the sacred watchwords were not love-and-marriage but love-and-revolution she felt immediately at home.

But if revolution was the theory, work was the practice, and without savings as a reserve the problem of making a living was uppermost in her mind. She took two jobs, one as a caseworker for a private charity in the Bronx, the other working nights as a bookseller, first at Gimbel's, later at Brentano's. Around the beginning of the new year she rented herself a room in an apartment at 98 Greenwich Avenue in the Village. It was a schedule leaving little or no time for writing, but unlike her office jobs at least it got her out, around the city, into contact with people's lives, and it provided considerable fodder for observation. Organized charity was "abominable": "[all] this uplift stuff and asking questions that I'd never answer if put to me. Some don't answer — they lie and the Society attributes it to a bad character." Gimbel's: "They pay the girls so poorly that many live off the floorwalkers. In other words 'they make conditions for themselves,' as one girl told me." Rich and poor: "Thousands & hundreds of thousands of people live in N.Y. in the most terrible acute unbearable *unbelievable* discomfort.... And the few live in such insolent

54

magnificence on 5th Avenue and the Drive." "The more I see of the poor — of the underlying population — the more I believe in revolution & the class war," she informed her parents after attending a huge rally in Madison Square Garden for the striking coal and steel workers. "I never used to believe in that — the hope seemed somewhere else — but now it's the underdog's only salvation. Talk about labor's high wages — it's ridiculous — the vast majority in N.Y. are living precariously from day to day. I know of hundreds of families & of course there are thousands here where the man gets $60 to $75 a mo. & has 6 children. And the paper with their dirty lies about the steel strikers. I talked with the attorney for the steel workers who says that with double shifts & all night shifts the men are striking because they are dog tired & as for high wages — well, any wages they get are equalized by having to be idle sometimes for weeks & months during the year. The public doesn't know that but think what it means!"

At the end of February, 1920, when Josie had been in the city about four months, she was invited by an acquaintance named Margaret Anderson to spend a weekend with her family at their house in the country and she eagerly accepted. Her mood was momentarily low. With expenses so high that money was a constant worry and her apartment so drafty it was a struggle to keep it warm, she was having difficulty maintaining her health through the freezing winter, and she had just recovered from a flu all the more depressing as well as more frightening because she was alone. When she met Margaret's husband at Grand Central Station on Saturday, February 28, 1920, to ride up to Croton in company, she found they had much in common. At the time of their meeting, Maxwell Anderson, the future playwright, was a soft-faced, round-shouldered curly-haired boyish-looking young man, thirty-two, who had been married to Margaret, his high-school sweetheart, for nine years, and supporting a family for eight. Like Josie he was a small-town midwesterner by upbringing, though not technically by birth, an idealistic socialist who had been fired from two teaching jobs during the war for pacifism. Although in retrospect he seems clearly to have been headed for success, for he had moved quickly from piecework on newspapers in the West, to *The New Republic*, to his current job as an editorial writer for the New York *Globe*, he appears at that point to have been very discouraged about the possibility of doing anything he considered serious with his writing. In a civilization like America serious writing was a virtual guarantor of poverty, they agreed immediately. On the train he shook off his desperation enough to notice that his wife's new friend was spirited and intriguing. At least the weekend would not be as dreary as usual.

The Anderson house was on the Hudson among pine, beech, birch and black tulip trees and at least according to Josie's perceptions of it, it was decorated and run as something between a bohemian paradise and a bourgeois scandal, with Margaret herself occupying an unenviable position somewhere between an aging paramour and an inadequate wife. It was the first time Josie had left the city since she arrived there, and the outdoors seemed more appealing than the house. Josie and Maxwell walked through the woods watching great curled dead oak leaves drift on the crusty snow. They glimpsed the chasings of squirrels, tracked deer, tracked rabbits, followed the curves of the land down valleys and up over ridges where they saw smoke rising from distant villages, lights flickering from distant towns. They discussed the conflict between writing and having to earn a living. Only another writer could know how difficult it was. It was so hard for all of them. Especially for a man. Especially for a man with a family. The deadening routine of life. "He knew one bed, one woman. He would grow old and grey turning off alarm clocks, fixing furnaces, coming to meals on time," catching trains. What was happening to his imagination? What had happened, already, to his passion? Josie roughhoused with his boys. She rolled herself up like a snowball and tumbled down an embankment. "Aren't you afraid?" he shouted down after her. "No I'm afraid of nothing, are you?" she shouted back. Margaret and another visitor stuck to the open paths.

When they got back to the city, his notes started coming. Lightly penciled, in a delicate script, on thick paper, elegant. Lunch at the Three Steps Down? She telephoned the *Globe*, yes. By coincidence it was her twenty-eighth birthday. At lunch they dished out to each other the appropriate philosophies. He had never done this before, in all the years. . . . Neither had she, but she let him think she had. It was vital to the onset of the affair. It was, of course, to be a free affair. There were to be no attachments. Maxwell and Margaret had even agreed in principle. . . . Odd that those discussions should seem to lead straight back into the marriage bed and make him realize what a remarkable woman his wife was. For Josie it was going to be free or it was going to be nothing. "We are all alone anyhow." Life is impermanent, love is impermanent, a "blinding exquisite moment of companionship" is all you can expect. She flicked her cigarette into the ashtray in a way that made him see the ashes of a thousand cigarettes before it growing long and cold and finally forgotten on the ashtrays of a thousand tables while the lovers swooned passionately on a nearby couch. Her imaginary experience made him bold, he nodded, she nodded, he reached for his hat. They went to her apartment and made love, Josie for the first time in her life. When it was over, she was in love with him and he was worried.

So much for the ideology of the 1920s. Not even the most radical wishes could long hide the news that beneath this unconventional romance lay a classical triangle with all of the possibilities for anguish hidden in such affairs. It is as if everything that happened during the course of their relationship took place on at least two levels at once. First there are the lovers against the backdrop of their own time, walking the crooked streets of Greenwich Village, smiling across tables, coveting the sentimental letters exchanged almost daily in their respective offices, speaking and writing to each other in the vocabulary of "free love." Then there are the emotions. Maxwell seems to have spent most of the affair in a paroxysm of ambivalence: simultaneously telephoning Margaret, looking at his watch, pulling on his pants, racing for a train: Josie in a paroxysm of unexpected unhappiness, standing alone in an empty doorway, wiping away her tears. It is hard to be sure about the depths it reached on Maxwell's side, for he played the last-chance scenario with considerable poignancy for a man who was going to have two more wives after Margaret died in 1931, and many affairs, and to attach profound implications to what was, after all, her first affair, would be to overanalyze Josie; but if, for her, the affair stirred up jealousies dormant since childhood, for him it appears to have kindled loyalties he seems not to have known he had. If anything their ideology intensified their suffering, for it tempted them to tests of insouciance difficult to survive. But it could not explain the pain of reality. Josie told Maxwell he could bring Margaret to sleep in her apartment after a party in the city, then lay awake on the narrow couch while the couple took the bedroom, fearing she would not be able to breathe after their light went out. Maxwell stayed up reading. She visited Margaret in Croton while he was away on a trip and found a loving note he had written to his wife, and she burst out to Margaret in a bitter attack on the self-deceptions of married women, saying she was having an affair with a married man and coming so dangerously close to the truth that when Margaret described the incident to Maxwell he was furious with Josie and began to think of bringing the relationship to a close. From the evidence it left behind it appears that the affair consisted largely of a series of subterranean eruptions impossible to account for by the ideas they were trying to apply. For an "incorrigible gypsy," Josie made a lot of demands.

Yet whatever the pain involved in Josie's romance with Maxwell Anderson it is hard to resist the suspicion that it was exactly what she wanted. Revolutionary comrades: a Village apartment: the scenario plainly called for the addition of a lover, and presto, as soon as she was ready for one, one appeared. As for the heartache, that too was part of the story. It was a terrible affair, it was a wonderful affair, but at least it *was* an affair, and for a woman more interested in experience than in marriage it is hard to imagine a better companion than this unavailable married writer who kept her mailbox filled with poems. If it reads today like a bohemian caricature that is less my predisposition than their clichés: it was something of a caricature when it happened. "[I had] happily fallen in love unhappily," Josie wrote to a friend years later, and if the affair had stood alone in her life, unrelated to anything that happened after, her own words would serve as an adequate summary. There was something not especially serious about it. The failure of love was blamed not on the limits of love but on its circumstances. The way she felt was precisely the way society intended to make her feel. "It's not love, but marriage, respectability, people believe in," she protested.

Unfortunately for Josie, the affair did not stand alone.

## CHAPTER SEVEN

# "Grief Castle"

ALL DURING the months following Josie's arrival in New York letters traveled back and forth between herself and Helen like diplomatic communications from the emissaries of sister states. After so many years of moving in the same direction, it seemed their lives were suddenly starting to diverge. There was Josie, in New York, conducting herself by will right into the center of the life she had always imagined, and there was Helen, still in Detroit where she had been reunited with Andrew, surrendering herself unhappily to a series of unsatisfactory circumstances. To Helen, living in a boardinghouse, working every day in a hospital clinic, her emotions bound up in a marriage she was not even sure she wanted, all Josie's experiences sounded exciting. Josie did not simplify for Helen any more than she simplified for herself. She was not "happy" and she did not pretend to be. She did not deliberately boast. But she was in the capital and Helen was in the provinces and the fact is that even a list of department stores would have sounded inviting. The people she was meeting at parties were people whose work they had both been reading since before the war. "Washington Square" — "Union Square": the very locations had a fabled, romantic ring. Night after night returning to the boardinghouse for a depressing supper, Helen would reach into the bowl at the center of the table for a letter with the latest from New York, and respond with a generous commentary on the things she found there. Genevieve Taggard was publishing poetry in *The Nation*? Why didn't Josie try it? Her sister's poems would surely be better. Her love affair was painful? At least it was intense.

In the summer of 1920 Josie left the city for a job as a cigarette clerk at a Jewish resort in the Catskills, the Hotel Glass. Maxwell had broken off with her, over her opposition; the charity appeared to be going bankrupt; all in all it seemed a sensible opportunity to take some time away. She had not been there very long before she realized she was pregnant. To Josie's surprise she was not sorry that it had happened and she wrote Maxwell she intended to have the baby. He replied at once: don't: the knowledge and responsibility would weight him down. She said yes: he said no: she gave in: and nothing could illustrate better the state of relations between the sexes in the radical circles of the moment than that both of them accepted as natural that his freedom was worth more than her maternity and that it was his welfare, not hers, that was at stake. The abortion was arranged by a young Russian chauffeur working at the resort. It was done by a fashionable doctor in New York City, and she recuperated, alone, in a hotel. Apart from the chauffeur and Genevieve Taggard, who was now her closest friend, Josie told nobody what she had done. Her ambivalence, her fears, and her suffering, were much too real. In the years that immediately followed, she thought with longing of her missing baby and wondered if she would, or could, have another, which was never certain, but her maternal feelings seem to have crested with this opportunity, and she never felt as strongly about it again. She buried the memory of her abortion in a graveyard reserved for her most private memories, and in a long life in which most events were reviewed with a puzzling frequency, she referred to this one rarely. To Helen, and in her letters home, she remained the sophisticated radical alien dropped into an amusing environment. She quoted from *The Nation* and *The New Republic*, noted the progress of the Bolsheviks, recommended D. H. Lawrence's *The Rainbow*, commented on the illusions of the guests. A few times, after the abortion, she hinted to her mother she was very unhappy and inquired, if she could not pull herself together, could she please come home, but she gave no details. It was what she did not say that summer that mattered, much more so than what she said.

Soon after Josie returned to New York, in the fall of 1920, a job was advertised in the magazine empire of H. L. Mencken and George Jean Nathan which consisted not only of the famous *Smart Set* but a number of sleazier publications called *Les Boulevardes, Saucy Stories, The Parisienne,* and *Black Mask* — more or less the ancestors of today's sex and detective magazines, popular and lucrative. Out of a hundred applicants for the position, Josie and one other woman were invited to take on trial assignments; Josie got the job. Appearances to the contrary, it was not exactly a literary breakthrough. The magazines for which she worked were not magazines for which she was eager to write; the directions her writing took and the publications it led her to were not directions in which Mencken had crowning power; and the fact that, as it happens, Mencken did publish her first two stories in *Smart Set* shortly before it was replaced by *The American Mercury* does not make the link more significant because to avoid his favoritism she submitted those stories under a false name and he did not know till later that she was the one who had written them. But it was the first decent job she had had in New York, the first job she had anywhere that had any connection with her literary interests, and a valuable association besides. At about the same time she got the job, she had an epilogue to her affair with Maxwell — a romantic evening in which she cried and he cried and they swore to return to one another and have a child in two years if they missed one another as much as they thought they would, and the new ending pleased Josie much more than the original. She was just on the verge of recovering from her ordeal when something happened which deepened the impact of the abortion on her life, and gave it a different meaning. What happened had to do with Helen. A few months before, in the spring of 1920, Helen and Andrew had decided that the only way to save money was to return to Sioux City and now they were home again, living in the gable room they called "the tower" of the current Herbst household, almost as if they had never gotten away. If Helen had not been in Sioux City, perhaps Josie would have told her about the abortion, for she told her everything else, and while that would not necessarily have changed the outcome for Helen, it might have made Josie's burden easier to bear. But Helen was home and no secrets were possible and Josie, though she did not fear her mother's disavowal, was in much too much turmoil herself to court her probing. Thus it happened that Josie began writing only her good news precisely when Helen began writing about troubles of her own.

"I hesitate to take any work," Helen wrote to Josie in late September.

I am in a fearful quandary. The totally unexpected may have happened to me. Certainly I hadn't planned on a child yet — not for a year or two — but I'm in doubt. It *may* be.

If it *is* that I don't know what I should do. It will mean utter catastrophe as far as my plans go. Plans for everything — my whole future. I had wanted to go to Chicago in Jan — I wanted to try it away from A. for a year to see if we cared to keep on or not. Now it happens this way. I am caught in this net — such tyranny!

Do you by any chance know something to do. I went to the Dr. — he gave me medicine. It didn't help. I'll try it again when "Gramma" is supposed to be next due but it may not work.

Tell me if you know anything.

Funny what queer turns life takes. I had planned it (having a child) so differently. I wanted it to be such a beautiful thing.

If it happens now Lord knows how long I'll be stuck in this blasted town.

"I keep thinking about you," Josie replied in a letter just after she had told Helen about the likelihood of getting the job with Mencken.

Something *must* be done. It isn't fair to you or Andrew — who both are still trying to get a foothold — to say nothing of being fair to a child. Oh life is stupid. But I know women who have done something even as late as 2 months without any danger. Doesn't Alice know any doctor — some of her women friends ought to know. In either S. Francisco or N.Y. it would be so simple. There is some contraption the doctors use — insert it in the womb to dilate the womb gradually & it produces results painlessly — just passes off in the night — Maybe I could find out if it's anything anyone could insert.

I'm worried myself about my job which hasn't been decided yet & no clothes & money going like water. But what can I do.

M.A. sent me the little verse below. It's about the evening we were together after I came back. Isn't it beautiful. Ah why must life be so hard —

EVENING

This earth of me is swept with whispering wings
And all my life whirls upward like sweet fire,
And woods and sea are kindled with murmurings,
And the long new night shot through with white desire;
And noon is mine and night is mine, and the morning
Pierces me as the hills are pierced with springs.

Let me know how you are. Castor oil should be taken in big doses of course.

"Hope you got the position with Mencken," Helen replied.

It *would* be a fine opportunity. Tho of course the Smart Set is a snobbish mediocre thing with a few redeeming bits of poetry now & then. I know how rotten the suspense of waiting to get something is. To see your money dribbling away and no job cinched. So I'm hoping something will turn up soon.

Things are just the same with me. I can't expect anything till next month. Then I'll start in dosing myself in earnest again. I took Chichesters at first, then some stuff (stronger) that the Dr. gave me. I was going to continue it all month but it was impossible — it made me horribly sick. Alice once took similar stuff 2 mos. & it finally worked. So I haven't lost hope yet. I shall do all I can short of an operation for the idea of having a child is simply impossible. Did you find out about that dilation thing? *It sounds too easy to be true.*

By the first week in October, Josie knew that she had landed the Mencken job. On October 7 she sent Helen her first letter on office stationery, *The Parisienne* written in dashing script across the top, risqué drawings of the cocktail-napkin sort running along the border. "It seems characteristic that Sioux City should be so ineffective & unable to get you out of your dilemma," she began.

> It never gave me anything I wanted . . . its whole nature was mean & barren. I do think though that there ought to be some way out. I don't mean a child would be a disaster — you might even be glad — but it certainly seems as if both you and A. would stand more of a show in life without that just now. . . . If you were only here — I'd go with you to the doctor Genevieve had & that would be the end of it. Genevieve got over it in no time & it was about a month and a half. . . . Oh I wish there was something I could do. It's terrible to seem so ineffective. Do try to find a doctor & let me hear from you.
>
> I like the new job — it's amusing. You ought to see the stories I get — some are imbecilical — so stupid — so silly. I just read them all day long & talk & gossip & eat & smoke. It's huge fun. I'm on the editorial staff & the job really has possibilities. Of course all the magazines are flippant & "smarty" & superficial & cynical but it's good experience & will get me somewhere better afterwards. So far I've had only bluff & it's time I had something else to back me. Mr. Mencken is first rate if his magazines aren't. Hardly a publisher in NY accepts a book without Mencken first approving it. He *is* a real critic.

Why even then, with Helen's desperation clearly increasing, did Josie still not say she had just had an abortion herself? In mentioning Genevieve Taggard she was edging toward the truth, attributing her experience to a friend, but she came no closer to it than that. The most plausible explanation for her silence is her confusion, for to tell the truth would have meant exposing her wretchedness about her own abortion at the very moment she was urging her sister to go ahead. The bravado required to undergo the ordeal in the first place cannot have run very deep. She was afraid to face her own feelings. There were also practical reasons. She was apprehensive about setting an example. As encouraging as she was in everything that she wrote, news of her own safe abortion would have been more encouraging by far. She knew that conditions in New York and Sioux City had little in common and it was important for

Helen to make her decision based on the local situation alone. With money so much a factor it was unlikely that Helen would consider traveling elsewhere, even if she had some place to go. It is not that the responsibility was only Josie's. Mary, Frances, and Alice, who had herself once had an abortion, were also involved. But Josie's relationship to Helen was special, what she said was bound to be taken seriously, and even as it was, she feared she was influencing her more than she should. As busy as Josie was with her new obligations, her sister was constantly on her mind. She did not hear from Helen for several days, and on October 13 dashed off another note. "I've talked to more people," she wrote.

> In the apartment where I am for the present is a girl who had something done after 5 months. She knew all about it. *Said not to worry or get nervous* and NOT to take any more medicine. It's that which causes trouble because the system becomes poisoned. . . . But all the doctor does is dilate the womb & there's very little pain — you're over it in a short time — why she was & it was 5 mo! And Jed didn't even stop work. . . .

On October 16, Helen wrote again. "I have been so distraught by this business that I couldn't even write," she said.

> I've spent days & days going to Drs. trying to persuade them to do this — they are all too pious & in fear of the law. That's the trouble in a small town. . . . All of them told so many terrible stories that I began to get cold feet — But pinned down they admitted that if *done right* there was little danger. The trouble is finding an expert physician who will do it. I have finally located a Dr. whom I think will but his rep. isn't of the best. Still I could find out nothing definite against him. So if he'll do it I expect I'll let him. You see there really is a risk of blood poisoning from incomplete abortion. I remember women who had to come to the hospital & have the uterus scraped. An awful operation & as a result you can never have children. So I must be careful.

October 20. Josie to Helen: Parisienne stationery.

> What hypocrites doctors are. Hope you find one soon but I've known so many girls who had it done. Just get a good Dr. I suppose you might have gone to Omaha. It's bigger.
> Everything is so high & I'm so dowdy I feel so low spirited. You know how clothes do affect you — particularly when life is sad enough as it is.

64

## "Grief Castle"

On other side is a copy of some verses M.A. sent me the other day. You will understand them. We get so desperate — & I think he tried in them to see ahead some beauty in the end out of it all that might save us. *The Nation* has taken all his epigrams. He is starting a new poetry magazine to be called *The Spade* or *New Yeares*.

### GRIEF CASTLE

I keep my darkness though. This cloud is mine,
This memory of a sun that passed and turned.
If you had told me then there would be one spring
And then no more spring — no, for the whole earth burned,
And the sky was a flame, and winter was shriveled away —
I would not have believed. But now I believe and know.

And out of the dark you left me there has risen
A wide cloud palace topped with domes and spires
That shelters me from a world of streets and faces
Hides me and shields. For a year it was a prison
And its one close room a torture chamber where fires
Were lit for the branding of souls, your soul and mine.
But the walls gave way to the winds of old desires.

Gave way, withdrew, with the dark still covering them
Back to the bounds of grief, to the hollows of time
   Until there was place for music, place for rest,
     And I go warily, fearing to disturb its beauty,
     Lest at a word the battlements fall, lest
      The foundations crumble, the fragile night be broken,
      The sun come in from the West.

And I have forgotten how it was in the winter,
How it was in the early spring,
And I have forgotten the sea and the forest places,
The laughter of lovers, and lovers' lips that cling.
You I remember, and all my grief is above me,
And all my grief is about me, barring the days,
And I hear only echoes, and see men going and coming
Dimly, along dim ways.
High and deep and still, builded of cloud and shadow,
Hung with shadows, fold on fold,
   My grief has covered me from weeping, covered me from madness,
   Has shut out the cold.

I think the last verse showing the reality of love against the unreality of life is very effective.

But Helen never read Maxwell's verses. For her indeed the unreality of life had become fact. Exactly as she feared, an infection had set in after the abortion and there was nothing that could be done about it. When "Grief Castle" reached "the tower," she was dead.

The news reached Josie, as she was sitting in her office, in the form of a phone call from Genevieve Taggard who had opened the telegram that arrived at 12 St. Luke's. "It's my little sister. I did it," she said. The night before, Josie had suddenly been aroused from a deep sleep by the sound of someone calling her, "Jo," clearly, almost laughingly. She either answered "yes" or thought she had, because she wondered if anyone had heard her speak, and she felt, before she realized that she was dreaming, that she was in Sioux City, rather than in New York. It took several minutes of looking around the room before she knew where she was. The voice had been so familiar, so challenging. It left her in a happy, confident mood. She laughed at herself and went back to sleep — and understood the next day that it happened at just about the time that Helen died. She went home for the funeral and stayed in Sioux City a week and it was so . . . Sioux Cityish . . . that she could hardly bear to remain even that long. The house was filled with sentimental bouquets and people milled about constantly offering saccharine condolences for little sister's tragic appendicitis. Mary and Bent, Frances and her husband, Ben Wells, Alice and her husband, John Hansen, Andrew, Andrew's parents, Josie — all who knew the truth were pitted against the others in their awful secret and they sat close together when the callers had gone home, consoling each other with instances of courage from the family's past and reminding themselves of the one fact that was undoubtedly true: Helen would not want them to mourn too much. But for Josie there could be no consolation. Maxwell soon faded to the proper place for a first lover in her mind. The scars from her own abortion would in time have healed. But when she lost Helen she lost part of herself and the most important relationships of the rest of her life were attempts in one way or another to bring her sister back.

When Josie returned to New York she tried hard to resume life as she had left it. Too hard, thought Genevieve Taggard. Evidently Josie's efforts at brightness were not very convincing. She went to work every day reading manuscripts for Mencken and won his permanent respect for her competence. She had dates, she went places, she read books, just as before. But it all seemed empty and meaningless. Nothing could penetrate her private despair. "It seems to me as if my sister's ashes cover the wide world and everything looks grey," she wrote to Jed.

Her body, as well as her mind, was suffering badly. Always given to the physical manifestation of her emotions, she could scarcely eat, she was sleeping poorly, and her feelings overwhelmed her at unexpected moments — even on the subway — and left her dissolved in tears. In January, 1921, when Helen had been dead three months, a doctor diagnosed "nervous exhaustion" and told her she required rest. She borrowed money from friends, Mencken kicked in her salary, and she spent two weeks in a sanatorium in Clifton Springs, New York, taking baths, having rubdowns, and getting plenty of food and attention. "It hasn't been that I've consciously grieved about Helen — but I couldn't help the feelings that came unbidden — as if a hand were clutching my throat and choking me," she wrote to her mother. "I miss her so terribly and in so fundamental a way . . . I know I shouldn't blame myself, but I can't help it."

Even after her stay at the sanatorium, she continued to feel worn down. She was extremely dependent on her friendships with Genevieve Taggard and Robert Wolf. Jed was an intelligent, strong-minded, and sensuous young woman whose determination to make a life for herself had much in common with Josie's own. Bob was an intense, sensitive, and lightly whimsical man who dedicated himself with equal fervor to writing and sex. As a couple they were romantic and modern. They wanted love and work, freedom and commitment, involvement with other people and absorption in themselves. Today, Bob's reputation has altogether disappeared. He published only two books, poems, called *After Disillusion*, in 1923, and a novel, *Springboard*, in 1927. Nor has Jed fared much better, though she published many volumes of poetry, some prose, and was active in radical as well as literary circles, and as a teacher, all her life. Ultimately, their life together was not successful. At some point Bob was committed to a mental institution, and in 1934 Jed and Bob were divorced. The following year, Jed married Kenneth Durant, an American who worked for the Soviet news agency, Tass. She died in 1948, long after she and Josie had ceased being close. But in the period Josie knew them best Jed and Bob were young and strong and they seemed to have a future separately and together, and she was comforted by their example. Of all the people she knew in New York, only they understood the complicated interrelations of everything that had happened to her in the way she understood them herself. Jed and Bob were not her only companions. She had other friends among the women of 12 St. Luke's, and men were in constant pursuit. Alan Gardner, a Canadian she had met at the sanatorium, wanted to marry her. Albert Rhys Williams, a minister turned radical who was one of the leading American publicists against Allied intervention in Russia, had been attracted to her from their earliest meeting, and was endlessly attentive, and they often spent weekends together, out of the city, at the Brookwood Labor College, or on the Long Island or New Jersey coasts. Even Mike Gold let it be known that he was available, despite Helen Black, if she were interested. And there were others. She simply was not interested. The Canadian, she felt, was in too much need — she was bound to hurt him. Albert was "too uncertain a child." About Mike she could never bring herself to be serious — "he confuses me about writing, for one thing," she wrote to Bob. When a married organizer from the Brookwood Labor College tried to persuade her that a husband and wife should be free to accept beautiful spontaneous moments, "I agreed and added they were the only ones really who could afford to be spontaneous and free. The other people risked too much," she said. After looking for love on the trail that had led from an affair to an abortion to her sister's dying, for the moment, friends were enough.

In the spring of 1921 Jed and Bob married and moved to Connecticut to work on their writing undisturbed. Not long afterward they moved again, to California. The next year they had a baby daughter, of whom Josie was named the godmother and the writer Floyd Dell, a friend of Bob's, the godfather. She missed them very much. She thought very often of her family in Sioux City, maintaining an intense correspondence not only with her mother but for the first time with her sister Frances, and she wished, very often, for a family of her own. In September, 1921, less than a year after Helen died, something happened which revived all her associations and grief. A note arrived at the office from Margaret Anderson announcing that she had come to the city to deliver their third child, which was expected imminently, and wouldn't Josie come up and visit her? Josie ran from the office, stuffed the note into an envelope and scrawled to Jed, "Oh Jed — won't somebody help me . . . I can't bear it . . . It is so unfair. That's *my* baby. She is having my own baby. Oh Jed I do need help so. *She* didn't need another when she had two." She stayed out of the office the entire day and by the end of it she was feeling more calm. "I don't want to seem foolish & think that because I was in Maxwell's life, nothing should happen in his ever after," she wrote Jed again. "But this is all too ironic & terrible. I wanted my baby so much and only gave it up because he had so many burdens all ready. But it would have made such a difference in my life. He might have helped me and money was all I wanted. But he was so quick to advise *me* to get rid of it. It's only wives who can have babies — no matter how dear the baby may be . . . I'm just limp tonight & its foolish I know but O I can't bear it. It's so cruel . . . If it hadn't been successful with me I wouldn't have told [my sister] — and now it is all so bitter. Don't mind this Jed dear. Only I'm so ill at heart and so tired of pretending to be gay."

Being ill at heart was more than a metaphor. She began having palpitations so frequent and intense that a doctor told her she must lie down for twelve hours out of twenty-four and forecast a life for her as a semi-invalid. That evening was one of the few times in her life she considered suicide. But it is as if imagining death in the form of her black gas stove made her reckon for life again because suddenly she realized that she knew more about herself than any doctor and she refused to accept the verdict. What she needed was not rest. It was excitement. "Here, everyone I know runs to Europe or takes prolonged vacations because they have to in order to keep up & going the rest of the time," she wrote to her mother. "They need a change or they'd go stale & mad . . . If I can feel a sense of adventure about this, I'll gain 20 lb. in a month & no one will know anything was ever wrong with my heart." Abroad, she could live cheaply enough to write. From the day after her interview with the doctor to the day she set foot on the boat she concentrated singlemindedly on saving money for Europe. Her mother came east to spend two weeks with her, and together they visited Mary's childhood haunts in New Jersey, then roamed the city like sisters. Josie left New York on May 13, 1922, on the Cunard liner *Caronia*, stayed some time in England with acquaintances from San Francisco, and spent the summer traveling on the continent with Albert Rhys Williams and Max Eastman. In the fall, her companions went on to Russia. Josie settled down by herself, in Berlin.

# Following the Circle

SAY "BERLIN — 1922" to anyone who knows its story and the image you will evoke before any others is the image of money: worthless money. Every story you have ever heard about the German inflation is true. One woman sold her furniture to raise money for postage to send a letter to relatives in America: ten women did: perhaps it was a hundred. One child followed the coal wagons picking up bits of coal so small they were scarcely more than dust: a hundred children did: perhaps it was a thousand. The dramas of a period in which the value of the mark fluctuated so wildly that the price of a sausage was not the same in the afternoon as it had been in the morning unfolded on every avenue, daily. Josie was sensitive to the people's desperation: she recognized her position: she felt uncomfortable about the fortunes of currency that left her a "dollar princess" while a suitcaseful of German money could not buy bread: she stayed anyway. For $20 a month she could cover all her expenses, including extras, and it was not an opportunity she could afford to lose. She "mingled with the rich in swank hotels and spas . . . or shared black bread and cabbages with students in their unheated Studentenheim . . . or paid ten cents to take the train to Dresden to hear the opera . . . or reveled at a different theater each night"; and between the American radicals passing through and their European acquaintances she felt well enough connected to assure her parents airily that in the event of a revolution she would personally be safe. Yet contrary to the impression created by her eventual memoirs, which focused more on external conditions than on herself, during the period she was actually in Germany her experiences were largely private. She spent most of her time in a suburban boardinghouse, writing her heart out.

The novel that Josie began in Berlin is a bitter portrait of marriage from the point of view of a single woman. Called *Unmarried*, it follows her recent experiences so closely that it is literally impossible to tell whether a notebook labeled "New York" among her papers is a diary of her affair with Maxwell Anderson or a workbook for the novel. It could be either or both. An unmarried woman falls in love with a married man, becomes pregnant, and has an abortion, and her sister also has an abortion, and her sister dies — but you have just read the story yourself. While she was writing it she lived her life with deliberate sexual desperation. She walked by herself, better dressed than any but a few German women, down streets that belonged after dark to the prostitutes, almost waiting to hear the footsteps falling in alongside her, the tug at her coat sleeve, "Guten Tag, Fräulein." She went by herself to fancy restaurants where animals male and female sat two by two and she saw herself as an outsider from an aberrant species doomed to extinction. She went to cafés where even couples seemed doomed to extinction. She slept with a number of radicals and journalists who could not possibly have had particular feeling for her — one, a man committed to one of her friends; another, who was traveling with his wife. "It seems as if all I get were men's passions — as if on me they wrought all the fantastic extremities of their imaginations," she complained to Genevieve Taggard. Yet she invited those very passions. Her Berlin adventures constituted the logical extension of the fate of the unmarried woman and she wanted to be reminded. It was only by heightening her alienation that she could begin to see it clearly, and it was useful to have a literary rationale. "There isn't any man in all this world who can give me very much any more . . . Now I go to them pretty much as men go to prostitutes. And that's the way my book ends," she wrote to Jed.

*Unmarried* was never published, nor, from a literary point of view, did it deserve to be. Its tone was unmodulated, its characterizations simplistic, and its story incomplete. But more important than its literary flaws was the fact that its entire framework was not only outside publishing law, it was outside social understanding. Although similar in a generic sense to the confessional novels of some of her male contemporaries, such as Floyd Dell's *Briary Bush* or Bob Wolf's *Springboard*, Josie's novel was exceptionally intimate, and of course it was a woman's story. Its harsh representations of relations between the sexes read like the notes of a consciousness-raising group from the feminist revival of a half-century later. Nearly fifty years before Martha Quest had her interview with the sanctimonious Rhodesian physician who denied her an

abortion in Doris Lessing's A *Proper Marriage*, "Claire Stahl" had an almost identical one in the American city of "Iroquois"; and the abortion
scenes in *Unmarried* are so affecting that the writer Claude Mackay, who
read the manuscript in Paris, told Andrew Bernhard that he could feel
the scraping of the knife. Never mind that everything that happened in
the novel happened in life. An abortion in a book was in effect twice the
crime of an abortion in the flesh and a novelist would be far more likely
to be prosecuted than a doctor. As involved as she was with writers and
books I think on some level at least Josie must have known this and on
some level at least she must not have cared. When she failed even with
Mencken's help to find a publisher later she did not seem too disappointed. It was the writing itself that was important to her. "It seems as
if it were my blood going into it," she wrote to Jed. "As if at last I'd found
a lover who knew all and understood all."

After she had been writing for more than a year her self-absorption
was jolted by the arrival in Berlin of her brother-in-law, Andrew Bernhard. Andrew was family, practically brother, for he had been living
with Mary and Bent since Helen died, continuing to try to save money by
working in a Sioux City packinghouse, and he and Josie were companionable and close. By then she was ready for a change. Together they did
everything she had not already done and did again some of the things she
had — walking excursions, boating excursions, side-trips to Dresden, to
Marburg, to Cologne. Another winter was coming: a cold fuelless chill
was in the air. She packed her trunk and went with Andrew to Zurich
where he had relatives, then on to Florence on her own. She settled into
a pensione by the railroad, and there she celebrated Christmas, 1923.
Andrew came to join her and so did another friend, Ruth Allen, an actress with whom she had briefly shared an apartment in New York. Hour
after hour she sat in front of the typewriter and page after page was
added to her manuscript. But it was hard to sustain two realities at once.
It was so comfortable here, so satisfactory. The pensioners were so eccentric, so entertaining. At dusk every day the sun came streaming
through the window and with it the jabber from the neighboring café
and the wine was so cheap . . . Once she saw a man just sitting who reminded her of Bent, and for the first time she understood her father and
his Royal Arcanum Lodge. In late winter or early spring Andrew and
Ruth went to Paris, where Andrew found work first as a tour guide, and
later as a proofreader for the Paris edition of the *Chicago Tribune*, a step
toward the successful newspaper jobs he was eventually to hold. Josie
stayed in Italy trying to write. But now it was no longer enough. In April
she faced the fact of her restlessness and went on to Paris to join the
others, beginning her stay there with a smashing debauch consisting of a
dozen parties with barely time out for dozing in between, and drinking,
and doing things, as she wrote to Jed, that "I never thought I would do."

And after that, and after she had slept for a while — I should say she was awakened by a kiss on the lips from a handsome prince. It wasn't that exactly. But it was close enough.

Of all the cafés in Paris none was inhabited by the American set more regularly than the Café du Dôme in Montparnasse and it was there on an April afternoon in 1924 that Josie first met John Herrmann. He was sitting alone at a table in the rear balancing a stack of saucers precariously in front of him. Andrew introduced them. She never forgot how he looked that day: his brown hair tousled where his fingers supported his hungover head: the leanness of him: his eyes. John Herrmann was twenty-three. The son of a conventional Lansing, Michigan, businessman with whom he had long been at odds, he had been in Munich for two years, studying art history at the university, but literature interested him more. He was working on a novel about his adolescence. His European travel, his ambition to be a writer, his affinity for culture and art — whatever it was that mattered to him, his family viewed with alarm. Their attitude undermined him. If he became a famous author he supposed he might do as he pleased and still remain in the family circle. Otherwise, it was the family business or out. In Paris he had the reputation of being "good company." He drank much more than he wrote. Josie was thirty-two but in her heart she was twenty-seven. Also on her passport: she had taken two years off her birthdate when she entered Berkeley and another three when she left New York. He saw a woman different from any he had ever met — not "silly," like the Lansing girls. She saw an endearing boy so tender beneath his cockiness that for the first time since her relationship with Maxwell Anderson she could be vulnerable too. "I've known older men and sophisticated men for such a long time — men who never quite wanted to lose themselves in any but a physical way that I had quite forgotten what young love was," she wrote to Jed. "I didn't know I wanted it. I had forgotten or was sceptical of the way it can flood your veins. But I met a young and beautiful boy . . . who looks like one of the beautiful Greeks . . . And this creature over a cafe table was young enough to fall in love with me. And to be adored Jed — not just loved but adored. I wonder how long it is since anyone has done that for me — it seems never." Soon she was spending most of her nights in John's little room with the death mask of Nietzsche on the wall and a paisley shawl over the trunk and a copy of *Ecce Homo* laid out like a private shrine, and whatever took place in those long dusky hours it made her feel she had found her truest companion since Helen. Everything that was true when they parted was true when they met. Josie was ambitious and John was not ambitious, he preferred the company of the cafés and she preferred the solitude of the typewriter, he had confidence in his charm but not in his book and she had confidence in her book but not in her charm. But what became difficult oppositions when things were dissolving between them were magnetizing complements at the time they began. Once again, Josie was in love.

Josie had a room of her own at an address so private she did not even tell Andrew where it was, and she continued to work on *Unmarried*. When she was through for the day she went out to the cafés. The people she saw most, in addition to John, Andrew, and Ruth Allen, were other writers — Robert McAlmon, Nathan Asch, Claude Mackay. A particular friend was the young Ernest Hemingway, whose camaraderie with John, based in part on their common Michigan boyhoods, was quickly extended to include his new girl. They did not much talk about their work. Writing was private — it was something that you did alone. Conversation was conversation. And parties were parties. Along with the men who in time became famous were the Parisienne Fritzis and Gigis who decorate their memoirs like parsley on soup and the Lillians and Marions from the old USA who — if the memoirs are to be believed — crossed oceans and continents to bring-their-sweethearts-to-their-senses and were always making scenes at restaurants. It was not really endlessly compelling. Josie and John exchanged infections. Josie got the mumps. John drank all night with Robert McAlmon and Nathan Asch worrying about whether he would ever be able to be a father, then went and sang to Josie beneath her window, as if she were a storybook queen. John was having trouble applying himself to his book; he was drinking too much and too often; he was on the threshold of giving up the idea of writing and returning home. His Lansing sweetheart was following him and while Josie was quarantined the sweetheart was at large. In a moment of sweet confrontation Josie and John decided together: whatever the influences beckoning him to respectability, John was going to resist. He would go to Brittany and rent a room by the sea and write and live more healthily, and she would come when she was better. He wrote her charming, piteous letters about the roll of the bed and the roll of the sea and how difficult it was for him to be without her. He called himself "your boy."

When Josie joined John at Le Pouldu in June, 1924, she entered upon one of the loveliest moments of her life. Everything was wonderful. The village was perfect and the inn was perfect and the Breton fishing boats with their red sails were perfect. Even the sex was perfect: perhaps the first she had ever really enjoyed. When they were not walking or talking or making love they were working on their respective novels and that too was perfect, the very model of a bohemian romance. John's novel, *What Happens*, is a series of episodes in the sexual enlightenment of an adolescent boy, with emphasis on the adolescent. You love the girls from whom you don't get any and if you do get any then you don't love the girls anymore. Those girls are whores. It is as real a reflection of his experiences with women as Josie's novel *Unmarried* is of her experiences with men, but compared to *Unmarried* it is juvenile in the extreme. Where one is the story of a profound and fateful attraction, the other is the story of a succession of meaningless affairs. Where in *Unmarried* the women are self-willed beings who court experience on its own terms and wrestle with the consequences, in *What Happens* the women are man-centered twerps and the only wrestling that does not take place on davenports occurs in cars. For all its weaknesses, *Unmarried* breathes like a woman. *What Happens* pants like a boy. They are not opposing viewpoints in an ideological sense so much as manifestations of completely different beings. Why didn't they realize, typing away back to back at the opposite ends of their room by the sea, that the stories they were telling about relations between men and women were incompatible? They came from opposite sides of the double standard. The answer is simple. They did not want to know. They were happy together that summer. Between his ease and her intensity they made a perfect pair. They used their novels to share their intimate histories and if their histories were difficult for one another to take, how could they quarrel with the truth of experience? Its importance was the closest they had to a shared literary idea.

As long as they were in Brittany the idyll continued, but as soon as they were back in Paris, it began to fade. It was one thing to face "experience" in a novel, but Josie's was in the past and across the ocean and John's was in the present and still in Paris. In addition to the matter of his girlfriend, there was also the matter of his book. Somehow in the trading of manuscripts and the reading aloud and the mutual criticism that had gone on over the summer, *What Happens* had gotten most of the attention, and it was now ready to be sent to publishers. Never one for fidelity, then or later, John was considering gathering up girlfriend and book and returning to Lansing. Josie was in the opposite position, for under the influence of love her manuscript was undergoing changes. Instead of ending with the heroine going to a man for sex as a man would go to a prostitute, the novel ended with her coming back from a sanatorium resolved to begin anew, and for the changes to be integrated much work remained to be done. She found herself in a dilemma. What she wanted she was hardly certain, but she did not want to be separated from John. Although she had always intended to complete her book before going back to America, she now followed his schedule rather than her own, and nothing will tell you better how she felt about him at the time. When they sailed together on the *Rochambeau* in October, 1924, her novel was still unfinished. It was now called *Following the Circle*.

# An Even Race

WHEN JOSIE and John returned to New York, they stayed together for only a short time. They saw *What Price Glory?*, Maxwell Anderson's successful new play, visited with Genevieve Taggard and Bob Wolf who were back in Connecticut, met enough of each other's friends to establish some common ground, and then they separated. Josie was eager to get back to Sioux City where she could visit with her family and finish up the novel without worrying about money. John was going to take his novel around to publishers and then return to Lansing. Their understanding was definite — sooner or later they would get back together — but the details were vague. It depended.

As long as John was in their common world, things were all right between them. He wrote warm teasing letters encouraging her about her work — "Somebody has got to support the family and the Lord knows I can't" — and criticized sections of her manuscript. When he got back to Lansing around Christmas, things began to change. There was something to be said for the old town after all, he realized. Despite the interest of a number of publishers he had not sold his book, and although he was greeted by his acquaintances as something of a celebrity, in his parents' eyes he seemed to be heading for failure. Naturally easygoing, preferring comfort to pain, John was far from committed to starving for the sake of a literary ideal, and he could see their point of view. The family tailoring business looked as odious to him as ever but the idea of owning a bookstore someday did not. He could always write a novel or two on the side.

Receiving John's letters in her distant Sioux City outpost, Josie was dissatisfied with them and it is easy to see the reasons. There was a lot going on between them, none of it resolvable by mail. Anything could lead to a misunderstanding. If one letter began "Dearest Josie" and the next did not, a storm of denunciation would follow. John Herrmann was nothing if not candid. If the Lansing girls were after him, if there was necking at parties, if his mother, sensing a rival, found ways to put her down, he duly reported it all. But if John was too honest, Josie was too blunt. She was perfectly right about it — he *was* under his mother's thumb — but was it necessary to insist he had a "complex" about it? He turned aside her worries with his usual touch: "I am not serious sitting here writing but feel like smiling." That was the trouble — he was never serious. Would no one ever understand the pressures she was under? Why couldn't he be reassuring? Why did he always have to say things like that? Like what, exactly? Like *that*. Beneath the surface quarrels there were serious issues. Did he really want to be, was he going to be, a writer? Were they going to be together? It suddenly seemed very uncertain.

Even apart from her difficulties with John, life in Sioux City was far from rosy. Josie, too, was treated as a celebrity, lecturing the local drama society on, of all things, *What Price Glory?*, but at home there was a lot of strain. A financial scandal involving her sister Alice's husband, John Hansen, who had "borrowed" money from his lodge treasury, been found out, and had had to borrow in turn from the rest of the family to escape prosecution, had left them embarrassed and strapped. Her own sworn intention to continue carrying on with this boy from Lansing, yet never to marry, evoked considerable disapproval. And more important than anything, staring them all in the face, was the fact that her mother was ill and though no one, even the doctors, knew how ill, it was obvious that something was radically wrong. Always a stalwart, Mary resisted as long as possible, trying to keep going, but it was a losing struggle. Between the swelling of her stomach and a terrible itch for which there were only surface balms she was more tormented every day. Josie was increasingly distracted from her book. Between her anxiety about her mother and her anxiety about John, she was getting very little done, and what she did write she felt was inferior to what she had written before. In March, 1925, she left her mother to visit with John in Detroit — a visit in which everything that could go wrong did. He acted as if he were frightened of her coming and stuck her away in a hotel where his mother wouldn't know and he had another infection which made it impossible for them to make love and she made a scene in a bookstore in which he had taken a job and all in all it was much more distressing than satisfactory. Josie had not been there very long before she got a telegram that Mary was worse. She went back to Sioux City before anything improved with John.

When Josie arrived in Sioux City she found her mother on the edge of death. Mary kept "sinking and reviving," sinking and reviving. She was swollen and disfigured, practically putrefying. Only her eyes and her spirit remained bright. "One moment we thought she was gone, the next she was sitting up asking for ham & eggs & wanting to brush her teeth & actually *doing* it," Josie told Jed and Bob. Next she wanted mashed potatoes. "Something beyond her will" held her to the earth, as if life were still so intense for her she could not bear to let it go. Watching the family, watching the patient, the doctor said it was wrong. Someone must make her stop fighting death. Josie drank a tumbler of whisky and went upstairs and began to talk to her mother. "In whose voice?" she wondered later. "Why don't you just let go? We all have to let go. Sometimes. The birds. The grass. The leaves fall. Just be easy and let go. It's only a little time, we all go." And Mary took Josie's advice and she squeezed her arm so hard it hurt and she looked at her daughter out of her poor swollen face and she said "You're my sunshine" and Josie took it as her benediction and the hired nurse in the background was swaying and bawling "ho to Jesus," "ho to Jesus" and Mary smiled firmly and said no, she was still not interested in Jesus, and she told Josie she wished she could have seen John and she wanted John to take care of her and she called in her husband and her other daughters one by one and she told them of the other things she wanted done and then she said nothing else and not right away, but not long afterward, she finally died. "It was hard slow laborious work, like a dreadful birth," Josie wrote Jed and Bob, but it was "strange and wonderful," too. To the family history of noble endings which she herself had so often recounted, Mary had now added her own.

Josie stayed in Sioux City for several weeks longer, comforting her father and helping to initiate him into life on his own, and then she was ready to move on. She was in a highly euphoric state. Stopping off en route to New York for a visit with John in Detroit she found things just as difficult as the first time but now she was less affected by it. For the moment she knew what was important. Arbitrarily she declared her book was finished. She would begin taking it to publishers in New York. The more she thought of it the more she was certain that what she wanted was to live with John in rural Connecticut, near Jed Taggard and Bob Wolf, and the more she thought about that the more she was certain that the only obstacle was money. Carrying out an idea she had had a long time, she got in touch with Maxwell Anderson, who had not helped pay for her abortion, and asked for some, and in what spirit the transaction occurred it is impossible to say for the correspondence has vanished, but that was probably part of the point. By the end of the summer, 1925, Josephine Herbst had some money and Maxwell Anderson probably had his letters. As for John, he was delighted to be rescued, for the attractions of living near his family had rapidly started to pall. Several months earlier during their wintry correspondence Josie had toted up all the factors involved in holding them together and concluded that, all in all, it was relatively equally balanced. "I want to keep to myself. I want to love, not too much. . . . It will be an even race between us or nothing," she promised.

# PART FOUR

# THE HOUR OF COUNTERFEIT BLISS

# Connecticut

WHEN JOSIE was fretting in Sioux City and John was flirting with other women in Detroit he typed her a copy of a poem by James Joyce: "And soon will your true love be with you, Soon O Soon": and I like to think she was thinking of it now as she lay in the Connecticut hospital bed covered head to toe with poison ivy — revenge of the strawberry patches on the hill behind Jed and Bob's. For John is her true love, at least as far as love is ever true, and she is his, at least of anyone he has met so far. Whatever struggles they have just passed through, the important fact is that they have passed through them. They mean much more to one another now than anyone else has ever meant to either one. He has decided he will be able to settle down, give up the girls, trade popularity for serious writing as the basis of his being. She has accepted the risks she knows loving this boy entails. The life they are beginning cannot possibly be easy but it has something better than ease: it has belief: they are creating a life close to the lives they have both independently wanted. It is a honeymoon but it is better than a honeymoon. The couple will remain unmarried.

*Fall, 1925.* They rent a small wood farmhouse for $6 a month near the town of New Preston in a valley called Merryall and the old tobacco farmer who owns it is so happy to see life in his place again he gives them a cookstove and a coalstove and tables and chairs besides. Jed and Bob produce a bed and a quilt. John puts up shelves and paints the walls white and the sashes red and Josie makes curtains, red and white, to hang in the windows, and when the painting is done they put flowering geraniums on the windowsill overlooking the porch. It is too late to begin a garden but John has only to walk the route to town stopping off along the way to make the acquaintance of their neighbors before he has promises of enough surplus tomatoes and carrots and onions and squash to last the winter. The apples are free and plentiful and lie so thickly on the ground bushels can be gathered in minutes. While Josie works at Jed's, canning chili and mincemeat in amount and in quality something to be proud of, John tends to the cider — two fifty-gallon kegs — which he rolls into the cellar to harden with the hanging beef.

*Winter.* They close off most of the house to save fuel and use only three rooms. Josie works all day in the kitchen getting heat from the stove and keeping an eye on dinner while John works in a front room upstairs, she on a novel, he on stories. At night they read aloud from the moderns or the classics, the reader sitting up by the kerosene lamp in the only soft chair, the listener curled in the quilt on the bed, most often he the reader, she the listener. They see only the milkman and the mailman. The pages pile higher with the snow.

*Winter. Version Two.* The neighboring men have discovered both John's cider and his sociability. He can recite "The Shooting of Dan McGrew" as well as he can recite "The Waste Land." As Josie is interrupted in her writing for the . . . time by these loutish drunks who can never say anything to her but "here's to your bonny blue eyes, my lass" as they refill their glasses for the . . . time, she stomps upstairs to John's office thinking "If I hear 'A bunch of the boys was whoopin' it up in the Malamute Saloon . . .' one more time I'll . . ." and sits down at his typewriter and dashes off a funny furious bitter story called "Dry Sunday in Connecticut" about exactly what is taking place at that moment and two writers who are deluding themselves with images of peace in the country, and when it appears as a reprint in the *Hartford Courant* a short time later it is not the disclosures about their insensitivity but the revelations about their drinking the neighbors find unconscionable: After all it *is* Prohibition, and it *was* Sunday. But Josie and John reread it and laugh: because the story was precisely true: because "Mrs. Sherman" was still too much in love with her "husband" to stay angry at him for very long, just as the story said: and because the money from *The American Mercury* didn't do the budget any harm. Besides, it is spring. Everything looks worse in a New England farmhouse in the winter anyway. Now the blossoms have burst forth from the trees again and the people have burst forth from their houses and they see that they are not the only writers in the valley anymore. Nathan Asch and his wife, Deane, friends from Paris, have turned up not far up the road. Jed and Bob have separated and Jed has left, but Bob has returned to the barn with the swallows and has rented the main house to a new couple, Katherine Anne Porter and Ernest Stock, she a writer, he a painter, and Josie and Katherine Anne take to each other as neither has taken to another woman in some time — serious women writers are precious to them both — and John carves a model of a Brittany fishing boat and races it on the lake with a model of Stock's. The garden is in early: John's peas are the talk of the countryside. The neighbors forgive them and they forgive the neighbors — at least on the surface — and soon they are going to barn-dances and swapping recipes again as if they really belonged.

*Summer, 1926.* The days are getting shorter again. They count the pages of their manuscripts. The work is coming along despite everything. They count the money in the bank account. They have spent less than $600 so far. Standing in the garden with their arms around one another's waists while the katydids fiddle and the toads burp percussion they think "Why not buy it?", the obvious answer — that they are penniless — evidently not striking them as a serious obstacle, and they go inside and sit down at the table and compose John's father a letter asking for money. When it is done they put on their visiting clothes and walk to town arm in arm to put their proposition in the mail: thereby initiating a series of events that will have exactly the opposite effect of the one they want — and more besides.

*The Father:* To Henry Herrmann money is love, love is approval, and approval is obedience, and why John thinks his father will help him is hard to guess because in his father's view John has done nothing right since he got out of knickers and if you follow it backwards beginning with obedience you will see that the request is not very likely to lead to cash. But: *The Son:* John has put it cagily — a "real estate deal" — and Henry thinks: "ah, wise investment — maybe the boy is all right after all": and he sends off a check for one thousand dollars without consulting Mother, who, when she hears of it, hits the roof, because: *The Mother:* if Mr. Herrmann is interested in his son's equity Mrs. Herrmann is interested in his morality, and when John was at home on his long recent visit she had gotten the scent from his belongings of an aroma not her own. Accordingly she snooped: accordingly she discovered some letters from Josie she found most remarkable: and accordingly when John had left — precipitously, in her view — for the East, she had put a detective on his trail who had turned up not only Josie but either the manuscript or at least the gist of *What Happens* — all of which, for reasons of her own, she has not yet told Father. Now she does: one thousand dollars is serious business: and now Henry Herrmann stops the check: and now he sits down and writes to his son on his own father's stationery — John

Herrmann's Sons — a letter in which questions of love and questions of money are so shamelessly intermingled that: *Josie:* could use it intact when she was writing her trilogy as a caricature of the essence of fatherhood under capitalism — because it was. But: *Josie and John:* now it is not parody it is reality and now they are not writers they are only children and now Josie is angry and John is humiliated and the angrier she gets the more humiliated he gets because: *Josie:* is demanding to know just what are those "deprivations" the father refers to with his two houses and six bathrooms and his son not even having running water and what is so "criminal" about writing a book and you would never catch her family carrying on like that — poor as they are, they help when they can — and: *John:* what can John say? — he is sick of comparisons — and now it is not just the house in the valley that is at stake anymore, it is something intangible — his parents' respect — and now: *John:* instead of saying to them what he probably should have said: "Love me as I am or let me alone": he tries one more time to be the manikin his father wanted and writes home a letter claiming "We are married" and: *Josie:* Josie does not stop him, perhaps she even leads him to it, because she has already told *her* father when they moved to Connecticut that they *had* gotten married because Mary would have wanted her to and she regrets not carrying out her mother's wishes and: *Josie and John:* the point is they are in it together: it is her lie as well as his: and it is on both of their lives that its consequences will fall.

Why?

Because when: *The Father:* Mr. Herrmann gets that letter he turns to his wife and says "What shall we do now?" and: *The Mother:* Mrs. Herrmann says "Ask for the license" and: *The Son:* when John gets that letter he types on the bottom "My wife and myself do not wish to be further insulted. Your conduct has made my wife suffer a nervous shock that has forced me to put her under doctors care. John." and: *The Parents:* when Mr. and Mrs. Herrmann get that letter they decide to investigate and drive east one thousand miles arriving unannounced on a matrimonial stage set that could not have been better if it had been designed for the purpose while Josie is in cooking in the kitchen and John is out hoeing in the garden and the curtain ne'er rose on a scene so domestic and John's mother cries: out of guilt for her suspicions?: and Josie cries too: in the spirit of forgiveness?: and: *The Parents:* the parents leave satisfied only to blame one another someplace on the turnpike for how easily they most likely have been deceived and to issue an edict: The License or Else. And: *The Young Couple:* as Josie called them when she was writing about it later: now Josie and John draw up a marriage contract and predate it to the time they arrived in New Preston and now they get Katherine Anne and another accomplice to sign it and now they hand it to the parents in New York claiming it is legal and now: *The Parents:* refuse to believe their gobbledegook and haul them off to an attorney who attests it is, indeed, gobbledegook: and now there is an Ultimatum involving money and now it happens in the middle of the night in the Hotel Brevoort that Josie and John face one another with the question they have been avoiding: Will they marry or not? And: *Josie:* Josie is afraid John's parents will disown him and he will blame her for it and: *John:* John is afraid Josie will think he doesn't love her and: *Josie:* Josie is afraid he doesn't love her and: *John:* he does love her and: *Josie:* she loves him and: *Josie and John:* they conclude "If we love, why not marry?" and thus it happens on September 2, 1926, that Josephine Herbst and John Herrmann are unduly married and: *The Biographer:* I think it is too bad because they hadn't ever decided to get married they had only decided to live in the country and write and marriage is complicated enough without beginning in coercion. After which they return to the Hotel Brevoort, tear the license into tiny shreds, and throw it into the toilet with their convictions as if they think the second deed will flush away the first and to show that they still do not understand why it was useless to have given in they make one more attempt to negotiate with the Herrmanns for money to buy the house, and it is only when: *The Parents:* continue to set impossible conditions — a high rate of interest and control of the deed — that *Josie:* not *John:* does what should have been done all along and tells them that she hopes their righteousness will comfort them in old age because if they keep on like this their children are not very likely to. But now their contentment has turned to depression and now the small farmhouse is a trap not a haven and now life in the valley is spoiled for them and though they could make other arrangements for the farmer is kindly they leave the country and move into the city to find work, leaving the deposits of what was probably their happiest year together rotting in the Connecticut countryside like vegetables after frost.

# New York

THEY RENT an apartment at 92 Fifth Avenue and it is just what they are worried about — $45 a month for a three-room sixth-floor cold-water walk-up where the sink cover doubles as the eating table and there is scarcely space enough for one, let alone both, of them to write, but they have finished the work they began in the country, they are looking for publishers rather than inspiration, they are not really bursting with energy to write. Life in the city has other compensations. The scene is very much the way it has been described in countless memoirs of the 1920s, Josie's included — the Golden Age of something, but what exactly? The Golden Age of a blackening age. The only original years possible out of the controlling cycle of War: Depression: War. What is true for the period is true for them as well. It is a time apart, its own zone, disconnected from the politics that anchor it at either end. Almost the entire action takes place below Fourteenth Street. The streets of the Village are thick with writers. They know one another from Paris, from the universities, from the very pages of their work and if they haven't met yet it is a detail, it makes no difference, they will meet one another soon enough. In those days a volume of Joyce or Stein carried under the arm was sufficient, like a political button, to establish membership in the modern movement. "I see you are carrying Gertie with you," remarked a young man to John, whose copy of *Three Lives* was lying face-up on the bar at Julius's on the night of the day they arrived in New York. The young man was Holger Cahill, novelist, art aficionado, eventual director of the Federal Art Project and director of exhibitions at the Museum of Modern Art, who became a lifelong friend. Josie, John, Katherine Anne Porter, Caroline Gordon, Allen Tate, Malcolm Cowley, Robert Penn Warren, Kenneth Burke, Hart Crane —: most of these writers are roughly at the same stage now. No one is wondering who will rise, who drop away. "Rising" is not particularly what they are after. They live in the basements of tenements, in the storerooms of penthouses, in the corners of lofts, casual nests they will not hesitate to abandon when the next opportunity calls. They inhabit speakeasies, cafés, the editorial offices of magazines and publishing houses, sallying out at peculiar hours to watch the sun rise over the Battery or the moon set down in Harlem, arguing without stopping, frequently — magically? — encountering an Italian workman with a cap and a lunch pail somewhere along the way. They drink: oh how they drink. They flirt: oh how they flirt. They spout Eliot spout Pound spout Dada poetry standing like herons on one foot: "Mama the man is standing there Mama the man is standing there Mama the man is standing there . . . They must be curious trees indeed where the big elephants go walking without bumping each other" — Kurt Schwitters's *Revolution in Revon,* a favorite demonstration piece of Josie's and John's. They write: they talk: they make love: oh how they make love. "A young man might phone his girl, 'I'll bring you asparagus in a taxi.' " It is a grand life, an exotic life, a communal life they have all separately invented. Josie and John take their places automatically. They are a popular couple, their writing admired, noted by the others for their good spirits, their literary and intellectual intensity, and their obvious romance, and if they are sometimes noted as well for her capacity for absorbing attention and his capacity for absorbing liquor, so much the better as far as the others are concerned — such gossip is the heart of a literary existence. But there is one peculiarity of the Village setting conspicuously unremarked on at the moment. There are a number of women present but for the most part they are Wives. Have you ever noticed that almost all of these writers-of-the-twenties are, as Josie and Katherine Anne Porter sometimes put it to each other, "Gents"?

Josephine Herbst and Katherine Anne Porter — "the two talkingest women I ever met," Malcolm Cowley told me — and why shouldn't they be talking to each other night after night in Katherine Anne's apartment on Hudson Street or Josie's near Washington Square? They have plenty to say to each other and very often none of their men friends is equally interested. When I think of them together I think of them first as characters in a story which either might have written but neither does, perhaps because different parts of it shame and sadden them both, but they see it that way themselves, save one another's letters, make their notes — of their literary self-consciousness throughout I think there is no possible doubt. "Shouldn't I be writing about KAP and myself? Where would it begin?" Josie asked herself in a literary notebook, probably in the 1940s. "Perhaps first intimations from GT and BW who described her so erroneously as a 'peasant,' drudging alone on a lonely farm, pregnant, poor, 'mad.' How different from her vision of herself as an aristocrat — her description of herself, 'she came down the stairs, a true aristocrat,' which she repeated to me from the mouth of [a German friend]." Similarly Katherine Anne, who in her last years told the woman she mistakenly thought was Josie's biographer, but was actually her own, that to explain Josie's "misled" and "misused" and "lamentable" and "disastrous" life as she really saw it, "I suppose I should have to write a book myself." The story has a number of elements in which both are interested, though in different degrees. There is the element of their personalities — really, of their characters: where they come from, where they are heading, their aspirations, their desperations, the lonely and tragic consequences of their solitary tangles with time. Then there is the element of the setting: their place in the world of men. History comes into it: what the world churns up to which individuals must respond. Politics. Social fashion. What a society values when. Artistic talent is involved, and its moral concomitants, if any. Attraction. Betrayal. The sheer influence of age and decay. If the story is large, grand, encompassing all the themes of the century, it is not a literary illusion, but a true reflection. It is both of their ambitions that it should be so.

At the time we are now in, Katherine Anne is by far the more beautiful of the two women. She is a small, bony, dramatic-looking creature with a fluid figure perfect for the styles of the 1920s; graceful; striking; her body incapable of a clumsy pose. Her face is delicate, cheeks slightly sunken beneath fine high cheekbones. She has fine hair, fine skin, fine eyes, fine everything, a luminous, colorless, almost ethereal aspect that can light up a room, conveying an impression at once delicate and strong. Josie is awkward, not so much because of her body, which is large-boned but well-formed, or because of her features, which are attractive enough and touched with distinction in her extraordinary eyes, but because of her attitude toward her body, which is mainly one of embarrassment. If Katherine Anne is the mistress of her appearance, which she is — in fact she will not look so different at eighty from how she looks at forty — Josie is the victim of hers. She flows between shapes like a concertina, expanding and contracting, in and out, largely in relation to the state of her emotions and her diet, and between her weight and her moods her appearance varies so much she can be unrecognizable from photograph to photograph even when they are taken a short time apart. In the city, when she has good clothes, she can look very sharp and striking. In the country she drapes herself in baggy rags like a scarecrow and usually looks as if she has been out chasing possums in the garden, as she often has. But between the two women there is basic physical liking. Energy, originality, sparkle, flare — these are the qualities that matter. Josie likes to be associated with grace: Katherine Anne reminds her, very slightly, of her sister Helen, six years dead. From Josie's presence Katherine Anne takes a relaxed, almost visceral comfort. Both women have knocked around, been on their own. Katherine Anne has been married as a girl at sixteen, run off, worked, run off, been married and divorced another time so far and why she married the latest she does not understand exactly — certainly she did not like him very much. With one stillborn child already, of whom she speaks very little, she is glad to be living in the city on her own. Josie has also traveled, held many jobs, had many men. She is over her first serious affair and is very absorbed in the one she is having now even though it has ended in marriage which is not what she expected and she fears may be more than the relationship can bear. Katherine Anne has lived off and on in Mexico among artists and revolutionaries and because of her associations she has something of a reputation as a radical, though her radicalism does not run very deeply, as her later history will reveal. Josie aligns herself with all the poor ravaged people of the world so instinctively that in her long life it is not a commitment she will ever really rethink. Nonetheless, politics is another bond. Both Josie and Katherine Anne spend a good deal of time in the company of literary people. Both are popular, others seek them out. Again their styles differ. Particularly around certain men of whom she may privately have a low opinion Katherine Anne will flirt like a schoolgirl — she is adept at the tricks she needs to secure admiration — but she does not mean very much of what she says to them. Flattery comes lightly to her. She tosses off the praises and is gone. Although there are many of them, the majority of her friendships do not engage her real self very deeply. Josie is a woman in whom the zest for interaction is truly deep. All her friends are important to her. All her relationships are lively. She declaims and decries in both private and public and if she sees someone with whom she disagrees she is apt to go right up and have it out at once regardless of circumstances. Argument is one of her greatest pleasures. The question of style raises the question of femininity — a sotto voce issue whenever the women are discussed. While Katherine Anne is always described as a "lady," Josie is sometimes described as "masculine," in part because she is often funny. It is an assessment with which she herself might have readily agreed: "I was never a little lady — and never wanted to be a lady — wanted to be a woman and a Mensch in Rosa Luxemburg's terms," she noted of herself to herself at one point. At a party Josie and Katherine Anne like to look across the room and see one another at it with all their diversity of tactics, the more to analyze later. Both are domestic — like cooking, like keeping house — both like solitude, and one of the things they like about these things and more is writing each other letters about how much they like them, whatever they might be. Writing is the heart of the matter. It is the thing of greatest interest to them both. At least half their correspondence and no doubt much of their conversation is about literature and their own writing. Neither has published much but what they have has been much appreciated by people who know them and more circulates privately. In a small but vital circle, both their reputations are on the rise. Katherine Anne is alternately a slow and an inspired writer, her stories forged mysteriously, even to her. She would never do in a literary realm what she would do socially: as a writer her integrity is absolute. Josie works steadily, journalistically, likes to be getting things done. If anything, the pipeline between her experiences and her writing is a little too direct. But both are intense intelligent women mainly committed to discovering what they themselves, and not anybody else, think and feel about things. . . .

. . . Of course they would talk to each other night after night and never run out of things to say. Between themselves they admit how it is. It is a man's world. There are conversations they are excluded from, speakeasies they don't go to, meetings to which they are not invited, magazines it is useless for them to try to contribute to. Love is not what it is cracked up to be, not an inevitability for either one, no hearts and flowers, a lot of trouble, only something they both hope to be able to manage in part because life on the whole is easier with a man than without one even if having one brings its own problems it is not very easy to solve. Take Katherine Anne. She was practically hewing the wood and drawing the water for that man in Connecticut. Why? Never again. The man was a child and a bore and if she is ever to marry again she will marry a man who will care for her and not the other way around. Josie's life is entangled with somebody scarcely beyond adolescence. She is trying to make him fit her mold, to be a writer, plausible enough on the surface — he claims he wants to be a writer — but she doubts it underneath, he isn't driven the way writers are, he will kill her with his drinking and flirting, he is holding her back yet on the other hand he is helping her, too, he is teasing and he is charming and he is an entrée into some things it is hard to get into especially for a woman like her because she isn't conventionally pretty and she isn't conventionally flirty and she isn't anyone's idea of a woman but her own and, she hopes, his. What a relief for each of them to have a woman friend who understands everything, particularly the contradictions. Between the two of them there are no deceptions except possibly one: everything is harder for both of them than they are usually willing to let on. Better to emphasize strength than to emphasize vulnerability is their philosophy: despite their modern styles they are nineteenth-century women at their cores. Their friendship, or certainly its particular quality, is invisible against the backdrop of the New York literary scene and dissolves into the background whenever anything public is taking place but to Josie and Katherine Anne it is dear, they depend on it. In their hearts they know they are not just two of the boys.

The interest of writers and the interest of publishers are two different things and as their days in New York lengthen it is more the latter than the former that Josie and John find lacking. From the little apartment they call the crow's nest their manuscripts are sent out, returned, sent out and returned again, but despite the urgings of their friends, they do not seem very likely to be taken. They do not worry about it so much. Publishers are Philistines interested in one thing only. Their friends like the books. Writers are the audience that matters. Unfortunately that one thing only is the thing in their lives in shortest supply and New York is so expensive that money is an immediate necessity if they are going to be able to stay on there at all. Josie takes a job with a research outfit investigating the conditions of women working in laundries and John gets a job with a publisher as a commissioned salesman of other people's books. In January, 1927, he goes on the road. Josie stays in the city alone, the first of many long separations that are as much a part of their marriage as the periods together. It is in these quiet months that her friendship with Katherine Anne really takes root. John is traveling everywhere — Rochester, Philadelphia, Baltimore, Cleveland, Detroit, Chicago, Sioux City, Kansas City, St. Louis, Indianapolis, Louisville, Columbus, Dayton — and he barely has time to recover from one journey before they send him out again. How things are going between them when they are together there is no direct way of knowing, but as soon as they are apart they act as if they are entering a competition for a world's saddest story award, vying with each other by mail about whose lot is the hardest: lonesome Josie climbing the stairs to their crow's nest all alone after her day in the laundries dowdy from poverty leafing through rejections all by herself and no mail from her boy; or John, running from town to town sleeper to sleeper hotel to hotel and no girl to come home to he can scarcely get through the days let alone write her about them surely a boy as good as hers deserves more than complaints: a characteristic whine in their relation to one another, so different from the spirit of Josie's friendship with Katherine Anne.

In Lansing, in the very bosom of his family, John collapses from too little food and too much drink and his old doctor tells him he must stop working and rest. What could be better news? When he gets back to New York they have an earnest conversation sorting out what is important from what is not. What is it that they want out of life? Not this. Not the way it has been. Not to feel nervous, to feel exhausted, to feel so burdened by the exigencies of existence that joy and pleasure no longer seem attainable to them. Neither one of them has done any writing since they came to the city and it is beginning to be too long. John's trips have served their purpose. They have money in the bank? They are rich. They need to feel free, to be light on their feet, to know they have not lost the battle with circumstance. To John at that moment freedom is the ocean. He wants a sailboat, his hand on the tiller, the wind in his hair. To Josie at that moment freedom is John. She wants him to be happy, and to be happy with her, and she wants it so palpably that his wish becomes hers despite the fact that she is as true a landlubber as the American prairie ever sent to sea. In the spring of 1927 they take a preliminary trip to the coast of Maine around Boothbay Harbor where John fixes his eye on a ramshackle cabin ketch which he buys and names the *Josy*,* and when the weather turns warm they abandon New York for a cabin on the shore near Wiscasset where they live equally tightly but more happily. They lounge: they make love: it reminds them both a bit of Brittany. John spends his time rebuilding the *Josy* and the real Josie spends hers listening to the stories of the villagers and the passersby and filling notebooks to use in the new group of stories she feels emerging in the summer sun.

On sea it is a different matter. For as long as he has been sailing on the landlocked lakes of upper Michigan John has wanted a cruise in the intricate New England waters and in the middle of August they leave on the *Josy* for a trip down the seacoast to New York, a journey they anticipate will take about a month. The *Josy* is lovely, a converted ship's longboat with a black hull, red mainsail, and white jib and jigger — "More seaworthy than the *Titanic*," John keeps insisting; "Why doesn't he stop saying that?" Josie thinks coldly. "How could she be less?" — but she is only twenty-three feet long and she has no auxiliary power. The cabin is so tiny that John has practically to double over to get in and out of it and if he doesn't smack his head against the hatch cover going one way or the other then Josie is sure to smack hers. The bunks are so narrow it is impossible to turn over without risk of falling and so short John has to dangle his legs over the side. They cook on the deck on a small one-piece stove called the NotABolt which, when the wind shifts, funnels odors and smoke back into their faces and, when the weather is bad, they cook in the cabin over a can. The toilet is a bucket and the sea. The *Josy* in short is a small boat for a long trip even under the best circumstances and these are not the circumstances at hand. On the other hand, why blame the boat? They are at the classical stations — man at the tiller, woman at the jib; in the classical relationship — man giving orders, woman fumbling them; in the classical frames of mind — man irritable and frightened but trying not to show fear, woman frightened and irritable but too dependent to be able to fight back. They are becalmed, caught in squalls, becalmed, caught in squalls again. They blame one another, apologize, blame one another, apologize again. They are trapped for two days in a terrible storm at Porpoise Harbor, the boat tossing about filling with

* "Josie" was often "Josy" between Josie and John, though usually "Josie" elsewhere.

water, everything soaking, hostility rising with the swells. Josie is miserable. She has not exactly predicted all this before the voyage but she has certainly hinted around about it enough to feel justified in implying I-told-you-so during some of the worst moments, which doesn't help, nor does it ease her own mind that she cannot swim. On the morning of August 23 in a fog so treacherous that the Coast Guard records more than the usual number of accidents they cross Casco Bay and head for the harbor at Portland, Maine, hoping to catch word that the execution of Sacco and Vanzetti has been postponed. They have not taken part in the protests themselves but Katherine Anne, John Dos Passos, and a number of their other friends are in Boston, and they have followed the appeals when they can. It is not postponed. They walk along the lonely beaches hand in hand glad to be together again in a reality that suddenly feels so frightening, and that night they decide to change their plans. Two weeks later they abandon the *Josy* in Cohasset and return to New York, expecting to be able to retrieve her in the spring, but they never get back. A few years later when John Dos Passos stops to look he writes them that without several hundred dollars spent on reconstruction, the *Josy* will never sail again. She never does. John's next boat is called the *Ruth Tate*. Out of the events of that summer Josie writes a number of stories, among them "A Bad Blow," an account of a married couple's mutual antagonism on a small boat during a long cruise that has some of the hard, undeluded, unromantic quality of "Dry Sunday," and from the juxtaposition of the trip and the execution of Sacco and Vanzetti she takes the meaning of a memoir of the twenties published late in her life, "A Year of Disgrace." In the later version a mist has rolled over the rough spots like the fog that rolled over Casco Bay and you might not think to read it that the rocks below the surface had ever menaced quite so much. John, too, writes a story juxtaposing the trip and the execution, "A Last Look Back," and he too writes a story based on the journey, "The Gale of August Twentieth." The date is approximately right for their traverse of Casco Bay. Only in John's story the boat is on Lake Michigan and the skipper is alone.

Now they are back in New York in an apartment on Carmine Street and things are not very different from before. Josie has a new job as a reader for the Dell Publishing Company and John is again selling books. In the fall of 1927 there is considerable excitement. *What Happens*, John's novel, has finally been published, in France, by Robert McAlmon, and, like many of McAlmon's Contact editions, it is seized from the ship by U.S. Customs officers and refused entry on grounds of obscenity. John and Josie protest and round up support from their friends and their friends' friends who sign a pamphlet on the novel's behalf and agree to testify for it in court, and they find a young lawyer, Morris Ernst, who is willing to take it on. The judge rules that the experts, who include H. L. Mencken, Heywood Broun, Babette Deutsch, Nathan Asch, Harry Hansen, Genevieve Taggard, and Robert Wolf, are superfluous — ordinary jurors are as well equipped as anyone to decide morality — and except for John, who explains that *What Happens* is about what happens in high schools and colleges these days whether the judge and jury like to think so or not, none of the witnesses is ever allowed on the stand. It is Ernst's first First Amendment case and he loses. The judge orders the books destroyed. *The New York Times* for October 5, 1927, reports that Ernst will appeal both the destruction of the books and the grounds of the decision but it is not clear that such an appeal is ever actually filed. The book is neither distributed nor reviewed: of course it is a disappointment. In November, 1927, John goes on the road again. Christmas is gloomy. John is not only drinking so much they are fighting about it, he is flirting incessantly with other women and a good many of his flirtations seem to end up in bed. Why there are so few traces of Josie's responses to John's affairs in the residues of their life together is something that will always leave me puzzled because I know that she knew about them — everyone else did — and a number of them seem to have their origin now. "Don't tell me that you love me, tell me that you could love me," one of Josie's friends told me John said to her in her apartment one afternoon — I think some variant of that: winsome, piteous: was his basic technique — and she said that he nested his other "little sparrows" there too. I have a copy of a remarkable love-letter written to John by a woman poet in 1937 citing the "4,000 days and nights" it has been since they met and the "3,000 of those 4,000 days you were constantly in my heart," which would place the beginning of their relationship between 1926 and 1929. Of course John is not alone. Infidelity is commonplace. Married or unmarried, the prevailing sexual ethic is still free love — in theory for the women as well as the men. But John, even in their circles, is known as a special case, and if Josie is making her peace with it any more deeply than as a necessity for keeping him at all, I would be very surprised. She drinks, she parties, she dresses up, she likes the company of other men, but for her part she is faithful to him, then. It is how she really wants their marriage to be. She attributes some of his restlessness to their life in the city. Who can blame him for feeling edgy in their dreary apartment, swimming around together like two chickens in a stew? She is edgy herself. Who can write under these conditions? Who can love? It was not for this tense narrowed life that she struggled so hard to leave Sioux City. On a gray day in February when she has decided to bear it no longer she goes off by herself, heading directly by train for the eastern Pennsylvania countryside she had been hearing about from her mother all her life, but has never seen, and soon she has located an old farmhouse in Erwinna, Bucks County, Pennsylvania, not far from the Delaware Canal. She knows almost as soon as she sees it that it is the place for them. In her long lifetime it is the only possession she will ever fight to keep.

# Erwinna

THE HOUSE in Erwinna is a plain stone farmhouse set practically into a steep bank which rises from behind. It is a small house built by poor people, perhaps even in the lifetime of the first Frey to come to America, perhaps a peasant's house, narrow, two-storied, everything about it is crooked, handmade. It has a big barnish stone-bottomed gristmill that was grinding flour for the freeholders of the valley decades before the Revolution, into which a more recent occupant has installed a still, and an assortment of other outbuildings, old and new, including a modernized chicken coop with solid flooring and brooder space for five hundred chickens. A small stream curves around at the front of the house running freely and sometimes fiercely through the flat open meadow nearest the road, crossed by a rickety cedar footbridge chained to a treetrunk and resting on the rocks. It includes fifteen acres of varied fields, hillside and woods, bare when Josie sees it first, but teeming with growth in the steamy, almost tropical, Pennsylvania summers and springs. There is no electricity and no plumbing: so much the better. The fewer the comforts, the smaller the bills. The price is $2,500. This time the senior Herrmanns are more helpful. They move in the spring.

In 1928 you do not move to Erwinna unless you are serious both about writing and about the person you are moving with because it is a remote rural hamlet — not a writer in sight — and the only life you can have there is the life you can make yourself. Josie and John are serious.

The move is an attempt to settle down. For Josie it has something to do with her mother. If there is ever a time when she is affected by her mother's dying to an almost haunted degree, as if she is trying to recreate her mother's life within her own, it is now, and a strong domestic life, which includes John, is very much at the center of the re-creation. John is ready to be made-a-man-of, to oppose his parents' expectations that he will never amount to anything, even if he is more or less counting on Josie to do the job. In photographs taken at the time of the move he looks manly, sober, responsible — at least he looks as if he is trying to look manly, sober, responsible — she looks matronly, they both look enchanted with their newfound maturity. The house requires a lot of work simply to make it functional for them and nothing could make John happier. He is a talented and ambitious carpenter — indeed there is no work, certainly including writing, he would rather do. On the question of the character of the house they will create together, there is no disagreement between them. They will subtract the porch, chip away the stucco, excavate the chimney, liberate the beams, restore it to the spirit it once had before generations of families altered it to suit their own needs. I think Josie felt as if she were the house's true owner, as if the fact that other families had lived in it all these years and hers hadn't was only an accident, as if her Iowa youth was itself an accident, as if now, prodigal daughter, she had returned. Now at last she can send for the old things that have been waiting for her in Sioux City — the silver Tiffany tea set Joseph Frey sent his mother from Atlanta, the frail painted eggshell Mary took out only at Easter, the sugar bowl of the errant Jacob — and they are arrayed around the house intermingled with things of John's. There is a rug braided by Mary out of Josie's and Helen's dresses, on the floor; a tool carved by John, replicating the net-mending device of Brittany fishermen, on the wall. There is a cloth, on a chest, handwoven in Pennsylvania one hundred and fifty years before, part of her family's relics; a barometer, token of his seagoing interests, hanging nearby. The ancient trunk, made in Pennsylvania, that had carried the children's wardrobes from Sioux City to Oregon that summer when she was six. His paisley shawl. A rug of the *Josy* in full sail . . . The house works, and it works even better as time passes and John is able to replace their first furniture bought for a few hundred dollars from the outgoing farmer with pieces of his own work — a trestle table, a corner cupboard, two Welsh dressers on which Josie paints some Pennsylvania Dutch designs. The Frey family papers are installed in the attic. In this genial pooling of pasts, even though it is dominated by Josie's, John cooperates. He visits her family twice in Sioux City while he is on road trips. He spends days driving her around the countryside looking for Frey landmarks, Frey relations, Frey graves. When her father visits, soon after they settle in, John spends hours listening to Bent's stories of his Pennsylvania boyhood which the old man, previously outtalked, has never brought to the surface before, and when Uncle Daniel, her mother's brother, visits later, again he is gentle and kind. If John had had more purposes of his own his incorporation into the Frey saga might not have been possible. He might have objected. Perhaps he secretly did. But John is nothing if not agreeable. He is pleased to be pleasing Josie. There is very little tension between them just now. It is a hopeful and promising moment. By fusing their pasts they think they have guaranteed the fusing of their futures. With more security than earlier, at last they can concentrate on work.

The next scene takes place almost entirely inside the house in Erwinna after Josie has recovered from the poison ivy which again lands her in a hospital for two weeks, after the sink is in, after the partitions are down, after John has returned from the road trip he goes on to pay for plaster and paint, after her father visits, after the Christmas holiday with its Pennsylvania-Dutch-style turkey dinner, after after after, after the last chores are finished and the first snows have fallen and given the fact of another winter there is finally nothing better for them to do than to begin. The atmosphere is reminiscent of that of Connecticut but there is a solidity about it the Connecticut establishment lacked. The interior is divided into two tiers, their places in it reversed from Connecticut, Josie upstairs in a small room next door to the bedroom, John down below at the table he has made himself. They meet rarely, but usually warmly — at the foot of the narrow staircase, in the kitchen, in the bed — but for the most part their lives are bisected by the physical space between them and each tier is shared by the constructed characters of the authors' fictions. Fictions? On both floors there is a lot of ghostly tramping and sometimes the real and the imaginary characters get confused. For Josie in fact the two are practically the same.

From her earliest published fiction to her latest unpublished memoirs the chief impulse behind Josie's writing was always autobiographical, and that impulse was never less diluted than now. When she put aside *Unmarried*, at the time of the move to Connecticut, she began at once on another book, *Nothing Is Sacred*, which recreates the events in her family in Sioux City at the time of her mother's dying, and with that finished she has now embarked on a third, *Money for Love*, whose plot bears a marked resemblance to her recent attempt to get money from Maxwell Anderson to begin a new life with John. Her short fiction shows the same autobiographical spirit. "The Elegant Mr. Gason," her first published story — submitted to H. L. Mencken from Germany under the name "Carlotta Greet" and published in *Smart Set* in July, 1923 — is about a chance meeting between a young woman traveling in Europe and the son of her mother's one-time suitor, in which even the name, Gason, is unchanged from the original; her second, "Happy Birthday!", also published in *Smart Set*, is about a minor adolescent heartache; and between the time of the move to Erwinna and the end of the decade she completed about a dozen stories on diverse themes ranging from "A Dreadful Night," in which an adolescent girl is thrown into a panic when her mother suddenly becomes ill, to "Once a Year," in which the editor of a New York magazine reveals himself as a transvestite during a Christmas party, all of which have in common, however, that they are taken, in one way or another, from her life.

The literary ideas that lay behind Josie's work at this stage are difficult to pin down because she rarely discussed them abstractly, but it is clear from her casual comments that the primary inspiration behind most of her fiction was emotional. When her family criticized *Nothing Is Sacred*, not for its portrait of the dying mother but for its portrait of the embezzling brother-in-law which her sister Alice found so literally rendered she was ashamed, Josie wrote her father that she "had to write that or never write again," and throughout her life, confronted by hostile people who found themselves in her stories, her justification was much the same. "I just had to do it, you know last winter and spring he was over so much and I had to hear the whole thing about his mother-in-law so much that I nearly went crazy and had to write it to get over getting mad about the wasted time," she wrote Katherine Anne about the story "A New Break," whose depiction of an Erwinna neighbor so distressed the neighbor's wife that she never thought of Josie without bitterness again. Given the tone of most of her stories the reaction of her subjects is not surprising, for with only a few exceptions her characters at this stage are so unsympathetically presented that they seem uninviting to know, let alone be. They have human reality, they have American particularity, they are embedded in families, towns, situations, social and personal circumstances that are always strongly drawn, but they have little soul. Their deeper reasons for acting as they do, unlike their self-deceptions, are usually not very clear. Why the characters in Josie's fiction are represented at such a distance that the most frequent complaint against her in this early period is flatness is not a simple question. Doubtless literary fashion and a young writer's difficulties with ambiguity played a part. Yet the very contrast between her letters on the one hand and her fiction on the other, and between the passionate storyteller she could be in person and the dispassionate observer she became in prose, suggests a more intimate answer. In 1929, in response to a series of rejections, Josie wrote a literary note in the *New Masses*, "Ignorance among the Living Dead," protesting the calls for "EMOTION AND TENDERNESS AND MOTHER LOVE" she felt were being demanded in her stories. Perhaps she protested too strongly. "The misery of it was crushing me," she wrote to her father about the feeling that lay behind *Nothing Is Sacred*. "I think myself I was too hard on [the heroine] . . . because I hate the memory out of which the story sprang," she wrote to John about *Money for Love*.

Given her direct involvement in the material of most of her stories, and her emotional nature, I suspect she was struggling for control.

The world into which Josie's fiction was received was exceedingly amiable and cozy. *Nothing Is Sacred* was brought to the attention of its publisher, Coward-McCann, by Ford Madox Ford; jacket blurbs were provided by Hemingway and Ring Lardner; and it was warmly reviewed by — among others — both Ford and Katherine Anne Porter. Following its appearance in the fall of 1928, Josie was cited by Sinclair Lewis in an article in *Pictorial Review* as one of a group of American women novelists "at least as important" as any men. Even outside their immediate circle the same warmth and geniality prevailed. Though it is impossible to be certain, it is a safe guess that *Nothing Is Sacred* was reviewed in at least fifty newspapers, and while some of these were repeats of syndicated columns, all contributed to the sense of genuine responsiveness from a real audience that a writer craves. What was true of the atmosphere of fiction was equally true of the atmosphere of criticism. When Katherine Anne, who loved *Nothing Is Sacred*, wrote privately expressing reservations about *Money for Love*, Josie was not offended but elaborated the point further in her letters and when Isidor Schneider, another friend, in an attack on the "Hemingway school" in *The Nation* called "The Fetish of Simplicity," complained similarly that Josie was leaving out of her novels the very qualities that distinguished her in person, she replied frankly, in a published rejoinder, that if he meant *Money for Love*, she herself "never liked the book, do not like it now, and have always considered it pinched." Such critical failure, if it was a failure, was not an embarrassment, nor did it lead her to change the direction of her work. When simplification suited her purposes she simplified, and when the time came to abandon it later she did. When Matthew Josephson, in a column in *transition*, criticized a story of John's published in the *American Caravan*, she wrote a letter to Katherine Anne about it that Katherine Anne found so amusing she asked Josie's permission to show it to Josephson, and it eventually ended up, slightly altered, as an item in *transition* itself. "I must say ... that we found the remarks of your gempmum friend Hochelhgeborener Josephson, provocative as they say in the press," Josie said to Katherine Anne.

> Personally his words on the Caravan had no more enlightenment for me than the opuses of Miss Izzy Patterson.* I even found in his distaste for John's characters the same squeamishness that characterizes Miss Izzy. She wants to read about people she would like to meet. There is also the curious moral survival of wanting a character elevated, if only in a poetical way. A sort of lunge toward fundamentalism which wants to deny man sprung from the ape. I don't know what all this shouting about the poetic in man

* Isabel Paterson, a reviewer for the *New York Herald Tribune*.

amounts to but I should think myself that it is a highly debatable article, especially in an age headed, as Herr Josephson contends, toward the Mechanical Millenium. The age of Zola is not the age we are living in, sewers notwithstanding. All in all I find myself pugging the nose at the Gelehrnter Herr. He seems to me in something of the same position as our friend Mike Gold, both are headed toward milleniums, the one communistic, the other mechanistic, both uttering hoarse cries to their cohorts, both pointing the finger of derision at other pathfinders or rather denying there are other pathfinders. Pathfinder Josephson is, in this circumstance, a somewhat limited gent. I wish he would just go ahead and turn out his stuff, although he can keep on yelling to the cohorts too for all of me. I did not write anymore for the Gobbler or whatever its name is, because I think I detect a male bias in favor of no ladies. The slightly — may I say — patronizing note in which Mrs. Herrmann was requested to enter the ring, has eat these here vitals and I see no reason to butt my head against a strictly verboten wall. Personally, I don't blame the gents. I can see where they like to mess around without skirts in one enterprise at least. But I seem to smell the same aroma of patronizing in the Caravan espousal, in which the only favorable allusions to the fair sex were undoubtedly guided by the very personal amorous animadversions of the said gent critic himself. These sly allusions to the secret troth are not exactly out of line with what I mean when I say patronizing, if you know what I mean. My admiration for Herr Josephson is still unbounded and his words I read with relish and not a little anger and hissing but all said and done more power to him. We thought the Murray Godwin answer to his declamation in No 14 was apt. More anon. Herrmann sends his best. We last night named Tato* transition and Mrs. Gummidge* Caravan and kicked them both out of the house.

*That* was literary life. *That* was argument. If it was not energetic, robust, good-natured, above all, fun — what was it for?

Josie was not the only one of them to have a literary break at the time of the move to Erwinna. The short novel *Engagement*, which John had written in Connecticut, about a girl named Ruth Mason who was "willing to marry George Harvey who was slow and steady and not particularly brilliant because she had been disappointed in a love affair she had been having with Harold Riley, who was not slow or stupid at all," appeared in the *Caravan* in 1928, and, having disposed of that trio, he was now at work on another book called *Woman of Promise* about how "Charlotte Dale had felt from her high school days that what she wanted most in life was a home and children, quite a few children, and for their

* Cats.

father she wanted Carl Yoeman" and how it happened that she did marry Carl Yoeman but did not have the children she wanted from the marriage, though to do John justice both books have a touch of genuine feeling in them somewhere, despite those beginnings. The difference between Josie and John at this point was not a matter of talent. John was a sensitive and delicate writer whose work was appreciated by other writers and publishers at least as much as if not more than hers, who had the support of their friends, particularly John Dos Passos and Katherine Anne, and who once won an important literary prize. The difference was a matter of drive. Where Josie wrote a dozen stories between 1928 and 1930 John wrote two or three. Where Josie persisted in offering stories even when they were rejected, John would retreat. When the critics howled, as Schneider and Josephson had, it was Josie who defended them. John would withdraw. Why John was the way he was he himself was not given to analyze and there is little independent evidence. Josie attributed it to his parents, who were always predicting his doom. In any case he was in a difficult position, trying to be a writer because overall he preferred it to anything else he could think of but not trying hard enough because it was impossible for him to believe he would succeed. In addition to the matter of ambition there was also the matter of position. John did not take writing as seriously as she did — it was not a matter of will, he could not take it as seriously as she did — there-are-other-things-in-life-besides-writing-for-chrissakes, his opinion is. While Josie sits tirelessly at the typewriter day after day John's attention wanders, he wanders, down into the village to hang around at the post office . . . up over the crest of the hill to visit a neighboring farmer . . . to his workshop . . . on out to the gristmill where the still has been refurbished and put back to work. . . . From time to time they put aside their respective labors to enjoy some common entertainments. Two beer trucks fall into the Delaware Canal bringing out in swarms all their supposedly teetotaling neighbors to salvage kegs and Josie and John find it so amusing they collaborate on a droll, lightly fictionalized, story "Pennsylvania Idyl," published under both their names in *The American Mercury* in 1929. Katherine Anne visits and the three of them sit up all night writing doggerel. Malcolm Cowley visits, Kenneth Burke visits, and they go away, in both cases, loaded up with beer. When the breaks are over they resume their usual pattern: sleep wake work and wander, sleep wake work and wander: and even if she is doing more of the working and he is doing more of the wandering, everything in Erwinna is fundamentally fine. They are carrying out their commitments to one another. Most of the action is of the imagination. The sound of typing is heard throughout.

In the spring of 1929, about a year after their move to Erwinna, Josie and John trade in their first car, an open Model-T bought from Caroline Gordon and Allen Tate, for a closed Whippet, rent out the house, and set off on a long trip across the country. They will do a lot of this for the next while: look at each other across the table, push back their chairs, and decide "let's go." It is important to them now that they have a house to come back to to be able to leave it as much as they choose. "Josephine Herbst will spend the summer in the Oregon mountains recuperating from the strain of writing her second novel, to be published next fall," announced an item appearing in several newspapers. "She delivered the manuscript to her publishers, Coward-McCann, the day she left with her husband, John Herrmann. 'We're going to the most remote pocket in the mountains that we can find,' she declared, 'as far away as possible from books and writers and publishers.' " Wrong in details, the tattler is nonetheless right in spirit. Josie has been working twelve to fourteen hours a day on the novel in its final stretches and she has not been exactly sweet. It is necessary for both of them that she relax. Still it is romantic: down the Jefferson and Lee Highway to New Orleans, Dallas, Santa Fe and Taos, the Grand Canyon, and Los Angeles, up the coast through San Francisco to Oregon where Josie's father is visiting her sister Frances who is temporarily living in Salem, in a circle in Oregon with her father, who enjoys it mightily, to Crater Lake, Bend, Mount Hood, and back to Salem, to the coast again, to the sacred Neskowin, where Josie shows John her beloved ocean, to Astoria, to Seattle, across Washington to Spokane, then up into Canada, down through Montana, North Dakota, Minnesota, and down again into Michigan for a reconciling visit with John's family at their enormous lakeside "cottage" where Josie is most impressed by the number of bathrooms — four — and poses for pictures beside one after another of his relatives including his stout sour mother while John stands usually off to one side as if he cannot quite accept the fact that all this respectability has overtaken his wilder upper Michigan boyhood: four months and about 7,000 miles of rugged travel. They returned refreshed, eager to cut away the weeds humming with insects that have seeded themselves between the house and the road, eager to tear down the cobwebs, eager for the routine of ordinary living once more. Alas, their good spirits do not hold. The reception of *Money for Love* is not very helpful.

It is not only criticism that darkens their mood. Alone, I doubt that it would have mattered very much. Josie is not particularly attached to her novel. Her powers are still growing and she knows it. She is already germinating ideas for a far bigger novel which will ultimately become her trilogy. The mood is about something more important than the book. It is the autumn of 1929. In New York the great bullbear, the American stock market, has suddenly rolled over dead crushing first those who have fed it most as they will now crush those who have been feeding them . . . feeding them . . . feeding them . . . until as many are crushed as are not crushed, as many are hungry as are not hungry, a line of backward-toppling, gray-faced, thin-bodied civilian playthings not stopped until they are turned into soldiers and marched to war. Josie and John have been living a deliberately private existence. Like the majority of their writer-friends in the late '20s they have placed themselves outside politics. Being outsiders is their politics. Now no one is outside politics — at least not outside economics. Josie and John are much too poor to be affected by the crash directly but as its effects widen it gradually makes itself felt. The money to be had from literary work is not much even in good times, nor do they expect it to be, but it is something, usually, and now even that something is under threat. Once published, *Money for Love* sells little more than a hundred copies and John's manuscript, *Woman of Promise*, seems unlikely to be published at all. There is no question about it, John will have to go on the road, but how it can be a worthwhile trip is more than either one of them can see. In the towns and cities that he travels books are the last things on anyone's mind. Josie and John are both depressed by the necessity of his departure. How can he write, even when he wants to, if he always has to be off on the go? They have begun that growing together that always takes couples by surprise: she will be too lonely to stay in Erwinna without him: she travels beside him as far as Syracuse. He continues his usual route through upstate New York, Pennsylvania, West Virginia, Ohio. Josie visits New York. She is alone in Erwinna in early December when sad news reaches her by telegram. Her father is dead in Oregon, of heart failure. He was eighty-one. John arrives home. Another car trip through snowstorms and ice across the country to Sioux City to gather up her father's ancient body from the train and put it into the ground beside her mother's. Home. This is the Christmas of the peppermints: pink and white pinwheels tied up in a little sack and left for Josie in a stocking by John exactly as her father used to do: a gesture she remembered all her life. She had never loved her father as she loved her mother, but she loved him just the same. It is a mournful beginning to the coming decade. In January John sets out once more on an even longer trip as far west as Nebraska and as far north as Wisconsin and when he returns he is gray with exhaustion. Before you know it there is another of those looks across the table: for this? no, not for this: and this time the picture is clear to them both from previous conversations: it is someplace warm and sunny where life is easy and cheap and all one's energies are not caught up in these endless household doings: in other words, the South. The house is boarded up again, the cats loaned, books, papers, typewriters, and clothes tossed into the back of the Whippet. The Herbst-Herrmann-Herrmann-Herbsts as they now sometimes call themselves are off again. The destination of the moment is Key West.

# Key West

THEY ARRIVE at Key West on the ferry after a four-day trip down the coast and drive immediately to a house they know already is for rent. Key West is the usual stopping place for travelers from Cuba and on one of his recent stops here John Dos Passos has written them about the place, describing it so perfectly they have no hesitation in picking it out. It is a large, bright, shambly two-storied stucco affair, simple on the inside but lush without, wound with tropical blossoms, and, best of all, cheap — $20 a month furnished, electricity included. They carry with them onto the quiet island all the accumulating toxins of their life together, having to do not so much with her relative recognition — no one could be more truly happy for Josie than John is — but with the difficulty finding a publisher for his novel, which is beginning to get him down. Josie believes in his writing but she thinks he must drink less and write more. In fact they have been quarreling on the way down. "I was all wound up with resentment against a certain party for encroaching his troubles day by day like pills down my gullet," she bursts out, "like boils," she says, to Katherine Anne, a few days after they get there. "My sole complaint against the aforesaid abovementioned affliction that just about drove me coockoo was that it was absolutely one sided and if by chance I interpolated a little of my own home brew just as an experiment it was met with such a glassy eye I knew it had fallen on worse than barren ground and a deaf ear. These long one-sided one lunged one tonsiled one balled chronicles get my gander and do me up worse than jaundice

. . ." but what better place than the one they are in for repairing the damage? They fall in love at once with the simple beauty of this poor unpretentious paradise where the only grocery stores are unmarked stockrooms carrying mainly beans and rice, where you buy turtle sliced from the beast itself before your eyes from a vendor in the street, where you take your fish from your neighbor's catch and share your own because trading is always preferred to selling among fishing people and the only commodity scarcer than fresh water is ice. The idea as usual is for them both "to write" but there is no particular direction to it this trip. There are no goals. A loosening, a getting down to sources, is what they are after. This means relaxing which means fishing which means walking the beaches which means collecting seashells which means lying in the sunshine which means love and rum. In the sweetsmelling perfume of the wild tropical garden which is the entire island their mild private dissatisfactions lose their aroma. Their troubles, like the corals, lighten in the sun.

Hemingway is on the island, they realize — it is from him, along with Dos Passos, that they learned of its charms — but they do not immediately seek him out. He has a new wife — Pauline; a new religion — Catholicism; and a new child — Patrick; and as friends from the days of his first wife, Hadley, in Paris, on these later intimacies they do not wish to presume. He also has a new reputation, based chiefly on *The Sun Also Rises* and *A Farewell to Arms*, and a new income larger than both of theirs. But a meeting is inevitable and shortly happens and soon they are a natural foursome, with John and Hemingway fishing, Josie and Hemingway talking, John and Hemingway drinking, Josie and Pauline talking, the baby sometimes along for the stroll. It is a freewheeling, companionable arrangement. No one is "handcuffed together." Among the four of them there are random attractions, random sympathies, random fun. Pauline and Josie become more or less traditional female friends: Josie looks out for the baby from time to time, Pauline counsels Josie on her hairstyle and clothes. John to Hemingway and Hemingway to John are something like each other's current boyhood companions. They look enough alike to be mistaken by the local people for brothers. Their mothers have been neighbors on the upper Michigan peninsula, they have similar backgrounds, they have only to say to one another a magic phrase like "Traverse City" or "Walloon Lake" or a word like "Charlevoix" to be reminded what the sources of their connection are. Between the men no explanations are required for the lure of the sea. Hem fishes as John sails: to be. Hemingway to Josie is something altogether different, a rare being in her life, a man she admires, and it is not because of his talent or his reputation but because of how he actually is, "like clear air," is how she puts it when she is thinking about him later; eager, intense; he is some kind of an ideal for her, not an ideal of being masculine but an ideal of being human that just happens to be male. Sufficient evidence exists to say that Josie to Hemingway is as much of a rarity: a woman he respects. He is interested in Josie and he is eager for her good opinion of him and as a man who has been through considerable upheaval he is interested in the consolations of a woman friend. Standing in the driveway with Josie one day after delivering a fish, "chatting about anything and poking aimlessly with the tips of our shoes at the sand" suddenly he begins to tell her about his marriage, how it was that Pauline had gradually made Hadley grow dim, how he had fought it, a "tough fight," "boxing was nothing to it"; it is the insects fornicating at their feet that bring on these confidences, Josie concludes. Had it always been as relaxing as it appears to have been on the surface it would have made a perfect vacation. A tropical paradise, two interchangeably compatible couples — what could be more idyllic? But it was not so idyllic. Tropical paradise or no tropical paradise, around Ernest Hemingway the perfect vacation is hard to take.

"If the undertaker's assistant had not been Jonathan Redding's Man Friday of the moment would the affair at the Dry Tortugas have turned out as it did?" Josie inquired later in an uncompleted novella she titled *Bright Signal*. "If you are thinking of a conventional situation with a woman at the center, this was no affair. The essential characters were male, with a woman in a minor role, acting at times like a Greek chorus of one. But don't get the idea that the men were involved in a vulgar complicity.... The conjunction of the three at that time and in that place was accidental. The drama had begun long before within the two main characters; in Jonathan Redding, himself, and in Lucas Heath, himself. As for Constance Heath, she could always say, if only to herself, 'I was the woman. I was there.'"

Forget the undertaker's assistant, who plays only a minor role in Josie's story. Forget, too, for the moment, that "the affair at the Dry Tortugas" happened on their second trip to Key West the following winter. It scarcely matters. The trips ran together in Josie's mind. The rest of the elements are important, particularly the woman who was only "there." However much Hemingway likes, enjoys, appreciates, admires — whatever — Josie, his particular affinity is with John. While the men are off fishing together day after day on ever longer, more rugged expeditions on which Josie, as a matter of course, is not invited, she insists she prefers to be alone, without them, but after teaching herself to drive the car, thinking all she cares to about her next novel, and strolling the island, collecting corals, and entertaining Patrick until she has had quite enough of the island, the corals, and, especially, Patrick, even *her* taste for independence begins to decline. "At present I am the only Herrmann in evidence and let me tell you this is a funny to-do," she fumes to Katherine Anne.

I thought this was going to be a kind of a vacation in my honor
being as it was with the money of The Golden Egg° but we were
scarcely turned around when the fishing began and the gents went
off day after day. I said nothing and held my peace and as long as
they turned up at bed time, it was all right but two weeks ago
they sailed off to the Everglades for a five day trip, and 2 days
after that sailed back bit alive with mosquitoes and no fish to
show. Max Perkins† at Scribner's is along and Hemingway and
Mike Strater.⸭ They were hardly here long enough to give the
wives a smacker when they started out again the same day for the
Tortugas, those reefs in the Gulf where the pirates used to hang
out. They were going to fish there four days and return. It is over
2 weeks and a northwest wind has been blowing so hard they can't
make the passage back. I laughed my head off when they went
taking 24 cans of spaghetti and 12 of beans for a 4 day trip but I
guess they knew what they were about. A yacht parked near them
until yesterday and wirelessed messages to us (Pauline Hemingway
and me, the other wives are in NY) but today she is gone and the
gents sent a last radio that the yacht was leaving and they couldn't
go until the wind changed. You know me under solitude, as tidy a
body as one could wish and one that goes about her business but
after all I had three months of it this winter when John was on the
road and this was supposed to be a vacation and certainly the hot
langorous climate and them moons and them gaudy sunsets are
best seen in company and a loving pair is better any day than one
when it comes to the good things like eating and drinking to say
nothing of them joys which can't be partaken of alone. . . .

As long as the friendship between Hemingway and John appears to
Josie to be more or less equal she accepts it — not necessarily gracefully — for she is glad of the fishing for John, but gradually another element emerges. Hemingway is so much in charge of things. It is his
equipment, his boat. He knows the fishing grounds. It is he who makes
the decisions when to stay, when to go. The origins of Josie's discomfort
with the implications of this relationship precede their visit to Key West.
John somewhat idolizes Hemingway she realizes, and she understands it:
she somewhat idolizes him herself. In Paris John had given his friend the
manuscript of *What Happens* for a critical reading and Hemingway had
pronounced it the best thing he had read in ten years, a remark which he
forgot but John remembered — treasured in fact — carried around inside him in quotation marks and quoted to others, right up until the mo-

° A story about a girlhood friendship published in *Scribner's* in May, 1930.
† The Scribner editor.
⸭ A painter, friend of Hemingway's.

ment a few years later at a party in New York celebrating *The Sun Also Rises* when Hemingway said exactly the same thing about E. E. Cummings' *The Enormous Room*, and not only that, about Cummings he eventually said it in print. "He suffered, his whole look showed it and his wife suffered for it — she could not show how she suffered for it for he had his pride," Josie wrote, fictionalizing the party incident, later. In Florida these feelings are rekindled. Nathan Asch, divorced from his first wife, comes to town with a new woman who calls herself a Countess and Hemingway enlists Josie and John in a campaign to make them go away. He does not want on his doorstep a footloose vacationing writer in the midst of a new affair. John, in particular, is flattered by the suggestion — *you* are serious writers, *you* are welcome — though he has barely cracked a postcard since they got there. Josie is more reluctant for she likes Asch though she is dubious about the Countess, but she can see Hemingway's point of view. They spend the day, without Hemingway, persuading Asch and the Countess of the superiority of Cuba — not so difficult after they tour the aquarium, knock at the door of the closed bowling alley, and eat a particularly tough turtle steak at the only restaurant. After a nightcap at the one bar with slot machines where the Countess plays "Believe Me if All Those Endearing Young Charms" on the broken piano for want of other entertainment, all retire early. Asch leaves in the morning, but he knows what is happening. Standing on the dock waiting for the boat to Havana he suddenly casts his cigarette stub down into the water with an angry motion. "Give my regards to the Lord Mayor of Key West," he says. At that moment John understands things also: he is just another of Ernest Hemingway's "Man Fridays." He forgets it that afternoon in a bar.

Yet despite such illuminating moments, the atmosphere of mutuality continues. When the fishing party returns from the Tortugas there is a great gathering at the Hemingways'. The table is heaped high with hams, whisky, and other luxuries supplied by the industrialist yachtsman who has relayed their messages. The men are tanned, bearded, healthy — clearly they have loved being stranded. The women relax. John and Katy Dos Passos, friends of all present, arrive unexpectedly from Havana to make it even more of an occasion. It is an evening of the kind Josie likes best, a tableau vivant of the possibilities she was seeking when she left Sioux City. There are friends, conversation, there is spirit, purpose. There is even more than she was seeking — there is a husband to go along. As Josie and John are departing the following morning for a return home that is already long overdue, Hemingway leans into the window of the car to offer them the manuscript of one of his recent pieces for *Esquire* which he says may bring them decent money in the North, and they take it gladly. They are still living by the codes of Paris: from each, to each; whoever has it, shares it. If their positions were reversed and Hemingway were in difficulty and they were lucky, they would do exactly the same. Between Josie and John nothing is any different than it was when they got there, but driving home they are in better spirits than when they arrived. The Key West vacation is catalogued "successful." Later she would call it "the hour of counterfeit bliss."

When they return to Key West the following winter it is another story. The year 1930 is over. Between their first and their second journeys the Depression has deepened and whatever has soured in the world in general since the previous season has soured in Florida too. Hemingway has taken over "their" house and the one that they rent has no garden or ocean view. He has also broken his arm — hence the undertaker's assistant, his official Man Friday — but there are more than enough errands to be run by two. There are more writers around but no one appears to be actually writing. Everyone is afflicted with one or another small ailment — irritations that will seem to Josie in retrospect like the omens of a world about to change. The heart of the problem as she sees it for the moment, however, is not so much economic or political as it is personal — specifically the mood of her husband, who is becoming more and more of an alcoholic every day. It is not only Josie who thinks John is overdoing the drinking. A letter to Katherine Anne from John himself written during this trip confirms that "the liquor flows so freely that I have not been entirely sober since we got here." As for Hemingway, in his published correspondence he refers to John most often as a genial "rummy." The psychological stresses for Josie in this situation are not hard to see. She is a strong woman seeking equality with a strong man, and her identification with a weak husband is making it harder to come by. Trying to maintain the image of John she herself needs to have she begins to shore him up in her own mind, if not in his, by referring to Hemingway ironically as "The Great Man," but John does not rise to her occasions. When it is Josie herself who is treated badly by Hemingway she fights back directly. On a fishing trip on which she is uncustomarily included a kingfish escapes from her line, Hemingway criticizes her for it, she defies him. I am not like you, she tells him. I fish for the water, the sky, the way the air feels. She dips her fingers in the water and holds them skywards, against the wind. John will not fight back. He will not fight at all — not for his writing, not in his friendships, rarely even with her. If they are disagreeing in letters during a separation he is apt to suggest that they stop writing for a bit and quiet down. He becomes even more smiling, more agreeable, even more anxious to please. Only later, to himself — and sometimes to Josie — will he admit how much something has gotten him down.

It is on this second trip that there takes place "the affair at the Dry Tortugas" on which Josie bases *Bright Signal*, officially "the story of Hemingway and the Dry Tortugas but really the story of a woman's disillusion with her husband — her effort to keep that illusion which is cruelly battered down by another man, who does not really care for her either, done just in spite — in what pattern of frustration — who knows?" The actual situation is another expedition to the Tortugas, on which the fishermen have run out of ice. It is a modest emergency — there are three hundred pounds of fish involved and genuinely hungry mouths in Key West who can use it — and Hemingway dispatches John and one of the fishermen whose boat they are using, Bra Saunders, to return to Key West in an auxiliary motorboat and bring ice back. The little mission is afflicted with difficulties. Between weather troubles, motor troubles, drinking troubles and domestic troubles John and Saunders do not get back to the Tortugas until the morning of the fourth day and they are carrying not only ice but Josie who thinks the expedition is not worth all the heroics it is producing. Although the fish are saved, all the way back to Key West Hemingway is mocking John for his failure. Look, the expert seaman, afraid of a little storm. Look, the hero of Lake Michigan, stuck on a sandbar. Look, the famous handyman, can't even get the motor repaired. At the request of the fishermen John is running the boat and he just keeps his hand on the tiller, smiling with his usual good-natured charm. Hemingway keeps it up, returning periodically to the stern of the boat, sometimes punctuating his comments with pistol shots aimed at birds in the sky. Finally Josie can stand it no longer. "If you don't stop talking that stuff, Hem, I'll take your gun and shoot you," she bursts out. Hemingway changes the subject and the rest of the trip back is peaceful but that night at the Hemingways' where Josie and John are staying before returning home he begins goading John again, and Josie, to her humiliation, bursts into tears of rage and leaves the room. Hemingway follows her, making excuses. His damn arm is bothering him, he tells her. Surely she knows how much he thinks of her and John. Later, alone with John, it is all covered over, but it is too late, she says in her notes, it is too late —: "He had already destroyed something, and it was terrible to feel pity for one she had adored. Terrible to feel she had stood up to his enemy — for was he not an enemy and would he not torture her by appearing in her dreams, as a loved one, he whom she should hate, bitterly, unremittingly and forever for stealing her happiness?" — and if there is more of the "little woman" in the fiction than in the life there is still much truth in the fiction, for the story reveals the meaning it is uncomfortable for her to see. John sees it anyway. The next morning as they are leaving Hemingway again sticks his head in the car window with an offer of $100 for the journey home, but this time John refuses. Hemingway seems to see very little. In 1935 in a brief reunion with Josie in Key West the fact of John's absence is not even mentioned, and it is odd, is it not, that when they meet again in the lobby of the Hotel Florida in Madrid during the civil war his opening comment is "Josie, I'll never forgive you for letting that 60-pound king off your line!", as if it is beyond his understanding that for her it was not only a fish but also a husband that got away.

# PART FIVE

# THE LONG TENSION
# OF LIFE

# "There'll Be
# No Distinctions . . ."

IN THE FALL of 1930, between their first and second trips to Key West, Josie and John went to Russia. More of a lark than a pilgrimage, the trip came about at the casual suggestion of their friend Mike Gold, who though spending most of his time in New York as the leading spokesman on literary matters for the Communist Party was also an Erwinna neighbor, and who told them if they could manage to get themselves to Moscow he could arrange for them to attend the International Congress of Revolutionary Writers in Kharkov, if not exactly as delegates, as guests. The invitation was not entirely on the up-and-up — in fact it was precisely the kind of irregularity Mike Gold always committed that did not endear him to his comrades, because Josie and John were not even members of the party literary organization, the John Reed Club, from which the official American representatives to the meeting were supposed to be drawn — but on their side they knew nothing of his jurisdictional problems, and on his side, he was able to bring it off. Considering the fact that at the time they made the decision they had exactly $14 in the bank, the trip was its own kind of economic miracle. They got cheap passage on a steamship in return for the promise of an article for the company magazine — "I would represent Kiwanis for less," Josie told Katherine Anne — sold their Hemingway manuscript, sold their first editions of *In Our Time,* sold their *Ulysses,* closed up the house, boarded out the cats and started for New York on faith alone leaving only two days to raise the necessary remainder and setting off with no more than $700 between them plus a note from John Dos Passos to his Russian publisher authorizing their use of $250 worth of whatever rubles might be waiting for him in Moscow.

Coming at a time when neither the extent of the American economic crisis nor the extent of the political response to it was fully apparent, the trip occupied a peculiar position in their lives, one whose meaning was set more by the things that came after it than by the things that had come before. For all their previous radicalism, they could not understand what they saw. They were there only a short time, a week or two in Moscow, another crossing the Ukraine, and a third at Kharkov; often housed separately, they did not even have one another for sharing impressions; and lacking any knowledge of the language, they were wholly dependent on translations. "You should have heard us making revolutionary speeches at workers clubs in factories with all the gestures and it didn't matter what we said because the interpreter got up afterwards and said what he thought we should have said and from the roars and applauds we knew damned well it was pretty good and quite unlike our speech," Josie told Katherine Anne. As for the conference itself, despite its glittering international composition, it was devoted chiefly to theoretical discussions about the "correct line" for revolutionary literature whose relevance to actual literature was hard for Josie to grasp. "Make no mistake about it, something is up in the Soviet Union," she concluded boldly in the short account of the proceedings for *The New Republic* that, except for her comments to Katherine Anne, was the only thing she managed to write about it for thirty years, but she was not able to convey what it was. You could hardly call Josie a convert. "Some of their new cities terrified me and convinced [as] I am that communism is coming whether we like it or not, and convinced also that it will save many while it damns a few, still I did shiver, being more of an anarchist and I am sure that as soon as it comes in the world little groups will revolt to get off by themselves and to be Alone," she wrote Katherine Anne. Yet whatever her private misgivings, she found she was genuinely moved. The shop windows in Moscow were surprisingly empty, but the people in the street looked so vital, so alert. The workers' kitchens were so shining. People were becoming literate by the millions, "they can listen to poetry all night," edition after edition of good books by good authors were constantly being published here and immediately sold out. On the way out of Russia, by contrast, everything looked blank. In Warsaw "suddenly the faces go dead like putty and seem actually degenerate in their bored and cruel sophistication." Vienna "is just a dead city . . . too many over-stuffed chairs in too many cafés" and too many people drinking too much coffee and whipped cream as if the only sweetness in life is in their cups. Even in Paris the Dôme has been modernized, "touristized," the very corner where they first laid eyes on one another destroyed. "I tell you none of us live enough, it's not enough, and I never felt it so much as in Russia, where everyone is alive and writers are not just observers huddling around with their little feelings but are actively in a thousand things," she told Katherine Anne. It was not exactly a vision of Utopia, but it was a vision of sorts. Against the collapse of capitalism which was coming to be felt with increasing force, the image of a society transforming itself in the opposite direction left its mark.

When Josie and John returned to Erwinna after the second Key West interlude, they found it very difficult to settle down. Everything was in a ferment. The area they lived in was a modest, self-contained, agricultural region seemingly remote from the major centers of business and population where the human consequences of the economic disaster were starting to make themselves known. Yet even in Erwinna the skeleton of the coming struggle was starting to rattle its bones. Those friendly neighborhood bankers who had been urging credit on the dubious farmers despite the drop in farm prices that had followed World War I had started to call in their mortgages, and those self-sufficient, idiosyncratic and hitherto law-abiding dairy farmers who were their neighbors had started to refuse. Not only that, but the entire circle of writers and intellectuals they were part of was itself in an uproar, ending its isolation, involving itself in politics with a steadily increasing fervor. Despite the complexities which would soon begin to become apparent, the early years of the decade were a good time — in fact they were a wonderful time — to be an American radical. There had been desperate moments in human history long before this particular Depression. Invisible linkages between region and region had always gone awry. Mysterious changes in the weather sired famine. Diseases bred who knew whether by fate, sin, filth, or poverty had murdered millions. Within tribes, within towns, within cities, between nation and nation, the strong had always vanquished the weak. But there had never been a time, not even during the period of the French Revolution, when so many people — especially so many ordinary, everyday common people — believed that these things did not have to be. Out of the wretched of the earth, the main thing the earth then seemed capable of producing in any abundance, the Soviet Union was creating a new society whose ultimate purpose was to answer every human need. It was the antithesis of the United States and its fulfillment simultaneously. Thanks to the laws of Marxism, everything was going to be all right. Objectively speaking, by every measure of the statisticians, things were as bad as they had ever been for a large proportion of people the world over, but subjectively speaking, particularly from the viewpoint of the intellectuals, things were not always necessarily so bad. Everything was explainable. Everything could be cured. Why it became such an issue that there had once been a moment when they had actually

117

had faith in the future of humanity is part of the public and the private tragedy of every twentieth-century radical, but there was such a moment. A "New Deal"? A likely story. Socialism? As John Dos Passos put it — "near beer." If capitalism was the problem, Communism was the solution. That the solution was itself a problem: that transformation of the dialectic came later.

However much she welcomed the return of a radical atmosphere, Josie had little desire to become actively involved. In addition to all their other travels, when John's mother died of a heart attack in the summer of 1931 they made another journey, to Lansing, and with all their comings and goings she had found relatively little opportunity to work. Ever since the time of the move to Erwinna three years earlier Josie had been immersing herself as much as possible in the Frey family papers she intended to use as the foundation for her next novel. Exactly what she was going to do with the material she was not yet sure, but that the book was to be the first of a trilogy, that it would have an American theme, and that it would be larger, grander, and infinitely more ambitious than anything she had previously attempted — that much was already decided. The more she considered the more she saw that the hero of such an epic might well be the tragic adventurer whose misfortunes dominated the family letters as they had dominated her mother's stories, the luckless nineteenth-century carpetbagger for whom she was named, her mother's favorite brother, Uncle Joe. On one of her return trips from Key West with John they had stopped in Atlanta so she could supplement her personal archives with published corroboration of Joseph Frey's part in the financial scandals that followed the Civil War, and she was so excited about the prospects of a novel with a southern setting that her letters to Katherine Anne during and after her Russian travels were in fact more about the novel than about the trip. Invited through Theodore Dreiser in the spring of 1931 to become a member of the executive board of a new organization, the National Committee for the Defense of Political Prisoners, an affiliate of the legal arm of the Communist Party, Josie accepted, but, invited a few months later to join Dreiser and others in a firsthand investigation of violence against miners in the Kentucky coalfields, she declined. Nor did she go to Alabama at the time of the Scottsboro trial, another of the defense committee's major interests. For an article on the case in the *New Masses*, "Lynching in the Quiet Manner," she appears to have worked from transcripts. Josie identified herself with the radical movement, she made her contributions freely, and as her work itself took more of a radical direction the lines between her literary and her political interests were at times obscured. But her overwhelming intention, right from the beginning of the decade, was to keep her agenda her own.

John was very nearly in an opposite mood. He believed. After their trip to the Soviet Union he believed in Communism, he believed in the possibility of revolution in the United States, and he believed in these things with so much the same radiant buoyant enthusiasm with which he believed in everything he believed in that he was able to make other people believe in them too. He had no definite plan to stop doing one thing and start doing something else, but simply by following his instincts, that was approximately what happened. Soon after their return he began giving lectures on the subject of Russia, and as 1932 progressed he joined with other writers and intellectuals in the League of Professional Groups for Foster and Ford supporting the Communist presidential ticket. Few things made the transition from the 1920s to the 1930s more gracefully than John's powers of elocution. His voice was as gentle as the rustling of dune grass and his language so flexible he could make Communism sound as subtle as "The Waste Land" or as rugged as "Dan McGrew," depending on the audience. When he was not out with one group he was out with another, rushing from an angry meeting of the poor to a guilty meeting of the rich, soothing unity into one, charming money from the second, sometimes in the space of a single evening. "John has developed into a magnificent speaker and talks at Cooper Union, etc., with a fine dramatic conviction and all the oratory of a first rate soap boxer," Josie informed Katherine Anne. It is true that John was discouraged about his writing. It is true he had been drinking and drifting. It is true that he found in Marxism both a theory and a practice of escape. Yet to attribute his politics to escape alone would be an error for it is just as true that there was an irreducible quality of goodness in John Herrmann, an irreducible sympathy for the sufferings of others, that his enthusiasm for Communism exactly expressed. When he ran into Malcolm Cowley at the May Day parade in New York in 1932, Cowley found him "exalted." He did not altogether stop writing. If anything, along with his general sense of himself, that improved. The same determination that went along with his commitment to revolution seems also to have stiffened his prose so that it lost the little-boy whine that had characterized it so often and took on, at least temporarily, the voice of a man. What is by far the best writing of his career was done now — the portrait of a ruined salesman called "The Big Short Trip" for which he shared, with Thomas Wolfe, the $5,000 1932 Scribner's literary prize — and it is also the piece of work most directly influenced by radical ideas. John's career in the radical movement gave him a confidence in himself and his usefulness which nothing he had done before ever had and nothing he would find to do afterward ever would. In a context where his basic amiability was not a distraction but an advantage he found a sense of purpose. Perhaps as early as 1931 he joined the Communist Party. It was something that Josie never did.

There was another difference between Josie and John as they took their positions in the radical orbit: in a word, sex. Not to put too fine a point on it, the radical movement of the 1930s was a male preserve. "There'll be no distinctions there" promised a song about heaven popular during this supposedly egalitarian era. But there were here. "Listen I must write you a long letter about the Scottsboro case, the miners strike and Revolution," Josie wrote Katherine Anne in the summer of 1931, but what she actually wrote was:

> Speaking of the latter, a few gents, including Herr Herrmann, and some of our well-known talk-it-overs such as Edmund Wilson, Malcolm Cowley, Slater Brown, Burton Rascoe, Murray Godwin, Mike Gold, decided to meet to talk things over, over beer, as you might know. I, being also an ardent talk-it-over longed to partake of this wordy feast, in fact showed a good deal of longing for same but the usual masculine retort, such as we well know, and I have only to recall to you the same gestures made by some of these same gents reenforced by the redoubtable Josephson, at the time that little journal which was to see but never saw the light, for which us three, you, me, and the Grist Mill himself labored with delight, was scheduled to appear, at that time, Misz Porter you and me received much the same gentle stay-in-your place which may or may not be the home, as I received now when the new and proposed talk fest was projected. Mister Herrmann departed for thence full of a masculine importance you and I will never know, alas, and came back somewhat boozy but so far as I could see with not one idea the smarter. Another meeting was proposed for which I continued to long to partake but said nothing, no even urged the Grist Mill to go and lap up his masculine delights along with the beer. He did and returned a sadder and wiser man, forced to report that very little in the way of conversations had been accomplished. At the second meeting the brilliant Bob Coates adorned the gathering contributing to what was meant to be a revolutionary round-about such glowing points as Aw you dont want a revolution, and various little gems of thought picked up from the New Yorker. This seems to have dulled the gathering. Malcolm left in the midst without explanations. A smart man, say I, and just what I would have done, but Herrmann stuck it out with the beer. All and all the conversations peed out along with the beer and there has been no more of such. I told Mister Herrmann that as long as the gents had bourgeois reactions to women they would probably never rise very high in their revolutionary conversations but said remarks rolled off like water.

Funny, wasn't it? How did Josie actually feel about it? How could Josie possibly have felt about it? The men in question were men she had known at least since her return from Europe in 1925 and in some cases earlier and she was involved with them both as writers and friends. Not only had they read her stories, argued with her about literature, and solicited her contributions to their magazines —: both in Erwinna and in Connecticut earlier they had eaten her cooking, drunk her liquor, and slept in her beds. Now here they were at the beginning of a new political epoch reducing her to that very caricature she had sworn all her life to avoid: "John's Wife." How did Josie actually feel about that? She hated it, naturally. She was furious about her exclusion, she was jealous of their luck, and if she was able to get a good letter or two out of it now and then as she sometimes managed to do, it was never really adequate revenge. If she had ever for one instant attempted to communicate to any of her male companions the true measure of contempt with which she sometimes privately viewed their actions it is hard to say whether she or they would have been more surprised. Comic antics were the closest she could come in public, a murky kind of reproachfulness in private, to its expression. Part of her difficulty was exactly that: she did not fully recognize her feelings. The psychological ideas that would explain to women the interior corollaries of their subordination did not exist. There was no explanation except "selfishness" for her dislike of running the house single-handed, no explanation except "masculinity" for the ambition that drove her to the typewriter day after day, no explanation except "temper" for the rages she let fly at John sometimes, no explanation at all for the intense but unidentified inner grievance she carried around with her all the time, a rage at the unstated accusation that it was not right to be what she was. Intellectual ideas about the subjection of women in general certainly existed and Josie was certainly aware of them, but with a few buried exceptions these were abstract, impersonal notions of relatively little use in interpreting personal relations because the phenomena they were addressed to were public rather than private. While her understanding of politics and economics had an intellectual foundation, her understanding of the position of women did not. Simply as a matter of personal experience it was Josie's natural assumption that women were the equals of men. So her grandmother taught her mother, so her mother taught her daughters, and as far as she had gotten in her own observations of the human species, she had found no reason to disagree. What Josie believed therefore was not that women were actually inferior to men but rather only that they were thought to be inferior to men and probably always would be, and the result was a contradiction that she never, ever, resolved. On the one hand she drew the obvious conclusion: it would be better to have been a man. On the other: what could possibly be a more fruitless notion? She struggled, as women have always struggled, against the intractable dictates of her own nature, to be "the kind of woman" that men have always wanted. So intense were the demands of this opposition that it cut right to the heart of her social being.

Whether the truest characterization of her relations with most men most of the time would be "hypocritical" or "ambivalent" it is difficult to say. Either way it did not leave her very much freedom. Like the work-songs of prisoners or the dancing of slaves, Josie's letter to Katherine Anne is essentially an entertainment of the powerless. Given her belief in the basic injustice of things, and in their irremediable nature, what better consolation was there than a joke?

Considering the terms of her participation in the radical movement, it is not very surprising that for her deepest investigation of the things that concerned her, Josie turned to her work. There she was unimpeded. As she examined her family's history for the first time through a Marxist prism, she came as close as she would ever come to that flash of understanding we call a revelation. The entire history of the Frey family from the events of her mother's childhood to the events of her own was an illustration of the breakdown of capitalism! The homely familiar stories that had been told to her by her mother for as long back as she could remember were not simply domestic diversions. They had historical significance. They had stature. They were just as important as Josie in her bones had always felt them to be. It was a discovery with a highly personal meaning for her — as if Marx and her mother had suddenly met and agreed, shaking hands over all the Frey bones scattered across Pennsylvania graveyards, that the economic afflictions of this one little family were part of the grand scheme of History! Nor was it only Josie's economic radicalism of which the trilogy became the chief repository. It was also her feelings about women and men. Present from the beginning and moving slowly into the forefront of the novels is an autobiographical heroine who is, in effect, a feminist. Named for Victor Dorne, the alias adopted by Joseph Frey as he fled the law, Victoria Wendel Chance was herself an alias, for she could explore all the author's perceptions about the fundamental tensions between men and women — without taking as many of the risks. "Don't be stupid and shut your eyes and imagine that the only things in life worth while come from men and what people call romance," says the fictional mother, Anne Wendel, to her daughters Victoria and Rosamund in the early pages of the trilogy, and it could be that Josie is writing these words at the very moment of a radical meeting after John and his cronies, ignoring her wishes, have marched out the door. In life she was more equivocal. Josie was never a systematic Marxist, nor was she a conscious feminist, but as the Frey saga absorbed more and more of her attention over a highly politicized decade, it was in the trilogy, more than elsewhere, that she tended to work out her views. It was the perfect answer to the insult of male rejection. At a time when the most characteristic social unit was a committee, the trilogy was a seminar of one.

If ever there were a better formula for domestic conflict it is difficult to imagine it because few kinds of work are less naturally compatible than writing and politics — the intractable frustrations of one and the erratic requirements of the other being equally capable of dominating any household — and it was less a divergence of principle than it was of practice that began causing troubles between John and Josie now. Imagine the scenes taking place in Erwinna at this moment —: each of them rationally supporting the other's involvement in activity unrelated to themselves, Josie insisting she was happy John was doing work she also believed in, John claiming to be pleased Josie had begun so important an effort as the trilogy, both agreeing there was no reason in the world they shouldn't each do what they wanted but emotionally resenting it, their convictions having little to do with their daily realities —: Josie alone in the period of her greatest literary and intellectual excitement, needing a listener, needing to share, John more independent than ever, off in the world, both uncertain about how much is serious, how much circumstantial, as they suddenly feel farther apart. All at once there are difficulties everywhere. Outside, the house and grounds are in increasing disrepair, first the autumn chores neglected and then the winter, the garden not properly bedded down, insulation skimped so that the winds when they arrive will blow straight through the house, and who-is-it-that-is-going-to-be-sitting-here-when-that-happens, she would demand of him, if-you-really-cared-about-my-work-you-wouldn't-expect-me-to-have-to-do-it-shivering-and-numb. In the kitchen. Josie has always done most of the cooking, that is no different from ever, but at least John was there in the past during the preliminaries, he chopped the wood, and now he comes barging in at mealtime expecting to be fed, or barging in with others expecting her to feed them too, or not doing any barging until dinner is long since spoiled, and sometimes never, leaving her to worry and fester long hours by herself. In the bed. Their sexual contentment has always depended on the simultaneity of her availability and his desire, and now he is often not present at the times when she might honestly say yes so sometimes she says no which makes him feel terrible because he is extremely sensitive to any form of rebuff and even if she says yes sometimes now it is worse than no because she can hardly open her legs she is so tense and dry and when he does manage to get inside her it is cold and quick and he falls asleep on top of her feeling more rejected than loved and she feels abused and angry and they lie there for a while in these classic silent postures finally stirring with apologies: She: I'm sorry, I was so tired, the book isn't going well: He: I'm sorry, I was so excited when I came in, I wasn't thoughtful: until finally they fall asleep together companionably and understandingly after all, certainly without undue worry, because they have had their ups and downs before, who hasn't?, and they see no reason despite their dissatisfactions to take the present phase very seriously.

To cover the inconsistencies of temper that so frequently characterize her these days especially when she is writing, Josie and John invent a
false personality for her known as "Susy" to whom they attribute most of
their household woes. If "Victoria" represents more or less the left wing
of Josie's personality — bolder, more self-reliant, and considerably sta-
bler than life — "Susy" is more or less the character on the right — a
morose, self-pitying accusatory creature blaming everyone but herself
for whatever difficulties have befallen her and making things out to be
considerably worse than they are. "Susy" is not a completely new creation. She had existed as a childhood scapegoat long ago in Josie's family
history and she appeared on occasion as late as Josie's letters from Berkeley under the same name. Nor is this the first time that John has seen her.
She is the woman who moped along back to their apartment in New York
and wrote him letters when he was on road trips — after Josie had spent
a perfectly satisfactory evening with Katherine Anne. But the resurrection of Susy at the present moment, her official adoption, is an indication
that between the pressure of her character and the character of her oppression those quintessential fluctuations of emotion that have always
characterized "Woman," if only in the eyes of the beholder, are indeed
characterizing Josie now. Under the circumstances the introduction of
Susy into the household is a considerable domestic convenience. If Susy
is complaining about having to do the chores again, Josie can be independent, self-sufficient, loving even the hardships of their splendid life
together in the country. If Susy might at times almost be accused of
being hostile to the radical movement so sceptical is she whether John's
activity in it stems more from a fear of writing or a love of revolution,
Josie is the comrade who endorses every bit of what he is attempting and
is proud of him for doing it so well. If Susy is nasty, Josie is considerate. If
Susy is malicious, Josie is contrite. If Susy is doubtful how they will make
it through another winter if something doesn't happen, Josie is passionately loyal, declaring of course they will make it, haven't they always?
aren't their freedoms, their commitments, precisely what they mated for
before they married? In fact Susy brought a lot of comfort to them both.
"I can't blame poor Josy for going all Susy on me," John wrote Josie tenderly once when he was away, though disliking hostility as much as he
did it must have been exactly then he liked her best, Susy being far easier
to live with as a literary amusement than she was at close range, when
Josie would kiss him good-bye in the morning and there was no telling
who would greet him at night. As for Josie, Susy took a lot of responsibility off her shoulders. Whatever her dissatisfactions, if it was only Susy
and not Josie who was complaining about them, she was safe. Besides,
Susy was a joint invention, a character they coauthored, a member of the
family, another joke between lovers. Funny, wasn't it? It wasn't.

From the time of their return to Erwinna after their second visit to

Key West, in the winter of 1931-1932, until the following summer, 1932, this was their pattern: Josie primarily involved in writing and only secondarily in politics, John primarily involved in politics, increasingly leaving his writing behind. In addition to all their other problems they were also increasingly anxious about money, for apart from a small amount coming in from various stories neither one of them was earning any — less than ever before — and given the combination of their other interests and the national economic picture, neither one of them was much inclined to try. Sometime during the spring they heard for the first time about an old estate in Saratoga, New York, which had recently begun to open its doors to a small number of writers and artists, and when they inquired into it they were both invited to come. It seemed to both of them an ideal arrangement, for room and board was provided and they could save the money gained from rental of their own house over the summer to get a head start on what they needed for the coming year. Josie could complete a draft and begin revision of her novel. John could plunge ahead into some of the stories he had not been able to get to. The household responsibilities which seemed to be so much at the heart of their quarrels could be left behind. Before the moment of departure actually came, however, John changed his mind. Whether it was uneasiness at the solemn way Yaddo sounded, lack of desire to be there with Josie, or the positive lure of a Michigan vacation it is impossible to be sure, but in any event it was decided that she would go to one place and he would go to the other. It was not a separation in any emotional sense they had decided on and in fact would not be any longer than many another time they had been apart. Neither one of them believed that anything between them was seriously wrong. The last two weeks before they left they spent working intently together around the farmhouse, fashioning a terrace with stones from the brook, painting and scraping, and creating the setup for the installation of electricity at last to meet their promises to the forthcoming tenant. In early June, 1932, when everything was finished, they set off together for Saratoga Springs. It was a pleasant, even a lush, drive, the eastern countryside irrepressibly flourishing even if the country was not, the relief of their impending separation, occurring, as it did, within the security of their attachment, leaving them both contented and relaxed. They spent a night together in a nearby town and then on a fine sunny morning, scarcely stopping off there himself to get acquainted, John dropped Josie off at Yaddo and went on by himself to Michigan.

# The Music
# Comes On Strong

IF JOSIE had seen the shade of her sister Helen traversing the Yaddo gardens and beckoning her to come as she sat alone on the porch of the old stone mansion one night when she had been there less than a week, she could not have been any more drawn than she was to the woman she actually found there, Marion Greenwood, a young painter, who moved her as she had never been moved before. In a sense it was always as much Helen as Marion that she saw. Marion was the more beautiful of the two women — she had a dark, lush, dramatic kind of beauty while Helen had been ethereal and fair — but there were the same slender yet ample bodies, the same sultry eyes, the same plasticity of expression that could transform the whole person from innocent to sophisticate simply by registering a change in mood. Nor was the likeness between Helen and Marion only a physical matter. It was also a matter of character. Marion, even more than Helen, was a strikingly erotic woman, as much in pursuit of romance as she was of her art, beset, in fact pursued herself, as Helen had been before she married, by urgent sexual desires which, while she did not wish to resist them completely, at times at least she wished to be able to discipline. Marion Greenwood was, then and always, completely serious about her painting. As a young woman she was regarded as having unusual promise which she in fact lived to fulfill. She was awarded one of the earliest fellowships to Yaddo in 1927, worked on murals in Mexico under the direction of Rivera and Orozco and later on her own,

126

directed a number of mural projects in the United States during the New Deal, and was well known throughout the country as an independent artist from the time of her first exhibit in New York in 1944 until 1970, when she died. Today her work is held by major museums, including the Metropolitan, which has a self-portrait, and a profile of her, by Alexander Calder, is owned by the Museum of Modern Art. At the time of her meeting with Josie, however, Marion was young and distracted. At Yaddo her affections had temporarily alighted on one of her fellow residents, a married writer named Philip Stevenson, and she was caught up with him in a cycle of attraction and rejection which seems to have left her in despair. Between her unhappiness over Philip, quarrels with her family, with whom she still lived in New York, and anxiety over where the money would come from to finance her further studies she was extremely wrought up emotionally most of the summer. How like Helen she was even in that — her tangle of lovers, problems with her family, money worries, and trying to get on with the business of a career. She was at an age in her life which for Josie was especially poignant — twenty-three — the age of hovering between triviality and seriousness, the same age John had been when she had met him in Paris, the age Helen had been when she decided to marry Andrew and Josie took her to the train station in San Francisco and said good-bye. "I watched you coming back across the room, and what there is about your face and body, whether it is your skin or heavy eyes or what, but just to see you brings back to me in some way all I ever loved and lost, the dreams a child has of a world that never quite comes true, the moment at twilight in our mother's homes, my dead sister and loves now dead and gone and somehow terribly sweet because they are gone forever, come back in you, they really do, they're there in you," Josie wrote her when they had known one another just a short while. It was only one of her many illusions.

From the time she met Marion Greenwood in the summer of 1932 until the time she left her in Mexico nearly a year later, Josie acted as if she had stepped out of real life into a circus of emotional possibilities in which the laws of nature and of society simply did not apply. Indeed in a sense she did step out of real life, leaving behind her usual commitments and routines for an exotic, highly sexual, romantic interlude that was unlike anything she had ever done before or would do again. Her relationship with Marion Greenwood is the personal secret at the heart of Josie's life and she did not speak of it herself. In the trilogy which is in so many other respects autobiographical, in the myriad memoirs and private memory-books that are part of the salvage of her later years, in the recollections of her recollections by her friends, the figure of Marion Greenwood, or a figure anything like her, most often does not even appear. The stories Josie told about her separation from John — stories from which she fed her friends and even nourished herself for years to come — indistinguishable as they were from her political stories of the 1930s, were always lacking the central factor, like a garnish served up without the main dish, albeit a garnish so attractively offered most of the diners failed to notice the meat was simply missing. Yet I do not think Josie wanted this story concealed. There are the letters, practically flagged, in the collection that she herself assembled for Yale, the latest in a long lineage of undestroyed "Destroy" files to whose importance she deliberately calls attention by references throughout her writing to the undestroyed secrets of other pasts through which she and her mother before her so openly enjoyed to riffle. And not only are Marion's letters, carefully marked "Destroy," safely secured with the rest of the collection, telegraphing their interest with that unmistakable sign, her own letters are there as well, indicating that whether she had asked for them back or Marion had returned them, she had at least once — but, I believe, in fact, several times — made a definite decision to keep them preserved. No one knew better than Josie the inevitable outcome of the command "Destroy." In the memoir of her childhood and youth, "Magicians and Their Apprentices," that was with her in the hospital the day she died, she had rested with pleasure on this particular point. "My mother had refused to be ashamed about prying into another person's letters," she wrote, retelling Mary's story about how she had scotched an undesirable romance of her brother Daniel's by this very means.

> "It's what anyone would do if they cared enough," she had put it. This was one of the last stories she had told me and hearing it I was certain that she had probably secretly regaled herself with letters not belonging to her all her life, including letters of my own. When she died, sure enough, I found among her papers a long envelope marked emphatically on the outside: *Private. Don't Open. Destroy.*
>
> How well my mother knew me, I thought. I'm her child and she knew I'd open it precisely because it says, *Destroy.*

In fact it was like a magician herself that Josie acted: as if she, John, and Marion were all capable of playing infinite parts in tableaux she could arrange and rearrange with a flick of her hand: as if unseen amulets dipped in the potion of her good intentions could protect her, could protect all of them, from harm. In one of the versions of the tales of King Arthur there is a colloquy between king and magician after the magician has told Arthur that soon he, Merlin, must leave the court. " 'This is beyond understanding,' said the king. 'You are the wisest man alive. You know what is preparing. Why do you not make a plan to save yourself?' And Merlin said quietly, 'Because I am wise. In the combat between wisdom and feeling, wisdom never wins. I have told you your certain future, my lord, but knowing it will not change it by a hair. When the time comes your feeling will conduct you to your fate.' " He follows the maiden Nyneve where she leads him, reveals to her the "tools of enchantment," and after he has given her all the secrets that she wishes to extract from him, she traps him, forever, in a cave. Among the many photographs from Mexico is a picture of Marion, dressed in a cape, standing at the mouth of a cave, eyes closed, as if some important work is now behind her. It could almost be illustrating the story.

Two women. One is forty years old, though she admits only thirty-five, established, respected, already noted if not actually famous, a woman popular among writers, known for her vigor, for her mind, a great deal of living already behind her, capable of giving advice on a variety of problems, outwardly philosophical and yet inwardly stormy, a lonesome woman despite her many friends, shy, awkward, and uncomfortable in her body — for years she has certified her femininity less by her actual feelings than by her marriage to an unabashedly masculine man whose attraction attests what it is impossible for her to prove — lonesome physically, perhaps more than any other way, for a contentment, a satisfaction, that almost always eludes her, for that natural climate of spontaneous affection she remembers from childhood, not exactly wishing she had children and yet missing them all the same, missing the warmth and bustle of a family, a strained and driven woman despite appearances, a woman existing mainly among men, a woman who, even more than she realizes it herself, has more than a longing, has an actual physical necessity simply to relax. The other woman is in some ways the opposite, scarcely more than half the age of the first, a woman so pretty it is hard for her to see herself or get others to see her as an artist despite her talent, so passionate sex is almost another professional signature for her, sure more of her ability to seduce than her ability to create, profligate with her body and yet tormented by it too, bobbing around on the seas of sex, the seas of love, ready to leave her parents' harbor yet looking for another in which she can feel just a little protected and secure. One is intellectual; the other sensual. One is inhibited; the other unrestrained. One is settled in comparison to the other, with a home and a husband and literary ambitions she has worked all her life to be able to realize; the other is all future and possibility with no destiny, no direction, of which she yet feels entirely sure. One is accustomed to mothering while longing herself to be a child; the other accustomed to being babied while wishing to be like the other, so seemingly bold and so free. They have plenty of time as the summer enfolds them to understand these and their other differences, for they also have something in common. Among the several summer residents at Yaddo, there are many fewer women than men.

Sometimes I imagine it must have begun in tenderness between them: their conversation leading to confidences, confidences to confession, confession to consolation, consolation to physical comforting, Josie stretching out and lying down beside Marion one night to calm her when she was particularly wild after an evening with Philip. Other times I imagine it could have originated in lust: their different histories suggesting fascinating possibilities to them both, Marion incredulous about the difficulty Josie was having over such available pleasures, Josie envious of the very magnitude, if not the relentlessness of Marion's sexual desires. Who began it? I have sometimes asked myself that. Were they drunk? Were they melancholy? Were they playful? Did it have about it something of a dare? Either one of them might have spoken first, if words were the bridge that they traveled. They were both reckless enough to have taken the initiative, fearless enough not to refuse the possibility when it appeared. I suppose that away from John, and from the continuing mutual reassurances that their life together had always demanded, Josie began to have a clearer awareness of some of the disappointments of her marriage. I suppose that fundamentally she was very angry at John. I suppose that she had been so tense for so long, not only sexually but in other ways, that she would have been just as ready for an affair with a man that summer as she was for the one that she actually had, if any of the men who had been at Yaddo with her had happened to strike her interest or she theirs. I suppose that, finishing a book, she was already experiencing the first tremors of emptiness that are almost indistinguishable from the earliest moments of relaxation: I suppose that, being at Yaddo, she had that illusion of immunity from reality that has offered itself to many residents before and since: I suppose that the atmosphere sanctioned experiment: I suppose that Marion Greenwood was a tease: I suppose that there are a hundred reasons why the things that happened happened and the things that did not did not: but what it is not necessary to suppose, because it is beyond supposing, is that within a few weeks of their meeting Josie and Marion Greenwood were together in bed understanding one another with their eyes, with their lips, with their hands, and if for Marion the feelings it aroused were at least in some respects familiar, for Josie it was something of a revelation. For, gentle or passionate, fierce or tender, whoever began it, whatever they said: when she was lying in bed beside Marion Greenwood she felt at ease.

While Josie was following her instincts at Yaddo, John was following his in Michigan, visiting with his family, sailing a little, writing a little, and just generally keeping himself amused. Mail, as usual, was the shuttle between their separate lives. Josie's letters from the summer have not survived, but from John's it is possible to get a distinct impression of the progress of events. Throughout most of the summer they were writing to each other every day. As attentive as it was possible to be to Josie long distance, John was. He sympathized with the details of her adjustment to Yaddo, he emphasized the importance of her work, he mailed her package after package filled with clothes she very much wanted, both old ones belonging to his sister and new ones he would buy himself, hovering with a comfortable familial intimacy over such details as size, what alterations she might need to make, and fit. John's letters were scarcely passionate but they were affectionate, they were endearing, they were filled with the natural assumption of their common interest in various items of news, gossip, and opinion that reflected so many years of a common life. When word came during their separation of the boon of John's Scribner's prize, the exchange of fantasies about how they would use the money was one of their last simple moments. But after that, some of what was really happening in their relationship began to rise to the surface of their correspondence. To what did John attribute Josie's increasing crankiness and irritability despite an agreement between them not to write each other nasty letters? how interpret his inability to do anything to her satisfaction, whether criticize her manuscript or balance the bank account? how account for his sensation that despite the familiarity of their cycle of complaint-apology-complaint there was a new catch in it this time, something he didn't quite get? At some point Josie obviously mentioned Marion's name and told him something about their friendship, but what exactly did she say which made him reply, "Painters are awful stupid people as a rule. I hope I got all your love always like you end up the letter. I'm jealous and have funny feelings since you wrote me how you've begun to have somebody make you feel on your own feet and not feel like you felt with me. Maybe I'm just silly about it but the last three nights I've been feeling awfully sad as if something had happened . . . "? What anxiety made him start to pile up more insistently the loving phrases, the sexual reassurances, in the closings of his own letters — "I love you with all my heart and want you all the time," "All of my love ever your boy keep on loving me," "I got to have my baby in my arms," "Wanting you in my arms and loving you so," "Your boy loves you, never forget that," "I want my baby in my arms." To what outpouring of ambivalence from Josie did John reply at the beginning of August that he was forgoing a long sail because on the boat he did not hear from her for days "until I get a nice stack of letters in one saying you want to leave right away in the next saying it is fine there and you want to stay until Sept and in the next you could shoot yourself if you don't get away immediately and in the next it is such a lovely place the work is going good and you are getting along fine and in the next you will just run away and go see your boy friend and go back cause you cant no longer stand it and next day everything is going famous and there never was a better place to work etc." "If I had a little idea of what my baby wants [I] would be right on the job giving it [to] her," this one continued. "So I figured after yesterdays letter and the wire maybe you will crystallize your views and then I will know what to do etc. But I love you so much and am worried for fear if I don't get a letter off each day you will stop loving your boy or something that I hated to start this cruise . . ." With what obfuscations had Josie alluded to the discoveries she was making about her body, how explain how she came by the things she must have been trying to tell him she learned, to make him say the day before he left to pick her up, "It will be swell to see you, I suppose I better not mention how swell it will be to have you in my arms any more since your letter. I'll try to get myself on a higher plane so as you'll love me. And I'll try to learn to love you with my imagination the way you want me to. The old body love days will have to be over I suppose. I used to think you liked it . . . I'm glad you learned this summer that your body was all right all along and it was my way of loving you was bad for you. You'll have to show me the way and when I get there in the morning Sat. I hope the gal I meet will be my same Josy and not the gal as wrote me that letter. Nothing I say seems to make you know how much I love you so I'll just have to try to show you with my actions. All my love including that of the imagination is yours, John." With what trepidation of emotion had she then softened her previous declarations so that his final note before arriving was more confident, almost teasing, "I'll try to be very romantic when I meet you at Yaddo if I know how it's done. I may not be very good stuff at that but I sure will try and anyway I shouldn't fall down an awful lot . . . Well I'm loving you [with] all my might and I hope you too will be a little romantic when we meet and no hard looks or any of the old greetings I sometimes get from Josy after being away a few days. Just the good old love and romance from now on." But when they did finally meet, in the driveway at Yaddo, what could either of them have been expecting?

On the surface their reunion was unexceptional enough, their reactions no different than on many another occasion they had come together after being apart. They left immediately on a trip through eastern Canada, Cape Cod, and Long Island in the new car that was the sole durable embodiment of John's prize money, then stopped off in Erwinna for only two days before heading west to Iowa where the first major farm strike of the Depression was in progress. On the second part of the journey they were traveling in company with none other than Philip Stevenson, who had acquired the status of a family friend, and the journalist Mary Heaton Vorse, who had also been at Yaddo. Both the women had arranged to write articles on the farm strike; the men were investigating the politics. The Iowa trip was an important juncture for Josie for several reasons. It was her first return to her home state since the deaths of her parents. Her article, "Feet in the Grass Roots," which appeared in *Scribner's* in January, 1933, was her first major contribution to the journalism of the

Depression. And with the emergence of militance among previously conservative western farmers, the politics of the Depression itself entered a new and more radical phase. Her exploration of these events —as an Iowan, as a radical, and as a writer — added a new dimension to her public identity which lasted the rest of her life. Yet despite the significance of the trip, it was internal rather than external events which interested her most. Almost as soon as she had left her behind at Yaddo, Josie's thoughts turned to Marion and the question of how and under what circumstances she would be able to see her again. From Canada, less than twenty-four hours after they parted, she wrote:

> We got into Montreal at ten and drove around the crowded streets with tiny stores that all looked cluttered and like second hand clothes stores and we got us a good room in this hotel and had ale & sandwiches in the room and laughed and did things and I thought of you all the time and in the night woke thinking of you as if you were all alone in that great house and it was very painful thinking of you so. And now it's morning and you are just now having breakfast and we are going to soon & then we'll drive today to Quebec. This is just a hurried note, I'll really write you later. But be patient, my sweet thing, and life is going to be as good to you as I should love to be. And we will have good times together this winter. John likes you; with a strange intuition he has talked about you. I'm going to tell him all about you someday. Be good darling . . . and take good care of yourself and write me.

From the next stop, Provincetown, she wrote a peculiar letter, oddly off balance, as if feeling the conflict of trying to live in her two emotional worlds at once.

> I wonder how you are. You were as lovely as a Greek vase but I see much more clearly now why things did not go well with you. I am tired and indescribably sad and will write no more but we had a fine afternoon at Dos Passos's house with wine and a roast duck and two swell Siamese cats and two Follies girls who had queer misinformation about science and oh, the eclipse was marvelous here, it was complete and the whole world died down with groups of people standing transfixed on hills of sandunes near the sea in tragic poses like the old Italian pictures of the Crucifixion and it had all the awe of that event, and a great sighing of birds flying as before a storm and the deepest shadows and one star came out beside that moon covered sun. Goodbye Greenwood — when you come away let me know, I will take you in this fine handsome easy riding car to our house and we will all laugh and have a great deal

of good food and fun together. Goodbye, my dear, and this is a lovely night outside with the water washing on the beach.

From Iowa her letters became even odder, as if her perceptions of the striking farmers, Philip Stevenson's relation to Marion, and Marion's to herself had all become fused. "Once I saw Philip walk off & look up at the moon. That's your moon and his. But the stars are mine," she wrote, in the middle of a description of a farmers' campfire in which almost the next lines are, "This whole business out here has been fine. These are the realest people you ever saw." Following the pattern of the summer, she did not lie to John exactly — it is obvious that he knew a great deal — but neither did she tell the truth, straddling instead a boundary between candor and deceit, hoping, it would seem, to gain maneuverability in ambiguity that full disclosure almost certainly would have ruled out, defining, as she went along, an unconscious strategy of vagueness whose purpose must have been to enable her to keep them both. It is apparent from her letters to Marion that her relationship with the younger woman kept recurring as a difficulty with John despite her circumspection. At some point during the summer Marion had made a painting of Josie which, after telegraphing John for his agreement, Josie had bought. What the painting looked like or what became of it there is no way of knowing but Josie must have been uncomfortable about it, because she intended to prevent John from looking at it until they got home, at which restriction he in turn must have become uneasy because he then insisted on seeing it at once. "Tried to keep John from looking at the painting . . . but he looked at it last night, so he told me this morning in bed, thinks it is *very good*, but you saw something he never saw," she reported to Marion only a few days into their trip. As long as they were traveling in company the issue was more or less submerged, but as soon as they were alone again, preparing to leave Iowa, it began to rise to the surface, with Josie trying to persuade John to return to Erwinna via Woodstock, New York, where Marion was visiting, John refusing, and Josie bending and twisting her arguments and explanations so that if they could not do that at least they could do the next best thing and invite Marion to visit them in Erwinna soon after they got home. From Sioux City, just before they set out, she wrote:

> I haven't shown your letters to anyone although it has made John more miserable than he has ever been by anything from me. I can't write more about this, but will tell you when I see you. I want him to know you, he won't feel this way. He is getting over it, he knows very little about you, as I couldn't tell him much about you and he is a strange boy when he gets an idea in his head. I'm going to have you come down to our place as soon as

you can, it will be fine — he wants you to also, we will make him feel better. I love him very much but I love you too.

After that she must have redoubled her efforts at persuasion so that she could write after they had been home only two days, "I want to see you a lot and so does John." When they had been home little more than a week, Marion arrived.

If there had been any possibility before the visit from Marion that Josie's feeling for her would wither in the light of her real life in Erwinna, once she had actually seen her again that possibility was no more. She was absolutely, unmistakably, and unequivocally hooked. She finished her article on the farm strike, she sent out the manuscript of *Pity Is Not Enough*, which she had nearly completed at Yaddo, and she even — with John — began an important new friendship with the novelist Nathanael West who left New York to live near them in the country and finish *Miss Lonelyhearts*,° but for all that it was Marion and not the rest of it that seemed real. "Every now & then the music on the radio almost disappears & comes on again and how seldom it is, in our lives, that the music comes on strong," she wrote Marion toward the end of the autumn. It was stronger than it had ever been at the moment.

After Marion had been to Erwinna much of Josie's imagination was occupied in exploring the possibility that the three of them could live together during the winter, perhaps abroad. Not only did she never have the intention of excluding John from the relationship, he was so essential a part of it almost from the beginning that it is hard to resist the idea that it was as much the threeness as it was the twoness of it she actually wanted. What was the original impulse behind Josie's attention to triangles it is of course impossible to be sure. The denial of the jealousy she had once felt for Helen, its transformation into the sanctification of noncompetitiveness, must have played a part. But whatever its psychological foundations, it was an additional powerful force. With Maxwell Anderson there had been a Margaret, with Marion, before John, there had been a Philip, and now again here she was in a threesome: Josie, Marion, and John. It is not as if she did not realize that what she was doing was risky. "We are going to Mexico and we will have a fine time because we are very lovely people and very unusual and wise even for danger," one of her letters said. It is rather that she was so relentlessly impelled toward Marion, and so instinctively determined to keep John by her side, that she seems almost blindly to have begun to make the effort to work it out. She was as much caught up in her infatuation with Marion as she had been in any purely emotional situation since the death of Helen, and the longer it continued the stronger it became. "It is get-

° See also pp. 283–284 and Notes.

ting harder all the time for me to go away and leave you and when I am away it is getting harder and harder to do without you. I can see the day coming when I will get up in the middle of the night and take the car and drive 70 miles and more to get you," she wrote later in the year. Between frequent trips to the city to visit Marion, Marion's visits to Erwinna, and an old kidney condition which acted up to leave her literally in a feverish state she had no energy to spare for what she had intended to make her principal work of this period — outlining the second volume of the trilogy — and consumed as she was by this passionate obsession, her nights were as feverish as her days. She dreamed she was standing in a garden of gorgeous flowers . . . she dreamed she was standing on a bridge over hot sand . . . she dreamed that she and John met Philip at a filling station as they were getting gas and then they were in a house where Philip was alone with Marion and she, Josie, was trying to keep other people out . . . Then there were the thousand little extras a relationship with Marion seemed to require: buying her envelopes so she would write Josie more letters, interceding between Marion and her mother, injecting herself into Marion's relationship with doctors when she had a stomach ailment, soothing her anxieties, particularly when, as happened often, because of her continuing sexual activity with men in New York she worried and wondered whether she would get her period or not. "Write and tell me if you are all right the 15th. Don't worry if you aren't . . . ," Josie told her on one of those occasions, in a tone full of echoes of her final letters to Helen. Between John and Josie Marion was emotionally omnipresent even when she was not physically there.

"Dear little Crocodile," Josie wrote Marion during a period they were temporarily separated by their respective physical complaints:

> Here we are, in bed, but not in bed, alas, together. Could anything be funnier than the lives of women? John & Pep* are out tramping the fields for pheasant — why, God knows, Philip is no doubt pensive & brooding but quite comfortable. . . . Here you & I are, — heaven knows you may be throwing up at this moment — and I have begun this letter in a desperate race with a pain literally like a knife that stabs me & makes me know just how it would feel to get a knife in the back. John called up my New York doctor who asked to see me — he has seen every crack, corner & crevice & God knows what good it will do him to take a peek again. However, pinned down, he told John I could get cured of this plague once & for all & be all right again & the news was as good almost as health itself. I have been lying here, leading a dozen lives, all grand and robust in sunlight with a great deal of laughter & drinking & swimming and loving. John just came in & is going to get

* Nathanael West.

136

my supper. But in our next lives, let us be males. At least one of us. Pep had a letter today from a gal he has been quietly screwing & she is in the hospital, says she has had a miscarriage & needs some kind of operation. He was really worried, got off a telegram, & yet I laughed & laughed. God — here are the women, always on their backs. Even in defeat, on their backs. And the men can walk upright & sound. . . .

So, bitch, you did not write me even a line for today, especially after I was foolish enough to ask you to be good to me. You don't need love, but a whip. After all the trips I've made to town & all the running & all the evidences you've had of real anxiety, you can't give me that much. Well don't. See how much difference it makes. None, at all. Don't. But I'll teach you yet, you little tadpole. Just a rudimentary lover, that's all you are, got all the wriggles and the tail twistings & that's all; still just a tadpole. I love you anyhow and wish we were both well right now, very gay & savage.

Struggling out of the most horrible depression caused by this bloody sickness has been like trying to get out of a marsh, every step you sink deeper. But I pulled out at last, here I am, on a dry bit of land, covered with mud but free.

Darling I could laugh I feel so contemptuous & so happy.

I will pretend now that you and I are in beautiful clothes, driving someplace very fast & as long as I can choose, why I'll make the car a cadillac & dress you in a grass green dress. But I'd rather get on to the undressing. Goodbye sweet crocodile, till we meet in mud & sun by deep green water.

I'll be in town soon & out to see my girl. Get well, I can't bear to think you may still be throwing up, but why won't you tell me? Why are you so bad? Just a tadpole, that's the answer.

But an awfully sweet delicious one.

This is a very smudged letter. I can't help it. Try to like it anyhow, ungrateful one. What do you do with my letters? *Tear them up.*

Marion seems to have been intrigued enough, responsive enough, perhaps pliable enough when they were actually together but by no means as passionate in pursuit of their connection as Josie. Since most of Josie's letters drew either no response or letters that were apt to be a little cool, if not actually callous, Josie must have been pleased when the crocodile letter at last drew something of a response in kind:

How is my blue-eyed buxom bitch today — and the bad bad kidney? I hope and pray it is all gone. I feel today your better because as you see I'm feeling so good today no pain no nausea, Old

Greenwood will be up an at em soon, I might be able to be
smacked down easily at present, I might be wobbly and leak like a
sieve when vertical but it won't be long now and believe me
baby — all the goddamn males on earth won't be able to push me
over, without money down and a room of my own. But how I
would give up all sensual pleasures, if I could be free of them and
not need them, if I could throw all physical desires in the sewer or
the sea, how peaceful and calm and beautiful life would be — I
could then give myself up wholly to the serene and contemplative
study of Man's evolution thru eternity, inquire and gain power
over the most secret and occult laws of Nature, Yea verily seated
on some glacial peak of the Himalayas, having become incapable
of tears, and killed out all desire, having triumphed over the
painful wheel of re-birth — being and becoming — I could gaze
unmoved as the aeons rolled out Man's destiny before my eyes —
great civilizations, races, cultures would rise and fall, immense
continents would sink beneath the sea — shall I go on — or wait
till I see you — alas you are not ready — you refuse to see the
light — I weep — having not yet become incapable of tears. But
when the pupil is ready the Master appears —

I would love to see the mood this letter has put you in do you
want to wring my neck, baby? Do you love me?

How is John, the sweet thing? I bet he's taking good care of you
but I hope you're well enough to take care of yourself. I enjoyed
your letter of Wednesday night, I'd like to have more — No — I
don't tear up your letters, funny —

God when I'm well every time I might feel like weakening I'm
going to get hard — females, women have to be *hard* in this world,
I'm going to think of pain and get hard — write me soon — Adios,
Chicita Mia — Your Crocodile —

Well, how was John, the sweet thing? It was a reasonable question.
After Marion's visit he was right in there with them, doing just what they
wanted, concerned less that the two women might possibly love one another than that either of them, but especially Josie, should stop loving
him. This is not to say that he was happy about it. It is obvious in retrospect that he was not. To sleep with other women himself was one thing,
but his own philandering was so traditional it was practically respectable, and despite his own participation there was an atmosphere of per-
version to the affairs of the threesome he did not fundamentally accept.
Nevertheless he went along with it, even to the extent of trading his own
political activities for Josie's vision of a winter in the sun, not only because he was weak, although that was certainly a factor, but because he
loved Josie, and just as she was unable to imagine her affair with Marion
without including him, he was unable to imagine abandoning her to her

unexpected passion, no matter how unnatural he found it. By accepting Marion into the household, he even helped it along. What with Josie and Marion so involved with one another, Josie and John, John, Josie and Marion, and Marion and John, and with it all being given a parental cast by Josie and John playing Mother and Father to their Baby Girl, Josie and Marion playing Mother to their Baby Boy, and Marion playing Baby to them each alone, all in all it was quite a little family that they created.

The story they gave out about their departure from America during the critical winter before the inauguration of Roosevelt had primarily to do with work. It was too distracting in this country: there were too many demands on their time: they were writers, first and foremost, whatever the political season: there was nothing that they could be true to if they could not be true to that. Josie would be beginning the second volume of her trilogy. John would be working on stories. Marion would be developing her art. While banks were closing, bread lines were lengthening, and talk of revolution was reaching wider and wider circles than it ever had reached before, John and Josie closed up the house in Erwinna, stopped off for Marion in New York, and headed south to a new location where they expected to be able to live out their private adventures undisturbed. On Christmas Eve, 1932, after a rough ride over a new and not yet officially opened highway spanning the two countries, they crossed the border from Laredo, Texas, into Mexico.

Nowhere in Josie's life is the record of what actually happened thinner or more elliptical than for the months she spent in Mexico. "You say, tell me ALL. Would that I could," she wrote to Katherine Anne in February, 1933, but even for herself she seemed unable to write things down. Two decades later she would be able to keep a journal savoring her emotions concerning another woman, but the journal she kept in Mexico is scarcely more than a collection of Mexican impressions full of fires flaring, priests mumbling, Indians with long faces, and the smell of tequila always in the air. It was for the living and not for the writing about it that the winter in Mexico was all about — and live they did: in a charming villa in the village of Taxco, complete with a cook and a houseboy; in a comfortable and careless way with no household chores, no political responsibilities, and almost no work to distract them; in an atmosphere of indulgence, in a mood of abandon, in a state of so much relaxation, however fleeting, that at least for Josie it illuminates more than anything else could the deprivations hidden in the years on either side. "Give me your hand, dove, and let me climb into your nest/ If last night you slept alone, tonight you will sleep with me," is an approximate translation of the Spanish verse they found carved into the hand-painted, dove-decorated red and blue bed that was waiting for them in Mexico. It is not very surprising that she found it "wonderful."

Photographs, more than the usual sources, tell the story. First the villa itself, a simple and graceful abode belonging to a friend of Katherine Anne's, with a courtyard and patios and balconies rising up above a twisted cobbled street. Here is Josie lying in a hammock in the living room, a whitewalled, stonearched, plainly furnished room, with the sun streaming in the windows over flourishing tropical greenery in handsome ceramic pots, and here is Marion, on the floor or a cushion beside her, her legs in wide flowing pants draped up over Josie's in the hammock, a tangle of gently rocking limbs. Here are the two women outdoors in the sun, Josie in a long loosely hanging white dress with colorful embroidery on it, a robe different from the matronly styles she usually wears and very becoming — she looks graceful and pretty, her face soft and smiling, not stiff the way she often does when she poses. Now they are clowning, going up some stairs, Marion entering a doorway with her rump deliberately sticking out, Josie smiling and playful, bending over behind her holding something up to it, a framed picture or perhaps a book — it could be a genial spanking. Again they are sitting in the sun, outside the villa, on either side of a stone statue, perhaps of a maternal god, Marion with an arm slung about the creature's head, Josie, still in her pretty clothes, looking amusedly on. Here are John and Marion beside the same statue, John standing, Marion sitting, only now she is not only caressing the head of the statue, she has reached over and with her other hand is seductively squeezing its breast. Here is Marion posed theatrically against a mountain cavern — the Merlin photo — and here she is in the same dark dress leaning against a tree, a picture hand-framed by Josie in the way only one other photograph in her possession — of John sailing — was ever framed. Finally here are John and Josie alone together, more formally got up for conventional exploring, staring out across a valley with the mountains behind them, and here is another, also outdoors, against a pile of rocks, John sitting, Josie standing, with her arm around him in a decidedly maternal fashion, pulling him toward her so that his head is against her cheek. But there are two flaws in Josie's tropical idyll and the flaws are Marion and John. In most of the photographs John looks not only not-happy but actively miserable, as if while she is flowering he is fading, and Marion looks not only indifferent, at times she looks positively glum.

How precisely things were among them, what were their specific tensions, there is little evidence, but the atmosphere emanating from the general tone of their notes and letters is one of constant suspicion. Although much was open between them, much was secret. Josie and Marion betrayed John by referring to Marion by a private nickname known only to them. Marion and John betrayed Josie by wanting to go off alone. Josie and John betrayed Marion by using her as a foil for themselves. By typing out for Marion unbeknown to John some of the very poems he had typed for her in the earliest days of their romance, Josie betrayed even her past. Another difficulty was the problem of appearances. The Taxco house was owned by Moisés Sáenz, an official of the Mexican government whose involvement in a conspicuous circle of Mexican and American homosexual intellectuals, artists, and politicians was well known. When tirades arrived from Katherine Anne denouncing the whole "slimy tangle" and praising Josie's safe alliance to John for the protection it offered from the little world of "pederasts" and "fairies," it can hardly have been cause for joy. At last, after about four months, there came a moment when nothing worked. Reversing the logic that had brought them to Mexico in the first place, they concluded it was too lush and lazy there while all of them were together and that for anything to be accomplished they would have to part. John would go to Texas and begin his stories. Josie would stay long enough to make some progress on her novel and then rejoin him. Marion, who had been offered a mural commission in Taxco, would stay on indefinitely alone. In April, 1933, John left. They treated it as a practical matter.

Almost as soon as there was physical distance between them, however, there was emotional distance as well. Alone in a Galveston boardinghouse, John was trying to work, but though he wrote often, and his letters were ostensibly friendly — to "Dearest Josy" or "Dearest Josy and Baby" — he became terser, more mechanical, and steadily more short-tempered in his communication, as if, without actually confronting it, he was undergoing some revulsion of the soul. Soon he was drinking heavily, and before long he became both too sick and too wretched to do almost anything at all. Left alone with Josie for the first time without the semblance of normality automatically conferred by the presence of a man, Marion too, evidently, began to balk. "We cannot talk to each other today," began a note that Josie left for her, perhaps under her door, on a short trip they had taken together to Mexico City.

> Perhaps if we remembered that the time we shall have together
> will be very short, when you think of a lifetime, it will be short as
> all the other passing things that have happened and that you re-
> gret, it would be easier to be happy. If you could be happy with
> me as you were with [a former lover] but sometimes I feel that it
> all flows over you like water. I love you so much, too much, and
> too much love is never lucky. I wish you felt as I did about love,
> that it happened like a crater or a rock and was a phenomenon no
> matter where it came from. But unless it comes from a man it
> means so little to you that it means now, just only beginning, to
> mean almost nothing to me but pain. When I think how all the
> time we have known each other I have never had you out of my
> mind or body, you are as much a part of me as anyone or thing
> could be, as what I breathe and drink and eat, and it is very hard

to think of life without you, or of being someplace where you will never be. But I can go to such a place, as I shall, and I know that is surely going to happen and I will surely do it because that is the way it has to happen. But while we are together for such a little try to remember how much I love you and that it will be over soon and I have to remember now that so far, at Yaddo, everywhere, I have no power to make you dream and I shall have to go away from you feeling I have not really touched you. If I were a man and had taken a lover to a country where I longed to be happy, it would be easy for you to understand. . . .

Whether it was anxiety for John's health, Marion's withdrawal, internal promptings to resume her ordinary life, or in what proportion it was all of these, it is hard to tell, but faced with the unmistakable evidence that John's inexhaustible agreeableness might finally be giving out, Josie made a rational decision: she would return to him at once. Marion was young. Her natural inclination was toward men. And she was so fundamentally self-absorbed that one of her chief interests in Josie was for discussing her other lovers in any case. Nor was Josie's only a negative decision. Josie had loved John for nearly a decade. He was devoted to her. By the deepest values by which she had ever set out to live it was to John and the life they had painstakingly built for themselves that she really wished to belong. There was a highly emotional parting. From the train Josie wrote to Marion at every stop. In letters which continued for several months Josie spoke of her anguish, of her craving, of a cascade of physical longing such as she had never imagined before. "If I had taken a spoon and scooped you out and crawled into your little hide, I couldn't live more completely in you." "I am as obsessed as if it were only starting between us." "I hunger for that country where your blue veins are." Yet she never felt that her decision had been wrong. She had made her choice and she intended to live it out. What she did not realize then, what she never realized later, what she refused to realize the rest of her life because realizing would have called into question her entire understanding of both her character and her fate, was that it was not only hers to make.

## CHAPTER SIXTEEN

# Feet in the Grass Roots

As Josie was going home she made another decision: she would get back to her book. "The only thing that will save me is my work and I will cling to it like a raft in a flood," she wrote to Marion from a stop in Lansing with John. In a way it was hardly too soon. While they were in Mexico she had done almost nothing on the second volume of the trilogy and her relationship to the volume she had previously finished had become remote. Her negotiations with the publisher, Harcourt, Brace, had been handled by her agent, Maxim Lieber, in the first place; it appears she did not even meet her editor, Charles A. Pearce, in the flesh, until the book was already out; and she was such a stranger to the whole operation that when a photographer sent in a jacket photo from Mexico without her name on it, she was afraid no one in the New York office would know who she was. Josie had always been casual about her publishing arrangements, but this was excessive. When the proofs arrived she was practically indifferent. Coincident with her return to Erwinna *Pity Is Not Enough* was about to appear, and she wanted to negotiate a contract for a book of short stories to be published in conjunction with the second volume, which she hoped would be soon. If ever there were a time for her to consolidate her literary position, it was now.

The publication of *Pity Is Not Enough* in the late spring of 1933 established Josie, in the words of Horace Gregory writing in the *New York Herald Tribune* literary supplement *Books*, as "one of the few American important women novelists" of the day. Magazines and newspapers from the *Saturday Review of Literature* to the *Springfield Republican* all carried reviews of it, and while the discussions were by no means uncritical — the criticism varying with the critic — it is obvious that between the author and her readers there was a considerable rapport. Among her acquaintances who wrote enthusiastic letters to the publisher about it were John Cowper Powys, Newton Arvin, and Granville Hicks, and she also heard directly from friends. "Ever since I can remember, people have been shouting for *the* American novel. I doubt there is any such thing really, but if there is, here it is. . . . Josie, darling, it's just too damned good 'for this world' . . . ," said a long, exuberant letter from Katherine Anne.

> It makes everything written for years just seem a little tripy and futile. You'll have to let me just splutter a little. I'm not up to a calm pointing out of virtues. It's not necessary anyway. Everything about it is right. The way you have got your avalanche of material controlled so it rolls down a great groove to the exact stopping place: and the way you have told the whole story of a historical period, and related it perfectly to the miserable fortunes of one little, confused, struggling family. What can I say about your language, that breathing American talk? And your people, who live so clearly and close by I could hear them moving in the room. The destroying corrosion of simple human pity in them — poor bird, poor Joe! and their real helplessness before the elements — of flood, of change, of political and economic movements . . . You know how much I have loved your work, first to last, short stories, all, with one exception, (and I think you agree with me) but this is finer by a dozen times than anything you have done. It's a wonderful book, you should be easy in your mind about it. It will wear and wear.

Certainly the publishers were pleased. Despite the fact that they expected and got very small sales — about 1,500 copies — because of the book's soberness, they accorded it the advertising budget of a book potentially selling four or five times that number as an investment in Josie's future.

Broadly speaking it was as an historical novel that Josie had written it and it was as an historical novel that it was received. Although the American "success story in reverse," as another of the reviewers, Bruce Catton, described it, had many aspects, perhaps its central achievement was the re-creation of both the atmosphere in the South during the Reconstruction era and the atmosphere of the western mines. Since these are seen largely through the effects on his mother and sisters of the decline of Joseph Trexler as he makes and loses a southern fortune, is partially blinded, and finally loses his mind, the consequences for ordinary families of the great social and economic forces that dominated American life in the nineteenth century are also very humanly explored. Yet *Pity Is Not Enough* is not only an historical novel. With a series of inserts which reveal the later life of Joe's favorite sister, now Anne Wendel, it becomes autobiographical as well. "At least once during the cyclone season, Anne Wendel and her four girls raced through the pouring yellow rain to the cellar," the novel opens. "The littlest held to the bigger girls. . . . In the cool damp cellar they lit the lamp and shut out that dreadful yellow sky and the red barn a monstrous red looking as if it lived and breathed in grass that was too green and living. Down there, they huddled around and Anne brought out to still their terror old Blank and his fits, the dead and gone Trexlers and Joe, the most generous brother, poor Joe." The entire novel takes the form of daughters listening to stories at their mother's feet — and they are all Mary's stories. "Poor Joe": her brother Joe. Poor "Mem": her mother Mem. The fictional "Catherine" who dies of "brain fever" is the story of Mary's sister Priscilla. The frustrated "Hortense" is her sister Alice. Little "Victoria" and her sister "Rosamund" want to hear every word. In addition to carrying the autobiographical core of the novel, the inserts also carry its intellectual meaning. The historical action takes place between the 1860s and the 1890s but the inserts take place between 1905 and 1918. By parallelling the troubles of the past with the troubles of the present, particularly Amos Wendel's failure in business, the novel makes the abstract statement that America is in need of change. *Pity Is Not Enough* is not a political novel in the sense that the characters have any awareness of their situation beyond a kind of puzzled acceptance of their fates, but it is political in the sense of the trilogy's overall design. At the very end of the novel, just before he lapses into madness, Joe reads in a newspaper the final words of one of the Haymarket anarchists executed in Chicago — "I believe that the state of caste and classes, the state where one class dominates over and lives upon the labor of another, and calls this order, yes, I believe this barbaric form of social organization with its legalized plunder and murder, is doomed to die and make room for a freer society" — and is moved to thought for the first time. Receiving Joe's old clippings from their mother during the general strike in Seattle in 1918, Anne's adventurous daughters Victoria and Rosamund are also stirred.

The lives of the two young women throughout the 1920s are the principal subject of the second volume, *The Executioner Waits*, which Josie began now. Since in the second volume, Victoria meets and marries Jonathan Chance, a young man from a conventional middle-class family whose biography very closely resembles John's, and since Rosamund dies while pregnant, the autobiographical character of the novel is even more striking than in the earlier volume, but it is given a political and economic cast by the use of the inserts which here consist of forecasts of the collective protests throughout the country in the 1930s intended to suggest that the tentative dissatisfactions felt by Victoria and Rosamund individually would eventually crystallize as a political force. The book also carries forward the histories of Anne Wendel's brothers and sisters begun in the first volume, most notably the story of the self-righteous businessman David Trexler — as close a portrayal of Josie's uncle Daniel Frey as Joseph Trexler is of Joseph Frey and in a sense "Poor Joe" Frey-Trexler's opposite number — and the story of Anne herself. It is in the counterpoint between the rising radicalism around the country, which draws in Victoria and Jonathan, and the conservatism embodied in characters such as David Trexler, that the political excitement of the novel lies. At the dramatic climax — a funeral of a fallen striker that is observed accidentally by the successful capitalist — they are neck and neck. Like many of the writers of the period Josie was combining direct reportage with a conception of fiction greatly expanded from her earliest novels — no doubt under the influence of the times. What is most intriguing from a biographical viewpoint, however, is her abandon. Not only in her use of political developments, but also in her use of her life, she was tossing things into her book almost as soon as they happened, and she did not know how it might end.

John too wanted something to cling to, and he turned not to his writing but to political work. All during the time they had been away the nationwide farm crisis that was one of the key features of the Depression had been deepening, and the crisis of the farmers around Erwinna was no exception. There are as many ways of describing what was happening as there are statistics — wheat, which had been $1.03 a bushel in 1929, was $.38 a bushel in 1932; hogs, $11.36 a head in 1931, $4.31 a head in 1933; per capita income of farmers $162 in 1929, $48 in 1932; purchasing power, in 1932, only 60 percent of what it had been in 1929 — but the gist of it stated in nonstatistical fashion is that the prices of everything emanating from the countryside sank: sank absolutely, sank relative to the prices emanating from everyplace else, and sank farther and faster than at any other period of American history. What was sinking around Erwinna where the majority of farmers were dairymen was the price of milk which was at an all-time low of a few pennies a quart by the summer of 1933. As purchasing power fell in the cities because of unemployment at the same time that the farmers were attempting to maintain their slender foothold in the economy by producing more, there was literally a glut on the market. Unable to make their payments on the various debts contracted at better periods the farmers were in danger of losing their houses, barns, acreage and animals to assorted creditors. At one point in Bucks County there were 5,000 houses on the auction block for back taxes alone. The Bucks County farmers were by no means radicals, but they were increasingly militant. Like farmers in the West they responded to the threat of foreclosure with a spontaneous array of collective devices only barely this side of the law. When they learned of a foreclosure or repossession about to take place because of missing mortgage or insurance payments they would appear en masse at the scene of an auction, systematically control the bidding, and return the property to its owner for as little as a few dollars or cents. There was often a threat of force. About the overall situation and what might be done about it there were as many shades of opinion as there were individuals. What should be the role of government in regulating supply and demand? What about relief? Should there be a moratorium on debts — an idea popularized in the West by Milo Reno's Farm Holiday Association — or should the debts be wiped out? Among the farmers who traded theories as the disaster intensified, a few were Communists.

To understand what follows it is necessary to accept the premise that, as far as any central organization is concerned, in the context of the agricultural upheaval of the first stages of the Depression the word "Communist" or the phrase "the Communists" refers to a handful of members of the Communist Party who had maintained an interest in agriculture throughout the previous decade despite the indifference of almost all of their fellow members, and, more specifically than that, primarily to three people whose interest extended beyond the office and into the fields: Ella Reeve Bloor — "Mother Bloor" — throughout the '30s the reigning matriarchal figurehead of the Communist Party but a figurehead who often sprang to life on her own; her son, Harold Ware, a farmer and expert agricultural economist and engineer; and Lement Harris, a well-to-do graduate of Harvard who had cut himself off from his family, worked on a Quaker farm in Pennsylvania, eventually met Ware, visited the Soviet Union, and turned from an espousal of a kind of Tolstoyan idealism to an espousal of Communism. Of the three the most famous was Bloor, who led the rallies and made the speeches; the most efficient was Harris, who followed up with organization; but the most important was Ware, who was literally the only American Communist who understood both what the problems facing American farmers actually were and how the crisis related to the other interests of the Communist Party both abroad and at home.

Harold Ware — "Hal"— is one of the most interesting figures in the history of the American Communist Party and that until recently he has been either absent from discussions of it or only fragmentarily presented tells more than the missing volumes about the effect on American scholarship of the anti-Communism of the Cold War. Personally "shy and retiring," "muted" — photos show a straitlaced, conservative-looking

fellow with a scholarly aura — perhaps overshadowed by his indefatiga-
ble mother, he appears to have preferred to remain in the background
and leave the shouting to others but he was not that elusive: he coauthored a lead article in *Harper's* — a critique of the New Deal's farm policies — and it appeared with accurate biographical data only shortly
before he died in 1935. Not a bureaucrat, not an ideologue, he was essentially an intellectual farmer with an interest in scientific methods who
had been the first in his area to use a gasoline-driven tractor, apparently
as early as 1913. As much as any American alive in the 1930s — certainly
as much as anyone John and Josie personally knew — he was involved on
a practical level in the effort to revolutionize farming in Russia, for, frustrated by the lack of interest of the American party in agricultural matters he had spent most of the 1920s in the Soviet Union participating in a
number of projects involving the collectivization and mechanization of
farming there. At one point he organized a delegation of American
farmer–tractor drivers, together with twenty tractors and the equipment
required for their upkeep, to join him. In 1922 he received a commenda-
tion from Lenin. Several times during the '20s he had returned to the
United States to try to persuade the American party of the importance of
agriculture, even documenting, in exhaustive surveys, the rural distress
which would later be so clearly highlighted by the collapse, but the
American Communist leadership, its eye on the urban masses, declined
to find itself moved.

By 1931, with farm agitation in the United States clearly mounting,
the need for his knowledge was obvious, and Ware — together with
Harris — was summoned home. During the next year they completed a
survey of farm conditions, appeared at the scene of the 1932 farm strike
in Iowa and Nebraska — which had also drawn Josie and John — and attempted to develop a specifically Communist following, particularly
among the farmers of the West. At a moment when the farmers were so
far ahead of the radicals that it was practically an embarrassment, how
"the Communists" could have possibly assumed the leadership of the
farm movement is a good question. In fact, their purpose was more to
keep up with the situation than it was to influence it. They coordinated a
national demonstration of farmers, the Farmers' National Relief Conference, which met in Washington, D.C., in December, 1932, and in turn
led to a permanent organization, the Farmers' National Committee for
Action; they started a newspaper, the *Farmers' National Weekly;* and as
a kind of intellectual headquarters to follow what was happening both on
the farms and in Washington, and communicate with the farmers by
bulletin about it, they established a research and information bureau, in
Washington, called Farm Research.

To the extent that the Communist activity was anything more than a
simple presence scarcely distinguishable from the Farm Holiday move-

ment or others at any of the countless acts of militant resistance to the Depression that continued to take place, it consisted mainly of an attempt to persuade the farmers to understand their problems from a Marxist viewpoint. Extremely modest on the central level, it was a working-on-your-feet, seat-of-the-pants kind of movement in the field where people who were inclined to take a radical view of the crisis, finding themselves side by side with, enmeshed in action with, people who didn't, would seize the moment for one of the most truly vital actions of the Depression: Talk. Talk about the relationship of capitalism to the present crisis. Talk about the inevitable recurrence of the crisis despite all temporary remedies if the basic structure of the system did not give way. Talk about the way to change the system, by the unification of the protests of the workers in the country with the protests of the workers in the cities. Talk talk talk with the endless conviction and enthusiasm endemic among converts was what Communists did, their talk ranging from the most detailed dissection of the relationship between the "Milk Trust" and the class struggle to the most general representation of a rosy Utopia where swords would be turned into ploughshares and nations no longer make war — the one gripping in its precision, the other breathtaking in its hopefulness. What John was was one of the talkers and he did it very well. When the little group of farmers known as the United Farmers' Protective Association joined with others in a march on the county seat at Doylestown, their radical slogan "Revolution, Not Relief" was one of many placards in part thanks to his talking, and once Josie wrote him that long after he had left Bucks County "the people at Appelbachsville still talk about you — they don't know your name, just wish the man — the tall man with the smile — had not gone away." No doubt John would have met Hal Ware anyway because Hal was married to one of Josie's friends from the Village, Jessica Smith, and they had once or twice visited Erwinna, but when they began to meet more often, after Hal and Jessica had settled in Washington, they had their mutual interest in the farm situation in common.

Josie also was becoming involved in the farm movement, not on an organizational but on a personal and intellectual level. The trip to Iowa during the farm strike had given her for the first time in her life an appreciation not only of Iowa but of farmers, and she was looking at her neighbors with different eyes. When Lew Bentzley, a militant farmer, who had no money and five children became ill with ulcers she took the lead in collecting money from the "summer people" to help him out and she helped out personally — with meals or clothes or blankets — in other emergencies when she could. She found these connections refreshing. "The trouble with us and our kind is that under this system we are such isolated bastards. . . . Once we are grown we have too little contact with real struggling people," she wrote to Katherine Anne who was in

Europe and eager to hear what was going on. "My head gets foggy if I hang around the intellectuals but if I go out where the farmers are talking turkey it all gets fairly simple," she commented another time. The connections were also useful. Material from the Iowa trip not used in her *Scribner's* article was going right into the inserts of *The Executioner Waits* and scenes from around Bucks County were going to follow. Bentzley became a model for a farmer in the final volume of the trilogy, *Timothy Robb*. The whole trilogy, in fact, with its strong rural flavor, represents a recovery of her Iowa past that is very much a product of this period. Between a snobbish, more-sophisticated-than-thou discussion of Iowa culture that Josie wrote for Mencken in 1926 and the respectful compassionate accounts she wrote of the farm situation in the 1930s there is a definite difference of spirit and between her early novels and the trilogy the same distinction applies. Crisis had revealed resistance and — of all things — imagination. Now she could be an Iowan. There was another factor in Josie's growing involvement with the farm movement: of course, John. It gave them something to fall back on. When the United Farmers' Protective Association, which was affiliated with the Farmers' National Committee for Action, decided to send a delegation, including John, to the second national farmers' protest meeting in Chicago, she made an arrangement with *The New Republic* to write about it and went along.

The Farmers' Second National Conference, which met in Chicago from November 15 to 18, 1933, was the peak of rural protest during the Depression. It was also the peak of Communist influence. Over seven hundred farmers — white, black, rich, poor — representing thirty-six states and fifty-eight farm organizations ranging from the conservative Grange to the militant United Farmers' League — debated and ultimately endorsed an extremely radical program including cancellation of debts, cash relief without collateral, an end to evictions, reduction or elimination of rents and taxes and — the distinctive contribution of the Communist Party to the politics of the Depression — an end to Negro oppression. A woman's auxiliary demanded birth control. What role John may have played either in articulating the issues or in shaping resolutions there is no direct evidence but according to the most recent historian, Harris and Ware were preoccupied by a factional challenge, and with Ware so ill-suited to conventioneering, and John so good at it, it is probable John did some of both. For Josie it was not only her moment of greatest identification with the farmers but of consonance with the Communist Party "line." Her article "The Farmers Form a United Front" emphasized what different elements of the farm population had in common, and had in common with workers — which was very much the position of Ware and Harris — and she stressed the farmers' opposition to the New Deal's proposed destruction of crops. When *The New*

*Republic* rejected the article chiefly on the grounds that she was falsely generalizing from the radicalism of the poorer farmers to the position of the middle farmers who in fact supported Roosevelt, she not only submitted it to the *New Masses* instead, but gave them as well her entire correspondence with *New Republic* managing editor Bruce Bliven in which among other things she denounced him as a "liberal" — a word that had never been an epithet in Josie's vocabulary nor would be later. The whole tenor of the controversy between *New Masses* and *The New Republic* on this point reflected the aggressiveness of the Communist so-called "Third Period," which was about to go out of style. There is no doubt how much John and Josie believed in what they were doing. On a visit to Lansing after the conference they risked alienating John's father forever by reading out the demands. At the very moment of the conference the current farm strike "was failing miserably; government checks were about to fall on the farm belt like a gently nourishing rain; and the vast majority of farmers were sincerely ready to allow the Roosevelt administration to have a fair try," but no one quite realized it at the time. "The Communists" were just gearing up. Whether it was respect for John's performance, appreciation of his charm and sincerity, envy of his other personal qualities or something else altogether it is impossible to say, but, not long after the November meeting, probably early in 1934, Hal Ware invited John Herrmann to come and work with him in Washington.

## CHAPTER SEVENTEEN

# "The Most Unhappy Woman Alive"

HAL'S INVITATION to Washington precipitated the crisis between John and Josie that both of them had been trying to forestall. Entangled as they were with one another, loving one another despite all the complications they had shared, neither one of them had yet seriously considered the possibility of giving the other up, yet the fact is that since Mexico the tenderness between them had been more habitual than real, and their bond was becoming more and more their mutual misery instead of, as it had sometimes been in the past, their mutual joy. Outside of the house, in their separate spheres, they both continued to function, John in his political world, Josie with her work, but in it they were rapidly reaching that stage in the degeneration of love where the mere sight of the other party changes compassion into self-pity, self-sufficiency into helplessness, acceptance into rage. John was finding it impossible to live with the recognition of Josie's love for Marion and the recollection of what he himself had done. Josie was finding Marion impossible to forget. At the heart of John's suffering was the feeling that Josie had revealed a sickening abnormality in which he had taken part. At the heart of hers was a sorrow for her loss. There was no way in this circle for them to help each other out. Of the two sufferings Josie's was perhaps the worse because while John felt pain and rejection Josie felt pain and guilt. Caught between his anguish and her own mourning she found herself stranded on a disappearing island until finally her passion itself was extinguished and she began to discover an absence of desire that would remain with her for years. She continued to write Marion letters, but by the time Marion returned to New York, nearly a year after their parting in Mexico, their relationship was very largely over.

Unable to talk to each other about what was really happening to their marriage, Josie and John focused their tensions on a series of nagging trivial recriminations that left them both depressed because they both knew the hopelessness of substituting these quarrels for the one quarrel that was real between them but that they did not dare begin. When Hal urged John to come to Washington it was not only the opportunity John was interested in: it was the relief. But far from lessening their problems by suggesting the possibility of escape, the Washington offer only made things worse because it opened up for the first time a political difference between them: their relationships to the Communist Party. While John had by now become wholeheartedly involved, Josie had kept her distance in part because of a long-standing suspicion that what the Party wanted from its members, at least from writers, was not necessarily what they wanted for themselves. She interpreted the Washington business as a case in point. Here was John, with a life of his own, doing excellent work, which he loved, with the farmers of their own region, and now he was expected simply to drop it and follow Hal. In terms of its relation to their ongoing domestic power struggles, the weakness of Josie's position was — sour grapes. John was a member of the Communist Party: Josie was not a member: she had never been invited to be a member: and leaving aside for the moment the question of the exact status in Communist politics of fellow-travelers in general and Josephine Herbst in particular, the fact of the matter is she felt excluded. Hal's activities in Washington had a peculiar aura — there was something beyond the obvious about them, something mysterious, unexplained — and apart from being party to the secret of a secret, Josie was kept largely in the dark. She did not want John to become a part of it. Her insinuations that he was weak, incapable of sticking to what he started, a tool of others, added to the tensions in the air. Yet it was not perhaps so much the substance of their arguments as it was their range that was responsible for dragging them down. With so many sources of estrangement, little remained. They were relentlessly depressed, the despair of one immediately equaled by the despair of the other: they lurked sullenly about the house, each waiting for the other to do something wrong so as to provoke an attack: they could not meet each other's eyes anymore: after so many years of living together as both comrades and lovers suddenly they were scarcely even friends: they were enemies.

All during the early months of 1934, the crisis intensified. In May Josie fell sick with the old reliable kidney ailment that could usually be counted on to contribute its share to her agony in times of trouble, and argument abated while John acted as he often had in the old days, a tender nurse. In June she smashed up the car. Understanding as they both did the connection between their desperation and her near destruction it was easier to make an agreement: it was time to stop. Josie would go to Provincetown to stay with Mary Vorse and try, in the relative peace there, to finish *The Executioner Waits*. John would take an apartment in Washington. The house, the symbol of their relationship, would temporarily be closed.

In August, 1934, her book still not finished, Josie went to stay with John in Washington, with predictable results. It was a small, stuffy, one-room apartment, with no place in it for her to work, and her characteristic last-minute tenseness, combined with his busy schedule, meant that they rarely saw each other in any peacefulness, only in a rush. The degeneration in their relationship to one another continued. As unable to talk as they had been before, yet constantly rubbing up against each other in the most unsatisfactory ways, they took to communicating by a series of accusatory notes, as if they were still apart even though they were actually in the same place, of which the following — Josie's — is a fair enough sample of what was going on.

*3:30 AM John*
I've just called up to find out the time after sitting & walking here & crying. I can't stand it and am going out to walk around the streets. You shouldn't have let me come back here to stay here all alone. I *wanted* to go to the meeting & hear you speak & if I'd had a ticket I would have followed anyhow. But you seemed so glad to leave me & perhaps you were. If I hadn't been let alone so many times like this, or seen you when we are with people put me to one side, I would never have got into the state I've been in the last few months, the most unhappy woman alive. I've struggled hard to make a good life but I feel as if everything were against me & tonight as if you were pushing me into insanity. You've been good to me these last weeks and I love you more than anything else in the world. If I hadn't, I wouldn't suffer all the time. But you've never . . . bothered much for a long time to take pains making love to me or to call any part of me beautiful. You never really did that, until *she* did & that's what's so painful, that I never would have gone to a woman for caressing love if I had got it much from you.
  I don't know where I'm going but I can't stay here. Leave the key in the lock. You might have called me on the phone if there was a good time somewhere, or thought of me at least, here all alone.

Nor was it only their intimate relation that remained a problem between them. Their political differences, presaged in the debate about John's coming to Washington in the first place, once they were in Washington took an increasingly concrete form, adding their own share of difficulties to the ones they already had.

One of the purposes of Hal Ware's being in Washington, in addition to the political and economic activities that were specifically connected with Farm Research, was to help make friends and contacts for the Communist movement in important places: not a very difficult process in the early days of the New Deal but neither, as far as Hal was concerned, a very congenial one, because far from being involved with either numbers or farmers, what he liked best, it consisted for the most part of a kind of intensive socializing, which he did not like at all. Congressional smokers, fund raisers, cocktail parties, private meetings — nothing out of the ordinary, just the usual routines of the American capital before and since the Depression —: these were the centers of action. "Neither an orator nor a glad-hander" is the way one farm historian describes Hal. John was both. A good part of his labors consisted of using exactly those characteristics of oratory and glad-handedness in exactly the same sort of hail-fellow and alcoholic social settings to which he naturally gravitated in any case and which Hal just as naturally tended to eschew. It is not the case that the farm work was a front for another activity. There was more than one activity. As a writer whose literary and political credentials, as well as personality, could make him welcome almost anywhere, John was the perfect assistant.

The Communist work in Washington in the 1930s has never been adequately characterized. It took place in a curious zone between openness and circumspection difficult to define precisely because it was never precise in the first place and most later accounts of it, whatever they claim, are based more on the imaginations of the narrators than they are on facts. My own formulation, based on the primary sources constituted by the correspondence between Josie and John, and related materials, is approximately this: while neither the political activities nor their radical orientation were concealed — indeed, that would have been contrary to their overtly political purpose — at times, though by no means always, the specific connections between particular activities and the Communist Party were both privately guarded and publicly played down. It was a clumsy and inconsistent policy which had as much the effect of inhibiting personal communication even between intimates such as Josie and John as it did of promoting security with respect to outsiders. Indeed, security was scarcely an issue at this moment because not only was the Communist Party legal, Communism was fashionable, and it was more anomalous in Washington if government officials did not express an interest in Communism than if they did. "Was invited to the Sov. Embassy last night for buffet supper and to meet Ossinsky head of state planning board there in Russia . . . the entire new deal was there with the exception of the president. Tugwell, Frank, Howe and etc etc": a typical comment to Josie from John, this one late in 1934.

There was, however, still another aspect to the Communist effort in Washington in which John was also involved, about whose secrecy there was never the slightest ambiguity or doubt: it simply was secret. This consisted of the transmission of materials between Party officials in Washington and Party officials in New York — a courier operation — for which John, along with Hal himself, was one of the drivers. In the summer of 1934 both John and Hal went back and forth between Washington and New York very often. What was the material being conveyed on these missions it is not clear whether John ever actually knew, or Josie either, but Josie at least took it for granted that like nearly everything else either one of them came in contact with during this period it had to do with agriculture — the area central to them personally, to those parts of the Communist Party they had the most to do with, and to the New Deal. It was information about the administration's agricultural program that could be used politically by the Communist Party: that was her understanding. What she did know about the operation, however, even if she did not know its exact content, was its form, and its form struck her as ridiculous. Sometimes while she was in the apartment the telephone would ring or a visitor would come and John would ask her, in a voice thick with innuendo, to leave: other times she was permitted to remain: but either way: staying or leaving: she was close enough to whatever transactions were taking place to witness what she regarded as a lot of self-important revolutionary hocus-pocus and she was irritated by it in the extreme.

Of all the people that Josie met in Washington that summer the most conspiratorial in style, the most melodramatic, the most "vainglorious," as she would later put it, was a slovenly, rotund, and yet oddly cherubic emanation from this underworld whom she knew only as "Karl." "Karl" came to the apartment both when John was present and sometimes even when he was not — the latter, as far as she could see, simply to chat with her awhile to no apparent particular purpose — a boastful and paranoid character who always made enough allusions to his *Friends* and *Relatives* struggling for justice abroad so that Josie might have known even had she been much less sophisticated than she was that he was doing something subterranean, something dangerous, to which he immensely enjoyed making reference. Apart from this affectation she found him pleasant enough — literarily inclined, articulate — and on the two or three occasions when they were alone they gossiped companionably about this and that, Josie even sharing with "Karl" some of the aspects of her problems with John, problems to which she found him surprisingly sympathetic.

The surreptitiousness of the original meetings, the circumspectness of any references to them at the time, and the political circumstances affecting all subsequent recollections, make it foolish to attempt to pin down in a legalistic spirit what Josie's impressions of either the structure or the function of the underground operation were — let alone what they may have been — but at least as far as organization is concerned it appears from the correspondence that while most of their routine, daily contact on agricultural matters was with Hal Ware, the voice of authority on such practical details as assignments, the timing of vacations, and leaves, was "Karl's," so she would have had to infer that "Karl," rather than Hal, was the ultimate boss. As to the function, the gist of her understanding seems to have been that while Hal's activities included the recruitment of a group of lesser New Deal officials who would provide the agricultural information being transmitted to New York, "Karl" was aiming at a higher governmental level. But whatever its structure, whatever its function — other than that it was intended generally to promote the interests of Communism in the United States — Josie could not bring herself to take the Washington underground seriously. It appeared to her to be a case of people playing at revolution when they could be accomplishing the same things better working openly. Because of a pamphlet she had written for a refugee organization attempting to bring German Jewish children to the United States, because of her correspondence with Katherine Anne, who was still abroad, and simply because of her general continued interest in Germany and things German, she was well aware of the difference between a country where political opposition was permitted and a country where it was not and for the Communists to function underground when they could function perfectly well above ground she believed was a mistake. Yet many people Josie knew seem to have been involved with it. In Washington there were not only Hal and John but the new acquaintances who appeared to be part of the network. In New York, there was Joe North, an editor of the *New Masses*, sometime Pennsylvania neighbor, and friend, at whose apartment John often stayed on his trips, as well as their literary agent, Maxim Lieber, whom both Josie and John had come to regard with affection in the years since the early '30s when he had begun handling their stories. At least by implication, there were also the wives and families.

While knowing about the underground activity without being part of it was a measure of the confidence in which Josie was held by leading Communists, from her own point of view the situation was more of an inconvenience than a compliment, because the overlap of the secret with the open activity made space for evasions between herself and John at a time when evasion was the last thing they needed, and it complicated her position as a journalist by making her privy to information she had no reason to know about, and could not use. She responded to this dilemma by finding out as little about the operation as possible. When such an item crossed her earshot as that "Karl" was interested in meeting Alger Hiss, a young lawyer with the Agricultural Adjustment Administration who he hoped would likewise be interested in meeting him, her brain recorded its passage as her notebooks more circumspectly did not, but she deliberately did not pursue it for fear it would tie her thoughts. Nor did it seem very interesting. It hardly seemed worth the mystery with which "Karl," Hal, and John all seemed to invest it, and if it was worth the mystery of their theatrical performances, she would just as soon not know why. When Josie separated from John after Washington in the fall of 1934 she separated as well from her connection with the American Communist underground, and she was never close to it again. Hal Ware died in the summer of 1935, not long after Josie's return from Cuba, in a car accident, driving, as he often did, the route from Washington to New York. As for "Karl," except for a party at Joe North's, also in 1935, where he consoled her with real affection for the loss of her mate, until she saw a photo of Whittaker Chambers in a news magazine many years later, she scarcely thought of him again.

Important as these political disagreements were in contributing to the coldness between Josie and John, there were still other sources. Their day-to-day living complaints returned with a vengeance and during the last weeks of Josie's working on *The Executioner Waits*, things were as hostile between them as they had ever been. In September, 1934, when the manuscript was finally finished, Josie was invited by Farm Research and the *New Masses* to make a trip west to look at the results of Roosevelt's farm policies and get some feeling for the present status of rural protest — an opportunity that, since the state of their marriage was well known to their immediate circle and their immediate circle included all the parties relevant to the invitation, was probably not a coincidence. The trip was to be in the company of another Farm Research employee, an economist and journalist named Webster Powell; it was to take them through Iowa, Nebraska, North Dakota and South Dakota; and it was to result both in articles for the *New Masses* and a pamphlet for Farm Research. Even more unhappy in Washington now that she had nothing to do, Josie accepted, despite the fact that traveling would complicate her relationship to the production of *The Executioner Waits*. She deputized John to manage the details, which he faithfully did: supervising the correction of proofs; rushing to New York at various times to help maintain an atmosphere favorable to the book at Harcourt, Brace; even using his best salesman's skills to preserve the Victoria Wendel–Jonathan Chance story, from the editor's inclination to cut. "I told him . . . that it is the only case where the so-called lost or present generation is shown in relation to its background and is shown as moving in a certain direction . . .

[and the] Vicky Jonathan stuff . . . not only completes the lost gen. but will also end for all time any writing about either of us as nobody could go beyond what you have done," he assured her loyally. The author herself spent most of the fall of 1934 on the road.

Apart from the satisfaction of simply being on the move again, Josie's trip was not a pleasant one. For one thing, what she saw was not very encouraging. A superficial optimism largely attributable to government intervention was undercutting rural radicalism, but between the support programs, which tended to strengthen larger farmers at the expense of smaller ones, and the drought, which hit the smallest hardest, the small poor farmers were still suffering badly and in fact were being driven from the land. Fields empty of all but thistles: one-third of the population of South Dakota on relief: cattle killed, hogs killed, even chickens killed for the sake of government relief checks that went straight from the farmers to the banks: these were the sights of the journey. Then too there were personal problems. Josie and Webster Powell, together almost all the time, did not get along very well. He was inclined to look upon her as a secretary, which she resented. He found her temperamental in the extreme. A difference of opinion arose between them over her notes, Josie wanting unequivocal rights to them for stories to appear under her own name in the *New Masses* and elsewhere, Powell feeling that they belonged to Farm Research for the future pamphlet. All these incidents and more she reported to John, ostensibly soliciting his arbitration as a spokesman for "the movement," but they became in effect occasions for her continued criticism of the Communist Party, and his defense of it, and therefore an extension of their domestic quarrels as well: *Josie:* "the movement" is selfish, using people up for its own ends; his activities in Washington and hers, wearied by this terrible mission, are good examples of it: *John:* he is doing what he is doing freely, if he had anything better to do on his own he would be doing it, the "using 'em up" theory of attack on the Communists is evidence of her own bad character, bad temper, bad faith. Through John she was also in contact with Hal but Hal's supervision was confined to the practical level: he sent her factual material, possibly emanating from his groups of government employees, having to do with county-by-county allotments under the corn and feed program and with the slaughter of hogs. Josie attached them to her notes and thought nothing special of them. She felt pressured by the responsibilities of her assignment. Yet the trip had its compensations despite its difficulties because Josie was affected by what she saw. Her notes and her articles are vivid documents in which the voices of the real people she met mingle with objective analyses of the prospects they faced to precisely capture the moment, and it is obvious from their spirit that however constricted she was feeling in the confines of her marriage, apart from it she was very much alive. Others seemed to sense it also. Among the farmers she met in that autumn of backwater travel, was at least one who would write to her for years. Then too her political loyalties were strengthened. Whatever private reservations she might have about the Communist movement, in the field, where the farmers were struggling, it made more sense.

In Nebraska Josie was bickering with Powell: in New York *The Executioner Waits* was being rushed into print: and in Washington where John was still by himself in the stuffy little apartment on New Hampshire Avenue, the inevitable happened —: at one of the myriad parties to which his duties required him to go he met another woman to whom he was suddenly, strikingly, drawn. Her name was Ruth Tate: she was a small soft gentle wide-eyed compliant beautiful blonde woman: everything Josie was not: who even liked drinking and partying as much as John did: which was saying a lot. He told her he was separated from his wife, giving "separated" a more definitive cast than their stumbling comings and goings had actually had, and on Ruth's side she had no reason to disbelieve him — there was no wife in the flesh, that was certain — and she fell "instantly" and "joyously" in love with him with a love she says lasted "forever." John did not tell Josie about it right away. If anything he redoubled his efforts to please her at least in the intellectual department by increasing his solicitude for her book. When Josie returned east she stopped off briefly in Washington en route to Yaddo where she intended to work over her material, but even during their visit while the fact of Ruth emerged, the seriousness of John's interest in her did not — indeed, he seems to have been of two minds about it himself at this point, telling Ruth he and Josie were finished for good, telling Josie Ruth was just a passing attraction, theirs was the love that mattered — as if, though he wanted the freedom to do what he wanted, he was far from reconciled to the idea that his long relationship with Josie might be coming to a close. The news made Josie even more desperate than she had been before: she knew it was serious even though John denied it: and from Yaddo to Washington their struggles continued by mail with a vindictiveness on her part and a defensiveness on his that could not have been better calculated to bring about their parting had it been consciously intended to do so: Josie, far from attempting a real appraisal of the situation, blaming John for everything rather than herself, misrepresenting circumstances, casting about like a wounded animal for a way to pay back the pain she must have felt she received: John trying to stay cheerful, even remaining affectionate, but cringing more and more, and finally pulling himself back altogether out of the range of her attack. Toward the end of November, after receiving a particularly recriminatory letter, John seems to have stiffened himself to fight back, beginning by constructing a "Chart of John Based on letter of Nov. 19" in which he itemized her accusations against him as if he were trying to get them into a court where they could be clearly examined. Under "Negative Aspects" he listed 24 points: "(1) Sole interest not Josy. (2) Constantly accusing. (3) Refuse shelter to J. (4) Desert you when sick. (5) Refuse to give vacations. (6) Self-indulgent spendthrift. (7) Yammer constantly. (8) Sabotage J's work. (9) Imprison her in cage. (10) Destroy her. (11) Never talk to her. (12) Never notice her. (13) Sex & bed only interests. (14) Treat like stone. (15) Indifferent and insulting. (16) Persecution mania. (17) Works for anybody but J. (18) Spends money on self. (19) Getting TOO FAT. (20) Dishonest. (21) Bed only interest. (22) Cruel. (23) Willful, selfish. (24) Not human, just tail." Under "Positive Aspects" there was only one item: "Husband — occasionally sweet and wonderful but only when in bed." "How in hell either of us will ever write spending all the time and energy on letters like these last is more than I can see," his letter concluded. But the bitter exchanges continued. Though they planned to have a real holiday in New York at Christmas in the hope that it would help them get back together, their reunion, at the Hotel Albert, only made things worse. A thousand small pains afflicted them whenever they tried to be together. Ruth was on her toes for ways to make her own claims weigh in to whatever was going to be decided: she left a bracelet under the bed at Erwinna: *under our bed,* Josie thought wildly: which Josie, on a stop to pick up clothes for the winter, of course discovered: Ruth called up, during their very reunion in New York, asking John to come over and help her: she had the flu. Josie, her passion aroused by jealousy, was attracted to John once more but now it was his turn to be unresponsive: it was too late: he could not, with all that was happening, become aroused for her: a shattering moment.

In the midst of this turmoil during the late fall of 1934 came the publication of *The Executioner Waits,* an odd event, though neither of them treated it that way, this public celebration of the early days of their involvement with one another, just as things were falling apart. Again there was rapport between writer and reader for, with its broad exploration of the roots of the present's radicalism, it was a book very much of the moment. Not only were the reviews largely positive — Horace Gregory dropped his qualifying "women" and proclaimed Josie "one of the few major novelists in America today" — there were all the other earmarks of a book that had found its audience: praise from friends — "the best novel I have read in years if not the very best I have ever read," a letter from William Carlos Williams —; waiting lists at libraries; reorders at bookstores; even rumors of a Pulitzer Prize. Josie paid little attention. Except for a reply to a negative review in *The Nation,* which in turn earned the comment of an anonymous newspaper columnist that she was a poor sport, and a little correspondence with her editor, the fanfare more or less passed her by. Still, between her recognition as a novelist and her recognition as a journalist Josie's reputation as a writer was higher than it had ever been and her talents were much in demand. A political situation of particular interest to radicals was developing in Cuba and the *New Masses* asked her to go. Josie and John talked it over and agreed that being apart appeared to be best and although they still did not call it a "separation" in a final sense, the fact that it might be was becoming harder and harder not to see. Beside herself, not really herself at all, still attaching herself more firmly than John did to the possibility that her marriage was not really over, yet knowing, without admitting, that it was lost, crying even while packing —: Josie nonetheless managed to get herself to Miami and thence to Cuba where the new assignment was to begin. She felt that her heart was breaking, but she was moving through the world with ease.

## CHAPTER EIGHTEEN

# Empty Mailbox

*Havana, 1935.* Ruddy-cheeked gentlemen beneath Panama hats. Starched white linens. Drinks over the table and deals underneath. Shops laden as the horn of plenty. Shoestores with shelves full of the latest offerings. But outside the cafés where the deals are being made, beggars, hundreds of them, pleading for pennies. Prostitutes, hundreds of these too, on the lookout for work. Outside the grocers', hungry children hoping for a bite of bread. Outside the shoestores, shoeless peasants with bleeding feet. It is the second year and the third government since the dictator Gerardo Machado was driven from power by a popular uprising that included even his own army, protesting three decades of vassalage to the United States — two years in which American involvement to protect the sugar interests which dominate the island has been continuing at a steady pitch. What in the decline of imperialism will usually be accomplished by clandestine agencies operating in the dark, in Cuba, while colonialism flourishes, operates boldly in light of day. There is scarcely even a pretense of nonintervention. "Diplomacy, as I interpret it, nowadays consists largely in cooperation with American business," remarked Roosevelt's second Ambassador, Jefferson Caffery, successor to Sumner Welles, on his arrival in Havana in 1933. Guided by American interests the conservative countercoup has been practically consolidated. The liberal Ramón Grau San Martín has been toppled after four months and power now rests with an army colonel, Carlos Mendieta, who is in turn dependent on another colonel who has seized military control, a protégé of Welles named Fulgencio Batista, whose career in Cuba will last many years. Meanwhile the economic situation on the island has been growing worse, not for the giant companies who benefit from the guaranteed markets of the newly renegotiated Reciprocity Treaty with the United States, but for almost everyone else, because under the terms of the treaty which rests on a logic similar to the New Deal's domestic program, sugar production is not permitted to return to the levels of its pre-Depression high and for sugar workers the quota means that the short season of ill-paid, back-breaking labor that for years has been their only source of cash income is going to be curtailed. If sugar continues to be King, the army is now the Regent. The reforms of the Grau period have been wiped out. In the countryside the closed sugar mills have been reopened to house government soldiers with orders to prevent a renewal of unrest. In a country with an overall budget of $56 million, the military portion is almost half. The revolutionary opposition, smashed forcefully by Batista in a second general uprising in January, 1934, is not yet dead — it is waiting its chances — but it has been driven, for the moment, underground.

Following arrangements made before she arrived, Josie checks into one of the big tourist hotels in Havana, the Hotel Plaza, as a free-lance journalist, for she is officially representing not the *New Masses*, which could be dangerous, but moderate publications such as *The American Mercury*, from which, among others, she has letters of accreditation. Her job is to go through the motions of preparing a conventional series of articles — interviewing Cuban and American officials, studying the political and economic situation — while at the same time awaiting the appearance of a contact from the opposition who will begin to introduce her to people in the revolutionary underground, which constitutes her real assignment. For reasons of safety she cannot initiate these contacts herself. In some ways it is a situation in which it is useful to be a woman because when her sympathies show, as they are inclined to do, she is apt to be perceived less as a radical than as a bleeding heart, but in other ways it is difficult because there are few women alone in Cuba in 1935 and almost everyone she meets assumes she is vulnerable, as indeed she is. In the pitting of herself against an alien setting, she is doing almost what she had done in Berlin, in the 1920s, only the German men then only looked and leered while the Cuban men now reach out to touch and between the men reaching for sex and the men reaching for money every walk down the street can be filled with uneasiness. Her Mexican Spanish, far more different from Cuban Spanish than she expected, keeps all conversation at a somewhat stilted level. There are no easy confidences of a kind that might happen at home. Contrary to her understanding of the agreement between them when they parted, she hears scarcely anything from John. A couple of cables, an evasive letter, and then no more. Faced with both circumstantial and fundamental isolation at a moment when she is also in a political situation far more complicated than any she has faced before, Josie seems to divide herself in two. On the one hand she plunges down into a sewer of desperation clogged with all the emotional garbage of the years with John and around and around she swims in it like a wretched sewer rat snapping now here, now there, at a familiar blob floating by, sending letter after letter to John, and sometimes to John and Ruth, letters so obsessive, so repetitive, that it is possible simply to lift one paragraph from one and another from the next without losing any of the threads. These hopeless epistles are most often dated "Sunday" or are written in the evening. On the other she is functioning not only with intelligence but with finesse, grasping the facts and figures of the U.S. domination of Cuba, meeting with the Ambassador, with Cuban politicians, with businessmen, playing the role of the softish but knowledgeable lady journalist, eliciting the official positions on various questions and transcribing the conversations afterward with so much thoroughness that in her notebooks not only the policies but also the personalities of the various characters emerge intact. This activity takes up most of the daylight hours, Monday through Friday. To explore the bifurcation of Josie's experience in Cuba is not to say that she was not truly in despair there. She was. A tiny notebook intended only for herself suggests in a scrawl very nearly a poem how much the sheer quantity of writing she did of both kinds is itself the principal clue to her state of being: as if in a situation where there is no chance of companionship she can keep going only by talking to herself.

O god
Write it down.

Write anything. don't cry, Josy, please don't cry, it
will be all right, eat your dinner, dry your eyes, this
is life as Depesey says.

Case of a reliable
comrade gone nutty from
personal worry and despair
unable to do the job right.

[Later, a few pages.]

Everything is very hard
Because no one is ever here
& it is almost impossible to

see anyone. A very difficult
business & my handicap of
language complicates every
thing together with the
burden
I brought with me of personal
troubles very hard to throw
off & very hard to bear
with cheerfulness & pleasure.
I'm tired of Cuban music
that sounds here very raw
& brassy. Tired of people
who want tips. I'm just a
tourist so far — no way to
penetrate this mind. Yet it has to be done.

I wonder when this night-
mare will end. It's always been
like this
except when
I was a child, very
small, & with John. I feel
our life together all over, he in one local
body spot. I think that
is it. It colors everything.
Can I ever see out of this
dark again? It is
impossible at present.

Yet in many ways this production with its dramatic alterations between matinee and evening performances is the quintessential Josephine Herbst. For if Josie was sinking further and further into sloughs of desperation, "Victoria" was rising grandly to the occasion.

### From the Letters

Am writing this in a cafe. I sent off an airmail & cable to you. You have been flooded with letters from me, far too many. I can't understand why I haven't had a letter from you. I know I see it all in a crazy unreal haze but I can't help that. I wouldn't mind not hearing if we'd parted in an ordinary way but after all, John darling, we

### From the Notes

*Sugar.* 80% of sugar industry belongs to US citizens, balance controlled largely by Am. creditors. Tobacco same. Banks, railroads, streetcar lines, electric plants, telephone systems and other utilities owned by US capital. . . .
*Medical.* Dr. Gustavo Aldereguía, director of La Esperanza (Sanitarium). All medical approach pene-

166

didn't. I had a lot of hard things to face and even if my letters displease you, you must know my terrible need. You knew *her* need, even when it displeased you to have her phone, and I knew it and I urged you even though it meant real pain to me to phone her even to see her in a Christmas holiday that was to have been all mine. I don't blame you for anything you do, but I don't want to live or be in a world that makes it seem right for us to hurt each other so. We're hypocrites, you & I, when we cannot help one another, to try to help a world going down. I know I've wearied you and frightened you with scenes before I left, but you did the same to me not so long ago. I know I tried to comfort you then as I could & your wire was comforting. But it seems so *long* and not to know what you are doing or anything about the job in Washington is unbearable. I've written so often, not to make you write to me but to try to pull myself together. I don't care what you write, only if you had only written. . . . What is so terrible is not to have you want to write me but still you never did write letters much except those nice ones in Brittany & the long poem. I want that poem. I want to go home to Erwinna. I am very very sick. . . . I was kind to her John. I didn't want her to suffer & I asked you to phone her the day she phoned when I was there. I was. Won't you help me? Forgive your lost lost unhappiest. . . .

I am afraid. Tomorrow is Sunday and I don't see how I will ever get

trated by imperialism. . . . TB question of hunger and air. No more negro tb than other races, only poorer, hungrier, so attacks more. Worse sight of hungry children on streets two years ago than now.

*Historical* (Portell Vilá): If 80 cents legal rate per day, even then man has 4 cents a day for a year to live on. Caffery thinks island should devote itself to sugar. In 1861 raised 20,000 tons of rice. Even raised wheat at end of last century. Could raise crops but policy is not to. (Am policy that is). Mills at Preston. Owned by United Fruit. . . . Hennequen or sisal plantation near Cárdenas owned by International Harvester controlled by Rockefeller interests. Here a man has to provide his cart and mule, feed the mule and after buying fodder has about 16 cents a week for himself. Now burning and sabotage there but people are very desperate. . . . This is a dangerous job, it has thorns, cuts the hands, many workers lose fingers. Only raw fibre made here, the rope is made in US. The profitable task in US, like sugar.

*At the embassy.* Commercial attache very solicitous. Wears a rose in buttonhole, tall goodlooking moron. Suddenly becomes disturbed at my questions, hunts for papers, says he has to get letter off. I offer to come again, is obviously relieved, worried, when I challenged his statement that Cubans are benefiting under reciprocity treaties, he blinks, says oh he can prove it. Shows chart of prices. I through it. I hoped, I literally prayed that you would write me today. I have been here over two weeks. It probably seems a short time to you. That's because someone loves you and you have someone to sleep with and someone to touch and help keep you human. It's only simple human things that keep one sane and able to talk as if it were easy to live on high planes.

I read your one and only letter over and over. I'd like to believe in the future. Maybe, as you say, it isn't dark. But if it is so hard for you to say even a few words to me, I see no reason to be sure. What is it that makes it so hard to say a few words. No one asked for long explanations. If you had wrapped up a newspaper, anything, forwarded mail, just scribbled a line, saying, how are you Josy, are you all right, this is your boy speaking.

No. I just sit here. Don't think this is the first letter I have written today. Two long letters are written and in my desk. Why should I struggle for such terrible control? What is it in my life that puts such a heavy burden upon me? Do you want me really to be of stone? Only a woman with a heart of stone could be so aloof, so content just to go away, never to hear a word. . . .

John John I want to die. I swear I want to die I want to die. I can't think of anything else tonight, it just sticks in my head. I've been sick all day, feverish, there isn't a movie I haven't seen, it's so horri-

ask what about standard of living. Says workers getting 80 cents a day now and factories glad to pay it as they can afford it under new rates. Says Cuba would be sunk without reciprocity treaty. . . . Says he doesn't think Cubans appreciate what is being done for them. I laugh and ask why should they? Afraid I showed my hand too much.

*Interview with Ambassador Jefferson Caffery, February 16, 1935.* Do you still think that the government of Mendieta is the best one to solve the problems of Cuba as you stated at the time it was initiated?

C replies that of course his answer must be off the record but he thinks that Mendieta is the only man that can guarantee elections. Asks who else could do it? I ask if anyone really thinks elections will take place in July as announced and he says he thinks so. I say opinion on the island seems to be that elections only announced to fool the people, C shifts uneasily, looks away, answers that he believes elections will take place. . . .

Do you think that the tendency of various revolutionary groups to insist on agrarian reform is justified?

C says oh yes, that is one of the things he is most interested in. Says hopes the people will be "able to buy back the land." Reminds me that after all the people who now own the land paid for it. . . . Says that Cubans do not like or understand agriculture. . . . Repeats lit-

ble to have to feel so forlorn, so neglected when a little letter, even a
paper in the box would save me
from this desperation. To be alone
in such a city surrounded by people who go together, who are not
alone, is bad enough, every time I
see my mailbox with nothing in it,
it is like a punch in the face....

Tell her to keep away from me, I'll
surely kill her. You didn't want me
to be human, kept your little, darling isolated, she was too good for
me to meet. No, it was only
Greenwood whom you fell in love
with yourself that was good
enough to meet. You loved her, not
me. You haven't loved me — I can
see that, you only pretend to now
to keep away so you can be happy.
I'm finished. I hope I die with all
my heart and soul. Life's ended,
work is nothing but a pile of shit,
love is something to be turned
out in the cold and kicked in the
tail.

... John, I think you are paying me
back for all the times I didn't take
you in bed, for the times that I'd
give anything in this world to live
again. Don't blame me for them
John too much, I really have never
loved anyone but you or never
ceased to love you, it was only too
hard for one person that was all,
too hard to work and be responsible and never to be without anxiety for saving. Needing to save
money, made me somehow save
*that*. ...

Just remember I love you now so
much that what seems cruelty

tle stories and this and that person
who gave a man a chance to garden and he didn't garden. Sees no
connection between this condition
and general economic situation,
seems to think it purely a matter of
"temperament."

What would be the reaction of US
government to a really revolutionary movement in Cuba?

C very nervous at this question but
answers at once, Oh hands off by
all means. Realizes the extreme un-
popularity on the island of US
warships in harbor.... Asked why
US did not recognize Grau San
Martín and did recognize Mendieta, he explains rapidly that
Grau's government couldn't keep
order. In constant turmoil. I ask if
US had recognized it might not the
turmoil have stopped. Says no that
was the reason they didn't recognize it. I ask how he reconciles that
with his previous statement of
Hands Off as a policy. Says now
what would I do in his place. Says
he has to protect lives and property, doesn't he? Says that US can't
just let American citizens and
property be destroyed, order has to
be restored. ...

I ask him what is his opinion of the
repressive measures of the Mendieta government against freedom
of the press.... C says it is all
wrong and he has told Mendieta so
a hundred times.... Says it is a big
mistake.... Says Batista is a man
of the people, a fine fellow really
who wants to see the working class
benefited as much as I do. Why he

can't kill that love. I thought today of the night we spent at Joe North's and I didn't take you. Too tired, too frozen with responsibility. Oh I have given you the right to be hard this way but I never deliberately did it, I never set out to harm you in any way.

I'm just sitting here, with all I've got, every thought, every bit of living in another place. I'll hold out so long as I can but maybe the day will come when I got to have a word from you, just one word, if you just send your name, John, that will mean that you love me still that you'll try always to love me. I'll always love you, I know that, forever. You're part of me, I'm not myself anymore.

I know you won't ever again find what I have for you, but people and life are funny, many sell and lose for a mess of pottage. People's nerves aren't steel, they snap and break and the very thing that makes a person worth anything is often the reason that they are finally lost. I don't know what more to say, I'll try with all my strength every day to keep from writing, to be still. You make me feel very worthless and cheap — and yet I know you don't want to make me feel so. Yet what man treats something beloved as if they were made of something tougher than they themselves are made. Remember that hard as it was with G — yet I didn't cast you out for her, you had her too. I have nothing but an empty mail box, a future that may

comes from them and his men are all from the country, poor boys who are with the workers. . . . Says he is quite a character. Carries the conversation to negroes. Says they are likeable fellows, says his own body guard . . . is a great fellow. (I afterwards learn that this is Champizo, who broke up the tobacco workers union headquarters and beat César Vilar. . . .)

Appears to be a shrewd man with great limitations. His limitations also help him to be strictly man of action, able to work hand in glove with Batista under guise of maintaining "order." Apparently thinks I am a liberal pretty much to the left but nothing more. Does not follow through any of his statements, each one seems to contradict the other, his hands off policy contradicting his law and order necessity, and his insistence on sugar as central economy without any shift in the present setup being sufficient in his mind to maintain a standard of living, which he only wants maintained for the reason that not to maintain it threatens the "business interests".

*Street scenes.* Big almost empty square, men sitting, police with revolvers in blue . . . uniforms sallying up and down. Dog playing, barking at car with radio blaring past, kid with light curly hair, very pale, all pale thin kids, many beg, come up and hold out hands, at night on side streets women with kids, hold out hands, beg in soft voices as you pass. Sun with clouds never happen, because I am too tired. . . .

occasionally and people reading papers, yesterday boy of 17 killed, was carrying bomb, his corpse in paper, beautiful face, icy still, students arrested, yesterday police fired into air, no sign around here. . . .

Can't sit down someone asks for money, children, boy surprised to get a whole nickel, runs off delighted, waves looks back, looks at nickel, waves again. Negro woman from Barbados asks have I any work, willing for anything, wash clean cook. Says she just walks and walks. No work. . . . I give her 20 cent piece, she takes it with dignity . . . says hope you have a safe passage, lady.

Man wrapped in paper like old bundle in doorway for night. Perfumes, with proprietors coming out hunting customers, cheap clocks, belts, shoes. Woolworth's with guards hunting for bombs. Windows of shoes, big black man with tattered black shoes . . . turns looks mournfully at me, says slowly, *Shoes are very beautiful, lady*. Black boy in park, foot in bloodstained rag, other foot in sock tied with rope to sole of a shoe flapping. Shoes shoes shoes. Who makes the shoes?

At last, when she had been living in this state for almost a month, the event occurred which she had been longing for: a figure materialized behind a palm tree, bona fides were exchanged, and she began to have access to participants in the opposition movement whose struggle was the principal reason she had been asked to come. It was a complicated series of encounters. Addresses had to be memorized, devious routes taken, a watch kept for government agents who might be following her in an effort to follow her contacts; nor could she write up her notes as she was writing everything else, lest their inadvertent discovery endanger either others or herself. In workers' houses, in obscure cafés, in the offices of an opposition newspaper published secretly "Somewhere in Havana" she met member after member of the revolutionary labor unions representing all the forms of employment in the city and listened hour after hour while they all told the same stories of wages so low that even full-time work was not sufficient to keep a family alive, of repression so severe, especially after the second general strike, that only the most stalwart still had the courage to carry on. When she had been around the underground network long enough to have gained the confidence of its inner circles she began to press them for help in carrying out a trip to the eastern end of the island, Oriente Province, where the revolutionary movement was known to be the strongest, and after hesitating over that stubborn, irreducible fact that would plague her all her life — she was a good comrade, but she was, after all, a woman — they eventually agreed. In Santiago she visited the university where angry students protested the paltry offerings to education in a country more than half of whose people could neither read nor write, while Batista's army ate up the budget with its new barracks, its fancy new uniforms, its guns. She interviewed workers who showed her the scars blackjacks had made on their backs when they were beaten by rural guards for complaining about the conditions on the harvests, others slashed with machetes for being discovered as members of the union. Two high school boys brought her the bloody clothes of a comrade beaten to death by police on the suspicion that he was transporting a bomb. She learned from people who had seen loved ones murdered that by decree as well as by custom, the penalty for interfering with the sugar harvest was death. Immersed in a world where such terrors were not a metaphor, her own private terrors began to lose some of their grip. On her journey from the city of Santiago to the mountain stronghold of "Realengo 18" they were like so many insects, nagging sometimes, especially in the evening, but easy enough to brush aside during the daylight, as her horse swept off the horseflies that clustered around its tail.

"Realengo 18" was an immense tract of land in the mountains of Oriente Province, not far from where another band of Cuban rebels, twenty-five years later, would work out Batista's downfall. Originally belonging to the Spanish crown, the land had been given away to soldiers following the war for independence but the distribution had been unsystematic, and though the people of the area believed it was legally theirs, their claims had been periodically challenged. By the middle of the 1930s they had been living there for many years, about 15,000 of them — 5,000 men, the unit of counting, and 10,000 women and children — and they had made of their mountain enclave something a little different from the rest of Cuba. "Sugarcane administrators shrug their shoulders, complain of shiftlessness, of people not willing to garden," Josie noted of the clichés that so comforted Cuban colonialists. "One might as well accuse a man fastened to a ball and chain of not being willing to dance." But "Realengo 18" was an exception. Here, where the sugar interests had not been permitted to dominate,

> Coffee and bananas patchwork the mountainside in lines neat as machine stitching. Tall palms shoot to the sky from valleys and along the mountain tops. A hundred herbs flower and provide the only medicine that the sick in these parts know. . . . In "Realengo 18" on mountain sides so steep it seems as if only flies could cultivate them, the deep tobacco colored soil teems with food. . . .

— not enough to prevent malnutrition but as much as the territory would bear. Down below, around the sugar mills in the valley, the people's lives were controlled by the sugarcane reaching practically into their doorways, by the sugar police making certain that they did what they were told, by the sugar economy which kept them hungry because hunger was the "electricity" that drove them to work. In Realengo these positions were also reversed. No sugar agents penetrated without anxiety over the possible loss of their lives. No soldiers traveled through except in numbers large enough to be sure they would get their way. Except for the efforts that were made to reclaim it,

> "Realengo 18" is a country the government forgot. It is even hard to find, lost in the mountains at the end of narrow trails. No road ever came here, no teachers and no doctors. To reach "Realengo 18" one rides a horse, takes trails that go steeply up a mountain side through thick virgin forest and jungle, sprouting ferns and vines as tangled as hair. . . .

But relative to the rest of Cuba life was free there and the people of Realengo intended to keep it that way. Just now they were under mounting pressure because the sugar interests were attempting to take over the region for themselves and they appeared to be determined about it.

> In August, 1934 the army started to attack after Realengo men had driven out surveyors perched on mountain tops measuring the land. León Alvarez, at the head of some thousands of men, filled the forest, waited for the soldiers who could see the men behind the trees in the deep wood, machetes in hand. The officer at the

head called out that he had orders to attack but he was afraid to attack; there were so many trees that bullets seemed useless. At this moment, León Alvarez answered that he, too, had orders. His orders were to defend. The captain and his men withdrew from such stubborn resistance . . .

but they were expected to return. Originally only separate house-holders — "shackholders" would be more accurate, for these were hardly palaces that the men would die to defend but windowless one-room shelters with thatch sides and mud floors and roofs that were open above the hearths — under the pressure of events they had discovered the necessity of cooperation and had now become something like an agricultural collective: they had an organization, with a title, to which everyone belonged, the Asociación de Productores Agrícolas del Rea-lengo 18 y Colindantes,* which even had a letterhead stationery and that most unlikely of mechanical implements, a typewriter. In part because of the crisis generated by the government's attempt to oust them they had made contact with students and workers in Santiago, who went out on strike to support them when the military entered, and also with radicals in Havana. Stirred by what they had begun to learn of the Soviet Union they had taken to calling themselves a "Soviet" — "the first Soviet in America" — but they stirred, too, to their own traditions in Cuba and Latin America; they spoke of Antonio Maceo, of Pancho Villa, of the great Nicaraguan rebel, Augusto Sandino. Alvarez, their leader, was a strong, stocky, newly literate former teamster, a black man, who had been working with the mountain people since 1920 when he was asked by his employer, one of the large sugar proprietors, to help drive them out. Like a growing number of Cuban radicals during the 1930s, he had become a Communist.

> Talk is fine, and here where no trains have come, autos have
> scarcely been seen, the words "imperialism, struggle, united front
> of workers and farmers" are common as sun and air. Some farmers
> are slower than others, some do not see the clear implication of
> their tussle to hold the land . . .

but many do see it, Josie reported. In 1935 the link between this isolated struggle in Cuba and the revolution in Russia was difficult not to see.

With the exception of a Cuban journalist later killed in Spain, Josie was the only writer ever to have visited "Realengo 18" not only during its troubles but during its entire lifetime, and she seems also to have been the only non-Cuban ever to have been there. All the descriptions of the

* Association of Agricultural Producers of Realengo 18 and the Surrounding Regions.

life there in these pages come from her. She reached Realengo with the help of a comrade from Santiago and for five days and nights she traveled around, going from ridge to ridge, shack to shack, sleeping in gunnysacks on the floors the way the people did, sharing their meals, talking to them about their lives, and — mainly — watching them live. She loved it. She loved every minute of it. She loved them for being the simple people they were, enjoying the simple things that they did; she loved herself for being there, for appreciating it; and she loved them again for welcoming her so warmly among them. She responded to their lives not so much politically as viscerally, not so much with her intellect as with her heart. She noticed everything and everything had a meaning for her, an enlarging, symbolic, universalizing kind of meaning of the sort belonging usually not so much to living as to books. When a chicken was slaughtered she realized at once it was for a dinner in her honor — these chickens were regularly for eggs. When a goat settled under the table she found it "chummy" — she saw it was a member of the family. When a pig rooted around in the coat of another pig she understood that the first pig, like its owners, was on the lookout for crumbs. When a child produced a sliver of soap from a crack in the wall, Josie noticed not only how small was the sliver that was saved, but the desire of the poor for dignity; when she brought out a bit of broken comb, Josie saw not only the loveliness of the hair being combed, but the universal vanity of the tyke doing the combing. Alone with another woman awaiting the return of her husband who had gone to Havana, suddenly they were simply "two women showing each other pictures of our absent husbands." As for their end of it, it is hard to imagine how the Cubans could have possibly hosted a more satisfactory guest. They had the naive hope common to poor desperate people that publicity would help them . . . *if only* the world knew about their troubles it would not let them be driven from their land . . . and they treated Josie as if she were an angel from heaven arriving to take their message to the world. As close as they could come to conferring an honor upon her from their little territory, they did. On learning that she had been to the Soviet Union and even had a Soviet visa in her passport they decided that she needed a passport from Realengo, too, and lugging the typewriter up and down mountains to the house where she was to spend the night, they fashioned her one, a touching painstakingly contrived document now at the Beinecke Library: "We, the undersigned, members of the Association of Agricultural Producers of Realengo 18 and the Surrounding Regions certify that the comrade Josephine Herbst has appeared before us in order to investigate the struggles in which we are involved, in their many aspects. Anyone who wishes to question her has as proof this document which is being expedited on 24 February, 1935" signed by León Alvarez, Presidente, in a big shaky hand, for he was only then learning how to write his name, and two others, including Secretary Jaime Navarre, the only person in Realengo who knew how to type. It was here in the mountains of Cuba that Josie had the experience that she did not have in the Soviet Union and would never quite have again, the experience that can happen only once in its pure form, that transforming, radicalizing, perception that goes not so much "I have seen the future and it works" as "I have seen the people and they are good." It is a perception as old as the first idealist and as young as the last, and any revolutionary who does not have it at least once is a fraud. In Josie, as in others, it was fundamentally more anarchist than Communist at its heart, for what she actually experienced, beyond her immediate revulsion at the power of the sugar interests, was the feeling — whether it is more accurately called insight or conviction — that it was these people's birthright in this world, it was everyone's, to live exactly as they pleased. They could create plenty out of nothingness, find beauty in a humble stone, live out to their fullest the human destinies God and nature intended for them . . . *if only* they were left alone. If the politics of the moment specified that the route to Utopia was through Moscow, so be it. Compared to its promise of liberation for the people of Realengo, her own objections to the Communist Party were trivial in the extreme.

In the articles Josie wrote from Cuba, what she called the "implications" of the Cuban struggle were never entirely absent. Beneath the despair of the Cubans lay the hope of revolution on every page. Yet Josie's articles are more than political. They are beautiful. As natural and intimate as her letters, they people the landscape with individuals so definite they are given weight, historicity, by her accounts. The struggle for the "Soviet" in Cuba was a small moment in Cuba's history, lost as a mere incident in the post-Machado blur, lost even in the major texts, and to what extent it has been reclaimed even since Castro I do not know, but years later the people of "Realengo 18" are as alive in Josie's articles as any heroes of history, a direct light of determination linking the 1935 Cuban revolution that could not possibly have happened with the 1959 revolution that did. The *New Masses* made fanfare out of what was a major journalistic achievement. "Cuba on the Barricades," the series was called, and it began with a dramatic cover, "Eyewitness Account: The SOVIET in the Interior of CUBA," featuring Josie's name. That there was a "SOVIET" in CUBA was certainly what her audience wanted to believe. But far from simply asserting a position, Josie had demonstrated it. She had gotten below the politics of Havana to the movement of the people beneath, and beneath that she had gotten to a profounder question still: *Why* the people moved.

When Josie returned to Havana at the beginning of March, 1935, her personal situation was unaltered. After the lightening of spirit she had

felt in the mountains, the fleeting recovery of her unitary self, she seems
to have half-expected that John would sense how much better she was
via some subliminal message service and reward her for it with a letter — after all, had she not not-written to him for the ten whole days she
had been in Oriente, just as he wanted? — but no word had come from
him during her absence. Her mailbox was just as empty as before. The
political crisis, however, was intensifying. In the increase of bombings,
the blowing up of buses, the presence of still more soldiers on the streets,
the signs were everywhere that the general strike that politicians said
would not, could not, happen, was almost ready to begin. Again her attention divided. On the one hand she plunged directly back into the
mood of emotional hopelessness that had overcome her before, not only
resuming her letters to John but writing to their common friends, especially those who would see him in Washington, that she did not think she
was going to be able to pull through. At one point recalling a story John
had told her about a traveling salesman who carried in his wallet a lock
of his true love's pubic hair, she took a scissors and clipped off a lock of
her own and mailed it as if surely that would stir him when nothing else
did. According to Ruth she and John were both only appalled. On the
other hand she was right in the thick of things, functioning almost as a
clandestine adjunct to the strike committee, passing them military and
political intelligence gathered from her interviews with various officials
and in turn acting as their liaison with the outside world, for even the
strike leaders had the illusion of the Realengo men . . . *if only* their comrades knew what was happening in Cuba, surely a way would be found to
come to their aid. Suspended as she was between optimism and pessi-
mism, action and passion, the fullness arising out of her involvement in
the strike and the emptiness arising out of her failure to get a response
from John, the demands of one balanced out the despair of the other, and
if at one moment she was typing out wires to Joe North explaining that
between her internal confusion and the external chaos she could see no
way of sending anything more than scattered bulletins to New York, at
the very next moment she was tearing them up and sallying forth
through the streets to another interview with Ambassador Caffery or
with Batista in which a new dimension to her identity as a writer was
being forged. "I just found one of the envelopes where you wrote my
name in your own hand, not typed, I just licked every letter. I love you
and nothing really can be wrong. It can't be, that's all. Yours forever,
your wife and your lover, even if I am never able to write again I'm that,
I belong to you, I'll stand around like a broom or an old suit of clothes, I
got to be there, I got to, because I am yours. I am. Even if I never do my
articles or another line. This is Josy trying to make her voice heard from
hell to heaven," reads a letter she wrote to John on her forty-third birthday. "My impression is that B is ready to make a military dictatorship

and is expecting such a contingency to arise. He will use any force anywhere, and when asked admitted that strike breakers was first tactic and
after that they would make the workers work at the point of a gun if necessary. Said . . . he would stop at nothing. . . . An intensely practical man
without any ideology, not an emotional fanatic like Hitler or a schemer
like Mussolini but a pretty cold practical man who has one answer for
everything, force," reads a portion of her interview with Batista just
three days later. Her abasement as a woman was bottomless — but as a
journalist, she was very much on her toes.

In the last analysis, the officials were more accurate than the radicals: in early March, 1935, another general strike did begin but it was
crushed before it had barely gotten underway. Her notes chart the rising
violence —: March 9. "A big bomb goes off directly outside the movie
where I am . . . Group in lobby tells me man was blown to bits . . .
Shooting followed. Pools of blood on pavement when I left." March 10.
"Buses were blown to bits last night and street cars demolished when
scabs tried to operate after bus drivers went out on strike . . . Number of
people killed or injured unknown. . . ." March 11. "Few streetcars running, police manned. Milk not delivered — few wagons piloted by marine and soldier . . . No news . . . Last night soldiers took out several
students from a house and killed them . . . Government moves will not
quiet people but will further unite them. . . ." But however bold the revolutionary effort, its outcome was never in doubt.

By the middle of the month it was not only dangerous but pointless
for Josie to stay in Havana any longer. Most of the political people she
had been in contact with there had disappeared. Apart from the trifles
which had reached her during the first part of her trip, all Josie's out-
pourings to John had elicited only a single cable which arrived the week
after her return from the mountains promising that a letter would be
waiting in Miami. She left Cuba, stopped off briefly in Key West and visited Hemingway, without telling him what was happening, and then
went on. When she got to Miami there was another cable from John urging her to finish her work, and two letters, the first frigid, the second furious, reacting against her desperation, against her violence toward Ruth,
against the lock of hair. He is now utterly definite. He does not want to
see her again or for her to try to see him. As hard as it was for either of
them to believe that lives so completely entangled could be so fundamentally severed, that is what finally happened. Apart from a single encounter which took place about a year afterward, they never saw one
another again.

John's life after Josie was not exactly the paradise that she imagined.
He maintained his political ties till the end of the decade, resuming his
activities with the farm movement and later working with transport

workers in the South; he briefly had a cabinet shop in Manhattan where he made furniture for, among other of their acquaintances, Katherine Anne; and during World War II he served in the Coast Guard. His final novel, *The Salesman*, was published by Simon and Schuster in 1939, and he also published a number of stories. After obtaining an Arkansas divorce from Josie in 1940 he married Ruth. But according to many friends, except for the period of the furniture building, when he attempted to stop, he was drinking steadily for the rest of his life, and so was Ruth, giving a certain substance to Josie's belief that it was she who had helped him hold it at bay. In the late 1940s, when the FBI began investigating Communist activity in Washington during the 1930s, John and Ruth moved to Mexico where they remained until his death, from a heart attack, in 1959 — but that is part of a later story. As for Josie, she never really acknowledged what had happened to her marriage. Beginning with the trilogy she created a version of their relationship in which the political dominated the personal, and as the crisis receded more and more into the background she gradually substituted the fictional version for the real so that ultimately it seemed not just to others but to herself that it was a marriage broken not so much in the bedroom as in the field. Even to her closest friends she rarely told the inner story of what had happened. Of all the writing she ever did about it, the closest to the truth is a scene in the final volume of the trilogy, *Rope of Gold*, that she no doubt hoped was disguised. A man, Kurt Becher, the nearest approximation in all her writing to a character standing for anything like Marion Greenwood, has entered their lives, Victoria has had an affair with him, and Jonathan, recognizing the strength of her feeling, has started to withdraw. She tries to persuade him he is wrong about it, but she fails. Though it occurs well before their final separation, it is the moment of decision of the marriage. "She had not known it would be like this," Josie wrote, "that Kurt would haunt her as if he were in her very blood. It was with Jonathan she had made her bed, it was their life that counted. . . . She did not know how it had happened, only that the long tension of her life had suddenly snapped. . . . She saw that she would never be able to convince him, ever again, and it seemed the final treachery reserved in life was in one's own body," waiting.

# PART SIX

# TEARING PAST
# STATIONS

Josie's parents, Mary Frey and William Benton Herbst, at the time of their marriage, 1883

"Poor Joe," Josie's uncle Joseph Frey — the carpetbagger "Joe Trexler" of *Pity Is Not Enough* — 1881

Josie's christening photo, 1892

The visit to Oregon, 1898. Top row, left to right: Hettie Harbord Fry (wife of Mar'
brother Daniel), Alice Eppley (Mary's sister), Mary Herbst, Orris Fry (son of Daniel and
Hettie), and Daniel Fry, the "David Trexler" of *Pity Is Not Enough* and *The Executioner*
*Waits*. Second row, left to right: Hortense Eppley, Helen Herbst, Grandma Frey — the
"Mem" of Josie's trilogy — Frances Herbst, Charles Eppley. Front row, left to right:
Jennie Fry, Daniel Fry, Jr., Alice Herbst, Josie

The entering first grade class, Edith Everett Elementary School, Sioux City, 1898. Josie
is in the front row, fourth from left.

Josie and Helen, 1897. Josie is five, Helen, two

The four sisters, 1900. left to right: Alice, Helen, Frances, Josie

Josie's high school graduation picture, 1910

*From Josie's collections.*

Helen's high school graduation picture, 1913

Genevieve Taggard and her baby daughter, 1922

Maxwell Anderson, with *The Atlantic Monthly*, about 1920

"In my window, Basel, 1932." Snapshot sent to Josie by Katherine Anne Porter during her first visit to Europe

Hemingway and fishing companion in Key West, about 1930

Nathanael West at Erwinna, 1932

Josie in Berlin, 1922

Josie and John Herrmann shortly after their meeting in Paris in 1924, possibly at Le Pouldu

John Herrmann, perhaps on the *Josy*, about 1927

Josie and John at the time of the move to Erwinna, 1928

The house in Erwinna as it looked at the time Josie and John moved there, 1928

The interior of the house in Erwinna about 1930. Corner cabinet and trestle table, on the right, were made by John. A rug of the *Josy* is on the wall.

Erwinna, 1932. Marion Greenwood (left), with Josie, on front step; John and other visitors behind

Marion Greenwood in Mexico, 1933 or 1934

Josie and John in Mexico, 1933.

Josie and John Herrmann en route to the Soviet Union, 1930

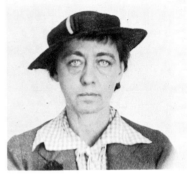

Josie's first passport photo, 1922

Josie en route to Germany, 1935

Josie's 1955 passport: the passport of the passport case

Josie's final passport, 1963

Courtesy of Ann Reeve

The Collection of American Literature, the Beinecke Rare Book and Manuscript Library, Yale University

CUERPO DE EJÉRCITO DEL CENTRO
ESTADO MAYOR
2.ª SECCION.—2.ª NEGOCIADO

Se autoriza a la camarada JO-
SEPHINE HERBST, periodista Nor
teamericana para que pueda circular libremente por Madrid, tan
to de dia como de noche.

Rogamos a Autoridades y fuer-
zas armadas no le pongan ningún
impedimento.

Madrid 3 de Abril de 1937
El Jefe del Negociado

BEHIND THE SWASTIKA
*By JOSEPHINE HERBST*

PUBLISHED BY
THE ANTI-NAZI FEDERATION
168 WEST 23rd STREET, N. Y. C.

5c

Courtesy of Renée Ralph

The young man with the glasses is Hal Ware, 1890–1935. The photo of Josie was taken by Katherine Anne Porter at the grave of Henri Barbusse, in Paris, the day following his burial in 1935. The document dated April 3, 1937, is one of Josie's several safe-conduct passes from Spain. It authorizes her to circulate freely about Madrid, day or night.

## The Farmers Form a United Front
### JOSEPHINE HERBST

## Cuba—Sick for Freedom
### JOSEPHINE HERBST

## THE SOVIET IN CUBA
### JOSEPHINE HERBST

## Farewell and a Promise to Barbusse
### JOSEPHINE HERBST

JOSEPHINE
HERBST

Caricature from the *New Masses*,
1935, at the time of the
American Writers' Congress

# Former S. C. Girl Is Leader of Delegation
# Demanding Lifting of Spain Arms Embargo

## Josephine Herbst, Novelist, in Fight Against U. S. Rule

Washington — (AP) — Spanish-
ed by po-
the State
nand that
shipment
d.

ed in the
State de-
the south
se. They
r speedy

gation to
t and see
S. Mes-

of Rep-
d, farmer
rs. Jerry
esentative
Montana,
erly di-
versity li-
n Ameri-
nen Con-
Josephine

**JOSEPHINE HERBST**

uled to call on members of Congress.

### HIGH SCHOOL GRADUATE
Josephine Herbst was graduated
from Sioux City high school about

## Masses
### Eye-Witness Account!
# THE
# Soviet
## In the Interior of
# Cuba
## By
## JOSEPHINE HERBST

Yaddo, September, 1939. Bottom row, left to right: Frederico Castello, Jerre Mangione, Marjorie Peabody Waite, Nathan Asch, Elizabeth Ames. Second row: Nora Holt, Josephine Herbst, Eleanor Clark, David Diamond, Delmore Schwartz. Third row: Newton Arvin, Marc Blitzstein, Rudolph Von Ripper, Richard Berman. Fourth row: Morton Zabel, Unknown, Prudencio de Perida, Arthur Cohn, James Still. Fifth row: Unknown, Helen Muchnic, Blanchard Gummo

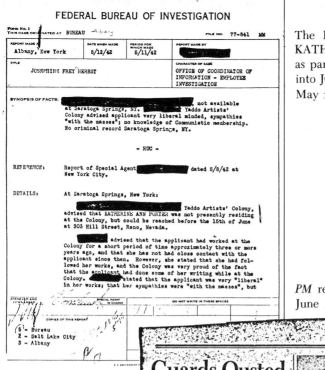

FEDERAL BUREAU OF INVESTIGATION

FORM NO. 1
THIS CASE ORIGINATED AT BUREAU - Albany     FILE NO. 77-841

| REPORT MADE AT | DATE WHEN MADE | PERIOD FOR WHICH MADE | REPORT MADE BY |
|---|---|---|---|
| Albany, New York | 5/12/42 | 5/11/42 | |

TITLE

JOSEPHINE FREY HERBST

CHARACTER OF CASE

OFFICE OF COORDINATOR OF INFORMATION - EMPLOYEE INVESTIGATION

SYNOPSIS OF FACTS: ▮▮▮▮▮▮▮▮▮▮▮▮▮▮▮▮▮▮▮▮▮, not available at Saratoga Springs, NY. ▮▮▮▮▮▮ Yaddo Artists' Colony advised applicant very liberal minded, sympathies "with the masses"; no knowledge of Communistic membership. No criminal record Saratoga Springs, NY.

- RUC -

REFERENCE: Report of Special Agent ▮▮▮▮▮▮▮ dated 5/8/42 at New York City.

DETAILS: At Saratoga Springs, New York:

▮▮▮▮▮▮▮ Yaddo Artists' Colony, advised that KATHERINE ANN PORTER was not presently residing at the Colony, but could be reached before the 15th of June at 303 Hill Street, Reno, Nevada.

▮▮▮▮▮▮ advised that the applicant had worked at the Colony for a short period of time approximately three or more years ago, and that she has not had close contact with the applicant since then. However, she stated that she had followed her works, and the Colony was very proud of the fact that the applicant had done some of her writing while at the Colony. ▮▮▮▮▮ stated that the applicant was very "liberal" in her works; that her sympathies were "with the masses", but

APPROVED AND FORWARDED: ▮▮▮▮▮▮ SPECIAL AGENT IN CHARGE     DO NOT WRITE IN THESE SPACES

COPIES OF THIS REPORT:
5 - Bureau
2 - Salt Lake City
3 - Albany

The FBI tries to locate KATHERINE ANNE PORTER as part of its investigation into JOSEPHINE HERBST, May 12, 1942.

*PM* reports Josie's firing, June 15, 1943.

PM, MONDAY, JUNE 15,

# Guards Ousted Liberal Writer

### COI Worker Interrupted While Writing Boast That U. S. A. Has No Gestapo

*Fourth of a series on the "Red" witch hunt now being conducted by Federal agents among liberals in public service and in certain war industries.*

Josephine Herbst, the well-known novelist who abandoned the comforts of her Bucks County home shortly after Pearl Harbor to join the staff of the Co-ordinator of Information (COI), was fired three weeks ago, for no other reason, apparently, than her activities in support of the Loyalists during the Spanish Civil War.

On the day of her dismissal the *New Republic* reports, she was sitting in her office, tapping out copy for transmission by short wave to Germany describing the

Josephine Herbst, novelist, who lost her job with the COI apparently because she was pro-Spanish Loyalist.

...to establish he... She was co... the *Daily Wor*... about Spain. ...had written the... and the *Daily*... without perm...

She was als... Madrid in wh... from John D... fessor emerit... noted anthrop... same progra...

#### Merry-Go-Round

"On June 4 I went to Washington and called on Col. Donovan's office to learn what had happened to my appeal. I failed to see the Colonel, although I called there and telephoned several times during the course of the day. A secretary finally told me that Col. Donovan had finally left a message to the effect that I was to take up the matter with the Civil Service Board of Appeals 'as was customary in such cases.'

The next day, after intervention on the part of certain influential friends, I talked with Civil Service Commissioner Fleming, asking for specific information about the charges against me and the date of a possible hearing. I told him that it was impossible to postpone the hearing as I no longer had a job in Washington and that it would take unlimited private means to linger indefinitely. He promised to let me know within three days.

"On June 8 I called Commissioner Flem-ing's office and could only reach his secretary, who asked me to call again the next morning. I did so and was told once more there was nothing to report, but that she would call me back the same day. She did not do so.

Miss Herbst... unsympathetic... friends can... the Spanish... rather than...

Eleanor Roosevelt wonders why. June 17, 1942

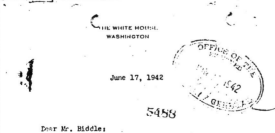

THE WHITE HOUSE
WASHINGTON

June 17, 1942

5488

Dear Mr. Biddle:

This story about Miss Josephine Herbst seems to me extraordinary, and I should be interested to know the real facts in the case.

Very sincerely yours,

Eleanor Roosevelt

Courtesy of Julia Older Bazer

Josie and Clair Laning, New York, 1945, in a photographer's street studio on Broadway

Josie and Gustav Regler at a brief reunion in the early 1940s

The surviving Herbst sisters — Alice, Josie, and Frances — in Sioux City, 1943

Josie upstairs in Erwinna, probably in the late 1940s

Josie and Hilton Kramer at Erwinna, 1964

Josie and Jean Garrigue dressed as tramps during a spring festival in Erwinna, 1957. Josie is probably reading from Schwitters.

Josie and Jane Mayhall at Erwinna in the early 1960s

Jean Garrigue in the early 1950s

Josie in the garden at Erwinna, 1965

## CHAPTER NINETEEN

# Floating Feather

JOHN WAS gone, but there was work to be done. Love had fled, but revolution was rising to take its place. Her personal life had failed her but politics would keep her going until the end. If only it could have been as simple as Josie longed for it to be. But it was far from being that simple. Fundamental things that had been settled in her life for almost a decade had suddenly come apart — at least she felt her life had crumbled suddenly, even if the relationship of creation to destruction was not necessarily exactly what she thought — and when she first reached the East again at the end of March, 1935, she felt herself wholly at a loss. "It's wrong to be a feather floating in the sky," she had written John from Havana. Now she was one. The very structure of the life she had been leading — always, whatever else was happening, in some relation to John — was suddenly missing and she was much too bewildered to know even in a practical sense, let alone a political one, what to do. Chief among the uncertainties to which she had to turn her attention was the problem of money, of which she had none, nor any prospects for getting any except what she could earn herself, which particularly now, at this midpoint in the Depression, was not likely to be very much. Second was the problem of work. Between the second volume of the trilogy and the Cuba articles her name was better known than it had ever been and obviously the time was right for her to write and publish the final volume, but it was much too soon for her to face in prose the denouement of the story of Victoria and Jonathan that was still so fresh in life, and she knew she did not have either the energy or the capacity for isolation such a task was surely going to require. Another difficulty was the matter of friends. Toward the Communist circles with whom she had been in the closest contact before and during her months in Cuba she felt that neurotic suspicion endemic among separated spouses, for not only did she hold the Party as an organization responsible for drawing John into the activities she associated with their downfall, these very friends had accepted her successor, welcoming Ruth into their houses, their apartments, their parties, the Party, and while Helen North, who was married to Joe, Helen Black, who was still involved with Mike Gold, and Jessica Smith, in particular — all old friends — were sympathetic to Josie's suffering, they expected her to be able to bear it, as part of the common lot. Other old friends were geographically scattered. Nathanael West was in Hollywood, Katherine Anne was in Paris. New friendships were materializing, particularly ones with John Cheever and James Farrell, both of whom she had met at Yaddo shortly before going to Cuba, but Cheever was only twenty-three, twenty years her junior, and Farrell, separating from his wife Dorothy, was involved with his own affairs, and coming as they did at this particular moment, the relationships had neither enough history nor enough intimacy to be very sustaining. Unable to face Erwinna where these problems and others would rise up before her undiluted she remained in New York for some time after her return, sleeping on assorted living room couches, in borrowed apartments, or at cheap hotels. For the first six or so weeks of her officially "separated" existence, she scarcely unpacked her bags.

The literary atmosphere with which Josie was surrounded during her temporary residence in New York was an atmosphere almost wholly dominated by politics — specifically the politics of the American Writers' Congress, which took place a month after her return. Indeed, Josie was nominally one of the sponsors of the Congress, for her name appears on the original "Call," published in the *New Masses* during the time she was in Cuba, and she was later on the national committee of the League of American Writers, which grew out of the Congress, although there is no evidence among her papers that she was ever more than marginally involved with either one. The American Writers' Congress was the product of the coming together of two forces. The first was the mood that was common to many writers at that moment that it was time to get serious about politics. The second was the position of the Communist Party at the threshold of the Popular Front. Earlier the Party had cultivated the earnest but unpublished "proletarian" writers who made up the bulk of the membership of its John Reed Clubs; later it would cultivate the famous; but just now it was interested in the broad category of more or less middling writers, well-known but not necessarily popular, who had proved willing to associate themselves with the cause. Thus Waldo Frank but not Sinclair Lewis, Genevieve Taggard but not Pearl Buck, were among the signers of the "Call." That the Communist Party should seek openly to strengthen its position through a political alliance with sympathetic writers was not something to which Josie objected. In fact she took it for granted. Temperamentally uncomfortable with partisan extremities, the more popular the front, the more she felt at home. The literary implications of such an alliance, however, were another matter. Despite the assurances of Communist Party secretary Earl Browder who addressed the gathering that the Party wanted nothing more than that the writers should be good writers, the very agenda of the conference was a set of Marxist-theoretical questions which, in Josie's long-standing opinion, had little to do with literature. "The Worker as Writer," the talk by Jack Conroy; "Proletarian Poetry," the talk by Isidor Schneider; "The Dialectics of the Development of Marxist Criticism," the talk by Granville Hicks — such topics might fascinate Mike Gold or Joe Freeman or others who had more taste for abstraction but they had been boring to Josie in Kharkov and they were boring to her again in New York. She was also put off by the climate of suspicion surrounding her new friend James Farrell whose literary talent she genuinely respected and whose policy of cooperating with the Communists on political issues while criticizing their literary ideas was, at this point, roughly similar to her own. She and Farrell spent most of their time with a third ally, Edward Dahlberg, making fun of the solemnity of the proceedings, rechristening the League of American Writers the League Against American Writing, and otherwise caricaturing the goings-on. Appearances to the contrary, Josie was far from being an insider at the Congress. Stuck up on the platform opening night at the last minute because the organizers belatedly realized that there was no Woman on the program — Richard Wright was the Negro — she gave a blazing speech, mainly about Cuba, which the young women in the audience — Tillie Lerner,* Meridel Le Sueur, Rebecca Pitts — would remember the rest of their lives, but she herself knew exactly what she was doing there. Between the portentousness of the official proceedings and the pettiness behind the scenes she found the entire experience disheartening. Where was the spirit of Realengo? In the alliance between writers and the Communist Party it seemed that not only literature but revolution could get lost.

Shortly after the Congress Josie went back to Erwinna and it was just as difficult as she had feared. The house was physically run down. There were debts. Even the title to the property was in doubt because of their separation, as a result of their ambiguous financial arrangements with Mr. Herrmann. Not long before John had passed through briefly with

* Later, Tillie Olsen.

Ruth, and there was also the gossip of neighbors. Not feeling up to reestablishing herself there at a time when so much was uncertain she decided instead to fix up the house only sufficiently to rent it out, but — other than the fact that she did not want to go back to New York — she did not know what she wanted to do. Of all the things that were happening in the world in the spring of 1935 nothing seemed more important to Josie, as to other radicals, than the situation in Germany, where the Nazi Party, led by Adolf Hitler, seemed to be establishing itself ever more firmly in control. Every day, every week, every month, every two months, the newspapers were releasing their shocking reports — Hitler had renounced reparations, reincorporated the Saar, sent troops into the Rhineland, sanctioned the killing of the Austrian chancellor, murdered his own men — and even though the Communist movement did not yet officially oppose him, taking the position that the advent of Fascism would hasten the advent of Communism, what was happening officially and what was happening unofficially were not identical, and the rise of the Nazis and specifically the fate of the German left held the attention of almost all radicals in its thrall. In June, 1934, New York was visited by the German Communist publisher Willi Münzenberg, later killed by Stalin, who was attempting to persuade anyone who would listen, first, that the Nazi government was the most terrible government ever to exist on the face of the earth, worse than anything under the Kaisers, worse than Russia under the Tsars, and second, that it could yet be overthrown. In fact there was an underground opposition to Hitler flourishing even now but such was the control of propaganda exercised by the Nazi Party that word of it never got out. No matter what actually happened in Germany — no matter what strikes, sabotage, demonstrations, whatever — the newspaper stories remained the same. The opposition was dead. The Nazis had unified German society. Long live the Thousand Year Reich. Heil Hitler! Although it is not clear whether or not Josie actually saw Willi Münzenberg she certainly talked with other people who had seen him and she later met with at least one other German Communist refugee, Hede Massing, who was also in touch with the German underground. The possibility of returning to Germany to investigate for herself what was happening in a country to which she still felt closely tied loomed up for her at the moment as the most compelling alternative to her life in the United States, but at the same time she was full of doubt about her ability to undertake such a journey on her own. To travel alone, given the state of mind she was in: to risk again the isolation she had experienced in Cuba: to face the dangers that would automatically follow from the kind of investigation she had in mind: how could she possibly even consider such a trip now? In this period of indecision about her only source of comfort was her growing friendship with James Farrell, and it was as much from the confidence in her reflected in his eyes as from her confidence in herself that she eventually came to her conclusion. Of course it was not wise to go to Germany but since when had wisdom been the clarion call of life? It was action and not wisdom that made her blood stir. The very idea of going off again made her feel more like herself. By June she was thoroughly ready and it is a measure not only of the importance of the subject but of the influence of the movement with which she was so closely identified and of her own prestige that she could practically no sooner crystallize her decision to go than she was able to negotiate a choice assignment from the *New York Post* to do it. At no other time in her life did Josie undertake a mission that ran so high a risk of failure and at probably no other time was she emotionally so ill-suited to carry it out, but daring herself as she had dared herself on the eve of her first trip to Germany years before, she plunged ahead. If it was something larger than herself she needed to lift her above the petty wreckage of her life at the moment, surely in the story of the resistance to Hitler's Germany she had managed to find it.

# "The Italian Front
# Isn't the Hardest . . ."

HER FIRST stop was Paris, both to further her preparations for the German assignment and to visit Katherine Anne whom she had not seen for several years, and it was to Katherine Anne's that she went immediately after her arrival in July, 1935. At the time of the visit Katherine Anne was living with her third husband, Eugene Pressly, in a small old Parisian town house on the left bank, a little sanctum of genteel elegance made even more elegant by touches that were distinctively Katherine Anne — a polished table shining out of a long passageway, a tall vase with tall flowers, a Chinese bowl, a painting hung just so where the light would strike it rightly at a certain hour. It was the perfect setting for the real life counterpart of her fictional incarnation, Miranda Gay. There was a charming kitchen, a tiny garden with a stone cobbled walkway and thick foliage, separate writing studios a floor apart for husband and wife, even a music room where Katherine Anne practiced faithfully on her virginals every day. Out of politics, out of time, after years of ill-health, poverty, and wandering in Mexico and Europe, she seemed finally to be settled and secure. Though her appearance had changed, for her hair had already turned white, physically she was just as lovely as ever. In addition to her marriage to a young man who adored her, she was the center of an admiring circle of American expatriates including writer Glenway Wescott, publishers Monroe Wheeler and Barbara Harrison, and photographer George Platt Lynes, and while her work, as usual, was coming slowly she was flourishing as she never had flourished before. Every day, when Gene had left for the American Embassy where he worked, Katherine Anne would occupy herself about the house, writing for several hours, pottering in the kitchen and garden, which she loved, working on her finger exercises at the virginals. In the evenings there would be apéritifs, a candlelit dinner, late night strolls by the river, the gathering of friends at a café. Into all this domestic tranquillity Josie stepped as happily as if she had entered the very Kingdom of Heaven itself, and between the two of them it was soon much as it had always been: the endless discussion of people and books, the exchange of domestic tidbits, the instructions for jellies and jams. "Josephine Herbst arrived practically out of a clear sky the other day . . . and we've about talked ourselves hoarse," Katherine Anne wrote to Caroline Gordon, their mutual friend. "I have so enjoyed having her. . . . She's a grand guest in all the ways. Eats and drinks what is set before her and praises the cooking, and goes to bed and sleeps, and lolls around over coffee in the morning taking up the conversation where it stopped the evening before, and goes about her own business when the time comes, and likes the house and is getting a good rest and in fact is God's gift to the hostess." Katherine Anne in turn was God's gift to her guest. She knew Josie and she knew John, and if she did not guess correctly at exactly what had happened between them — nor did Josie tell her exactly — she could see from Josie's condition that it had been disastrous, and from the most elementary female assistance such as supervising a restorative haircut to the deepest emotional reassurances, she performed all the offices of a friend. Of everything that happened during their two-week reunion in Paris nothing was more comforting to Josie than her friend's example, for if Katherine Anne was succeeding in marriage — or so Josie thought of it — perhaps she herself had not been so foolish to try. In the circle of Katherine Anne's apparent security Josie slept more soundly than she had in months, and how could she have known — though Katherine Anne must have suspected — that Gene Pressly, always a self-effacing man, would soon be effaced altogether from Katherine Anne's life, that there would soon be another ideal husband and another perfect establishment and another romantic setting and another circle of friends and so on into the future until even the beguiling "Miranda" could enchant them no longer?

But now Josie was in Berlin and the circle of her protection was shattered and she was left facing her own life, with the consequences of her own choices, once more. Apart from her knowledge of Germany in the past and her present instincts she had very little to go on. There were some names, provided by the Germans she had met in New York and Paris, a few addresses, a telephone number or two, but the reliability of these was uncertain because the exiles by the very fact of exile were out of touch, and the gravity of the cautions with which they surrounded their information made Josie feel not more secure but more nervous. She took a room in a comfortable hotel on Unter den Linden and tried to get started but the atmosphere around her was even more impossible to penetrate than she had thought it might be, her own uneasiness far more formidable to overcome. At the beginning her inner terror and the outer terror were strangely matched. Unsettled by the unfamiliar aura of the familiar sights around her, at times actively scared, her mood thickened and darkened again and she wrote often to Katherine Anne, as if trying to maintain the normality of her communication with her friend. "Dearest Katherine Anne," she wrote on July 21, 1935, shortly after her arrival,

> Here I am in this hotel — much too dear & yet only $2 a day in my money, & I am here until I can feel my way a little. Everything very quiet, muzzled in fact but no more of that until I see you again. I felt dreadfully depressed at first, did even this morning with a kind of horror of being alone that goes to the very bone. I'm not sure I can pull off the business here & am not going to be frightened if I don't. I am not going to be terrified of failing for the moment. You don't know how wonderful it was for me to be there and to find you so happy and so secure. Nothing better could have happened. In all these months those days are the only ones I have had that haven't been nightmares. The nightmare comes & goes now & I have to figure out some way to beat it if I can. . . . You won't mind I know my writing like this, kind of thinking in a way out loud, you've been alone so much & so bravely. I think that you know much more about "bravery" than Hemingway who was so glib with his definitions & talked of bravery being "gallantry under pressure" — My God there are wars and Wars. The Italian front isn't the hardest. I could have gone to jail or been beaten easier than this and you have stuck through worse things than gunfire. You're out of it now Gott sei dank & if I can pull through the next year — sometimes I think I can't — . . . .

Though her moods continued to alternate, stalwart one moment, melancholic the next, gradually the external reality overcame the internal one and she began to work.

To understand what was happening in the German underground Josie had to function almost as if she were a member of it herself. It was essential to keep no names, phone numbers, addresses, or notes of any other kind, to meet people surreptitiously on train platforms and public benches, to avoid the telephone, to do precisely what had been agreed upon in advance and no other lest a deviation provide even the smallest link in a chain the police might be waiting to wind around someone's neck or even around her own. In all of her papers there is little that provides clues to exactly where she went during a specific period, whom she visited, how it had been arranged, and when once she made a mistake, leaving a note under the door of one of her contacts so that there was such a record, news of her misstep reached all the way back to the refugee network in New York. Only her articles themselves record how she proceeded, in what ways information registered itself on her, how she reasoned, on what basis she constructed the impressions she formed. The only way to comprehend the reality was to feel it, to use all her senses simultaneously, like an animal tracking another animal that is trying to lead it away. What was absent was just as important as what was present. The discrepancy beween appearance and reality was very great. "One must know the lay of the land, have been familiar with an earlier Germany to get the scent," Josie wrote in her articles in the *New York Post.* "The newspaper, the radio and the newsreel repeat that all is quiet in Germany, everything is in order. To the eye, streets are clean, window boxes are choked with flowers, children hike to the country in droves, singing songs." Yet "by word of mouth, in whispers, the real news circulates steadily through the German world. From hand to hand tiny leaflets inform the uninformed." "When people go to movies, a voice tells them that under their Chancellor Hitler everything is being done for the betterment of conditions, while in other countries chaos is ruining the masses." Yet "the housewife going to market the next day cannot buy butter." "The old system is attempting to work within a changed world. The strain is great upon it but on the surface things appear cheerful. Boys bicycle on country roads. Who sees a concentration camp? Yet silence is over the very countryside, in little inns where one is sharply scrutinized, in trains, along streets. Talk does not bubble up any more."

Everywhere, there were silences. "In restaurants, where the host used to exchange bright words with guests, only those hosts firmly established as Nazis beam and chatter." "In cafés and trains the familiar greeting of 'Guten Tag' is lacking. If it is heard, the voice is timid." It was as much a matter of what was not in the bookstores any longer as what there was — "works about our animal friends, the birds and the bees, and pictures of Hitler smilingly accepting a nosegay from a little girl" — as much a matter of what newspapers excluded as what they put in. "The butterfly is a major subject in the new Germany," Josie concluded, and in a newspaper that would formerly have scorned to give even a line to such trivial business "A thunder shower in Berlin is described on page one as 'Cloud Burst Sweeps Berlin' with lavish details of water-filled gutters and broken branches of trees." She looked at the movies, at the posters in the railway stations, at the advertisements in the newspapers, at the nightlife in the cafés. She mingled with the people around her, participated in their conversations, contemplated the meaning of their jokes. On the rising birth rate, the pride of the Nazis but the scandal of the people who believed that the government was deliberately impregnating young girls. Two women meet at a shop in Berlin. "Good morning," says the one. "Is your daughter going to the country on a government project?" "Oh no," replies the other. "She already has a baby." Or on the situation in general. Hitler goes to a barber and complains, "Look at my hair, how flat it is. What can I do to make it stand up a little?" "Stick your head out the window and look at what is going on in Germany," the barber replies, "and your hair will stand on end for the rest of your life." She befriended a Nazi family in Munich, interviewed Nazi officers in Berlin. Nosing her way through the misleading detail of the surface of German life she arrived at the fundamental situation — the incipient "coordination" of the economy, the destruction of the unions and the churches, the development of the Terror against the Jews — and of the persistence of opposition to it, despite all obstacles. The political convictions of the eleven million citizens who had voted for the Communists and Social Democrats in the election of 1933 had not simply vanished overnight. Something had happened to those people. What?

Slowly, carefully, cautiously, she collected the opposition stories. The stories of the illegal strikes, involving hundreds of thousands of workers. The stories of the illegal newspapers, involving hundreds of thousands of readers. The story of the leaflets printed surreptitiously and set up at a certain signal to rain down a waterspout, tiny pages reaching the streets with their big messages . . . "Down with Hitler" . . . "Remember Thaelmann"* . . . "The Revolution Lives." The story of the workers in Wedding who would not wear the Nazi work badge on their work clothes; of the workers attending the funeral of their comrades blown up in a munitions explosion believed to have been staged by the Nazis, who did not salute Hitler when he came to console them; of workers at the funeral of union leaders shot for treason, who braved the intimidating photographers and placed a floral tribute around their leaders' graves. The stories of the unsung unnamed ones who defied the Nazis individually in their daily lives. Of the Catholics who put up wall posters calling on their following to remember that "there is only one true leader and He was born more than 2000 years ago." Of the Salvation Army woman "arrested for carrying the Nazi flag, enforced on every gathering, with a snooty expression that looks like contempt." Of the woman who, commenting from a passing bus about the construction of a circus tent on

* A German Communist leader caught and imprisoned by the Nazis in March, 1933, after the Reichstag fire.

Tempelhoferfeld a few days after the May Day celebrations staged by the Nazis said, "Well there's another circus," and when asked by an official just what she meant, stood her ground and said "I said, there goes another circus," much to the satisfaction of the other riders nearby.

Out of all her experiences, all her sources, all her intelligence, all her memories, Josie put together a portrait of life "Behind the Swastika" in 1935 that is unrivaled in both depth and accuracy either by the journalists who were her contemporaries or by historians reconstructing later what was happening at the time. In addition to documenting the continued instability of the Nazi government — a vital point if there was to be any hope of undoing the political circle in which Hitler's ostensible invulnerability inside Germany reinforced the circumspection with which he was treated abroad and his successes in foreign policy continued to reinforce his acceptance at home — there is a haunting element to her descriptions whose meaning is also moral. The German opposition to Hitler: suppressed by the Nazis, underestimated by historians, usurped by the aristocrats: is alive in Josie's pages in very much the way it must have been: not the aristocratic resistance, the military resistance, the belated resistance of the complicit whose urns officially bear the ashes of whatever German "honor" is conceded to have survived in those years, but the plebeian resistance, the democratic resistance, the early and ordinary resistance of ordinary people whose memory has been obliterated from history as its participants were soon to be obliterated in the flesh. It may have been insufficient, but it was something. It may have been futile, but it was brave. Josie's articles, a six-installment, front-page series in the *New York Post*, reprinted as a pamphlet by the Anti-Nazi Federation in New York, played a small role in the unsuccessful international campaign to influence the democracies to apply sanctions against Hitler while there was still time, but it is as more than an artifact of a lost diplomatic possibility that they take their force. Like her articles from Cuba, Josie's series from Germany is a rare portrait of an otherwise missing moment: a kind of graveside taps ceremony: a salute, a tribute to the fallen: like a permanent bouquet of roses placed up against the fences at Auschwitz.

When Josie returned to Paris after more than a month in Germany her attention was divided, as it often had been before. On the one hand she was saturated with politics, in a blur of identification with everything she had thought, felt, seen, and heard, so much so that even her relationship with Katherine Anne was affected. On the other hand, she was worried about herself. She had expected the same satisfactions in her friend's company as she had had before, the same comfort in her surroundings, but Katherine Anne's detachment from her own political passion transfigured her very perceptions of her friend. The contentment that on her

journey into Germany had looked so enviable, now, on her journey out-
ward, appeared almost obscene. The apartment which had looked so
elegant now seemed pretentious, the circle of friends which had seemed
so sophisticated now seemed superficial, the life that had seemed full
now seemed empty, what had seemed true seemed false, what seemed
innocent, wrong, as if her very organs of sight and hearing were receiving
information in a manner different than they had before. In spite of the
fact that their friendship was in some ways deeper than it had ever been
as a result of Josie's unconcealed wretchedness and Katherine Anne's
loyal support, Josie became critical of Katherine Anne in a way she had
never previously been. If Katherine Anne prepared a festive dinner she
was gourmandizing: if she mentioned wine, she was putting on airs: if she
and her homosexual friends discussed literature and art they were "precious," as ignorant of the true conditions that make art possible as they
were of any other knowledge of the world. At a garden party held shortly
after her return she became furious with the lot of them for failing to
treat the situation in Germany with the seriousness it deserved. "My very
voice changed in their presence," she wrote Jim Farrell. "Got flat. Just
went dead. I had just returned from Germany, was still full of it. No one
asked a single question. They discussed ancient music, gossip, drawings,
etc. Many of the names constantly on their lips were the talk in 1924
when I lived abroad and it was right to be concerned about them. Now
somehow it is not right to be *only* concerned about these things. I could
not go to galleries any more as I once did although I still go now and
then. It is different. One cannot just live in the world of art when Germany and Italy have made it quite impossible for artists and writers to
live or work at all." She has left other images of herself from that same
occasion, her skirt accidentally having become unhooked, causing fastid-
ious eyebrows to be lifted in her direction, "making me continually long
to do something vulgar — fart for instance"; the conversation continuing
around the refrain "How *is* Italy? How *is* Italy" — meaning "How are all
the art restorations proceeding?" — until she wanted to cry out to stop it
that the Giotto they were so endlessly discussing would have hated their
guts, "Giotto having been an able workman, a busy man, and a democrat
through and through"; presenting herself as a kind of political mongrel at
a showing of pure-bred aesthetes, condemned to sniff out the vapors of
decadence that had somehow gone undetected before. She could argue
with them, and did, pointing to the throngs of refugees on their very
doorsteps, press them about the whereabouts of individual German and
Italian writers and artists they knew, insist that they face the realities of
the present instead of exalting the achievements of the past — "Where is
so-and-so now?" she would demand; "I suppose he is in jail," would come
the reply — but she could not make them see the situation as she did, a
frustration which only sealed her own position more strongly, and —

perhaps because of the contrast between her previous appreciation and her present indignation — in turn seems to have irritated Katherine Anne.

Yet at the same time Josie was defining herself more and more by her politics, her private sorrows absorbed her scarcely any less than before. In Munich she had not only interviewed Nazis and members of the resistance but had visited relatives of John's who lived in the vicinity, exchanging photographs with them, cuddling their babies, and otherwise constructing an illusion of a continuing family life. Another time she made a pilgrimage to the boardinghouse where he had lived before they met and she stayed there awhile "with dead John's ghost," as she put it in a letter to him, as if the fading establishment were some kind of private shrine. Alone in Paris in the apartment Katherine Anne had sublet for her from a friend, her anger against John erupted with all the bitterness of before, and she continued with a stream of denunciations of John, Ruth, and "the movement" in letters not only to John and Ruth but to "the movement" itself in the person of a woman who worked in the office of Farm Research, as if she would no sooner tear out of her typewriter one page that might contain a draft of her articles than she would roll in another on which she could vent her rage. She was tormented with loneliness, filled with sexual suffering. The wailing of cats upset her: she was envious of the lives of prostitutes: occasionally she picked up men. Once she must even have dropped a hint to Katherine Anne that a little physical comfort would do a body no harm, a hint not taken and never referred to again, though in Katherine Anne it rankled, she confessed it to Gene, and it made another edge between them on Katherine Anne's side that paralleled the one coming into being on Josie's own. In the same letters to Jim Farrell in which she criticized the revelers in the garden she gave equal attention to passionate distorted evocations of her life with John, and these letters show her as concerned above all else with the question of where and how to live again when she returned.

Alienated from the present, terrified of the future, obsessed with the past: which was it she was hearing louder, the clicking of the Nazi boots in Munich or the tapping of her own footfalls in Paris? Stalking up and down in a stranger's apartment, smoking, drunk, what was it she was really seeing, the machinery of History marching onward or the machinery of her own life breaking down? The Nuremburg Laws were promulgated shortly after Josie left Germany, but was it the tragedy of the Jews or the tragedy of herself she felt most strongly? It was easier for her to face the Nazis from behind a typewriter than it was to face her own image in the mirror just now, as if what was the onrush of fate for the Germans had been a respite from it for her, and in the heroic images of the German resistance she was fashioning was she not also fashioning, if only for her own purposes, a heroic image of herself? Shortly before Josie left Paris she witnessed the immense funeral of one of the most popular figures of the French left, the writer Henri Barbusse, and she was so moved by the outpouring of solidarity and love that she returned to the cemetery the next day with Katherine Anne to leave bouquets of red and purple asters on his grave. Again her dedication was strengthened. Josephine Herbst was as genuine an opponent as Nazism ever had, at least among those who were neither German nor Jew, and she did as much as she could to help defeat it. Still it is fair to ask the questions: how much? in what ways exactly? did she care what was happening in Germany. For that matter, how much did anyone?

## CHAPTER TWENTY-ONE

# "Custer's Last Stand"

WHEN JOSIE returned from Europe in September, 1935, she was entering a far from pleasant situation. Political disagreements among the writers and intellectuals she knew were not as rancorous as they later became, nor as weighty, but already there was a suspiciousness to the atmosphere that made relationships far more complicated than before. Defection and the fear of defection were already in the air: already if X lunched with Y too often at the Brevoort it was not so much a friendship as a faction that was perceived by the passersby: already there was such a profusion of private motives behind public actions and public motives behind private ones that to distinguish when one was being courted personally from when one was being courted politically was no easy matter, yet it was a distinction no one — particularly no woman — could ever afford to ignore. Privately shaky and yet publicly much in demand, Josie was in a particularly vulnerable position. After a brief period of sharing a small apartment in the city with Jim Farrell and an actress named Hortense Alden, whom he later married, she retreated to Yaddo where a small number of writers, including John Cheever and Nathan Asch, were spending the winter, but she was frequently called upon to make speeches, help raise money, or come to meetings, and she more or less commuted to New York. Previously she had scorned such activities as much for their ceremonial and bureaucratic emptiness as for their polemical spirit. Now it was not only all the radical movement had to offer her: it was all she had.

Nothing better illustrates the convergence of the political and the personal that characterized the period than the stories of Josie's relationships with James Farrell and William Phillips. Indeed in a certain sense it is a single story for the friendships rose and fell against the backdrop of a single season, the winter of 1935–1936, they were affected by the same issues, and they came to their conclusions, albeit for different reasons, at approximately the same time. In fact it was Farrell who introduced Josie to Phillips, shortly after her return from Europe, probably in November, 1935. At the time of their meeting William Phillips was a young man in his twenties who had entered the radical movement via the New York John Reed Club and with another young man, Philip Rahv — Malcolm Cowley called them "the kids" — was attempting to transform its magazine, the *Partisan Review*, into a journal which, while still within the Communist Party orbit, would, unlike the political *New Masses*, focus primarily on literature. It was a project with which Josie felt an immediate kinship. "Politics is about swamping literature and the Partisan Rev. is an attempt for Custer's Last Stand," she told Katherine Anne. To help it along she initiated contacts on *PR*'s behalf with friends and acquaintances such as John Dos Passos and Edmund Wilson; she attempted to help raise money; she read and criticized some of Phillips' early articles; and in the issues that were published before its suspension at the end of 1936 and subsequent reincarnation as a Trotskyist journal the following year, she had several contributions of her own. But while her interest in the *Partisan* was perfectly consistent with her positions on literature and politics dating back a long while, her interest in Phillips personally was another matter, for if Phillips saw Josie as an important established writer whose support would be valuable in helping get the magazine off the ground, Josie saw Phillips as a very attractive young man. If he pursued her primarily for his political purposes, squiring her about the city when she came to New York, coming to see her, writing her letters in which flattery and solicitation are so disingenuously mingled that it would have taken a far less needy woman than Josie was at that point to sort them out, she responded not only without restraint but without consideration, ignoring the fact of his wife, keeping him up late at night talking, flirting with him with her mind, pouring into him as if he were a suitable vessel all the intimate feelings of her life since John — and then blasting him when he did not respond. Between her loneliness and his ambition their letters rapidly reached a crescendo of misunderstanding, and it is perhaps not surprising that after a few intense encounters at Yaddo and in New York their association came to an embarrassing conclusion of which Phillips would retain little recollection, but which Josie would remember all her life.

In her friendship with Jim Farrell a different set of misunderstandings developed. Farrell was not yet a Trotskyist but he was increasingly antagonistic to the cultural politics of the Communist Party which tended to endorse books either for their proletarian authorship or their political line, and believing that "the only way the ring of driveling mediocrity in our reviewing and criticism can be broken down is by a knock-down-and-drag-out fight," as he wrote Josie in January, 1936 — and having a combative disposition — he decided to start one. In late 1935 and early 1936 he wrote a number of unfavorable reviews of Communist favorites including one of Clara Weatherwax's *Marching! Marching!* — which he privately called "Stumbling, Stumbling" — that in one way or another all challenged the prevailing line. When an attack on Clifford Odets' *Awake and Sing* — this one Farrell called "Lay Down and Die" — provoked in turn an attack on himself by longtime Communist literary spokesman Mike Gold which also seemed to be attacking the very existence of criticism within the radical movement, Josie, at Yaddo, and a group of other writers including Phillips, Rahv, Nathan Asch, Horace Gregory, and Albert Bein, sent off letters of protest and the fight was on, but it was almost as quickly off because the show of division so disturbed the editors of the *New Masses* that they urged Josie to come down from Yaddo for a special meeting to straighten things out. Who persuaded whom of what and by which arguments there is no direct record but as a result of the meeting the group protest was abandoned altogether and when Josie's letter, altered to exclude a reference to Mike Gold's "anti-intellectualism" as "fascist," which seems to have been the key point, was published in the *New Masses* on March 10, 1936, it was followed by a rejoinder from Gold. Farrell was disappointed. He had "loved" the "punch" of the first letter, felt that she had let it become "emasculated," and told her she had been "out-maneuvered by the boys." Forty years later he was still much concerned with the event, keeping a copy of her original letter at his fingertips and carefully instructing students of his politics, as well as hers, in his analysis of what he now called her "Stalinism."* Josie too was much distressed by what had happened. Although at first she defended herself, telling Farrell she was "amazed that you can think it possible to be let down by the kind of reply I made," within a few days she conceded that she had indeed been "outwitted"; and years later she too continued to brood about it, even writing one of Farrell's biographers in 1957 that although "I was persuaded to take out the word 'fascist' . . . because I was already tired of these words slung about [and] could even ask myself how much or how

* I have frequently been asked during the course of this work whether or not Josie was a "Stalinist" and there are those who believe, primarily on the basis of her connection with the Communist Party during this period, that she was. If her relationship to the American Communist Party and in turn its relationship to the Soviet Union automatically makes her a Stalinist, so be it, but for her long record of independent thought and action — albeit in association with the Communist Party — for my part I find "Stalinism" not only a meaningless, but, indeed, a misleading description.

little my own use of [it] meant," nevertheless, from this episode, "dated my own withdrawal" from the movement. While Josie's friendship with Farrell did not completely falter afterward, nor their mutual respect ever, from that moment on, it did begin to dwindle and die down.

What Josie concluded from the Farrell-Gold imbroglio was that politics was essentially beyond her. "I am inclined to agree with you about the business really not being on the level." "I have no business to play with them and don't intend to." "I don't know politics and don't want to. But I have learned a damned good lesson," she confided to Farrell. But "politics" was everywhere. Between the spontaneous mobilization of the people on their own behalf, which invariably thrilled her, and the direction of those protests toward specific ends by the Communist Party, there was a level of organization which was, precisely, "political," and this she invariably despised. "Came back from the marble strike area late last night," she wrote William Phillips in late February, 1936.

> The strikers were swell. They had a big meeting — two of them — in a union hall. I hadn't realized ahead of time what it was all about and found myself in the midst of the goddamned New York committee. Some of them are o k — Max Lerner's wife was there and she is very real, capable and all right but I wish you could have heard the speech that Rockwell Kent made. I wanted to sink through the floor. He patronized the strikers, and ended by calling them poor devils. But he gave them $100 so they cheered him. Percy Shostac made the most revolting speech I ever sat through telling the strikers all about the great celebrities that had actually gone out of their way to notice them. I was so angry I got up and left the stage and went into the wings where a marble worker was sitting in overalls with the swellest little kid on his lap. I had a chocolate bar in my pocketbook and gave it to the kid. The purpose of the visit was to "investigate", the first time I ever witnessed such a business. I think it will really help but I am so tired of petty striving ambitious little nobodies parading around and pushing. It was so funny. They wanted me to make a speech but I refused. I just didn't want to get up and call them "You" and if I couldn't identify myself with them I didn't want to say anything. All the other smuggies got up and told them "to fight" etc etc ad nauseam.

Another political irritant was the attitude of the Party not so much to the workers as to non-Communist, middle-class, intellectuals and professionals whose reputations were thought to be useful to the cause, and their relationship to followers such as herself. A case in point had to do with a project to create a new radical magazine of particular interest to women, to be called *The Woman Today*. Typical of many such efforts during the Popular Front period, the impetus for its establishment came from the Communist Party, but it was not to be an exclusively Communist operation, and the intention was to make it as broad in appeal and as popular in appearance as possible. The idea was that the appearance of influential writers in the magazine would induce the public to take it seriously and in turn that a magazine taken seriously by the public would be worthwhile for the Party to control. In this case the quarry were the most popular women writers of the day, including Pearl Buck, Kathleen Norris, Mary Roberts Rinehart, Fannie Hurst, Edna Ferber, and Dorothy Canfield Fisher. The project was proceeding on a kind of magnet theory of politics characteristic of the Popular Front. As a writer who was close enough to the Party to understand the value of the project and associate herself with it and yet respected enough beyond the left to be able to approach the popular writers on an equal footing, Josie was asked to send a letter to them inviting their participation, or, more precisely, to sign such a letter to them which someone else in the Party offices would draft. The draft letter, sent to her at Yaddo by a woman named Margaret Cowl, read:

> *December 7, 1935*
>
> *Dear Miss (name of writer)*
>
> *Believing there is a need of a publication that will discuss events and conditions in relation to and its effect upon women, a group of writers including the undersigned, Josephine Herbst and other famous women authors have organized to publish such a magazine.*
>
> *The editors intend to present articles with the express purpose of drawing women into the common fight for peace, for the defense of women's rights, and the fight against fascism. It will support the movement of women into the trade unions; demand equal pay for equal work; the right of married women to work. It will support concerted action by women's organizations for equal rights for women. It will wage a forceful campaign for the repeal of Section 213 of the National Economy act; it will co-operate with organizations fighting for the lowering of the high cost of living; it will promote cooperative efforts by various organizations for the maintenance of peace.*
>
> *This magazine will also include fiction, articles on health hygiene, fashions, cooking recipes, and other articles of feminine interest. A special department will feature letters from women (My Problems) and answers.*
>
> *Knowing that you are in sympathy with our aims, may I ask you to contribute to the success of this significant undertaking by*

*contributing a short story? The value of such a story by (author's name) would add immeasurably to the dignity and interest of our magazine.*

*Will you please write me if I can expect a contribution. I am hoping to begin our issue with a (          ) story of about 2000 words.*

*Thanking you.*

*Sincerely*

The identical letter, with a change only in the final paragraphs, was to be sent to a number of other well-known women being asked to serve on the Advisory Board, including Carrie Chapman Catt, Susan La Follette, Meta Berger, Mrs. Norman Thomas, Margaret Sanger, Mary Beard — or, as the notation to Josie on the top reads, "Etc."

Josie was apoplectic. "I am dead set against the letter to be sent to writers," she replied the same afternoon, as if she could scarcely contain her frustration with such amateurish fumbling.

This particular letter would, in my opinion, draw not a single response. It seems to me a mistake to imagine that merely because we want to draw these names into our work we can do so on our terms. The slogans that we have, as outlined in the letter, will only mean repetitious aims, and there is not in the letter one single direct appeal to the class of women called upon to respond. The assumption, contained in the last paragraph, that they would even send us a contribution, is preposterous. They will throw such a letter away. I would under no circumstances put my name to such a letter as it would be throwing away whatever chance I might have to accomplish something with these people.

These women can only be reached on a somewhat snobbish basis. They are popular writers and therefore respect an intellectual approach. If they are to be reached it seems to me necessary that we have at once some names for contributors that will impress them. . . . Concrete details such as this should be written within the letter. The letter should be very well written, informally, to give the effect of a real contact. As a matter of fact it is, in my opinion, useless to expect these women to reply unless some pains are taken. They should be written individual letters, to the extent at least that one paragraph seems to be written for them. The letter should really have in it the enthusiasm of someone who visualizes in this magazine a new outlet not only for the aims as outlined . . . but an outlet also for women writers who want to say many things often denied them in the regular channels.

You have not told me who the editorial board is and that is

highly important. The first paragraph of the letter would kill everything. I would not sign a letter with the phrase "other famous women" — no other woman should. The approach must be a taken for granted one, a very simple direct approach. . . . Also the next to last paragraph, like the first, is completely lacking in taste. One can not lay flattery on that thick with these people and have it mean anything. It all sounds too much like a circular letter asking for endorsements to cold creams. . . .

The manipulation of the famous: the haste and sloppiness with which many projects were conceived and put through: a kind of unthinking half-heartedness in which others were expected to be roused to action by rhetoric that the organizers considered a bore: this was one of the patterns of Communist activity during the Popular Front period — a pattern that *The Woman Today* story exactly fits — and it was one that Josie frequently saw repeated. Like others whose relationship to the Party was largely nonorganizational, she was torn between her identification with the purposes for which it was working and her scepticism about the way it went about getting things done. What was true of its attitude toward projects was also true of its attitudes toward people. The organizations and committees which openly solicited the use of one's name as the magazine had Josie's were not necessarily the most typical of the organizations of the '30s —: there were also the ones that didn't ask. Labor support committees, consumer committees, foreign policy committees, literary committees, film-making and film-distributing committees, anti-Fascist committees of innumerable kinds, were in a constant process of creation and cessation during this period and they all took their quotas of names for their letterheads. If your name appeared on the letterhead of a particular organization you were not expected to take any responsibility for its operation, merely to lend your prestige, and the less doubt you expressed about the system the better your reputation for reliability. But once you were on one list you were on them all, and between the transformation of one committee into another with a slightly different name, which happened often, and the genuinely new organizations always in the process of formation, the results in the case of any one person could be amazing. Josie was on the letterheads of the Prisoners Relief Fund, the National Committee for the Defense of Political Prisoners, the League of Women Shoppers, the League of American Writers, the Anti-Fascist Literature Committee, Frontier Films and perhaps a half-dozen other such outfits, all dominated by the Party, with whose day-to-day operations and overall policies she had nothing whatever to do — not even to mention the innumerable petitions of protest and denunciation among whose signers her name often appeared — and she was one of whom relatively sparing use was made. If you were willing at all to lend your support to the movement your name followed forever and you never knew exactly what organizations it had supported, what causes it had endorsed, or in what circumstances it was going to end up — one of the reasons why the very different committees of the 1950s could have such a field day. The *naming* of the 1950s was the mirror-image of the *listing* of the 1930s. Josie found the entire situation upsetting. "It seems to me altogether a wrong policy to connect my name with anything I cannot be actively identified with.... If I give my name to many projects ... I gradually make it so cheap it has no meaning," she complained in the letter to Margaret Cowl. "I am trying to get out of being on boards and committees etc where I am only a name — I dont want to be a front — if I cant actually work on all these things I gradually become a stuffed shirt and christ I'd rather be dead," she told William Phillips at about the same time.

Yet whatever her criticisms of the Communist movement, if ever there was a moment in Josie's life when she was so close to the Party that to say she was not "in" it would be to insist upon a legalistic distinction, now was the time. If the term "fellow-traveler" implies a distance from the center of things, she was more than a fellow-traveler. Her very criticisms, in fact, emerged from and were directed toward the inside. Precisely how she was regarded by the political leaders of the Party such as Earl Browder or by its intellectual and cultural officials such as Alexander Trachtenberg or V. J. Jerome there is no direct evidence, but the indirect evidence is that everyone assumed she was one of them. Mother Bloor and many lesser Communists addressed her as "Comrade." She was the nominal treasurer of a committee of intellectuals supporting the 1936 Communist presidential ticket of Browder and Ford. Her continuing relationships with Joe and Helen North, or with Mike Gold, or Joe Freeman, had a naturalness about them even when they disagreed that would have been impossible if they had thought her to be in any fundamental sense opposed to what they believed. Nor did she trouble to differentiate herself from them: the "we" was fine with her: "we" old friends, "we" the political cadre, "we" the harbingers of a just revolutionary future, "we" the Party. When she wrote Margaret Cowl about *The Woman Today* it was "our work" and "our movement" that she was referring to. As a result not only of her past work but of her continuing appearances in the pages of the radical magazines — and in the flesh — she was seen throughout the myriad networks of the movement if not as a heroine, at least as a leading lady, and as the Communists grew more powerful in the period of the Popular Front, her reputation spread. Under the circumstances, her identification with the radical movement was probably her greatest comfort. To appear on a platform in any city, any town, and sense within your eager audience the presence not of strangers but of comrades with whose efforts you believe the most ancient struggle of humanity against exploitation can be won is small compensation for the kinds of specific losses Josie was struggling with, but it is a real satisfaction nonetheless and it is one that she frequently had. A strike meeting could lead to conversations with the strikers or with their families, conversations to dinner or a cup of coffee, coffee to one of those ebullient all-night gatherings in which the very fate of the world appears to be in the hands of the talkers, a kind of gathering in which Josie got some of her strongest confirmations, not so much as a writer, but as a human being. Speechmaking, even "investigating," drumming up support for the *Partisan* or the *New Masses:* in all these things there was a sense of relatedness, of connectedness, of participation with others in a vital human enterprise. A letter from a reader in Nebraska: a discussion with a waitress in Saratoga: a meeting with some revolutionary students at Bennington: these things reminded Josie that there was a place for her in this world, that people looked for her work and responded to it, that there was a very substantial audience for the things she had to say. In her "politics" she found a certain amount of strength.

In March, 1936, Josie got the first good news that had arrived in a long while, the award of a Guggenheim Fellowship "in the field of the novel" — $2,000 — which, while not a great fortune, to Josie was a gift of at least temporary security. Although at first she conceived a grand plan to travel to South America by herself, she soon thought better of it and decided instead — as she wrote Katherine Anne — "to look the ogre in the face" and return to Erwinna and settle down. It was an awesome prospect with the house as decrepit as it was but somehow, after the snow melted, she was able to get it prepared and by late spring, 1936, she was back in her own house once more. The months that followed her return to the country were relatively peaceful ones. Partly for the money and partly for the company she invited two other writers who had been at Yaddo to join her — Nathan Asch, with whom she had a never-intensifying but always-enduring familial friendship, and Eleanor Clark, a much younger woman whom she had only recently met — and they all worked rigorously on their respective projects, Josie in the main house, Nathan in the chicken coop, and Eleanor in the barn, coming together in the evenings for dinner and conversation, three mendicants pooling their poverty in a mainly compatible fashion. If anything could illustrate Josie's relative aloofness from the factionalism starting to pervade the movement it is in fact just this relationship with Eleanor Clark, for Eleanor was a Trotskyist and Josie, generally speaking, defended Party positions, and despite the fact that this was the moment when these divisions were beginning to come to the surface, it was also the moment that their friendship took root. In the Soviet Union the first of the major purge trials that would permanently alter the way the world understood Communism were just getting started: in Spain the Fascist generals had begun their uprising against the Republican state: but in Erwinna, for the moment, the focus was largely personal. There are few traces in the residues of the summer of the upheavals that would later seem to have dominated the time. The garden blossomed, the chipmunks chattered, the copperheads slithered on the banks of the streams once more. When fall came and her friends had left her, Josie was flooded with loneliness again. Her niece, Betty Hansen, Alice's daughter, came east from Sioux City to join her for a while, looking like an incarnation of Josie's mother, Mary, with the family's blue eyes and red hair, but even though Josie had urged her to visit, Betty found her distracted and preoccupied and she did not stay as long as she had planned. A visit with Katherine Anne who was separating from Gene and had come to stay at an inn in Bucks County in order to work must also have been unsatisfactory, for though there is no evidence of a quarrel in their own correspondence, Katherine Anne wrote to Gene with a string of complaints about everything from Josie's voice to her driving, none of which seem ever to have bothered her before. Sometime during this period there was also a brief affair with a woman, an Erwinna neighbor, an affair which, while not documented in letters, was observed by both John Cheever and another neighbor. Fall faded. Intimations of winter were in the air. Although she had drafted several hundred pages of what was to be the final volume of her trilogy, she was finding it difficult to continue. It seemed pointless to be wrestling with isolation in the country when political events were rising to a peak of intensity both at home and abroad and she decided to join Mary Vorse on a trip to Flint, Michigan, where the occupation by the auto workers of a General Motors plant had just gotten under way. Moved as always by the strikers, her spirits momentarily returned. She would write a play about the demonstration, she thought, and even contracted to do one; she would incorporate the strikers into her book; but at home again her energy for writing faltered and the same mood assailed her as before. Whatever fortification she had gathered, it was not enough. As 1936 ended and the winter spread out before her there was a three-way internal contest. She could stay in Erwinna, just to prove she could do it. She could return to Yaddo or New York. Or she could do something else. From all over the world volunteers mobilized by the Communist Party were pouring into Spain to help the Spanish Republicans in their desperate struggle against the Fascist armies already on the very outskirts of Madrid, and it was tempting to want to be among them. Sitting at the familiar trestle table alone one day, her head in her hands, tired of herself, her morass, frustrated with the violent alternations in her spirit, with her inability to get anything done, Josie found herself with the same question she had asked so often before in her life, not only with John but before him: *"For this?"*: and in that invisible moment in which asking is its own answer: *"No, not for this.":* it is decided: she will go to Spain: if for no other reason, then as she says in the memoir which she finally managed to write about it years later, *"Because."* Of her relationship to the Communist Party on the eve of her departure for Spain there is perhaps no truer symbol than the fact that (a) she rented her house for the winter to the grand old lady of the Communist Party, Hal Ware's mother, Mother Bloor, who promptly took down all Josie's belongings from the walls and replaced them with pictures of Lenin, Stalin, Bill Haywood, Walt Whitman, Angelo Herndon and one after another of her own children and grandchildren; and (b) that the two women quarreled bitterly before Josie was even out the door.

## CHAPTER TWENTY-TWO

# Song of Spain

ONE DAY when I had been working on Josie's biography for several years I was sitting alone at the Oregon seacoast cabin thinking about Josie in Spain and feeling particularly dissatisfied with everything I had done. I had already written two versions. The first was a deliberately theatrical affair in which I had introduced the whole glittering array of characters who had populated the Spanish war and placed them against the political background. In the second I had started with a somber photograph of Josie and described that. The trouble with these two versions was not that they were not true to Josie or even that they were not true to Spain. Between the political passions and the geographic setting, the story of Spain was dramatic enough, as the very quality of all the writing about it testifies, and the photograph of Josie — sallow, unsmiling — I had always found particularly haunting. But they both left me someplace I did not want to be. In the play all the characters were so noble, or else so sinister, that once I had gotten them onstage I could simply not get them acting human again. In the photograph Josie appeared so desolate it was hard to bring her back into line with other people's recollections of how strong she had actually been. Walking along the beach to clear my head I found I was thinking not directly about Spain but about a conference on writers of the thirties I had gone to in Alabama sometime before. One evening a few participants in the meeting including its one genuine writer-of-the-thirties, who had been one of Josie's friends, a scholar of the thirties to whose work she had made a small contribution, and myself, had been invited to dinner at the home of one of the members of the university faculty. During dinner, the conversation had shifted to current topics — to Cuba, if I was recalling it correctly, or possibly China. Some writer of the others' acquaintance had recently been there and turned in a glowing report and the two of them were tearing him apart. "It's the thirties all over again," said the writer. "All that 'I have seen the future and it works.'" "Indeed," agreed the scholar. "The sixties were the same way," and he called the roll of distinguished American writers who had "compromised themselves" "forever" in his view by writing favorably about the North Vietnamese during the war. There followed the familiar denunciations. The intellectual world was peopled with sentimental muddleheads whose hearts were stronger than their brains. Could they not smell corruption when Power reeking with human blood was dragging itself right beneath their noses? Was there no skepticism? Was there still no moral discrimination? Would there never be any learning from the past? The only younger person present besides myself was the faculty member who had organized the conference. He had also been involved in the radical movement of the 1960s and he and I took the part of the radical writers of both the earlier and the later periods. I had personally once been a member of an American peace delegation meeting with the Vietnamese in Budapest during the height of the American bombing and I remember trying to explain how the power of such an occasion draws one in. Our arguments were scarcely heard, which for some reason reminded me of one of Josie's old high school debating topics: "Resolved, that if a Russian had had the Advantages of an American he would have been Equal in Rank." There was no doubt about it: the elders still held sway. Back at the hotel I avenged myself not by improving my own arguments but by improvising Josie's. She would have been loud, even thunderous, even violent, if she had been there, of that I was sure, for by the time she reached the ages of the gentlemen in question she was reckless in argument and I knew how passionately she would have disagreed. It was the same catechism she had been hearing at least since the end of the 1930s and she had said her piece about it many times. I could practically see her overturning the hominy and starting a scene, shouting out from the living room that it was they who were the historical illiterates who had forgotten whatever they had once known about everything that had been happening at the time, and yes, she had been sceptical, yes, she had moral discrimination, yes, she was continually learning from the past. Yet despite the consolation of such daydreams, the argument could hardly be settled so privately. Why was it so endlessly compelling? Why could it never be resolved? And what did it have to do with my difficulties writing about Spain? Far off in the back of my mind, from long before I had begun my actual chapter on Spain, there was an idea I had rejected many times, but in the aftermath of my Alabama reverie it returned again until finally I thought I understood why. It had something to do with the question of belief. Josie had believed before she went to Spain: she believed while she was in Spain: and she believed after she came back. *What* she believed exactly was difficult to categorize for it contained many contradictions: it was the state of believing itself that was important. Without feeling, she always insisted, you could explain nothing about the 1930s. Without recalling it, my readers could understand nothing of Josie's experiences in Spain. Perhaps I could have realized this earlier when I was lunching with an editor who had just decided against republishing Josie's Spanish memoir. "I just don't get it," he said to me exasperatedly. "What was it she was actually *doing* in Spain?" Which had reminded me of a time before that when another editor, reading a manuscript of my own about the 1960s, had said "I just don't get it exactly. What was it you were actually *doing* in the movement?" Now I *knew* what I was doing in the movement and I *knew* what Josie was doing in Spain, and if there was someone who had read her pages or mine and did not know, it was exactly this state of being that had to be explored. It was about the relationship between individual experiences and common ones: about the internal uses of external experiences and the external uses of internal ones: about the fact that within public experiences are private ones which political criticism never really touches. "There were two major reasons for my being there," wrote Alvah Bessie, an American volunteer, in *Men in Battle*, "to achieve self-integration, and to lend my individual strength (such as it was) to the fight against our eternal enemy — oppression; and the validity of the second reason was not impaired by the fact that it was a shade weaker than the first, for they were both a part of the same thing." En route to Spain Josie had written to Elizabeth Ames, director of Yaddo, that she intended to write about courage, "about the Spain that is living, in spite of the dying . . . how people hold together, live & eat & sleep under the barrage of fear": it was courage that impressed her while she was in Spain: it was courage she remembered when she returned. Nearly thirty years later when she wrote to Ilsa Barea, who, with her husband, Arturo, had directed the censorship office in Madrid, that Spain "put iron into me at a moment when I needed iron," it was something about endurance that she meant. It was beyond dinner-table argument. As far as the political issues were concerned anything simple about Josie's Spanish experiences ended almost before she had left. Forces were operating, events were occurring, and facts were emerging which made it impossible for her to see things as she had seen them before. But as far as her own personal experiences were concerned, nothing altered. Feeling was feeling — and it endured.

"Don't expect an analysis of events," she warned in her memoir. "I couldn't do it then, I can't now." Rarely did she write more honest lines.

Her journal is a useful measure of her confusion. Unlike many of the others she kept during her life, this one is strangely incoherent. It begins after she had been there for three weeks, more is attributed to one date than could possibly have taken place on it, and she wrote in it not systematically on consecutive pages but randomly, anywhere at all, as if she felt she could simply reach into her knapsack and pull out the notebook and write and the order would have no bearing on the point. A page somewhere toward the end is headed "Notes." It reads:

1. Ask Hem to explain who is fighting where.
2. Find out about women movement.
3. How much food allowed each day.
4. Health situation (?)
5. Tribune the people
6. *Hospitals*
7. *Get goatskin for wine*
9. What about court martial? Discipline?
10. Tribunals. Death penalty. Terror.
11. Composition of army = no of brigades etc
12. Shock troops in factories.
13. Collectives — cooperatives
14. Women's movement

In this sequence number 10 repeats number 5, number 14 repeats number 2, number 8 is simply not there at all and the most prominent item is probably number 7: *Get goatskin for wine.* I have a sense of her reaching out grabbing for things as they go by not catching them: the person passed over as the goatskin swings by. Other aspects of her trip to Spain have the same vaguely incorporeal character. In no place else in her papers are the details concerning practical matters so few. Usually there are a hundred clues contributing to the reconstruction of what she did, but here it is as if the physical details did not matter to her. I know that she sailed for Spain on March 19, 1937, and stopped in Paris, that on April 1 she was issued a Safe Conduct pass from Valencia to Madrid, and that at least by April 20 she was very much involved in the life of Madrid as if she had already been there for some time, but I do not know whether she entered Spain legally or illegally, how she got to Valencia or just what she did there, or for that matter how she got to Madrid. The same inattention to ordinary detail that characterized the logistics of her journey characterized her also while she was there. It is not only that I do not happen to know where she was when: it is rather that she often did not seem to know herself. Everything made her think of something else. Her writings are almost as full of Iowa as they are of Spain. The sound of shelling reminded her of an Iowa thunderstorm. Her hunger brought on dreams of her mother's bread. Even her own deepest reasons for being there in the first place had something to do with a conversation she had once had with Mary about nobility in the face of disaster and the way that conversation lingered in her head. One scene was a Breughel for her, another a Fra Angelico, the next a naive reenactment of a vision from the Quaker Edward Hicks. The whole experience had a fermented quality to it: and not only because of the wine. When I think of Josie in Spain I see that omnipresent but uncomprehending character, more eyes than flesh, who haunts our images of every war, wandering through the action directionless, almost deranged, looking for a meaning to what was happening that the events as they unfolded would not necessarily yield. Later she would distill it into the supple and beautiful memoir she called "The Starched Blue Sky of Spain," but for now it was an intense unintelligible blur. For most of the time she was in the midst of the action the fact of the matter is that she was lost.

The sources of Josie's confusion were partly political, partly military, and partly practical. That the war in Spain was part of the general struggle against Fascism and that the refusal of the democracies to assist the Republic was enhancing the influence of the Soviet Union, which did — that much she well understood; but the actual workings of Spanish politics presented themselves as an incomprehensible welter of parties and unions whose initials varied from region to region and whose positions constantly shifted, and her knowledge of the external situation did not clarify her understanding of the internal one very well. The military situation too was graspable in a general way for during the period Josie was there it consisted largely of the defense of Madrid, but between the government forces, the international brigades, and the militias of the individual parties — not to mention their periodic reorganization — the command situation was sufficiently chaotic to explain the Communist call for centralization and to ask Hemingway — or anyone — "who is fighting where" was to ask a very sensible question. Her immediate situation was also bewildering. Too distracted before she left to pursue a newspaper assignment — a self-indulgence she later regretted — her press credentials rested on vague expressions of interest from a handful of magazines which more or less consigned her to the "human interest" department. "Get the women's angle on Spain" is practically what they said. It was an inertia with serious consequences for her status in Spain. Throughout the war zone the fundamental necessities of the press were in short supply. There were few cars with which to get to the scene of the action. Gasoline, drivers, interpreters, the attention of Republican officials — all were sparse. Most of the time the correspondents from even the most influential papers were stuck in Madrid. The independents, like Josie, had the least mobility of all. Madrid was under constant bombardment from the encircling Fascists, being confined to it like sud-

denly becoming a trapped animal, continuously stalked. Every day people were being killed just in the normal course of things: buying a newspaper, standing in food queues, crossing the street. The correspondents
who filed the regular dispatches on which the Republic was counting to
bare its desperation to the world at least had a daily ritual out of which
they could manufacture for themselves the illusion of order. There was a
press headquarters to report to, articles to be struggled with, censors to
be placated, cables to be filed, a growling editor at the other end of the
line wanting to know what the hell was happening over there; but for
Josie for long periods there was no editor wanting anything, there was no
audience, the days were empty except for pointless rambles around the
city, the nights were terrifying, there was nothing to do except concentrate fearfully on staving off fear. Another element of her lot was as unfamiliar to her as her sense of irrelevance: in a word, the competition. In
most of her work, journalism as well as fiction, she had been the only
person doing what she was doing, or at any rate one of few. Who else
could write a trilogy about the Frey family? How many had covered the
Iowa farm strikes? What reporter had looked at Cuba, or for that matter
Germany, the way that she had? But Madrid was positively streaming
with reporters. There were American reporters, European reporters, and
Oriental reporters; there were news agency reporters, news magazine reporters, and newsreel reporters; there were male reporters and there
were female reporters; there were professional reporters and there were
amateur reporters; reporters reporters reporters: to look at some of their
recollections you would sometimes think that reporters were all there
were in Spain. They all lived together at the Hotel Florida on the Plaza
de Callao, ate together at a communal table in the basement of a Gran
Vía restaurant, observed the same incidents together, repeated the same
anecdotes together, kept track of the shelling together, clucked over the
rubble together, and they all studied one another like crows. Contacts
could be shared or not shared, rumors could be passed along or withheld,
an invitation to a particular correspondent to ride along here or there
with a particular official could be extended to include another correspondent or it could be reserved: it all depended. What were the threads
that bound together the correspondents in Spain into their tight little
nest? The strands were as much private as they were political. Who was
flirting with whom? Who was sleeping with whom? Who was funnier
than whom? Who was louder than whom? Who was respected by whom?
Who was trusted by whom? Who was last seen with whom? Who would
next be with whom? Whatever were the ties that held the correspondents together in Spain they had as much to do with the motions of the
flock itself as with the turnings of the earth beneath it. It was precisely
the kind of self-referring formation Josie had always tried to avoid in
New York and now in Madrid she was right in the middle of it.

If there was one member of the flock whose position she eyed more covetously than any other it was probably its captain, her old friend, Ernest Hemingway. All the competition she had ever felt for men in general she felt for Hemingway in Spain. He was the last person to whom she would have wanted to admit her confusion and, living down the hall from one another, they saw each other all the time. The contrast between their present situations was immense. Whatever the rules that applied to all the other correspondents in Spain, Hemingway was the exception to them. If they had a room: he had a suite. If they had no cars: he had two. He had sex: his affair with Martha Gellhorn. He had food: delicacies scavenged for him by his aide Sidney Franklin. He had friends: even the Russians liked him. He even had more reasons for being there than anybody else: deliverer of ambulances, correspondent for NANA, writer for *Esquire*, entrepreneur of the important propaganda film *The Spanish Earth*. Fame, fortune, a marriage, a mistress, even for the time being a purpose: Hemingway had them all. Next to him Josie was not only statusless and loverless: she was marginal. But it was not only the present Josie had to contend with in relation to Hemingway. It was the past. They had started out equal; they had known one another a long time; they were the kind of friends who, altogether without trying, knew more about one another than they necessarily wished. "Sometimes I wondered about Pauline and what was to happen" she wrote in a draft of her memoir many years later, "but nothing could be confronted outright, but had to leak in, as it might. As once when I had finally told him about John who was now gone from my life, and he had answered soberly, 'You were a good wife, a very good wife to John.' I couldn't resist answering, 'That doesn't mean a thing. You ought to know. Hadley was a good wife, too.' He had not answered directly but had looked thoughtfully out of the window, and only later that day popped the question 'What do you think of Martha?' When I replied that I . . . really knew nothing about her . . . he pounced back with 'But you don't know much about women. How could you? You're always with men.' " It was easy to be moralistic about his luxuries just as it was easy to be moralistic about his lusts but it was hardly an aspect of herself that she liked and she criticized herself for criticizing him as much as she criticized him. She was continually comparing herself to him, not in the spirit of novelistic inquiry into character she always relished but in just the spirit of petty psychological warfare she always despised. Her journal is full of references to him. Whether a particular opportunity comes her way because of Hemingway or in spite of him — she writes it down. When she loses in the physical strength contest, having to be carried across a damaged bridge over rushing water, she writes "Can't make it. Hem the strong man carries over." After a lunch at a brigade headquarters in which Hemingway is the center of attention, she writes "Hem good guy but I am going nuts at this fetish business." "Is it sour grapes?" she questions herself, and concludes "perhaps" but the contest continued. When she lost her voice in front of him in a moment of panic during a violent bombardment she described it so many times that I suspect she carried the shame of it to her grave.

Nor were the other threads of her life superseded simply because there was a war of principle going on. Some of them were more continuous than she would have wished. First there was the problem of her history, especially her history with John. With all the writers and intellectuals she knew there, she was always encountering some embodiment of the past. Then there was the problem of isolation. Cut off already from the people at home she was cut off still more by the objective situation: hardly anyone got letters from Josie in Spain. Another problem was the problem of sex. Given the fear, given the pressure, it was a time when for many people another body was a friend in need, but for Josie the very suggestion of desire only seemed to make her feel worse. A Hungarian commander, a Russian general, an American soldier: in part because of the shortage of women she was pursued all the time but she found she could only say no. For this too she rebuked herself. "A man about to die and she could not give to him what she had given to so many . . ." she wrote of one of her followers in a fragment among her papers at Yale. If it was deliverance from herself she was seeking in Spain, in Madrid at least it was not going to be easy to come by.

It was mainly when she was out of the city away from the claustrophobic intimacies of the hotel that Josie could feel connection with the fundamental political convictions that had brought her to Spain. In his autobiography, *The Owl of Minerva*, her friend, Gustav Regler, whom she first got to know in Spain, recalls standing in the woods on the outskirts of Madrid on a morning shortly after his arrival when he had just learned that a special Soviet mission had arrived in the city to begin funneling aid to the isolated Republic. Regler was a German Communist who had been in Moscow during the first purge trials the previous summer, had seen the very vans in which Kamenev and the other old Bolsheviks had arrived at the jail, and he knew better than most people — certainly he knew better than Josie — the terrible complications inherent in the news. "The good Russia had arrived," he remembered thinking. "Would the diabolical Russia follow?" In the field the good was plentiful: the good Russia: the good Spain: the good of the whole international radical movement as it had filtered down to ordinary people during the years since the Russian revolution: and it was mainly the good that Josie saw. It is probably impossible to recapture the special quality of her experiences there or why they mattered to her so much or to characterize the way individuals famous and humble glittered against the backdrop of the war. The world is too cynical now: at least the world of anyone reading this book. We have examined all the elements of the Spanish war so thoroughly that what it seemed to be while it was happening has been practically destroyed. Yet if the sleep of reason produces monsters the dream of revolution produces heroes and in a chronological sense the Spanish war occurred just before everyone woke up. The purge trials and the war in Spain were neck and neck. Neither in Moscow nor in Barcelona had the revolution devoured its children yet. It was a matter of all the hopes rising up from all the dispossessed of Europe at least since 1917: a matter of hopes plus action. Against the alternative of Fascism from which many of the volunteers in Spain were already refugees the revolutionary dream was sweeter than ever before. It was all that that Josie was somehow actually *"doing"* in Spain. Whatever her practical difficulties, whatever her personal moods, she was still spending most of her time in the places where this fundamental drama was being enacted. She spent several days with the international column near Murata in the aftermath of the battle of the Jarama, sleeping in the village café in the evening and sharing the life of the trenches during the day. She lived for a time in the house of the mayor of Fuentidueña, the village where *The Spanish Earth* was being filmed, getting to know the women and children and learning everything she could about their ordinary daily routines. Once she spent an evening in the Moorish caverns above Alcalá de Henares, where people had set up housekeeping as a refuge from the bombs. In all these things there was always something to be moved by. The candor of the American soldiers as they confessed their nightmares — and their dreams. The longing of the Fuentidueña townspeople for the varied vegetable crops that domination by the large landlords had always prevented — and their commitment to the little irrigation project that was bringing it about. The splendor of the mountain dwellers shaking their fists at retreating enemy planes and cursing — and their satisfaction that even here, even with the bombings, two little babies were being born. In and around the city she also went where she could. It was here that she saw Spanish soldiers in the scene she would always remember struggling to learn their own language, writing in their little blue books, in the trenches, "The cause of the proletariat shall win." Free of some of the obligations of the regular correspondents she was able to participate in government radio broadcasts, spend time with the soldiers on leave, pay visits to other trenches as well.

Of all the things she did and saw in Spain the one that best captures the feeling of the whole was a night spent in a little village whose name she never knew where an international battalion was struggling to make its relationship to the townspeople go more smoothly. It was not necessarily politics that divided them, it was trivial things too: the food, for example — olive oil or butter?: and it was these international differences they were trying to overcome. "One night driving out from Madrid to the Guadarrama under a quarter moon," she wrote in her memoir,

> ... I had a chance to see what pains the soldiers of the International Brigade took to reconcile the villagers to their presence. ... Not a chink of light shone from the squat dark houses and our feet rattled noisily as we walked over the rough cobbles and opened a door. A battery crew of Germans were eating supper on a table spread with a white cloth. Pitchers of wine glowed under the beaded lamp which swung from a useless chandelier, now shrouded carefully in green netting. They were all hard at work on a platter of eggs, with coffee in pink cups steaming beside their plates. The faces had a curious uniformity: I can only describe it by saying that they looked confident and joyful. One has to remember that these men had been summoned, as it were, from the shadow of a cellar. The whistle that the very air gives to every child at birth had been stopped up with dirt. Now they had cleaned the whistle and whether for a little while or for years they might be allowed to make the music of the living, didn't perhaps matter so much to them as the fact of the NOW which had restored them to visibility where they were actual men. They were no longer like sleepwalkers whose actions are mechanical and meaningless and who are haunted by menacing noises and phantoms of the dark. Inescapable as their private troubles may have been, *here*, at least, as if they had been on shipboard sailing from port to port, they could do nothing about them, and the saving grace was to use the NOW as if it were literally the forever.
>
> So it is not so farfetched to say that this one evening had a celestial quality, and that the little girls of the village, in their skimpy white dresses, sang like angels. Or that the schoolroom packed with many different nationalities had the benign air of those paintings called "The Peaceable Kingdom" made by the Quaker Hicks in Pennsylvania when he was trying to reconcile the animal world to the human, the invading whites to the Indians, and painted the Lion lying down beside the Lamb. If the soldiers' chorus of Yugoslavians with their leader rounding his O's and leaning forward with his hand transformed to a baton reminded me of the frescoes in Italy where Fra Angelico's band of musicians resembled the choirboys who sang in the big cathedral, it was because everything during this evening reminded me of something else, and that something always vibrant and living. It was a kind of enchanted world which was being kept suspended, like the colors in a soap bubble that may burst all too soon, but while it lasts reflects in gorgeous illusion every smallest object in the little universe where it will soon explode to nothing.

There was even an accordion solo — "Sole Mio" — of course — and a German recited a long narrative poem, filled with witty idiomatic allusions that nobody could understand except the Germans. But everybody applauded like mad and a mother stoppered up her bawling kid's mouth with a wine-soaked hunk of bread, which he blissfully chewed. The Czech soldiers sang Goethe's "Röslein, Röslein, Röslein roth" with the tenderness of men who were actually serenading a real sweetheart, and the evening was pitched so high that when the clown burst out, with a face whitened by flour and wearing a pink skirt over his uniform, and dangling a silly pocketbook from a stout wrist, it was almost unbearable. The audience moaned with pleasure. People at the back of the room clambered up on their chairs. Someone fell back with a squeal. It took a lot of shushing and hissing to quiet people down so they could listen to the violin solo played by a handsome Hungarian who had been the first violin in the Budapest orchestra and who was followed by two comic Rumanians, stamping and singing — of all things — "Who's Afraid of the Big Bad Wolf"!

Afterward we went to another house where the girls of the village had arranged roses and ferns in a little silver dish for the center of the table and where the soldiers, pressing around, produced a few bottles of champagne. Then they brought out photographs of groups taken with different nationalities all congenially intermingling, as if the photographs could substantiate forever the hope they had tried that evening to sustain.

"The whistle that the very air gives to every child at birth . . .": it was that the Spanish loyalists and the volunteers who joined them were struggling to defend. And it was Josie's cause too. It was her political and ideological heritage as much as it was anyone's. "The real *Brüderschaft*" she wrote that evening in her diary, with echoes of her own longings that went at least as far back as a night in Sioux City long ago, when, with her father and Helen, she had first heard the Wobblies sing, with echoes in the ancient longing of mankind for a brotherhood of the just transcending national borders that the singers that first night had themselves gotten from people who came before them and that they passed along. Now the slogans were different but it was the spirit and not the slogans that really mattered. Perhaps the hardest quality to regain about the Spanish war is just this absence of alienation. It was not *they* who were fighting. *We* were. *Fighting.* For Josie and the others there was little division between participant and observer, between subject and object, between us and them: it was all one. What she saw in others was exactly what others saw in her. If her own records are sparse, that is because of the military and journalistic circumstances: other people's response to her was not.

According to William Pike, the doctor of the Abraham Lincoln Battalion, her intercession with his troops at a crucial juncture was vital to their acceptance of the inoculations which shortly prevented the whole battery from being wiped away by typhoid, and when he accompanied her to those Moorish caverns to deliver aid "the women responded to her warmth and support even more than to the badly needed food." However modest she usually was about her own contributions in Spain, I have a whole fileful of unsolicited tributes reiterating this sense of the importance of her presence to others. From a correspondent: "She risked her life in the Spanish war much more than I did — or any other war correspondent." From a soldier: "One recollection that will never fade from my memory is the respect and affection held for JH by the anti-fascist volunteers who got to know her" at Murata. Her correspondence with soldiers and other reporters, some of which continued long afterward, suggests that she was seen as a concrete embodiment of that solid egalitarian womanhood in which they all would have sworn to believe. Even during the bombardment of the Hotel Florida in which she temporarily lost her voice she appeared to others as the incarnation of steadiness and aplomb, making coffee and serving toast while the shelling was shattering the very walls. "Shall always remember how human you looked and acted . . . that morning — amid many depressing circumstances that was one thing that made me feel good —," Dos Passos wrote her in 1939. In the presence of the real manifestations of a political force she too had been dreaming of all her life, she did, like the exiles, find a strength. Nor did she flinch from the consequences of what she believed. As she was leaving Spain she took it upon herself to communicate with the family of one of the dead Americans, a chore which had originally fallen to Hemingway and which he passed along. "The men of the International Column were an extraordinary group," she wrote. "I think we could not find more heroic types anywhere today. I saw a great deal of them on all fronts and I think, tragic as it ended, young Seligman was right."

But death was not only a military consequence of belief in the war in Spain. It was also a political consequence. For Josie the most intimate connection with the internal struggles on the Republican side had to do with the disappearance of John Dos Passos' friend, José Robles. The Robles story is so inherently dramatic that to resist representing it as an old-fashioned moral and political drama in which character and principle are hopelessly entangled is, after all, impossible. On the other hand perhaps that may be overdoing it a bit. Certainly Josie would have thought so. Too much was made of it in relation to the war, she thought; too much was made of it in relation to Dos Passos' changing politics; and Hemingway made too much of it in relation to himself, period. "I imagine the Spaniards may think it very odd to consider Robles the testing point" of anything, she wrote many years later to an historian asking her opinion of a manuscript involving the case, but then she too had reasons for her position. As far as the "guilt" or "innocence" of Robles — and of what — was concerned, she never claimed to know anything at all, nor were any facts about it ever subsequently established. But if it was one murder in many, one tragedy in many, or one error in many, depending on your point of view, that the Robles case was one of the hundreds of thousands of small events that somehow reflected the inner complexities of the Spanish war is a point on which no one could disagree. It just happened to be the one closest to home.

*The play opens* in an anonymous courtyard somewhere in the vicinity of Valencia in February or March, 1937, near where Professor José Robles Pazos, formerly of Johns Hopkins University language and literature faculty, lately of the Republican Ministry of War, has been held prisoner for several weeks. On vacation in Spain at the outbreak of the war, Robles, of a conservative family with whom he disagreed, declared himself for the Republic and was given a War Ministry post, in which he acted, among other things, as translator for the Russian military advisors. On this particular morning he is taken out and shot. We hear the sound of the rifle, see the blood spattering against the wall, watch the body slump. That is all we know.

Next, *the curtain rises* on a troubled Dos Passos trying to discover the whereabouts of his friend sometime not long after the execution. En route to Madrid to begin working on *The Spanish Earth* he has stopped in Valencia in part to attempt to persuade Robles to offer his services to the project but he has lost his address or never had it and in attempting to track it down he gradually becomes aware of a peculiar atmosphere. In a nondescript apartment in a run-down part of town he finds Robles' wife whom he also knows well, who tells him her husband has been taken away. Beyond that she knows nothing. She is poor and frightened. She asks Dos to help. At this point Dos Passos is in a very influential position. He is one of the most prominent Americans in any field who have identified themselves with the cause of the Republic; he has a long association with radical causes including the Communist movement which he has frequently served, independently but well; he is an old friend of Spain, his writing about it, like his friendship with Robles, going back as far as 1916; and most important of all, he is a central figure in the film project on which the Republican government is counting both to raise money from American supporters and if possible to wrest changes in the Roosevelt administration's neutrality policy. Nonetheless he can find out nothing. Republican officials including people he has known for some time assure him his friend is in no danger. Julio Alvarez del Vayo, the Socialist foreign minister who is widely assumed to be acting for the Communists, professes ignorance, concern, and promises to investigate. "The general impression that the higherups in Valencia tried to give was that if Robles were dead he had been kidnapped and shot by anarchist 'uncontrollables,' " Dos wrote in a letter to *The New Republic* in 1939. Meanwhile an unofficial rumor has reached Robles' son, a seventeen-year-old boy working in the information ministry, that his father is already dead. Frustrated, suspicious, determined to find out more, Dos Passos moves on to Madrid.

*Enter Josie* into Valencia following closely along Dos' tracks, possibly without realizing it. She too tries to locate Robles — she does not know him, but Dos has suggested a meeting — and she too is unable to find him, but here her situation and Dos' diverged, for unlike Dos, when she inquired after Robles, some forever-unidentified official somewhere in the offices of the Republic informed her that he was dead. Why someone would tell Josie when no one would tell Dos Passos is a good question and I can only guess at the answers. One is that, perhaps because of her articles on Cuba, she was regarded as more sympathetic than Dos politically, and she was not associated with the film, so that neither the likelihood of distressing her nor its consequences would seem as great. A second is that since she did not know Robles personally she would be unlikely to care as much. A third is chance. The last seems unlikely since whoever did tell her knew enough to realize that the news should not be repeated and pledged her to secrecy — especially secrecy from Dos. Dos Passos' biographer, in fact, infers that she might have been told specifically to help pacify Dos, though it is not obvious why telling her should have had that effect. She does not say in any of her discussions of Robles that I have found whether or not it was only Dos to whom she promised not to reveal it.

*The next scene* takes place at the Hotel Florida, Madrid, where against a background of rising political turmoil and constant military danger Hemingway and Dos Passos are arguing about Robles. The Robles case is not the only issue between them but it is an important one not only in itself but in relation to what each man is making of the Spanish war. Hemingway believes (a) that Robles is not dead; (b) that if he is dead he undoubtedly deserves to be — probably he had Fascist leanings; and (c) that in either case it is dangerous for Dos to inquire further because he is bringing suspicion both on them personally and on *The Spanish Earth.* Dos believes (a) that his friend is guilty of nothing; (b) that if he is dead it is Communists rather than anarchists who have killed him, probably because of his inside knowledge of the role of the Russians; and (c) that it may be compromising to be making propaganda for such a compromised cause. From Josie's memoir: "Dos Passos was worrying about his friend . . . who had been arrested as a spy, and Hemingway was worried because Dos was conspicuously making inquiries and might get everybody into trouble if he persisted. 'After all,' he warned, 'this is a war.' . . .

[Hemingway] seemed to be naively embracing on the simpler levels the current ideologies at the very moment when Dos Passos was urgently questioning them. On another level, Dos was absolutely right in refusing to believe that his friend could be guilty of treason; the bonds of friendship were not to be broken that lightly." But notice it is the others' positions and not her own that she analyzes and for good reason for the fact is that when she arrived bearing the one piece of information that could at least have eased the misunderstandings in the situation she did not reveal it. She must have watched Dos going around, even talked with him about his worries, and still kept silent. Finally it was to Hemingway and not to Dos she told the story. When Hemingway informed her importantly one day over drinks that Robles was safe and would be given a fair trial — a high Republican official he had reason to trust had told him so — she informed him just as importantly that he was wrong — and for the same reason. Agreeing with Hemingway that Dos Passos' inquiries were breeding suspicions, yet reluctant to break her promise to her informant, she contrived a story with Hem by which Dos could be told indirectly. At a luncheon that day to which all three were invited Hemingway told Dos Passos that he had learned from a German correspondent whom he could not name that Robles was dead, that Josie had also been told, and that more than that they were not free to say. Watching Dos Passos across the table Josie knew from his expression that he had been told, and when afterward he approached her "with a little coffee cup in hand . . . and in an agitated voice asked why it was that he couldn't meet the man who had conveyed the news, why couldn't he speak to him, too?", she could think of little to say.

But here is where an old-fashioned drama would fall apart and a modern ending would have to be offered because although Josie believed for the rest of her life that this was exactly how Dos' discovery of Robles' death came about, other evidence suggests that she was not necessarily correct. It is impossible to write it straight because there is no "straight." In Dos' accounts, he was also eventually told by a high Republican official, neither Josie nor Hemingway is given any prominence, and there are other discrepancies as well. If he did not find out then but he already knew, or he learned it later, what accounts for his responses on that day? It is also true that though the Robles issue does seem to have been a critical irritant in the deteriorating friendship between the two men, Dos never seems to have associated Josie with it negatively at all. Yet perhaps he ought, for she was in a false position in relation to him from the moment they saw each other in Madrid. When he came up to her, agitated, after the luncheon, holding his little coffee cup in hand, she must have realized that the roundabout mysterious manner of the telling, and particularly its delivery by Hemingway, could only have made his anxiety worse. On their ride home in a car together which she describes as hostile and silent she must have been experiencing guilt. On a long walk with Dos after they reached the hotel when he took her to the Plaza Mayor and they stared for a long time at the statue of a horse whose flanks bore the anarchist initials and whose rider waved an anarchist flag, it is hard to see how her consolations could have been so sincere. In 1939 when the Robles case briefly became a celebrated issue in relation to Dos Passos' frank disillusionment with the left, Josie wrote a letter to *The New Republic* personally sympathetic to Dos about it, but it was a letter not intended for publication. When she did write about it publicly later, it was the actors and the settings, rather than the issues, that seem to have held her eye. In her memoir she describes a lunch in the basement restaurant on the Gran Vía when Hemingway introduced her to Pepe Quintanilla, the Minister of Justice also known as "the Executioner of Madrid," one of the "high Republican officials" who had given Dos false reassurances about Robles. "When I heard his name I looked hard at him, as the man who had not told Dos Passos the truth about Robles," she wrote. But she had deceived Dos Passos herself. Now the fact is that the Robles case is the closest Josie ever came in Spain or elsewhere to the reality of political terror. The question is, was "looking hard" at Quintanilla enough?

Not long after the first of May, 1937, when the news from Barcelona about the open fighting between the government forces and the other left parties reached Madrid, Josie and several other of the Madrid correspondents went off to Valencia where the Communists were attempting to consolidate their control. Her journal shows her hopelessly confused. Several pages of the notebook, written with her old precision, record the speeches at a mass meeting of the Communist Party radioed to every village in Spain detailing their charges against the allegedly Trotskyist POUM, but a note at the bottom of the page says *"Quotes.* Don't believe." At that point, closer to a secure route out of the country, exhausted, and more than a little ill, for she had lost twenty pounds, she decided abruptly to go to Paris to recuperate, as many correspondents did, stopping off at Barcelona along the way. About the internecine fighting which was universally recognized, as she herself later put it, to "pinpoint the decline of the revolutionary fighting spirit," in her journal she had nothing to say. As if it were impossible in a situation of such intensity to imagine it would not always continue, she left thinking she would shortly return, and there were many people — soldiers and correspondents — awaiting her arrival, but she did not go back. There are three possible endings to the story of Josie in Spain and I want to offer them all. The first is the ending she gave it herself. In the closing incident of "The Starched Blue Sky of Spain," taken almost directly from her journal, she describes how on her final journey to Valencia from Madrid the car in which she was riding stopped at a little filling station halfway between, where she saw a young Spanish officer who remembered her from a visit she had made to the trenches at Guadalajara not long before. As they were talking "a simple townsman came up and listened in, enchanted. 'A commander?' he questioned the young officer, politely. 'No, no,' answered the officer. . . . 'American?' The officer nodded and we went on talking about his school. . . . The townsman was beaming and listening with all his might. Once more he plucked at the soldier's sleeve. 'But she understands everything!' 'Everything,' repeated the soldier, condescendingly, *'muy inteligente.'* *'Valiente'*, breathed the small townsman, *'muy valiente.'* But I was far from understanding everything," Josie concluded. "About the most important questions, at that moment, I felt sickeningly at sea. As for being *valiente,* who wasn't? If I wrote it down in my journal, it was to put heart in myself, if only to say, come now, be *muy inteligente,* be *valiente.* Just try."

The second ending belongs to Orwell. In the final pages of *Homage to Catalonia,* after he has recounted the last days of the fighting in Barcelona, his own wounding and recovery, his chasing about the country to get the papers necessary to leave, the anxiety of his wife, how desperately they were both determined to go, he records the story of the curious turnabout that took place as soon as they had actually left. "I think we stayed three days in Banyuls," he says:

> It was a strangely restless time. In this quiet fishing-town, remote from bombs, machine guns, food queues, propaganda, and intrigue, we ought to have felt profoundly relieved and thankful. We felt nothing of the kind. The things we had seen in Spain did not recede and fall into proportion now that we were away from them; instead they rushed back upon us and were far more vivid than before. We thought, talked, dreamed, incessantly of Spain. For months we had been telling ourselves that 'when we get out of Spain' we would go somewhere beside the Mediterranean and be quiet for a little while and perhaps do a little fishing; but now that we were here it was merely a bore and a disappointment. It was chilly weather, a persistent wind blew off the sea, the water was dull and choppy, round the harbour's edge a scum of ashes, corks, and fish-guts bobbed against the stones. It sounds like lunacy, but the thing that both of us wanted was to be back in Spain. Though it could have done no good to anybody, might indeed have done serious harm, both of us wished that we had stayed to be imprisoned along with the others. . . . This war, in which I played so ineffectual a part, has left me with memories that are mostly evil, and yet I do not wish that I had missed it. When you have had a glimpse of such a disaster as this — and however it ends the Spanish war will turn out to have been an appalling disaster, quite

apart from the slaughter and physical suffering — the result is not necessarily disillusion and cynicism. Curiously enough the whole experience has left me with not less but more belief in the decency of human beings. . . .

I think that is what Josie's *valiente*, what her *inteligente*, are also about.

The third ending comes from Josie again, many years later. As time passed her interest in Spain did not lessen but increased, and eventually she became something of a scholar of the war. As the new studies of Spain were published, particularly during the 1960s, she seems to have read them all, piling up pages of notes on their contents that rival in volume and exceed in lucidity the notes she took in Spain. But usually she found something missing. "I am of the opinion that what goes wrong with the best of research . . . is that the words can never convey the tune," she wrote in 1967 to two young professors who were soliciting her opinion on a manuscript about Spain. "It's like some old song that has died, and we can read the words but without the tune, no longer know what it really meant to the people who sang it." For Josie — and for how many?: so many — others, the song of Spain was never really over.

# Tearing past Stations

WHEN JOSIE left Europe at the end of June, 1937, after a stop in Paris, she did not really leave Spain behind her. For months, like Orwell, she "thought, talked, dreamed incessantly of Spain." She was in frequent contact by mail with some of the soldiers and correspondents she had met in Madrid. Anxiously she followed the news. Of everything she had seen during the period of her visit, somehow it was the children who haunted her most. Unlike many who brought out of the country luxuries bought mysteriously on the shattered Madrid markets or artifacts of war, she carried with her from her travels only two tangible extracts of her experience of the war. One was a roll of posters she intended to sell on behalf of orphaned children's relief. The other was a set of drawings by Spanish children, gaily colored and guileless revelations of their actual terrors of battle, probably elicited by Josie herself in her meetings with youngsters in Fuentidueña and Madrid. One of the drawings is particularly frightening. A left hand is traced onto paper at a small angle. On the hand is a swastika. Red flames stream from the fingertips. Below and above there are houses being bombed and the flames from the thumb reach the building below. On the side is written "Pasa el fascismo su huella" — "This is the Mark of Fascism." What Josie wondered, what everyone wondered, what the world wondered until events supplied the negative answer was: Was there any force that was going to be able to stop it?

Although she came back prepared to do everything she could to support the Republican cause, she realized quickly that being in Spain and being in America were two different things. In Spain the exalted aspirations of the original revolutionary movement and the human fellowship engendered by the pressures of war could lighten the oppressiveness of even the most treacherous political dealings, but at home, in the contest between politics and feeling, feeling was never enough. In part because of events in the Soviet Union, in part because of what was happening in Spain itself, the atmosphere on the left was full of suspicions and doubts. To the question of what was the cause of the suppression of the Trotskyist POUM and the assassination of its leader Andrés Nin, the Communist press gave only the unpersuasive answer that the POUM were traitors in league with Franco, and to the related question of the connection between the Spanish executions and those in Moscow it gave no answers at all. Josie was less distressed about the Soviet purges than many other people, but she was disturbed by the political atmosphere. "I would like to be able to question without having someone accuse me of disloyalty," she wrote to Granville Hicks at the *New Masses* in September. "There are many things in Spain that are far from simple. I could see . . . quite clearly the role POUM was playing but I ask what is responsible for [Nin's] assassination? Why are the documents claimed to have been found not published clearly so we can see them? If there was actual connection between POUM and Franco it would clear everything. While I think there were crooks in the leadership of POUM I know honest men followed too. Why are these things not cleared up? In the case of Russia, many developments leave me confused but I am willing to be patient. But this patience extends too far. . . ."

In the period immediately after her return she spoke often at the numerous Party-sponsored functions set up to gather assistance for Spain, but gradually a kind of mutual disenchantment set in. On her side, she was not only uncomfortable about the meaning of political developments in Spain, she was also doubtful whether even on a strictly humanitarian level the Party was being as responsible as it should, and she wrote an aggressive letter to officials in New York criticizing the efforts being made to provide for the children and to rehabilitate the wounded volunteers. In turn the Communists were uneasy about her refusal of simplifications. The same complications that affected her position as a speaker also affected her situation as a journalist. Again, at first her writing was in great demand in all the Party and Party-related publications and again the demand slowed down. Even *The Nation*, which had at first agreed to take several of her pieces, finally only took one — in part, she thought, because her reports on the collectivization of land and factories were more favorable to the anarchist, than to the Communist, position — and in the end she published only half a dozen minor and unpolitical articles about Spain. There was no break involved: Josie was still a part of the movement, as she had always been: it was rather that the movement itself was now saturated with these very suspicions and concerns. It was the beginning of a period of great frustration. To work for Spain it was necessary to work through the Communist movement because the Communists controlled all the vehicles of aid. But to work for the movement was suddenly to be working for an unknown.

Josie's frustration was not only political, there was a visceral edge to it, and in the absence of any other convenient outlet, she took it out on her friends. She was exceedingly short-tempered. She argued with Mother Bloor about the condition of the Erwinna house; she attacked her agent, Maxim Lieber, for inadequate work; and when poor Nathan Asch returned to Washington after a pleasant enough weekend visit to Erwinna a three-paged single-spaced letter listing every grievance Josie had ever held against him was right on his trail. Her friends were unaffected by her outbursts. Mother Bloor told her to buck up — wasn't she a good Bolshevik?; Lieber returned as good as he got, and received an apology; and Nathan Asch wrote her back a letter of such sweetness it is impossible to see how they could ever have quarreled again, although they did. It is as if her friends sensed that it was not really they she was criticizing, and they were right. It was friendship itself, not particular friends, she was starting to find lacking. "[I] have been so terrified at the indifference imbedded in people, their inability to respond really, the kind of deadness," she wrote to Katherine Anne. "What kind of a curse is it, a cautious inability to come out of one's shell. No wonder people have children." Whether she was in the city or the country the problem seemed to be the same. In the city life was all feuds and schisms. In the country it was all families and possessions. She was an independent woman with her own experiences and opinions and suddenly she was no longer young. Even in the supposedly progressive world in which she traveled, where did she fit in? She realized it was a social as well as a personal failure she was suffering: "[It] is a bad society that finds its only unity in family life," she had gone on; but such Marxism was small protection against the emptiness she felt surrounding her on her return. From the safe sweet-smelling households of her childhood to the intimate domestic life she had shared with John to her new solitary situation was too much personal diminution to bear, even in better political circumstances. For a person who relished people as much as she did, it was deadening to be so unconditionally alone. "How little control we have over some of the most vital factors of our lives," she wrote to Elizabeth Ames of Yaddo. "It seems to me sometimes as if only in the last few years have I really looked at myself and my life and even understanding many things did not give me control of everything. It is as if we had got aboard a train and suddenly woke up surprised to see it tearing past stations where we had expected to stop. Perhaps one should be thankful to feel on a speeding train and not in a station, waiting for the train to come. Both are rather painful." She thought of going to Iowa to visit her sisters and she thought about adopting a family of her own, but as Alice had still not forgiven her *Nothing Is Sacred*, and adoption, for a woman in her position, was very unlikely, the first scheme was more nostalgia for the past than a practicality for the present, and the second was less of a possibility than a wish. Travel, as usual — to San Francisco, the South — also entered her thoughts as a means of lifting herself beyond isolation, but in the end nothing came of any of her plans and she settled down into her usual antidote to depression: Work. The third volume of the trilogy, begun before she went to Spain, remained to be finished, and she took it down from the shelf. Except for a month at Yaddo immediately after her return to the United States, she braved it alone in Erwinna till nearly Christmas, 1937, and when she closed up the house to spend the winter away she got no farther south than Washington, D.C.

The literary-political world of Washington in 1938 was dominated by the Federal Writers' Project, the writers' relief section of the New Deal's Works Progress Administration, and though Josie was not employed by the project she mingled easily with those who were. It was a relatively convivial time. The Washington writers seem on the whole to have been more collegial than their New York counterparts — they ate together, drank together, lived together, it appears at times they even actually liked one another — and in addition to a few of her old friends who were among them, she made several new ones who would last her long into the future as well.[*] Regardless of her whereabouts, nothing was more important to her than Spain, and she continued to try to do what she could. Among other things, she was one of the leaders of a demonstration held at the State Department by more than a thousand women of Spanish descent, and afterward was part of the delegation that held discussions with government officials. "Former Sioux City Girl is Leader of Delegation Demanding Lifting of Spain Arms Embargo" headlined one Sioux City paper with a picture of Josie in a demure cloche and cape that managed to make her look like exactly that. Something of the constricted political atmosphere surrounding all work for Spain, and Josie's relation to it, in the spring of 1938, has been beautifully captured by one of her new Washington friends, the writer Jerre Mangione, who was working as an editor on the federal project. In his memoir *An Ethnic at Large*, Mangione recalls that when Josie came to Washington still full of

[*] Clair Laning, a congenial bachelor who was chief assistant to project director Henry Alsberg, was one of her new friends, as was Mary Lloyd, another Alsberg assistant. John Cheever and Nathan Asch were also working on the Writers' Project. Mary Vorse was another visitor.

the passion of Spain he persuaded her to write a play based on her experiences which could then be used by the local branch of the League of American Writers and other groups to raise money for the Loyalists. Josie agreed and, working with Nathan Asch, within a few weeks turned out a one-act documentary play called *The Spanish Road,* written in the popular "Living Newspaper" format. According to Mangione, *The Spanish Road* was enthusiastically received by the League, but when it was turned over to the local Theatre Union for casting and production "a ferocious battle of temperaments and ideologies" ensued. "The Theatre Union, which was closely allied with the Communist party, decided that the script suffered from 'some basic ideological flaws,' and demanded that radical changes be made 'to clarify the message.' " Josie and Asch disagreed. "The message was clear enough, the writers insisted, and they accused the producer of trying to reduce the script into a 'stupid propaganda vehicle reflecting a narrow Stalinist-Communist point of view.' " In the following ideological struggle, Asch quit the effort altogether, while Josie agreed to accept both a new collaborator and certain textual changes, but "the changes were not drastic enough to suit the producer and his Theatre Union associates" and her compromises appeared to be of no avail. "When both sides seemed to have reached a stalemate," Mangione continues,

> Josephine decided that the only thing left to do was to have a heart-to-heart talk with the producer in the privacy of his home, away from the pressure of his comrades. I agreed to accompany her. On our way she explained that her hope was to convince the producer that their mutual concern for the Loyalist cause was far more important than their differences of opinion about the script. While she could not have her name associated with a play that violated her integrity as a writer, she was prepared to make one or two more changes that would probably be to his liking.
>
> We had arrived without telephoning, but the producer did not seem to be surprised by the visit. He received us cordially, introduced Josephine to his wife and children as "a great novelist," then invited us into his study for coffee. When Josephine began talking, she sounded reasonable and in complete control of her emotions. I thought there was a good chance of winning him to her point of view. He listened carefully enough but as soon as she paused, he announced in no uncertain terms that the script would either incorporate all the changes he and his associates requested or there would be no production.
>
> Josephine stared at him for a moment, appalled. Then all the exasperation she had been enduring for two months erupted. "You stupid son of a bitch" she roared, and slapped him hard on the

face. With that, she made a beeline for the door and I followed. Outdoors, I expected her to verbalize her anger further but she became stone-faced and silent, hurrying as though she could not get out of the neighborhood fast enough. When she finally stopped, she burst into an uncontrollable fit of weeping, sobbing on my shoulder with an intensity I had not heard since the last Sicilian funeral I attended. I felt, as I tried to comfort her, that she was grieving for all the idealists thwarted by the machinations of political bureaucrats.

As a result of these conflicts, according to Mangione, the play was never actually produced, but it must have come very close, because among Josie's papers is an eight-paged Living Newspaper playbill for the play which includes several columns of articles about the collective nature of the project. "LEAGUE IN SUCCESSFUL COOPERATIVE WRITING VENTURE" is one of the headlines. "The Washington Chapter of the League of American Writers is the collective author of 'The Spanish Road,' the Living Newspaper," the article asserts.

> In bringing writers to Washington who were in the current of world events, the Washington Chapter was following the conventional (and worthy) pattern of most organizations with progressive aims. With the writing of "Spanish Road" it distinguishes itself as a writing organization that *writes cooperatively*. It is a unique accomplishment that few writing groups have ever achieved.

With the last opinion at least Josie certainly would have agreed. At the bottom of the playbill, in a thick, dark, hand, as if on whatever day she found it in her papers again she was roaring still, she wrote:

Idiots! Nathan Asch and I wrote and directed it.

J.H.

In such an atmosphere it was increasingly difficult to think freely about politics. There was little space for thinking. As the quarrels within the left sharpened over both the implications of the Moscow trials and the controversial reappearance of the now independent *Partisan Review*, complexity in discussion of literature too became a thing of the past. "I wish that we could keep from yelling 'thug' and 'crook' at everyone who does not agree with us," Josie wrote to Granville Hicks in the fall of 1937, complaining about a *New Masses* editorial which because of the original connection of the *Partisan Review* with the Communist Party had described William Phillips and Philip Rahv as "thieves"; and when she wrote Phillips a thoughtful letter criticizing what she viewed as an over-dependence on European standards in an article he had published with Rahv on American writing, he replied that while he did not think "for one moment" that Josie intended to endorse the "gangster" attacks on them by the Communist press, that was nonetheless the emotional impact of her letter. "Maybe my morality is becoming sectarian, but I simply cannot understand how anybody can stomach the dirty, stupid, and vicious *literary* regime of the Daily [Worker] and the [New] Masses," he wrote. There was no longer any opportunity for individual positions. From now on one was either a "Stalinist" or a "Trotskyist," period.

Of all Josie's friends, the only one with whom she could honestly probe her reactions to what was happening was Katherine Anne. Katherine Anne, divorced, was now living in New Orleans where she was about to marry her fourth husband, Albert Erskine, then an editor of the *Southern Review*, and evidently she felt the same need as Josie for, whatever the reservations of the recent past, their correspondence resumed with a fullness that had been absent for several years. "I am up writing after several days in bed with what is grippe if not general disheartenment," Josie wrote Katherine Anne from Washington in the spring of 1938.

Anyone writing today should either shut out the papers or get chronic hardening of the heart. The Spanish business is so shocking and so horrible and having been there I feel as if I had watched a boy grow up through sickness and with much promise only to be run over by a streetcar — the horrible treachery involved, the sheer lack of ammunition, all of it, is something one might as well harden oneself to, as the worst has only doubtless begun to happen in the world. . . .

I find it very hard . . . to live in so impersonal a world. In the nineteen twenties the world seemed better to live in. I suppose it is what everyone feels in time. But at least people did have personal ties, people exchanged visits, had friendships that meant a great deal. Now it seems as if nothing existed except committees. In such a flinty plane as I now live I find it difficult to breathe . . . The air is so thick one would have to live in the wilderness to offset it. We used to talk about literature, I would give years of my life for a little literary talk again, with some feeling for it. This may seem strange from me, who am supposed to have in particular been absorbed in politics, but I never was absorbed in organizations and only in politics so far as they were giving me some understanding of the world. At the present moment, politics has ceased to illuminate. . . . I saw your letter in Partisan Review, and feel as dismayed as you about the Russian trials although I am much more dismayed by other conditions, which I do not under-

stand. It is possible that there are traitors but if there is again a
widespread growing class differentiation and oppression, it is far
worse for me to look at than the killing of any dozen or even fifty
men, old bolsheviks or whatnot. I don't want to get frantic but to
try to find causes if that is the truth, and to try to understand. Is it
totally mad to want to understand so passionately at this hour? It
is all I ever did want, any place, any time, and throwing myself
into the movements that seem in the vital direction of history
were only to understand. Now I truly feel that the real thing
wrong in Russia is not its original aim, that is still the one aim
worth striving for, but that it has somehow been unable to work it
out, that we expect too much, that we understand too little, and
what I know is that Russia should not have let Spain down, not for
anything. Not for the threat of world war. Otherwise the cause is
all being lost, and the word democracy just a slogan to fool us, a
slogan that can't win because democracies will always cheat and
fool each other . . .

"Yes, you are right, there are things in the Russian situation more
dismaying actually than the trials," Katherine Anne wrote back a few
days later, ". . . but the trials are a symptom, a kind of obvious thing that
almost anyone can see. . . . We know a little about that, not enough, but
something. About the other things we cannot speak because we do not
know. . . .

Josie, you know well that the original aim of the Russian Revolution was the best thing that had happened to the mind of men . . .
in all the history of social theory. . . . But . . . all revolutions have
had noble aims, and without exception they have all collapsed and
gone corrupt and for exactly the same reason, over and over. . . .
The real revolutionists are betrayed and kicked out or killed by
demagogues, the dictator, the man, or the party, who will stick at
nothing to get power. . . . Stalin, who was a henchman of Lenin,
will not rest until he has wiped out every trace of Lenin in that
revolution except the embalmed corpse in the Kremlin. . . . I think
if he dared that madman would have Lenin's corpse shot and tried
as a traitor. . . .
    You know I have gone here and there, looking too for under-
standing, trying to know something of the causes of the disasters of
our times. . . . What else is there we could even want to do? And I
do not trust the people who profess to be working to make over
this world; they need only more power to be, themselves, the evil
they say they are fighting. I could not breathe any better in a
world they would make than I can in this present one. Democracy

is one slogan; revolution is another. . . . It has been a good while
now since I believed that Russia was any less corrupt than any
other government, bent on power, wealth, and prestige. If that is
Communism, believe [me], I am not in the least a Communist. But
I do not in the least believe that is Communism.

"I can't believe with you that those who long for a new world and a
different want only personal power," Josie replied about a month later.
"Two of the best men I ever knew, Gustav Regler, a German whose spine
was splintered in Spain, and Ramon Sender, are the least desirous of personal power and the deepest in hopes for another kind of world I ever
knew. I wouldn't have missed them for anything."

Another regular topic was the *Partisan Review*, whose increasing
identification with "Trotskyism" was taking it far from its original position in favor of the independence of literature from politics and, in Josie's
view, far from its original revolutionary aspirations as well.

*Josie:* [Apr. 5, 1938] I think Partisan Rev. has printed some good
things but on the whole stinks. To call themselves a revolutionary
magazine and print a piece like Elizabeth Bishop's in the last number . . . a piece using expressions like the pretty sight of a convict's
uniform against flowers, is inexcusable. . . .

It is a low time. They will all run to little fables because they
cannot bear to speak. Any good literature is dual, it uses an expression with more than one meaning, a pattern that is almost an alle-
gory, but the simple plain fable is, when it becomes the object of a
group, purely escape. . . . I am sick of all the labels, the Stalinite
label, flopped on from one side, the Trotskyite from another. I
don't doubt these things have some political validity but at the
present they have become more myth than fact, no one knows
anymore what the terms stand for. It is a great slander contest,
shameful all around. And the Trotskyists have less political leg to
stand on in my opinion, they are not able to do so much damage
as one would think, and actually many of their criticisms are valid
enough only they stop at that, one of the nay-saying groups of history.

*Katherine Anne:* [Apr. 8, 1938] Let us get the Partisan Review
off our chests. Of course I know that they are not a revolutionary
magazine and that they are, I suppose, Trotskyites, though much
good that will do Trotsky, and he'll need less weak-kneed cham-
pions before he's through. I mean to say, if that's the best support
he can get, God help him. . . . The thing that has troubled me,
kept me silent in so many situations and quarrels, is simply this: no

one can any longer give a simple opinion, or express a preference, or an opposition, in any question, without at once finding oneself acting, against one's will, as a stooge for somebody or some organization. . . . They had no business to print my letter (they ask for permission to print parts of it, and the only thing they left out was my saying I would subscribe. . . . Now it follows forever, I feel pretty certain, that for what it is worth, my name will be used on that side to beat up the New Masses — which did by the way behave like a jackass.) Insofar as they are opposed to the present reign of terror of Stalin, I am for them. But that doesn't mean I am for Trotsky, and if they behave as badly as the New Masses or print any more filth like Elizabeth Bishop's piece or Agee's poem, I shall be obliged to write them and take back what I have said. . . .

*Josie:* [June 15, 1938] I continue to think that our little squirt-budget, the Partisan Review, has its ass in a sling. I thought nothing could be more conflicting than the contents of the number in which William Phillips harangues Mann for not tearing off more masks from the world. A little nonesuch by Delmore Schwartz about ice statues in New York, told in the pretty form of a fable, informed I-don't-know-whom, of I-don't-know-what. It is now the slogan that betrayal is the watchword, but one cannot be betrayed until first one hath. It may be only a vision, a sense of life, but it must be something, and Eleanor Clark's story, beautifully written, of a boy who cuts his throat or does something to extinguish ALL seemed to be much ado about nothing. He cut it none too soon in my opinion. He was half dead already.

And so it continued, back and forth, on many of the vital topics of the day, an ongoing open forum of two, despite their differing views. As befitted their durable friendship, it was a remarkably free exchange.

The third volume of the trilogy, the one Josie had started before she left for Spain, was almost completely abandoned after she came home, and the version that was finally published as *Rope of Gold,* was begun again in Erwinna in the summer of 1937, continued in Washington in the winter of 1938, and completed in Erwinna again the following fall. Both as the climax of the earlier volumes and as a novel standing alone, it is one of her strongest achievements. Not only does she bring a large array of the characters and circumstances of the early 1930s to convincing fullness of life, she does so in such a way that while the necessity of revolution is demonstrated its likelihood is not, and the result is a tragic confrontation between the justice of the revolutionary cause and its futility.

It is a book of the heart and of the intellect simultaneously. Particularly from a documentary viewpoint it is a remarkable novel. But what is most remarkable from a personal viewpoint is that she could write it the way she did while caring about a different outcome so much.

If *Pity Is Not Enough* is "about" capitalism and *The Executioner Waits* is "about" the rise of resistance to capitalism, *Rope of Gold* is "about" a period of flourishing of the revolutionary movement. Continuing the stories of Victoria and Jonathan Chance at approximately the point they were left in the previous novel, the third volume opens with a long, painful, confrontation with Jonathan's relatives in his father's comfortable living room — a scene that will feel familiar to radicals of any generation who have suffered political estrangement from their families — and it follows them across what readers of this biography will recognize, with qualifications, as an essentially autobiographical terrain. Jonathan's difficulties in sticking to his writing, his self-doubt, his identification with the local farmers' protest, his elevation into a responsible position with the Communist Party, his dissatisfaction with being made into a fund-raising "Front." Victoria's obsessions with her past sorrows, her isolation in the country, her gradual development of a career as a reporter, her rising identification with the international revolutionary movement, particularly during a visit to Cuba, her increasing dedication to her work. What happens between them —: the recriminations that are a product of their poverty and disappointments, the complications of their conflicting schedules, their sexual and emotional infidelities, the long slow dissolution of their mutual trust and hope until their eventual, inevitable, separation. There are the near misses: *"The long ride to the West was as invigorating as a sea voyage but when she was in Chicago, Jonathan was in Milwaukee. In Minneapolis he had passed on to Omaha. . . ."* The long awaited reunions that go inevitably awry: *"By eleven she had the beginning untangled and was piecing it together. [Lester] had left great gaps which he expected her to fit together as usual. It was like a puzzle at first but afterwards fun. When she heard someone turn the handle of the door, she stiffened with alarm and sat rigid. 'Who's there', she called out clearly. 'Jonathan', said Jonathan. She got up and rushed to the door. He looked very brown and handsome and snatched her up before she could speak. 'Oh Jonathan, what a night to come', she said. . . ."* The ultimate revelation, on the day he arrived late for what she already knew would be their final Christmas: *" 'I want the book', he said in an indistinct mumbling voice"* of a handmade volume she had illustrated herself, *" 'it's a beautiful book',* and she wanted to thank him for saying that, for his tears, for his love, but she said instead in a low, bitter, voice, *'It's a woman, isn't it?' "* *"If only they could have had a garden,"* thinks Victoria, *"if the corn had had a chance to ripen. If the grapes had grown purple on the vine and she could have pulled them off in big bunches and the fragrance of boiling jelly and wine might have sweetened the air.''* If only they could have shored up the foundations of their love, like the foundations of a house, to shelter them against the world outside, but they are opposed to such shelters on principle, they want the world to come in, and soon their own foundations are lost in it.

It is essential to understand the fullness of the characterizations of Victoria and Jonathan earlier in the trilogy to understand the pathos of their collapse. It is as if not only their own lives but history itself falters when they do. From the great large families of the previous generation, whose histories have filled the pages of the trilogy, to Victoria's single stillborn son, from the material amplitude in which Jonathan was raised to the impoverishment of his psychological and revolutionary will, this — this terrible barrenness — is what it has come to. But if Victoria and Jonathan are the central emotional focus of this history, they are not its only focus. As in the other novels, there is a large cast of interlocking characters moving and swaying together, lives and destinies intertwined, as if a great frieze of the Depression had somehow acquired life —: Nancy Radford, Victoria's sister, traveling back and forth across the drought-stricken deserts of the West with her penniless family; Steve Carson, a farm radical torn between his attraction to the rising movement of striking auto workers in the city and his devotion to his pregnant wife on the farm; Lester Tolman, a vacillating but appealing radical intellectual who cannot make a political commitment; and many more, the reactionary as well as the revolutionary, the rich as well as the poor, individual, and yet representative figures of their time and stations, and not only the living but the dead as well, lovingly recalled throughout the story because they are present in the memory of the living.

It is in the contrast between the commitment of the radical characters and the outcome of their actions that the meaning of the novel is ultimately found. The book is more than the sum of its characters. Despite their desire for a new social order, despite their need, the book as a whole does not believe with them that therefore change will come about. There is a tension between what people want and what happens to them. Neither in personal nor in political life does justice necessarily win. In effect, despite the existence of the revolutionary movement, the destinies of individuals are as limited by external forces as they were in the periods of the earlier volumes, and radicals, despite believing otherwise, are no exceptions. If the passion of the book is in its people, the dispassion is in its design: both the forceful rhythmic alternation of scenes so that no one set of characters is ever allowed to represent the whole, and the use of italicized inserts which here carry the settings beyond the boundaries of the story in both space and time to indicate the ever-growing terrors, particularly in Europe, that the revolutionary movement must face. The principal action, including the story of Victoria and Jonathan, is set in the early '30s and is marked by its spirit of hope. The inserts are set in the later '30s and are marked by its spirit of doubt. The section of the book about Victoria's involvement in Cuba is preceded by an insert showing radical defeats in Italy and Germany. The climax of the text shows Steve Carson scaling a wall to join the strikers in an auto plant, but the climactic insert which precedes it is about the crushing of the popular armies in Spain. Throughout the novel there are two lines being developed at once, the subjective and the objective, and at its conclusion they are, at best, at a standoff. This is hardly the simple novel that its "proletarian" label suggests. In fact it is something like Brecht. Granted that the wishes of the author, like the wishes of the characters, plainly cry out for change, the judgment of the author — unlike the judgment of the characters — is another matter. Within its radical framework there is an authorial impartiality for which Josie has never been recognized. If emotional logic suggested revolution, political logic did not, and she shaped her fiction to history, rather than the other way around.

The isolation in which Josie wrote *Rope of Gold* was the greatest which she had ever so far experienced. For the first time since she had begun writing seriously there was not even the background presence of John to lend an ear to the daily bulletins on what she had, or had not, been able to accomplish. Nor was there anyone else to talk to about writing. With her editors her relationships had always been uncharacteristically formal, and though her Harcourt, Brace editor, Charles Pearce, was unfailingly, professionally, courteous, they did not get beyond the "Miss Herbst" – "Mr. Pearce" stage until they had been working together for several years. Except for Katherine Anne, there was no one to whom she could confide anything approaching her full ambitions for the novel, what she secretly wanted for it, what she hoped. In other ways too her isolation was greater than ever before. "I hardly get a single personal letter anymore," she complained to Katherine Anne in the summer of 1938, "only a shovel of demands, pleas, petitions and whatnots until I feel that all life wants of me is a rubber stamp with my name engraved and a trickle of pennies to drop in the appropriate slot." Even Erwinna was scarcely a comfort. "I would have made a good wife for a sea captain off chasing moby dicks and gone for five years," she wrote. "I would have wiped the children's noses and stoked the fires and kept the lights in the window burning bright, but when there aint no use putting a light in the window, the heart sinks low and gutters." Although she participated in some political activities locally, particularly by raising money for a workers' library from some of the wealthier writers who had moved into the area, socially she remained largely aloof. She rarely went to the city. What news she got came by way of radio. As the pattern of the democracies' capitulation to Hitler became increasingly clear she grew more discouraged, but at the same time there began to be an inner stiffening as well. It is as if realism were the mother of detachment. "I have only two hands and two feet," she said in August, as if a sobering recognition of her personal limitations were beginning. "I got so sick at the time of the Munich sellout and saw so clearly what would happen — I think most of us who know Europe did — that I have come practically to a resurrection where I am far from being above it all — but where I do not hourly bleed," she said in December, as if the process were continuing on. Toward the end of the year her manuscript was finished and delivered to the publisher in New York. She did not want to hover over the details of publication, nor was there anything else she particularly wanted to do, and soon she was faced with her usual seasonal dilemma again. Because she wanted to escape the winter in Erwinna, because she wanted to pay her bills, because, above everything, she wanted there to be a *Because,* she decided to accept a commission from Modern Age publishers for an ambitious journalistic survey of South America. This particular *Because* she might as well have left unheeded.

Josie's journey to South America in the winter and spring of 1939 was one of the emptiest of her career. Although she was gone for five months and visited Cuba, Colombia, Chile, Argentina, and Brazil, there is very little to show for it. One published article in a photo-newsmagazine called *Friday,* two unpublished manuscripts about Batista's regime in Cuba, and a packet of tiny photographs showing ragged families outside cardboard hovels in a city in Chile make up most of the discoverable remains. There are few personal letters, few personal notes. There never was any book. Whether the reason was political, as Josie later implied, or whether it was all simply too much for her, is difficult to say. I imagine it was some of both. The story the publisher wanted was a celebration of the New Deal's "noninterventionist" and "reciprocal" military and trade policies and an exposure of the dangers of Nazi penetration. The story she found was a story of contrast between rich and poor so great it was shocking even to her and an underlying hatred of "Yankees" and "imperialism" so intense that no alliance between north and south could be stronger than the police powers available to enforce it. It was a story that at that point not even the Communists, then supporting the New Deal, were especially eager to hear. But the logistics of the trip must have been overwhelming too. So many months, so much solitude, such difficult travel conditions, so little she truly understood. When Madrid fell, in March, she was probably alone. Sometime later, when political conditions changed, the publishers approached her again for the book she would have written in the first place and even replenished her advance, but by then, although evidently she tried it, it was too late. "You don't write when someone pushes a button," she told an inquirer many years later. "At least I don't."

When Josie reached home at the end of May, 1939, the political situation had deteriorated even further. War was on everybody's lips. The question was not whether it would happen but when. If, during most of the decade, literature had been dominated by politics, now it was becoming extinguished by them. The politicization at least of reviewing, if not of writing, was largely complete. It was the worst possible moment for *Rope of Gold*. Published while Josie was away, it elicited reviews that were not unfavorable so much as they were polemical, extensions of the reviewers' politics rather than examinations of the author's book. With the generalized radicalism of the early years of the decade on the wane, if you were still sympathetic to the movement you liked the novel: if not, not: it was more or less as simple as that. The politicized criticism which characterized newspaper reviewing in general characterized literary reviewing even more. A disdainful discussion by Philip Rahv accusing her of "rushing to and fro on the planet . . . in her anxiety not to miss any eruptions of the class struggle" was one she found particularly upsetting. It was not criticism in a narrow sense so much as the absence of criticism in a broad sense — serious attention to the literary and historical dimensions of what she was trying to accomplish — that she objected to. The authenticity of the trilogy and not its politics was what she herself felt to be its distinctive contribution, and she thought it was not taken seriously. When *Partisan Review* requested her participation in a survey of problems facing American writers she refused on the grounds that as far as she was concerned it had lost all claims to standing for a "disinterested interest in literature." "I agree with you it is a dark and dreadful moment but from every angle the Partisan Review is also part of that darkness," she wrote Dwight Macdonald. Yet not only was the political moment intense, it was also fragile, and with literature so subject to politics, it no longer had a foundation of its own. First because of the alliance between Stalin and Hitler, and soon because of the war, all writing reflecting the radicalism of the 1930s acquired a different aura. The practical possibility of a one-volume edition of *Pity Is Not Enough, The Executioner Waits,* and *Rope of Gold,* which Josie had always taken for granted, and its political impossibility, occurred virtually simultaneously. The intellectual, political, and emotional unities linking the nineteenth-century story of Joe with the twentieth-century story of Victoria into what Harvey Swados would eventually call the most "sweeping" and "ambitious" "fictional reconstruction of American life" ever to be attempted in our literature," could never be appreciated together. When the decade was over, it was over. As the publisher quickly realized, the audience had been swept away.

Nor was it only literature that was severed from its mooring, it was something more general, more like life itself, as if in the rising crisis the human meaning of things was dissolving irretrievably into the political, never to be re-formed. The uselessness of the sacrifice of the American boys in Spain was particularly painful for Josie to bear, a symptom of the cynicism, coldness, calculation she was beginning to feel everywhere, above all in the activities of the left. Scribbled fragments on the pages of political correspondence she received chart with an almost clinical precision the shriveling of her sense of identification with organizations with which she had once cooperated with an open heart. Item: Invitation to address the League of American Writers on Latin America. Note: "Invitation withdrawn after my return when it was discovered my position ran vs. the 'line' on S.A." Item: Invitation for five-minute address to the fiction craft session of the third Congress of American Writers. Note: "It is not possible to say anything of the slightest importance to writing in five minutes." Item: Request from the American League for Peace and Democracy to endorse a parade supporting Roosevelt's policy of avoiding "any action which will encourage, assist, or build up an aggressor." Note: a huge √ and ? suggesting both her opinion of the organization which had changed its name from the League Against War and Fascism and her opinion of the hypocrisy of the Roosevelt policy in relation to Spain. Long past the expiration of this radical decade her relationship with the organized left continued its progressive decline. 1941: Invitation from League of American Writers to participate in a symposium on the social novel. Answer: "No!" 1942: Letter from the *New Masses* expressing a desire to publish "more material of a cultural nature and especially more short stories." Answer: "Balls!" 1944: Invitation from Louis Budenz to become a regular contributor to *The Daily Worker*. Answer: "Any answer I could make would be the wrong answer." To the ardent free-flowing participation of the earlier years, this strained silent withdrawal was the solitary end.

Josie was at Yaddo during the late summer and autumn of 1939. She was there during the announcement of the Nazi-Soviet Pact. A group photo taken the day before the invasion of Poland shows her face dark with worry. Why didn't she "break" publicly with the Communist Party, to borrow one word from the vocabulary of the period, when she was so "disillusioned" with it privately, to borrow another? Why didn't she do it later? *Mea culpas* were replacing the "Internationale" on the lips of half the intellectuals around her. Certainly it would have been easy enough to join them. The answer is as much emotional as it is political and it rests more than anything on her identification with the past. "We are not only what we are today but what we were yesterday and if you burn your immediate past there is nothing left but ashes which are all very well for those heads that like nothing better than to be sprinkled with ashes," she wrote in the middle of the McCarthy era, but she was never the sort for ashes, never would be, never could, and she said the same thing, in different language, many times. The past was her family's history, it was her mother, it was Helen, it was John. It was her father's hardships, it was the Wobblies, it was socialism, it was Bolshevism. It was the Village, it was Berlin, it was Realengo, it was Madrid. It was literature, it was love, it was all those things that had once seemed to be moving in a common direction in her life — *it was all she had left* — and what actual motive had she to consider repudiating it? She had done nothing wrong. The life she had wanted had led her right into the middle of one of the biggest historical dilemmas of the twentieth century, but it was exactly the life she had wanted, it was even the reason she had wanted it, and she would not take it back. She felt far too keenly the stir of the revolutionary idea to be able to abandon it now for she had been young when it was, and if the course of the radical movement had proved complex, she granted it its complexities as she granted herself her own. She was not now, nor would she ever be, a revisionist. She was pessimistic, she was exhausted, she was sickened, and she was scared, but when war came she was everything that she had been before. Times changed, but Josie did not change. She ended the decade with her radical spirit intact.

# PART SEVEN

# IT IS REPORTED

## CHAPTER TWENTY-FOUR

# Measuring Sticks

*December 8, 1941. Monday. New York City.*

The War began yesterday around 2:30 in the afternoon . . . but so far as I am concerned I did not know about it until evening when Polly B.* came home from the movies and announced that they had asked all the service men to leave and report for duty. We went next door to [a neighbor's] and . . . sat around and listened to the radio, [the man] in bed with an upset stomach and all very pleasant and domestic with his lovely [wife] wrapping a blanket around his legs when he came out to sit with us while Clare Boothe, hound of the Baskervilles, had just trekked from the latest war zone, the Philippines, to report what it looked like and gave her report, slightly under the influence of liquor if you ask me, stuttering, as all the radio announcers did as for them undoubtedly this was THE DAY and they saw themselves being ushered into new realms of importance, and she gave her little tiddlewinks, the lowdown which was no lowdown but a mixed batter of what everyone knows with the air of a spy retrieving from the front line, and as if the Japs had held off a day or so on purpose to reward her with this Hour of Hours. Sheehan, Vincent . . . made little

* Polly Boyden, an acquaintance with whom she briefly shared an apartment in Brooklyn.

Guam intimate and touching as he could, heartening up the moment with tales of Coca-Cola and hitchhikes for the Boys in their monotony and those boys probably now prisoners. Meanwhile the radio came on, relentlessly, with rising crescendo, all the voices getting into stride as the hour progressed and one mention of Lindbergh erasing him from the map of history with the kind of righteous leavening which is a bitter foretaste, whether in this instance rightly or wrongly, of what is to come when we shall all be leveled to egg beaters for a cause which day by day and hour by hour will have to be simplified and oversimplified until the end. Great discussion as to the meaning of the attack, the radio announcing it was a suicide gesture on the part of the Japs and invigorating us all with the information we could lick em hands down and military experts said this and that and they had no fuel, no food, no sources of supplies, but have we not heard these tales before in other connections and has not war endured and the have-nots gradually become powerful through agencies unforeseen? . . . As usual everyone feels events have been going forward behind our backs and only time will reveal what has been going on these many days. Everyone puzzled, subdued, talking at once of death. . . . So natural when death has come creeping in this new general way of violence toward us all and today in the papers, 1500 were killed by bombs and machine gunning and so on in the Hawaiian islands and the first boy to have his death announced had a Polish name and his father who got the news lives in Michigan. The boy was 22.

Today all talk on street echoes war, and words Jap etc from all sides and at the hour Roosevelt broadcast war, girls and men pouring out of the Automat on 14nth Street, huddled around taxicabs to hear the radio. Polly came in from her meeting that was to have begun work on stop the war and they reconsidered how they could go on, under [what] slogans and for what purposes, many were against it even now . . . holding fast to their convictions, but the time is going fast and at last there *is* War again, so awaited by so many people, with all life suspended in so many ways so long as if it were not worth while beginning vast dreams when destruction or violence were near at hand. It is ten years since Mike Gold said to me, this is no time to write, general war is coming next year, it was said again all through 1934, every time there was a crisis, first Manchukuo, then Ethiopia, and later on, drop by drop, it came, everyone saying this is the war, now coming, and it was coming, too, just as we grow older without truly appreciating it, and near our dying without exactly knowing how.

—Wartime journal

In the period between the onset of the war in Europe and the onset of American involvement Josie kept very largely to herself. In spite of her public silence, she felt, privately, that she had "broken": "Escaped fire there, then broke. . . . Awoke from the long sleep. Cannot remain dumb or make love all the time," reads a note on the bottom of a piece of late-'30s political correspondence about Spain. Shaken by the Hitler-Stalin alliance, if not to the point of recrimination, at least of recoil, from politics she remained aloof, commenting about events only rarely even in notations to herself, seeing none of her political acquaintances, signing nothing, her withdrawal, in her own view, constituting adequate cancellation of the commitments she had upheld for so long. Nor was it only politically that she was withdrawn. She lived much as before, in her usual itinerant fashion, now at Erwinna, now at Yaddo, now in the city in borrowed apartments or in hotels, but if the form of life was familiar, the substance was strangely lacking. With the exception of Katherine Anne she had almost no private correspondents and even to Katherine Anne her letters were oddly toneless, vacant, without the energy that had usually animated them before. As if, though her eyes were continuing to register, her brain was refusing to analyze, nowhere either in her private or her public writing does she seem to have attempted to articulate the moment — which for Josie is saying a lot. On her forty-eighth birthday she must even have been reading the Bible because in the cheap tattered King James given to her by her father when she was small there are some uncharacteristic markings beside Isaiah 35 with a "March 5, 1940" date: "The wilderness and the solitary place shall be glad for them and the desert shall rejoice and blossom as the rose." In the confusion that followed the Nazi-Soviet Pact Josie was not alone but she did not share her confusion. The life she had fashioned for herself in the second half of the 1930s had everything to do with politics. Now it, too, was gone.

The narrowing that characterized Josie's life during this interval also characterized her work. Although she wrote one or two stories and had several ideas for plays, she undertook no journalism, and her major effort was a modest and unexceptional novel of chiefly regional interest about a rural Pennsylvania village very like Erwinna. Published by Scribner's in May, 1941, *Satan's Sergeants* is a loosely constructed portrait of modern rural existence in which oldtimers and newcomers alike struggle to find personal meaning in a life estranged not only from each other but from the land. Without much emotional focus, without much plot, it is a quiet, undramatic, village-gossip sort of a novel in which little of any importance actually happens. Restricted almost entirely to the life of the village, the novel is as unlike the trilogy as it is possible to be, not only in its absence of scope, but in its essentially nonjudgmental nature. Where in the trilogy a great deal of attention was given to the way characters reflected social or political forces, here they are more nearly left alone. It is far from being a trivial novel. Good-natured, humorous, perceptive, as many reviewers noted, it is occasionally even wise. Yet it seems to exist in a vacuum. Much is observed in it, but little is concluded. Much is experienced, but little is explored. "She understands . . . both the natives and the newcomers, and realizes that if the one have lost something they can never get back the others have come because they have lost something too," commented a reviewer in *The New York Times*. But it was not only the characters who had "lost something." The author had lost something too.

Immediately after the Japanese attack on Pearl Harbor everything changed again — almost as if a stopped-time panorama of the 1939–1941 period had suddenly come to life. Unlike many radicals, Josie had not sprung back into motion when Germany attacked the Soviet Union the previous summer. She had been visiting Mary Heaton Vorse at Provincetown, and the event seems to have passed her by. Now she awakened. The day after the Japanese attack she began keeping an informal diary. The next she began formulating a plan to offer her services to the government as what she called a "migratory listening post" to help gather and interpret information about countries involved in the war. The day after that she was contacting friends in New York to work out a line of approach to various writers, including Archibald MacLeish, who were already involved in the government's information program. By the middle of December, 1941, less than two weeks after the U.S. declaration of war, she had already taken herself to Washington.

The job which Josie landed by the traditional Washington mechanism of who-knows-whom was not with the Office of Facts and Figures (OFF) headed by MacLeish, which in any case was on the verge of being disbanded, but with the Office of the Coordinator of Information (OCI), better known as the Donovan Committee after its director Colonel William J. Donovan, an independent intelligence and propaganda agency, many of whose functions later ended up, via the Office of War Information and the Office of Strategic Services, in the CIA. Although the information services were in such flux following Pearl Harbor that *The New Republic* could describe them, in the summer of 1942, as being in a "state of untotalitarian confusion, a holy mess," roughly speaking at the point Josie was involved, domestic operations, including broadcasting, were under the direction of the OFF, and foreign operations, including broadcasting, were under the direction of the OCI.* The foreign radio operation, headed by Donovan's deputy, the playwright Robert Sherwood, consisted in part of daily shortwave radio broadcasts to the countries with which the United States was at war. Josie was on the German desk, and her particular mission was the preparation of radio scripts for the

---

* It is symptomatic of the state of affairs that even the initials of the agency were in flux. It was referred to as the OCI and the COI interchangeably.

daily transmissions in German. "Feel every day as if I were about to go into the operating room; same kind of calm submission to fate, braced nerves, clear half awake nights with rehearsal of the deeds to be done, the precise detail to be attended to before the incision is made; calm yet tensely nervous, just poised, not living, not dying," she wrote in her diary in early March, 1942. "Now it is my job to undermine what is left of the German will to live." But if the structure of the information effort was in flux during the period Josie was in Washington, its politics were in utter turmoil. Conservative political interests, routed by the early New Deal, were reconsolidating their positions. Liberals and radicals, affected by the counterattack, were carefully feeling their ways. Under the leadership of the conservative Martin Dies, chairman of the House Committee on un-American Activities, a great storm of attention was being given to the question of who was or was not fit to serve the American cause, and the information agencies were the leading target. What was the meaning of "fitness"? That was the underlying question. Although it was widely agreed even by liberals that actual Communists should not hold administrative positions because of the divided loyalties so embarrassingly demonstrated by the Nazi-Soviet Pact, the services of the large numbers of intellectuals whose convictions had brought them close to the Communist Party during the 1930s were now badly needed. Yet their reception was exceedingly hostile. MacLeish, the Librarian of Congress, and Sherwood — both friends of Roosevelt's — were criticized for their support of Loyalist Spain. Sherwood and his own deputy, former *Herald Tribune* correspondent Joseph Barnes, were denied formal clearances till they had been occupying their positions for nearly a year. Malcolm Cowley, who worked for MacLeish at the Office of Facts and Figures, was harassed till he finally resigned. Who had been what Then and what its political implications were Now were suddenly very much public issues. On May 21, 1942, when Josie had been working on the German desk only a few months, she was returning from lunch with another employee when she was accosted by uniformed security guards who padlocked her desk and locker, pawed over her handbag, and escorted her unceremoniously from the building. At that moment, she became a liberal.

What exactly took place behind the scences to bring about Josie's dismissal is something it was not possible for anyone to learn when it happened. "There was a great deal of speculation involved," Robert Sherwood testified at a hearing for another OCI employee fired at the same time. "It reached such a point in the case of Miss Herbst, she was suspected of being a communist and a Fascist. It seemed to me it was difficult to be both — but they could not specify which it was, or on what grounds their suspicions were based." About one particular "speculation" Sherwood was unequivocal: "As to the serious charge of taking secret documents out of the office, there was absolutely no legitimacy to that." Despite the release of material under the Freedom of Information

Act it is not possible fully to understand what happened even now, for while the number of documents is substantial, between the excisions, the internal contradictions, and the discontinuities between the files of various agencies there are innumerable gaps, and the precise combination of factors leading to the decision to fire at that moment we will never know. But if it is not possible to reconstruct every aspect of what happened in Washington, the general background of the dismissal is clear enough from the papers. It is not only not a very savory story: it is a story that Josie never knew.

It appears from the documents that Josie's dismissal was at least in part the product of an extensive security investigation undertaken by the FBI shortly after she began work. To say that the investigation "caused" the firing would be to go beyond the available evidence because the investigation both began before the firing and continued after it and Josie was ultimately "cleared"; but if it was not a case of simple cause and effect, it evidently contributed, for material from an informant in the field appears in at least one FBI memorandum discussing the firing more or less in the nature of a justification, and, apart from Sherwood's account of the oral rumors, there are no other plausible causes. Simply as a procedural matter the mere fact of the investigation seems unexceptional enough. It was one of many routinely ordered. Josie was handling "Confidential" information. During a massive war with political and ideological as well as military implications, certainly it was reasonable for the government to attempt to verify the backgrounds of its sensitive employees. But if the propriety of the investigation can at least be argued, its method was another matter, for it consisted of a full-scale mobilization involving offices and agents all over the country eliciting an undifferentiated hodgepodge of opinion of which the best that can possibly be said is that it revealed as much about the person being interviewed as it did about the person being investigated — with no sign whatever in the record of an objective intelligence attempting to sort it out. From the San Francisco office, whose report probably reached Washington first, came the incorrect assessment of confidential Informant SF-3 that Josephine Herbst was a "national character in the Communist Party" and had been a member of its advisory board since 1936. According to the St. Paul office she was "a good writer, honest, of good character, and no un-American tendencies." In Sioux City the "Women's Club heartily disapproved of the morals that appeared [in her] books," while at Saratoga "the [Yaddo] Colony was very proud of the fact that she had done some of her writing there." Confidential informant T-2, operating out of New York City, revealed the intelligence that "from her record and her writing . . . it appears that MISS HERBST is definitely a left-winger who is far to the left," while another, T-1, maintained that "if she ever belonged to the Communist Party, she must have been kicked out because of her intellectual honesty." From Boston, Philadelphia and Washington, from newspaper offices, publishing houses, and magazines, from the postmaster at Erwinna antagonized by *Satan's Sergeants* to a clerk in a Washington apartment house gratified by her friendliness, friends, enemies, acquaintances, strangers and spies spewed out pieces of gossip of which even those of goodwill were usually inaccurate and those of ill-will could unwittingly be truthful. But of all the interviews conducted by the FBI in its prodigious investigation into the character of JOSEPHINE HERBST the most provocative, the most extraordinary — and without doubt the one of greatest interest to the readers of this biography — was one conducted by the Salt Lake City bureau in Reno, Nevada, with a confidential informant who because of the derogatory nature of her information particularly requested anonymity in the government's files. Following the agents through their paces as they track their way to the individual in question, the evidence is unmistakable. This particular confidential informant was Katherine Anne.

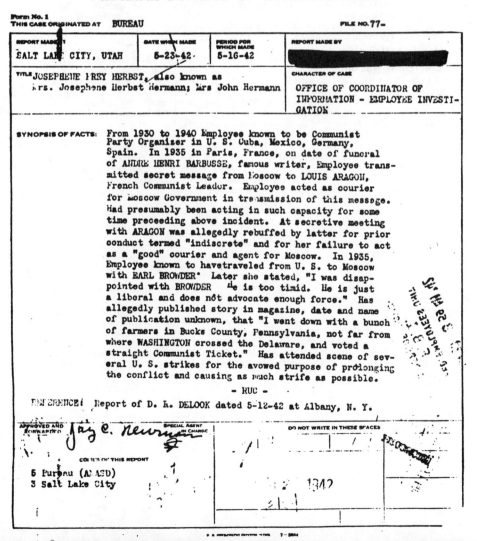

# FEDERAL BUREAU OF INVESTIGATION

Form No. 1
THIS CASE ORIGINATED AT **BUREAU**                                    FILE NO. 77-

| REPORT MADE AT | DATE WHEN MADE | PERIOD FOR WHICH MADE | REPORT MADE BY |
|---|---|---|---|
| SALT LAKE CITY, UTAH | 5-23-42 | 5-16-42 | |

TITLE JOSEPHINE FREY HERBST, also known as
Mrs. Josephine Herbst Hermann; Mrs John Hermann

CHARACTER OF CASE
OFFICE OF COORDINATOR OF INFORMATION - EMPLOYEE INVESTIGATION

SYNOPSIS OF FACTS: From 1930 to 1940 Employee known to be Communist Party Organizer in U. S. Cuba, Mexico, Germany, Spain. In 1935 in Paris, France, on date of funeral of ANDRE HENRI BARBUSSE, famous writer, Employee transmitted secret message from Moscow to LOUIS ARAGON, French Communist Leader. Employee acted as courier for Moscow Government in transmission of this message. Had presumably been acting in such capacity for some time preceeding above incident. At secretive meeting with ARAGON was allegedly rebuffed by latter for prior conduct termed "indiscrete" and for her failure to act as a "good" courier and agent for Moscow. In 1935, Employee known to have traveled from U. S. to Moscow with EARL BROWDER. Later she stated, "I was disappointed with BROWDER  He is too timid. He is just a liberal and does not advocate enough force." Has allegedly published story in magazine, date and name of publication unknown, that "I went down with a bunch of farmers in Bucks County, Pennsylvania, not far from where WASHINGTON crossed the Delaware, and voted a straight Communist Ticket." Has attended scene of several U. S. strikes for the avowed purpose of prolonging the conflict and causing as much strife as possible.

- RUC -

REFERENCE: Report of D. K. DELOOK dated 5-12-42 at Albany, N. Y.

APPROVED AND FORWARDED                     SPECIAL AGENT IN CHARGE                DO NOT WRITE IN THESE SPACES

COPIES OF THIS REPORT
5 Bureau (A ASD)
3 Salt Lake City

1342

(                                  (

DETAILS

          Informant I advised that in 1926 JOSEPHENE HERBST was a young
writer in Connecticut with very little money. At this time she was living with
her husband, JOHN HERMANN, who would often attend small literary meetings composed of young struggling writers in Connecticut. At these meetings the group
discussions usually included political questions of the day. At this time neither
JOSEPHENE HERBST nor her husband voiced any un-American political sentiment or
pro-Communist viewpoints.

          Sometime between 1928 and 1930 JOSEPHENE HERBST and JOHN HERMANN
traveled to Russia. The Russian Government had made an offer to the former to
have her books translated into Russian and placed on salt in that country. The
only condition attached to this offer was that JOSEPHENE must come to Russia
and spend all the royalties from the sale of the translated books in Russia.
This offer was presumably accepted by JOSEPHENE HERBST'

          Upon the return of these parties to the United States in about
two years, their interest in Communism was very marked. Both parties were in
accord with the theory of Communism and freely discussed the alleged advantages
within such system of Government. It was at this time, Informant believed that
JOSEPHENE HERBST and JOHN HERMANN joined the Communist party in the United
States. After this, JOSEPHENE HERBST became very close mouthed about Communism
and her affiliation, if any, with the Communist organization.

          From 1930 to 1935 JOSEPHENE HERBST corresponded frequently with
friends in Europe. These letters for the most part came from Cuba, Mexico, South
America, and Spain. According to Informant there was some intimation in all such
letters that the writer, JOSEPHENE was engaged in organization work for the Communist party in the respective countries mentioned above.

          In 1935, Informant advised, JOSEPHENE HERBST, traveled on the same
boat with EARL BROWDER from the United States to Continental Europe and thence
to Moscow, Russia. There is no evidence immediately available to show this trip
was pre-arranged by BROWDER and HERBST. Later in 1935, at Paris, France, in
speaking of BROWDER, JOSEPHENE HERBST said, "I was disappointed with BROWDER. He
is too timid. He is just a liberal and does not advocate enough force."

          Informant 1 further advised that during most of 1935, except for
intermittant trips to Moscow, HERBST was in Berlin, Germany, endeavoring to get
German Communists out of Germany and into the United States. During this year,
ANDRE HENRI BARBUSSE, famous French writer, died in Russia. His body was shipped
to Paris, France, for burial. At this time, HERBST traveled from Moscow to Paris
for the subsequently admitted purpose of transmitting a message from the Moscow
Government to a French Communist Leader named LOUIS ARAGON. HERBST stated that
she and ARAGON chose a public cafe for their meeting place on the day of BARBUSSE'S

- 2 -

funeral procession through the streets of Paris. HERBST stated that this day was chosen for the meeting since the cafes would be practically empty due to BARBUSSE'S funeral. HERBST and ARAGON had not met prior to this time. So that they could identify one another, each wore a red carnation and carried a newspaper under his arm.

It was further advised that in speaking of the above meeting, HERBST informed she was very indignant over the way ARAGON had treated her. She stated that ARAGON did not seem interested in receiving the message she had brought but rather spent most of the time rebuffing her for conduct he termed "indiscrete" in arranging for their meeting place. She also advised that ARAGON had told her she was not a "good" courier and agent for Moscow.

It was at this time, while speaking indignantly concerning her treatment at the hands of ARAGON, that HERBST implied by her conversation that she had been acting as courier for the Moscow Government for some time.

Informant #1 also advised that subsequent to this meeting, HERBST stayed in Paris for several months and attempted to obtain the right of entrance for German Communists into the United States. Her unsuccessful plan in this venture was to play upon prior friendly interests within the American Embassy at Paris.

The informant further stated that by the Spring of 1937, JOSEPHENE HERBST had returned to the United States. At this time she traveled from New York City to Detroit to be present at the scene of a large labor strike in the latter city. I" speaking of this strike prior to leaving, HERBST said that she had no interest in the rights of the strikers or in their physical comfort or discomfort. She said that her only interest was to cause as much dissention, strife and bloodshed as possible in order to prolong the strike. She said that it was the Communist purpose to try to prohibit a fair settlement of strikes and to arouse as much class hatred as possible.

HERBST is also known to have attended the scenes of several of mid-west milk strikes ostensibly as a union helper.

Informant #1 stated that HERBST at one time wrote a story for a magazine, name and date of the publication presently unknown, wherein she wrote, "I went down with a bunch of farmers in Bucks County, Pennylvania, not far from where WASHINGTON crossed the Delaware, and voted a straight Communist Ticket."

Informant stated that JOSEPHENE HERBST has a violent temper, a revolutionist attitude, and has caused trouble wherever the opportunity presented itself. She is described as having the utmost contempt for the American form of Government and for the so-called American "liberal". She is said to be a great follower of STALIN and a personal admirer of this man. She is not known to have been an admirer of TROTSKY nor to have been actively affiliated with the TROTSKY Communists.

- 3 -

Informant advised that JOSEPHENE HERBST and her husband JOHN HERMANN separated in about 1935. JOHN HERMANN is said to be a radical communist who at the present time is located in the South as an officer for a Communist Front Organization which has as its ostensible purpose the education of negroes and the bettering of condition for the share-cropper.

- REFERRED UPON COMPLETION TO OFFICE OF ORIGIN -

Why Katherine Anne Porter would spend hours with a special agent of the FBI creating a portrait of Josephine Herbst at such variance with reality is perhaps not such a singular mystery: she also invented stories about herself. The story of her aristocratic origins, the stories about her husbands and lovers, the details of the stories of dozens of different adventures — these could vary from time to time depending on the circumstances of the telling, but they had in common that they were all very often made up. Her friends recognized this tendency and made allowances for it. "I remember too much and she forgets too much," Josie complained to another friend at one point. Yet the story Katherine Anne told of Josie was hardly a case of "forgetting." Was it honest misapprehension? Wartime flag-waving? Simple malice? Could she possibly have believed what she said? It is true that they had quarreled a year earlier over who got preferred treatment at Yaddo, true that there was tension over Katherine Anne's failure to review *Satan's Sergeants* after promising she would, true that there was competition between them, growing rather than weakening with the years, that at times left one or the other of them uncomfortable; but it is also true that they had seen one another often in the last few years in their mutual crossings in and out of New York, that their rambling all-night dissections of writers and politics had never lost their zest, that they relished the image they made together, two aging ladies, pursuing the universe in hotels. "Our feeling for each other. Stood up this long, guess it will last forever. Believing friends," Josie jotted to herself after one such session only a short time before. Even the FBI appears to have found Katherine Anne's fiction farfetched because there is appended to the transcript a list of amplifications unusual in such reports.* I have ransacked my files attempting to see if there is any possibility the basic story could be true and I believe that the answer is no. Josie could well have traveled from the United States to Europe on the same boat as Earl Browder in the summer of 1935 and found him "timid." She could well have attempted to use her influence later that year to help refugees from Fascism gain admission to America — indeed, she did. She could well have met with Louis Aragon in Paris on the day of Barbusse's funeral bringing him messages from the German Communists she had been in touch with in Berlin, although the fact is she had known Aragon since 1930 so the carnation would have been rather a melodramatic touch. But there is no way — there is absolutely no way — she could have been traveling as a courier to and from Moscow. The times and places simply do not add up. Josie did not go to the Soviet Union in 1935; she did not live there for two years following her brief visit earlier in the decade; and there is nothing in her correspondence with Katherine Anne over those years that suggests she did. Kath-

* See Notes at on pp. 355–356.

erine Anne's story is purely and simply a malignant reinterpretation of everything she knew about Josie's history almost from the time they had met, and if destruction was her purpose it was also a particularly clever interpretation since it left Katherine Anne herself the only person in a position to prove or disprove what she said. Of the seven points listed in the amplifications, six have reference as sources only to Katherine Anne. Like the FBI investigations as a whole, Katherine Anne's interview cannot be said to have cost Josie her job for while the interview took place on May 16, 1942, the formal report was not made until May 23, two days after the firing, and whether or not the agent reported informally earlier and thereby fed the deliberations which must have preceded the event there is no way to establish.* But whatever its political consequences, Katherine Anne's interview with the FBI reveals an insidiousness in the relationship practically from the beginning which Katherine Anne never acknowledged and Josie only gradually sensed. When she learned about Josie's dismissal later in the war she was, Katherine Anne said, "horrified," and when the friendship did founder not long afterward on a very different question concerning literature and politics it was Josie, not Katherine Anne, who felt the burden and the necessity of repudiation. What satisfaction Katherine Anne could have anticipated from her invention is another mystery since the report was to be buried in a government graveyard for all eternity, but then she was accustomed to postponements. Her literary star was rising, her marital star was falling. In Reno for her fourth divorce, could it be simply that she was bored? In a heart that was festering with age, she must have enjoyed the knowledge that she was doing a foul deed.

In Washington, meanwhile, Josie was attempting to discover the charges against her to no avail. Colonel Donovan, who had ordered the firing, was uncooperative. Robert Sherwood was sympathetic but powerless. The personnel officers were unsympathetic and uncooperative both. It was not until three weeks after the dismissal, on June 11, 1942, that she at last heard some of the accusations in the course of an interview with Civil Service investigators, and when she did finally hear them she was appalled. She was "reported" to have been sympathetic to the Soviet Union prior to the 1939 Pact; she was "reported" to have endorsed Browder and Ford in 1936; she was "reported" to have contributed to a banquet honoring Mother Bloor. What was "reported" was nothing less than her entire political history. To almost all of the investigator's charges she responded with an affirmation. If the charge was complicated she explained it, if it was simpleminded she denounced it, but no matter what she was charged with even if she no longer remembered it,

---

* Such preliminary reports, often by teletype, were not uncommon, though neither were they universal, and none was released in this instance.

as long as she agreed with the principle behind the incident she claimed it as her own. "I am reported to have protested against the violation of various civil liberties . . . in the 1930s," she summarized almost immediately afterwards in the liberal newspaper *PM.* "Good."

> I am reported to have printed articles in magazines known to the Measuring Stick trade as "left". I am grateful that during the last decade I was not confined to the *Saturday Evening Post* for expression.
>
> I am reported to have been actively interested in the Loyalist cause in Spain, but in order truly to damn me they allege that I have taken part in a Communist Party broadcast from Spain. . . . My answer is: I would have broadcast from Spain under any auspices, including the Communist Party, in order to have one tiny chance of arousing people in England, France, and the U.S.A. to the danger that threatened not only Spain but themselves. History vindicates this position.

"History vindicates"? Sometimes. But history also condemns. Whoever controls the past controls the future. It was control over the past that was at stake in these charges and Josie would fight for it. In the interview with the gentlemen whom she later, in one of the finest pieces of writing of her life, called her "Interlocutors," she instinctively took the position she would take throughout all the investigations to come. They did not understand history and that was that. Everything she had participated in was not only justified but required by the conditions of the moment and the shame was not what had been attempted but what had failed. "I have [done] little really, too little," she brooded later that evening. Not knowing whether a transcript would be made available she returned to her apartment and attempted to record the session from memory, pausing at several junctures simply to think at the typewriter, trying to grasp the meaning of these vague and shadowy forces that seemed to be working their way through Washington. "Somehow this has to be brought out of the frame that the Civil Service has put around it," she wrote.

> Nothing sounds right within that frame. Everything is warped from its context. Actually now I see I am on the stand for trying to be truthful all along. The actual communists would never have put themselves in such vulnerable positions. I always expected truth to prevail somehow and in the end doubtless it does. But in a session such as this, how can it? . . . As I . . . indicated to the examiners, it would be necessary to write a book to make the beginnings of understanding the truth, to interpret the workings of even one individual in a time so complicated as the period since the first world war and this.

257

How is one to make people understand? How can these rigid frames be broken down to show the living person, how it is to be demonstrated that a life is not to be sized up by a few single acts which are not even rightly understood but are interpreted with prejudice from the word go? Why are people who had a few contacts with let us say communists, to be barred from this war effort of all effort, and not one word is said of people who did nothing but stuff their pockets and think of their own welfare during the last black decade? Why is reaching out a hand, not to conspirators about to throw over a government but to such people as I knew them, doing this thing or that, defending union labor or fighting fascism . . . why is that a criminal act? What is involved in all this? Why are Gen. Motors who deliberately preached Naziism in Lansing, Michigan during the last decade never investigated along such angles or the many people here in Washington whose one virtue has been caution and selfishness and therefore are fit delegates for fascism once it has swept before the winds?

"How is one to make people understand?" Who are these interlocutors and what is the source of their power? How does one hold one's ground against politically based interpretations of history so fundamentally hostile to one's own? Questions that she would return to again and again in the years to follow had their origin here. Sometime in the middle of this predawn internal reckoning her mind articulated the answer that her heart had known before:

> The measuring stick. That is the place to quarrel, not with defending myself at all. They cannot accuse me of acknowledged acts which I shall not allow myself to regret.

It was a strategy not only for the present but for the future and it was a useful thing to have one. What was reported this time would be reported another time. She would hear those charges again.

However isolated Josie would ultimately be, for the moment she was something of a heroine. Her colleagues at OCI signed a petition of protest contrasting the "peremptory methods" and "utter lack of opportunity offered . . . to present . . . [a] defense" with the "spirit of democracy" they touted every day in their broadcasts. *PM* and *The New Republic* ran articles echoing her question why it was largely Communists and not Fascists who were being investigated. Even Eleanor Roosevelt interested herself in the affair, writing to the Attorney General that she found it "extraordinary" and asking for more information, though why she was satisfied with the nonexplanation she received is something of a puzzle. Had Josie decided to do battle in Washington she would undoubtedly have succeeded in gaining reinstatement since she was later officially "cleared," but despite the existence of a small band of liberal friends who would probably have helped support her while she was doing it, to continue to live at Washington prices without a government salary was practically impossible and to hire a lawyer was out of the question. "I am not interested in trying to wrest anything from an unwilling government," she wrote Robert Sherwood. "Whatever odium there is, does not rest upon my head."

The rest of the war she treated as a personal reprieve. She had tried to serve and was not wanted. She was too unsettled to write. As far as she was concerned the war was over. She was free. With the house in Erwinna her only source of income she decided to keep it rented and go to Chicago where she had been invited by Dorothy Farrell, ex-wife of Jim, to move into her family's large rambling quarters in Hyde Park. It was exactly what Josie needed. Dorothy was living in the midst of a bustling, good-natured, and unconventional adult household into which the addition of another lively character was the most welcome thing in the world. From a group of black jazz musicians with one of whom Dorothy was having a romance to a group of classical composers, from the highly trained professors of the University of Chicago to the self-made intellectuals of the radical Abraham Lincoln School, from a household resident occupying a place somewhere between a second mother and a maid to the corner grocer, it was a house which attracted the most unlikely, eccentric, and incompatible personalities in the neighborhood and wove them into a temporary whole. In its warmth and casualness, in a family atmosphere that kindled memories of her own childhood, Josie relaxed. According to Dorothy Farrell, she was very much beloved. Since the financial situation was such that she did not even have to contribute, for a time she did nothing but rest and when she did go to work — for a salary, in a city venereal disease control project, and for a token, teaching writing at the Abraham Lincoln School — her jobs were practically entertainments. A friend from Washington, Mary Lloyd, was also nearby, in Winnetka, and they began to see one another often. Josie stayed in Chicago for more than a year, the woman who came to dinner, soaking up the pleasures of company, but eventually she had soaked enough and in the summer of 1943 she abandoned Chicago for a solitary journey west. Sioux City. Seattle. San Francisco. Back over the old territories she traveled, pausing here and there with familiar places or people, trying to find the old war in the new one, the past in the present, hoping to invigorate herself, by association, into some kind of literary awakening but nothing consolidated yet. She returned east in the fall of 1943 and took an apartment in New York in an effort to reestablish at least the conditions for work, but scarcely had she gotten herself settled when there was a new and serious diversion: John Herrmann, hoping to gain the property for himself, was trying to have her evicted from Erwinna. Advised by a lawyer in the middle of March, 1944, to resume possession at once to strengthen her own claim, she hurried to the country immediately and was there when the war began drawing to a close. Although much had happened to herself and the world since she had first begun keeping her wartime journal, the tone of her final entries had not altered very much.

*June 6, 1944. D-Day. Erwinna.*
  D-Day came early this morning. I got it over the radio at breakfast time. Yesterday the copperhead snake invaded here — was shot by [a friend] through a three inch crack in the terrace. I felt sick afterwards and had supper in bed. Today all sports called off. Roosevelt went to bed last night to compose a prayer. Ronald Colman read a prayer composed by Edna St. Vincent Millay at 7:30 — she had probably been composing it for months waiting the day. A gory stupidity about you mines in the dark earth, you workers at the plane's tip. A marine who won a jitterbugging contest in Los Angeles said he felt a little silly. Gambling dens were closed. The invasion held a 50 mile coast about 7 miles deep. Airplanes reported. Yanks leaning on the rifles awaiting mess — the parachuters went in first. The coast somewhere between Cherbourg and Le Havre. Flash from Quentin Reynolds about how beautifully all the British loved all Americans. First eyewitness report from Hicks broadcasting off a battleship on the coast. Sound of planes overhead and wind at the rigging. Wind at 18 knots. Getting stronger. An officer caught in a pocket screaming "They're on our necks —". Berne reporting the Germans amazed at news of our landing. Lots of quiet and ominous non-attack. RAF man said lack of German planes fantastic. Prayers over the radio — oily commentators, the same pleas for hair tonic. D Day — at last. Rejoicing reported in Russia. Calm in London. General de Gaulle may land on the coast of France. Here the woodchuck ate my morning glories in spite for my fencing the lettuce. . . . *June 9* Rain in the garden.

# "Somewhere The Tempest Fell . . ."

WHEN JOSIE returned to Erwinna in the spring of 1944 things were harder for her there than they had ever been. The place was more decrepit than ever. Unoccupied for a long period, the grounds were a jungle and the house was a zoo. With the war on not even the solvent could find help from among the neighboring villagers and Josie was practically penniless. To help pay the bills she had brought with her from New York a younger writer, Rebecca Pitts, whom she had agreed to house in exchange, and together they undertook the necessary restorations. There was a hot, dry summer. In search of water during a perilous drought, creatures of every description made their way through the overgrown territory. Birds flocked to the edge of the brook, the rivulets were choked with turtles, lizards insinuated themselves into the crevices between the rocks. On the land the garden was lost to the woodchucks, the squirrels found respite in the chimney, the copperheads were menacing, profuse. The fall was swift and pallid and all too quickly the winds of winter were rustling inside as well as outside the house. The walk to the village loomed longer and longer and what neighborliness there was in the vicinity dwindled as the population battened down. The house was still exceedingly primitive. There was no toilet, there was no tap water, there was no heat apart from the wood fires they had to supply themselves. The title to the property remained unresolved. They stayed on in the house together throughout the beginning of the cold spell, two women alone with a cat and a radio, but shortly before Thanksgiving Rebecca left, and then there was one. Except for an interlude in Florida the following winter, and occasional visits elsewhere, Josie remained by herself in Erwinna for several years.

The solitude into which Josie entered at the end of the war was as much an interior as an exterior condition. Companions and friends were as welcome as ever, but as far as any connection more intimate was concerned she wanted none of it, ever again. She was convinced of it. The outcome of her affair with Marion Greenwood had been too serious. Once during the summer she had given Rebecca a rare true accounting of the demise of her marriage, and when the subject recurred in letters she repeated what she had said before. "I am almost pathologically fearful of any kind of physical intimacy and for a good reason. I have been flayed to the bone." From politics, too, at least in the sense of active involvement, she was seeking shelter. The world was in a state of incomprehensible moral and political turmoil. The Nazi regime revealed the malevolent reaches of the human spirit: the Soviet Union demonstrated the indivisibility of revolution and reaction: the atomic explosions suggested the imminence of new catastrophes before the old ones had even been absorbed. On that trilogy of evils, who could lay claim to pronouncement? She still felt no need for the public renunciations and justifications emanating from many of her friends. She did not feel particularly guilt-ridden or sullied. She did not have any regrets. "When you say that all of us who were identified with the left merely stained ourselves to no purpose, I agree that we stained ourselves, but for myself I could by no means say that it was to no purpose," she wrote Rebecca in the summer of 1946. "A bad lover or bad political associates may actually give more in the end . . . for they arouse a more acute awareness of what the world is actually like. When things merely go well, one slumbers." Neither was she particularly unhappy. She was well over fifty years old. All of a sudden, for the first time in the decade since John had left her, she was free of him. She could see things again, watch the trees bloom, smell the flowers. One day, she wrote to Katherine Anne, she said to herself, "why there are the autumn leaves lying on the hill across the road like the shining scales of little fish." Her political disappointments too had been more painful earlier. Now she accepted them. History was what it was. Experience was experience. Participation had at least been an agent of knowledge. She was not going to assay any judgments. She would be stately and philosophical from now on. Call it shortsighted, if you will: you cannot really call it self-deception. She had every reason to believe her expectations. Her photographs from this period have a vaguely grandmotherly quality. There was nothing to belie the possibility of stateliness except that ultimately stateliness was not one of the possible positions.

The work which Josie attempted during a two-and-a-half-year confrontation with herself, human nature, and history is an ambitious philosophical novel, *Somewhere the Tempest Fell,* published by Scribner's in the fall of 1947. Set in Chicago during the war, the book involves a large number of characters each of whom is trying to reestablish connection with reality after the disintegration of a former dream. Against an almost surrealistic background individuals of every class, situation, and stage of life mingle and separate, pursuing their individual truths, attempting to resolve in action the inner and outer difficulties they face in accepting things as they are now. Adam Snow, a writer in a crisis of integrity: Ada Brady, a divorcée in a crisis of romance: Ralph Johns, a radical journalist in a crisis of revolutionary faith —: these and dozens of other characters at times only loosely related wend their ways into and out of the narrative, their encounters primarily the occasions for the revelations of their existential dilemmas. There are also a number of jazz musicians whose sessions in smoky basements and darkened clubs are important in setting the tone of the whole. What distinguishes *Tempest* from everything else Josie ever wrote is its explicitly philosophical content. Guilt and innocence in both a political and a personal context, expectation and disappointment — these are some of the themes of the novel. The world is far, far more complicated than one imagined — this is its essential conclusion. The difficulties with the novel lie not so much in its aspirations as in its realization. It has no central narrative, no definite story, and no sense of direction. It is as if in introducing certain problems on the level of idea, Josie ignored the necessity of concluding them in the flesh. "If the dangling ends of narrative had been caught up, if there had been a sounder proportion between important incidents and trivialities, if the characters had been better projected . . ." it would have been a stronger novel, commented Diana Trilling in *The Nation,* but whether its flaws proceeded from the "sense of urgency and [the] zest for experience and [the] acceptance of life" generously granted by Trilling, or whether Josie was still too overwhelmed by the complexities she was trying to describe to succeed in setting them all out clearly, not only on a philosophical, but even on a technical level, the book is a considerable muddle. Its plot and its characters are insufficiently integrated to sustain the philosophical interest. Its action is extremely difficult to follow. Its tone is decisive but its content is vague. It is difficult to summarize because it is difficult to be certain what is being said. If ever Josie were to produce a fictional reflection on the human condition that truly consolidated her understanding it should have been now because she had the experience and she had the intention and she still had the will, but in *Somewhere the Tempest Fell* she did not consolidate it. In his modest, concrete *The Middle of the Journey,* published the same year, Lionel Trilling, by attempting less, accomplished more. If Josie was trying to recreate the historical moment she succeeded but if she was trying to transcend it she failed. It is finally rather as an illustration of the confusion of the postwar period than as an illumination of it that Josie's last major fictional effort must take its place.

The literary situation that greeted *Somewhere the Tempest Fell* on its emergence was more dismal than any Josie had ever faced before. Compared to the response which characterized the reception of most of her earlier novels, the attention of the public in 1947 was not on books, at least not on serious books. Neither, it seemed, was the attention of the publishing industry. Promotion was scanty. The reviews were scattered and late. In fact the ill luck that affected the novel began even before publication when Maxwell Perkins, its editor, died unexpectedly of pneumonia, less than two weeks after Josie had turned in her final draft. Whether Perkins would have worked sufficiently on the manuscript as he did on others to pull out the central meaning at its core and so alter its destiny is impossible to say, but Josie was told by Perkins' successor, Burroughs Mitchell, that Perkins had found what he read of it "remarkable," so it is a plausible assumption. As for the reviewers, they were far from being negative about the book: it was rather that they were intimidated by it. Everyone commented on its complexity. "The question is . . . how hard a reader may justifiably be expected to work over a piece of fiction which, when slowly and carefully examined, reveals rewarding compensations," wrote a reviewer in *The New York Times*. It is a "sound and deliberate, scrupulous and valid novel. Yet it is difficult. In a time when so much fiction is uncraftsmanlike gush it is hard not to praise such writing as Josephine Herbst's simply because it is so complicatedly honest, and it is not at all a pleasant thing to have to decide, ultimately, that here perhaps the complexity has got a little in the way of the admirable seriousness and depth of the intention." In the *Saturday Review of Literature* Howard Mumford Jones made similar points. It was exactly this attitude that Josie found discouraging. "I ask you, isn't life complex and don't we have to struggle a little to find a light?" she questioned one of her Washington friends, Clair Laning. Except for occasional euphoria during the actual writing she had few illusions about the nature of her achievement. She was well aware of its flaws. It was the absence of any audience for the book even if flawed, the absence of serious discussion of its ideas, the absence of a community of people interested in books in general that she was depressed by. "There is a mysterious silence that seems to envelop books these days," she wrote Katherine Anne. "It is almost as if one should feel guilty for having produced one. Perhaps the child was a monster? Or perhaps it never existed at all. It gives one the feeling of a character in a Kafka novel, one is apparently guilty of something, but of what?" It was out of the emptiness she felt following the publication of her final novel that Josie first had the impulse to write about writers and what was happening to writing in America, an effort that through endless transformations would gradually come to dominate her days. And the precipitating factor of her literary speculations — in a way — was Katherine Anne.

"I found a lot of your old letters, — I certainly never destroyed even one," Katherine Anne wrote Josie about a year after the end of the war. ". . . Unless you claim [them,] they'll go in with the rest, to be sorted and used as part of a story." What story could she have had in mind this time, I wonder. In the literature department things were proceeding grandly enough. *Flowering Judas, Noon Wine, Pale Horse, Pale Rider, The Leaning Tower* — out it was flowing in a slow but steady stream, a body of work of such sterling character that it was hard to imagine reading it that its author might be otherwise herself, but it was rather the polish of sterling than it was its weight Katherine Anne imitated — so shiny, so stately, so showy on special occasions but rapidly tarnishing in the light. In her letters as well as in some of her criticism, the humor that formerly sweetened even her harshest observations was souring, her sharpness was becoming nastiness, the restraint which once gave a balance to her judgments was going or gone. The gain was all in the words: how they glittered and crackled and slithered across her pages. The loss was in the veracity: in the fullness of mind and heart. If she kept up appearances in public, at least in her fiction, in her lesser ruminations the malevolence that would later find expression in her final novel was steadily making its way. "When I heard Berlin was being reduced to rubble, I rejoiced," she announced as the Allied armies surrounded the city, and for Josie that seems to have been the beginning of the end. It was more than an argument about German character that was involved in the debate that followed: it was more than politics: it was a fundamental attitude toward the tragedies of human beings. As events proceeded their reactions to issues involving literature and politics grew steadily further apart. Consider the difference in their situations at the end of the war: Katherine Anne beginning to gather herself a following, moving toward the literary and political majority, identifying herself once and for all simply as an American and America once and for all simply with the Good: Josie losing even the smaller audiences she had once held as the possibilities she had stood for fell away, dividing herself still further not only from the mainstream but from the left, maintaining as she always would an instinctively international identification in which what she called "national maledictions" had no place. It was obvious who and what was pulling ahead. When Katherine Anne failed to review *Somewhere the Tempest Fell* as she had promised, Josie was humiliated, and when at about the same time she published an attack on Gertrude Stein in *Harper's,* Josie was appalled. In mocking Stein Katherine Anne was somehow mocking the entire modernist literary movement of which she herself, as well as Josie, was a part, Josie thought, and in mocking the literary movement she was associating herself with political reaction and worse. The article was brilliantly written, it was flawlessly argued, it was funny, it was subtle, the ideas and the characters simply leaped from the pages — but it was all wrong. "It reads so persuasively," Josie wrote her, "but it isn't Stein." Neither was it the nineteen-twenties as she was beginning to recollect them. In that era represented by Katherine Anne as a mindless muddle there was a hospitality to freshness that the increasingly stony present would do well to reinvent. She wrote to Katherine Anne honestly, if coldly, expressing both her disappointment about the review and her dissent about Stein, but Katherine Anne's conscience was clear. She had been too ill to review anything, she wrote back, and as for the Stein matter, it was nothing one of their famous conversations could not hash out. Unfortunately she never completed the letter. As far as Josie knew she was snubbed. A public rejoinder, "Miss Porter and Miss Stein," published in the *Partisan Review* a few months later, attacking the former and defending the latter, was the result. By now there were too many matters on the table between them and though I think they always wished to neither one had the strength left to try to sort them all out. They never saw or heard from each other again. Though it existed in both of their minds until their dying, with the first public installment in their continuous twenty-year chronicle, the epic of "Victoria" and "Miranda" was no more.

The act of articulating anything about the postwar period, however imperfectly, brought forth the gratitude of people who were experiencing the same confusions, and even in the absence of acclamation the publication of *Somewhere the Tempest Fell* offered satisfactions. For Josie the most important was the resumption of her friendship with Gustav Regler. Regler was a rare being in any era: a natural artist deflected into revolution by the desperation of Germany after World War I, a lover of justice who was also a lover of truth, a modern incarnation of the European chivalric tradition, a man in whom exquisite sensitivity and extraordinary strength were not at odds. In the film *The Spanish Earth* he appears at a political meeting tense, tough, and leather-jacketed, barking his Germanic exhortations at a pitch so grating you would think from the sound of it he was on the other side, but he was also the gentlest, most philosophical of men, with a radiance of mind and spirit that lightened everything it touched. His autobiography, *The Owl of Minerva*, is among the finest of all twentieth-century literary and political documents. He had lingered in Josie's mind for a long while after their meetings — throughout her life there was no man who moved her more — and although they had seen each other only once since the war in Spain, at a brief reunion at the home of some mutual friends, following the publication of her novel she began to hear from him often. Regler was in Mexico, exiled both geographically and politically, no longer surrounded either literally or figuratively by people who spoke his language, denied entrance into the United States by the government authorities, longing for contact with his own kind. His first wife, Marie Louise, the love of his youth and of the war years, was dead of cancer. In a second marriage to an American businesswoman living near him there was no real meeting of souls. He wrote Josie formally at first, then warmly, and finally with love, letters so revealing of the kinships between them it was no wonder one of them said "I told you so; heaven at last sent me my sister in blood and marrow, and if we have not met before on one of the planets in the curved space, I am wrong with everything." Pages filled with little drawings of nature that might have come from Josie's own pen; a shared cast of memory in which every event of the present was bathed in association with the past; an instinctively common language: only one thing separated them as the depths of their affinities were unveiled — she was afraid of them and he was not. In letter after letter following the renewal of their correspondence Regler wished, he cajoled, he tempted, he teased, he ordered, he commanded, he begged and he pleaded with Josie to come to Mexico to join him and week after week, receiving his entreaties in the isolation and loneliness of Erwinna, Josie vacillated over what to do. She would If, she wrote him. She would When. She would After. She was about to set off to see him several times, but a long string of afflictions from a sprained ankle to a strained pocketbook somehow got in the way. "I am no son and no brother and no needy husband, I am just a piece of this earth and the volcano broke out in Michoacan and it will break out every day newly at this table-desk, and therefore I wanted you here, because it is short what is left to all of us and I hear the neighing in the clouds, and am not morbid, but animated even more by it, and I wanted to animate you too . . . so this was the sense of my calling you like an owl calls the other owl" he wrote her in 1948 when he saw that she would not join him, but she could not return his call. Politics, yes: literature, yes: reflections about life and love, yes: she would speculate with him: she would pore over his manuscripts: she would pursue his wisdom across the pages: they could be each other's muses if they wished: but only by mail. What would have happened if they had seen each other again then, these celestial fellow travelers who even his wife believed would have done well to travel together, who can say beyond that in Gustav Regler Josie had undoubtedly found her match? As it was, it was another decade before they did meet, and by then it was already too late. For once she chose safety over the possibility of life. She remained in her exile in Erwinna contemplating the shadows on her own whitewashed walls until the substance of those shadows in the world outside her garden could no longer be denied.

# Witness

ONE DAY DURING the period of my work I was still spending most of my time in the archives I put aside my papers and went to pay a call on The Other Woman, the second Mrs. John Herrmann, a woman about whom I knew very little other than that in the years between his divorce from Josie in 1940 and his death in 1959 she had — indeed — been married to John. I was anticipating a perfunctory visit. Ruth had been passing into John's life at the very moment that Josie was passing out of it and their relationship, strictly speaking, was none of my affair, yet she had been intimate with him and I was writing about him and I felt she ought to know about it — that was all. I had scarcely been with her five minutes when she said she had been surprised to learn that a biography of Herbst was being undertaken so soon. Wasn't there a fifty-year stay on the papers? she inquired. "A stay on the papers?" I repeated. "Why?" "Why because of the Hiss case, of course," she said matter-of-factly, regarding me, with justification, as a political-biographical innocent who had no idea what complexities lay ahead. For the next day and a half we went over and over the points she thought I ought to know. John had been part of the Communist underground in Washington and he had been associated in the underground with Whittaker Chambers in his manifestation as "Karl"* — I knew that: but he had also been associated in his activi-

---

* Whittaker Chambers was always "Karl" in Josie and John's correspondence, though usually "Carl" elsewhere.

ties with a young Washington New Dealer named Alger Hiss and as a matter of fact Hiss and John had been friends. It was John, Ruth said, who had first introduced Hiss to Chambers, at lunch in a Chinese restaurant near Dupont Circle in 1934. By a conjunction of circumstances that was part contrivance and part chance this fact had never surfaced but it was nonetheless a fact, and Josie had known it as well as Ruth herself did. There were other details as well. It was this relationship Ruth supposed that Josie's papers had been garnisheed to protect.

To say I was distraught by her revelations would be considerably to understate my reaction. Why I cared so much about the innocence of Alger Hiss I could not have said exactly, but I did care. In the canons of American radicalism saints were of two kinds, heroes and martyrs, and that Hiss was one of the latter was a tenet I shared. Might as well call Peter Judas as to make Alger Hiss into Benedict Arnold. If he had not been falsely accused my entire interpretation of American history would be affected — and the interpretations of how many others, just like me? There was also a personal angle. I did not know Hiss well but I had once met him socially, and he hovered like an unrequited specter over the political lives of several of my friends. What's more I had heard from him only a short time earlier and on something related to this entire matter, a letter inquiring if there were any references to him or Chambers among Josie's papers at Yale that might amplify an interview he knew she had once given to the FBI. A cordial correspondence followed in which I summarized the few and seemingly unimportant items I had thus far found and in return asked some questions of my own, particularly about John Herrmann, whose later political life at that point I was still trying to track down. "I did not know Herman [*sic*] nor even know about him until Miss H's connection with the FBI came to my attention," Hiss replied. Now here was a contradiction. If Hiss had lied to the world at the time of the trials I had no way of knowing about it, but if he was lying to me personally in the present, perhaps I did. Could it be that because of my connection with the Josephine Herbst archives and Josephine Herbst's connection with John Herrmann the ultimate untangling of the relationship between Alger Hiss and Whittaker Chambers that had eluded so many others for so long was going to fall to me? I knew Josie was always at the center of things, but this was terrifying. That night I dreamed that an old woman with a cane who was undeniably Josie was beating me into silence at a political meeting and the interpretation was obvious, but by morning I realized that as far as my sources would take me I would have to go for it was not only Hiss's story, it was Josie's as well. The Hiss case is one of the greatest miasmas of American politics and there is no one who has been involved with it either as actor or scholar who has not in some measure been harmed. There are no arguments which have not been shaken, there is no evidence which has not been obfuscated, there have been no sentences either uttered or written that have not been parsed into nonsense. For this reason I want to speak as plainly as possible. There is nothing in Josie's witness that has direct bearing on the technical charges against Hiss which had to do with his relationship to Whittaker Chambers in 1937 and 1938. About espionage, about the transmission of State Department papers, about anything that happened in 1937 and 1938 Josie was not in a position to know. What she was in a position to know was whether Alger Hiss had met Whittaker Chambers in 1934 and had lied about it, and that is what she believed. She protected the secret out of a combination of loyalties, especially loyalty to John, and she paid a price for it later. It is time to invoke the statute of limitations on the political secrets of the 1930s, which, like most secrets, have gathered most of their power from being hidden from view. Reader: if your peace of mind is still dependent on a sacrosanct version of the Hiss case, this is not the chapter for you.

In August 1948 when the Hiss-Chambers confrontation occurred, Josie was in a very delicate situation. She had known that the underground figure "Karl" was the overground writer Chambers for almost ten years, since seeing a news photograph of him at the time he joined *Time* magazine, but suddenly it had become an important matter. She was not alarmed for herself, for in the former underground organization Chambers was exposing she had played no direct role, but she was worried about John. She had not seen or heard from him for more than ten years, she was not in touch with his family, for his unsentimental efforts to root her out of her only roost in the world she might well have chosen revenge, but her heart went out to him all the same. Almost universally among liberals and radicals alike it was held that the Hiss case was part of a governmental conspiracy to obstruct the resurgence of a radical movement in the future by discrediting that of the past, a position which rested on three points: (a) that there never had been any Communist underground in the 1930s in the first place; (b) that if there was an underground Alger Hiss had nothing to do with it, in the second place; and (c) if there was an underground and Alger Hiss did have something to do with it, it was a rightful, or at least inevitable, product of the period that it arose in and that there was nothing essentially wrong with it, in the third place. Josie was as certain that there had been an underground as she was of anything in her experience, she knew that Hiss had been considered a prospective contact during the period she was in Washington and she was clear in her recollection that John as well as Hal Ware and Chambers had said that they met, yet with the rest of the liberal dogma she by and large fundamentally agreed. She was convinced that the Washington underground was an innocuous domestic organization with no ties to the Soviet Union whose only function was to make its members feel important, and she was convinced she knew all there was to know about it. Yet here was the government taking it seriously. If it was "espionage" they were after there could be jail sentences, even death sentences, at stake. So careful was she in guarding her knowledge that I have found few places in her own papers where she appears to have initiated discussion of it herself, nor even at her most candid did she ever tell all she surmised, for from the reversal of values that accompanied the transmutation of the 1930s into the 1950s she would have protected even strangers if she could, and there were friends as well as acquaintances involved. Yet in a case of such public importance, and one being so thoroughly investigated, it was impossible to keep all her information to herself. It was inevitable that some of it at least would come out.

"So you knew Carl!!" a friend of Josie's wrote to her from Washington in September, 1948. "Did you know George Crosley? Your letter astounded me. I didn't know anybody knew Carl — when I asked if W. C. had crossed your path, I meant in a literary way. I read your letter twice to myself — passed it on to Blank who read it twice — then we read it aloud. Like all the testimony, it didn't contain many facts — but as interpretive material it was damned interesting — You were indulging in some very fascinating psychological matters which we long to discuss with you. We wondered why Carl was running from the police. Who said so? Carl? Was he a pathological character then, inventing lurid stories to dramatize himself & excite his cell members? What about our idea that even then he was an F.B.I. agent? Why so much monkey business in 1934? I was here in 1934 but I never heard of this business." Exactly what Josie had written to provoke this astonishment is not clear because her letter has not survived, but from the context it appears she was answering a question rather than volunteering the news. The woman in question, Ann Blankenhorn, and her husband, Heber, were longtime Washington liberals who had held a variety of responsible positions ever since the 1930s and they were appalled by the degeneration of New Deal liberalism into postwar hysteria. Moving cautiously between the parties, as the moment demanded, they made it known to attorneys for Alger Hiss that an individual of their acquaintance had indeed known Chambers as "Carl" and was willing to talk to them provided certain understandings could be reached in advance. While Josie was concerned lest in trying to help Hiss she accidentally implicate John, the attorneys suspected a government plant, and all in all it was not a simple matter to arrange. One point in particular made them choose to delay. "There was one rather ambiguous statement in Miss Herbst's letter, which Blankenhorn read to me, which seemed to indicate that she believes that you were in contact with Carl," one of Hiss's lawyers wrote him in discussing the pros and cons of setting up a meeting with Josie. "As I remember it she wrote, in connection with refusing to name names of Carl's contacts, that she made an exception with respect to you."

To judge from a memorandum prepared for the files by one of the participating attorneys it appears that, when they did meet with Josie in early January, 1949, it was not exactly a meeting of minds. There was a large political gulf between them. The lawyers believed that though innocent, Hiss had been charged with a serious crime that the government had a right to investigate. Josie believed that even if he had done what he was charged with he had done nothing wrong and in any case it was none of the government's affair. "I am very sympathetic to Hiss and think he is innocent. I would be sympathetic to him even if I thought he were guilty," she told them. From the lawyers' point of view it was essential that Josie be as specific as possible about the composition of what was now called the "Ware group" so that every clue that might lead to Hiss' exoneration could be followed. From Josie's it was essential that they understand that the government had gotten the "Ware group" all wrong. Whether Hiss or anyone else had participated in it was of small importance beside the fact that its activity was harmless, though she acknowledged it was her impression that Hiss had. They seem to have talked past each other for several hours, with Josie describing the operation of the underground in generalities and the lawyers pushing for more details, but despite her appreciation of their motives, in the end her own standard prevailed. "I do not recognize any higher duty to Government authorities and do not have any confidence in the Government," she told them. The lawyers were appalled. "Miss Herbst can perhaps best be classified as an international anarchist without any respect for government and with a completely confused set of political ideas," they concluded. ". . . She has no real concern about people working for the Government, taking papers, and supplying information surreptitiously to the Communist Party." Even if she knew the individuals in question were trying to promote revolution she would still find nothing immoral in it, they reported. "She said that revolutions had been going on for hundreds of years and referred to a volume of Lamartine, 'Revolution of the Girondistes,' which she was then reading. She indicated that the trouble with us was that we did not understand history." The trouble with her was that despite intending not to do so, she had inadvertently verified more than she had concealed. With friends like Josie Alger Hiss would not need many enemies. Clearly this was not what his lawyers had wanted to hear.

At almost the same time as the session between Josie and Hiss's lawyers, Whittaker Chambers was discussing John and Josie with the FBI. Why Chambers appears to have gone out of his way to protect John publicly — whether, like so many others, he simply liked John and was doing him a favor; whether John Herrmann, as an obscure writer, was simply not worth his attention; or for other reasons — is one of the lesser mysteries of the Hiss case, but in any case it was only a superficial courtesy for, though Chambers excluded John from *Witness* and from other public sources, he testified about him in private many times. Like most of Chambers' stories, like his pumpkins, his accounts of his association with John grew larger and larger as his situation demanded and were filled with inaccuracies, but the heart of his testimony was this. He said that John had been brought to Washington to serve as Hal Ware's assistant in the "Ware group" in 1934; that as a member of that group he had every opportunity to know what was going on in the underground; and that whatever John knew of Hiss's underground activities and connections he was certain that Josie knew too. With his characteristic alternation between details and delusions he also said that he had used John's Washington apartment to photograph documents obtained for him by Hiss and others; that on the Easter weekend of 1934 or 1935 he had driven with Hiss from Washington to pay a visit to John and Josie at the Erwinna farm; and that he had heard that Josie had recently defected from the Communist Party, which would make her a particularly valuable witness if true — all statements in the realm of the theoretically provable — and that John and Josie had both been members of the Communist Party and when they had separated from each other, an event he placed in 1937, instead of 1934–1935, Earl Browder had awarded possession of their nice place in Erwinna to her — a statement in the realm of the phantasmagorical. Ah . . . if she only knew.

Chambers' 1949 unburdenings set off a new period of intensive FBI investigation and within weeks of his confession two government agents came a-knocking at Josie's door. In a sense it was an unequal contest from the beginning: two youthful investigators with only garbled names, dates, and places that meant nothing to them at all, versus a competent older reporter, herself an experienced interviewer, armed not only with more of the facts but with the interpretation she wanted the facts to command. John had indeed gone to Washington in 1934, she told them, since they already knew; he had indeed been in contact with Harold Ware; he had even, she admitted, known Whittaker Chambers as "Carl" —: but it did not have the implications that they supposed. Really it was a very ordinary story. John was an independent writer with a special interest in farm problems and the purpose of his stay in Washington was to gather materials for his work. His contacts with Ware were undoubtedly in that connection, and, as for Chambers, while she could not say exactly, she presumed that he had had something to do with it too. It was a leftish sort of period, she reminded them, and the problems of the Depression made it inevitable that people would challenge the status quo. When she did meet Communists she could assure them she

273

thought nothing remarkable of it. She was not familiar with Alger Hiss nor a host of other individuals whom they named. If she seemed vaguer about her husband's activities than she ought it was because they had not been getting along very well and she did not question him about them. Marital discord. I imagine her giving them a sad wifely smile. She had also been finishing a book. She must have said it beautifully for the agents left satisfied and it is a fair measure of their sophistication and of hers that they recorded her exactly as she wanted to appear to them: "cooperative." As soon as the door shut behind them she sat down at the typewriter and wrote a long letter to John coded to tell him exactly what she had said to them without revealing anything she was covering up, a letter which would give him all the information he needed to make their stories coincide. She did not know where he was or whether he would get the letter, she only knew she was doing what had to be done, and whether we should call it "personal" or "political" is not an easy matter to decide, for the two intertwined. A man had done her wrong or she had done him wrong but it was long ago and far away and the details really didn't matter anymore. The things they had both believed in had not been wrong and she would shield him from their consequences if she could.

All during the rest of the year, 1949, as the Hiss case passed through various stages of litigation, Josie remained on her guard. First the lawyers came to see her again, then the FBI, then the lawyers again, each trying to see if there were some way she could be put to account. The defense at one point considered asking her to testify in court but decided against it. "My own impression is that neither the Government nor we would dare to put her on the stand," reads a note written by one of Hiss' lawyers. "She is likely to do more harm than good to anyone who calls her as a witness." The government was continually trying to track down Chambers' new details. "JOSEPHINE FREY HERBST interviewed at Erwinna, Pennsylvania," says the synopsis for the reinterview of November 7, 1949. ". . . She stated no photographic work done by CHAMBERS when she was present in Washington apartment. She advised she has never met ALGER or PRISCILLA HISS. She stated it was impossible for HISS to have been at her Erwinna home around Easter, 1934 or 1935. She advised she was very sympathetic to Communism from 1932 to 1934." Both the government and the lawyers were consistently asking her for the names of other people involved in "Carl's" network and she just as consistently refused to respond. And so it continued. In Mexico where he and Ruth had fled during the first round of the Hiss investigations and where he had indeed gotten her letter, John told a similar story and he maintained it, with variations, throughout a period of intense governmental pressure, until his death, a decade later, after a long slow alcoholic decline, minutely chronicled, down to the very ulcerations of his legs, in the government's files. From his continued residence abroad Josie gathered that he too was protecting the secret, but what he said exactly she never knew. "John was the big person in my life and to lose him was the most crushing thing that ever happened to me," she wrote to his sister when she learned that he had died. "I have never got over it." Not long afterward, passing through Michigan, she stopped to visit his grave. If she had not been faithful to him in one realm, she had, at least in another, and her loyalty lessened her pain.

"Anything you have stumbled on has already been stumbled on by others," a friend of Josie's who is also an acquaintance of Hiss's told me when I went to lay my story at her door. "However much you learn, you will find it will not take you anywhere." The introspection, the insomnia, the inexhaustible tracking down of clues familiar to any Hiss researcher: I have had my hours of them, and in the end I am not sure that it matters. Would Josie's position have made a difference to the Hiss case if she had revealed it? It is too ambiguous to be sure. In a case so presented that either Hiss or Chambers had necessarily to be lying Josie's position was that neither was being wholly truthful and it is not a position especially favored by the courts. She thought that Hiss knew Chambers *and* she thought that Chambers was unreliable *and* she thought that Hiss was not guilty as charged but what she thought did not correspond to any of the available choices. Then, too, much of her information was secondhand. As a witness to the "Ware group" whose very existence was often in doubt Josie's impressions would have had some importance because she was familiar with it herself, but everything she knew about Alger Hiss specifically had been told to her by Hal Ware, who was dead, by Chambers, who was practically on trial himself, or by John, who had disappeared. From an historical point of view her opinion is important because she was a good observer, but the lawyers could have torn her testimony apart. The same is true of my own discoveries. Neither from my conversations with Ruth nor from my examination of Josie's files is there any evidence which would withstand the scrutiny of the law. But if Josie's impact on the Hiss case would in all likelihood have been limited, the same cannot be said of its impact on her for it involved the one point in her political history on which she could not tell the truth. If it-had-been-reported in 1942 that in 1934 she had been close to the Communist underground in Washington, what would she have said? As the case continued to dominate and somehow even to symbolize the war of the 1950s against the 1930s she stood outside of it, critical of Hiss for his excessive denials of commitments which she believed ought to have been affirmed, sympathetic to Chambers if only because of the extraordinary vilification heaped upon him by others, contemptuous of the lawyers for their soulless re-creation of events in a way that had so little to do with their reality. Yet she never revealed what she knew. "I think the Hiss case was handled wrongly; he should have been more frank, as indeed I suggested to his lawyers all along," she hinted to her friend Clair Laning immediately after the first trial, in one of the few comments about it she ever seems to have permitted herself. "He should have boldly admitted to certain ideas now termed subversive but which were only honestly enlightened and leftish in the '30s. Instead he took too pure a stand, denied too much, admitted nothing. A jury isn't made up of lawyers, who in my opinion are verbal fools, they sense the truth. . . . You suspect a man who denies everything and is a pinnacle of proper conduct. . . . Admitting smaller things would have validated major denials. Any novelist could have told them that." She would do it otherwise herself. In a sense you could say that as the 1950s progressed, as she had more and more to protect herself and defend others, as the problem of "informing" became omnipresent and mixed up with the different problem of re-evaluating a political past now appearing very different from the way it had once seemed, she took her own advice, if the lawyers hadn't, yet it had its limitations. The difficulty has something to do with the fact that what in politics may be principle, in autobiography becomes evasion. It was part of the cost of commitment. Any biographer would have had to tell her that.

# Blow, Bugle, Blow

IN THE FALL of 1950, on the eve of an operation for a swelling of the thyroid gland whose outcome was temporarily in doubt, Josie surveyed her material possessions and in a rambling longhand testament beginning "In case of what is usually called the worst happening . . ." told "To Whom It May Concern" what to do if she died. She had little to give away and few people she wanted to give to. The disputed house she left to her niece Betty Davis who was charged with struggling for the title, and, if successful, selling it, preferably to John and Mary Cheever. Her literary affairs were to be handled by Clair Laning, a periodic companion who in the years following their meeting in Washington had become one of her closest friends. Token bequests of both money and goods were offered a handful of people she was seeing at the time with scarcely any of whom she could be considered truly intimate. There are few traces in this paper of any family affection, of political comrades or causes, of her friendships from her years with John. The chief beneficiary, recipient of a cornucopia of practical comforts and spiritual delights from a new Sears, Roebuck refrigerator to a trip to Europe, queen-for-a-day of her imaginary largesse, was a young woman poet she had met only months earlier, Jean Garrigue.

The place was Yaddo, the time was the winter of 1949-1950, and the situation was similar to what it had been once before: a brilliant and passionate younger woman momentarily forlorn and an ostensibly serene older one offering wisdom from a seemingly endless well. There was even a shadowy triangle to heighten the echoes, for there was a man in the background, the critic Alfred Kazin, also at Yaddo, who was drawn to both women at different times during a period when his second marriage was coming to an end. Jean Garrigue, then thirty-seven, was a midwesterner who had fled Indiana the way Josie fled Iowa and had been living in New York for several years depending on odd jobs to support her writing. A graduate of both the University of Chicago and the University of Iowa writing program, she was a poet whose earliest work had been featured in a collection of five young American poets in the early 1940s, and she had since published another volume of poems and a number of stories. She was now at a point of particular frustration, working on a novel that in fact was never done, in despair over the practical difficulty of keeping her work and her life afloat simultaneously. Talented and yet floundering, independent and yet in need, she was determined to make a life in art and willing to tolerate any sacrifice for it, and if it was that that first appealed to Josie in her, she saw it in Josie too. Whatever else overtook them as the years passed, there was always respect. Josie's relationship with Jean Garrigue is the most paradoxical — and perhaps the most painful — of her life. Though by far the most important involvement of her mature years — second only to her marriage to John, which was its closest equivalent — it brought easily as much suffering as happiness. It existed in full view of a circle of acquaintances who were constantly together, yet its intensity was unremarked by even her closest friends. It called forth voluminous writing, perhaps even as many as three thousand letters, yet there are no references to it in any of her published work, and with only a few exceptions the letters are the dreariest of her career. The story of John, for all its sadness, was part of the weave of her life, and long after it was over she kept it alive for herself and others by constant retelling in both conversation and in her work. For the story of Jean there was no audience and no place. " 'We are now men among men, we have brothers'/ Was not what you would have quoted/ But knew" read the lines of Jean's memorial poem published after they were both dead. It was as close as either of them ever came to an admission.

It began casually enough during the evenings at Yaddo in general literary conversation and if there were clues to the stirrings that soon came to dominate them they were well concealed. Later they would say "you wore that cap" or "that dress" or "the sun glittered on you that way" or "when you made a snow angel I felt such joy" but then they were romantic and they were ecstatic and if they noticed the deeper excitement that was coming to animate their rapport they did not choose to analyze it. The plot unfolded slowly, with a certain stealth, with a mutual interest disguised by one as solicitude, by the other as helplessness, yet it was unambiguous enough when it finally happened . . . a stumble in the grass, a helping hand . . . and if for Josie it was a tremulous moment, the first unloosing of her passion in many years, on Jean's side there was no such history of inhibition and her new love was neither her first woman lover nor her last. They were happy together their first summer, intoxicated, so secure in their conviction they shared a common understanding no negotiations were required. It was all taken for granted. They would live separately, they would be independent, they would expand one another's lives and not contract them, and as for men, far from wanting to obstruct Jean in any conventional desire, Josie would even teach her, by example, the ways of love. What enchantments were born in their first tender moments: ideas for collaboration, plans for travel, an imaginary island paradise they christened Bennville where both the forms of life and the customs of the inhabitants were eternally free. "Let us always be gay when we are together," Josie wrote her, but of course it was impossible. By the time Josie came to New York, after recovering from her operation without much assistance, they were already disappointed.

"She told me I talked too much — yes, yes. It is like blood pouring from a wound, such talk — it is simply one's life ebbing out — one cannot help it — it goes and floods everything with a dark swamp of wound, that is what it does. Does not clarify — no, its origin is dark and to dark it goes. Just bleeding. Not any more than that." Alas, both Jean's criticism and Josie's self-criticism are true. It was an affair that brought out the worst of a needy nature, and Jean, unlike John, seemed to have a steady appetite for it. Josie had intended to become her own Boswell, to keep a journal in which she and Jean would be "characters" seen from the outside, but by the second or third entry she was already lost in it and what began as an attempt at detachment became a record of confusion instead. A passage typical of both the journal and the correspondence, already severely edited, reads:

The waxy flowers, white, ivoried color, are here. They implore forgive, forget — and I should. But I am as weary as if I had come out of a sickness, weak as a convalescent. What am I to do? If I were as self-indulgent of my feelings, my ways or needs, this would now be finished. . . . Isn't it laughable to think of her as weak? Don't all the people who love me claim weakness and in the beginning have an appeal of touching need from me? And end by conquering? Let me be concrete. . . . She calls me to come to dinner. How I wish I were obtuse and did not at once take up into my very pores the atmosphere of the room. She isn't there, not really. I don't mean words. We eat, sit, but it is all empty — I might as well be alone in Grand Central Station. Then the strange evening begins. It is her place and with her kind of work she can work. I try to read . . . I feel she resents — not me — but her feelings for me. There has been the night before, presumably with the

Poppy Boy.° I do not think too much of this — I really do not — I
had dinner with her last night too and was there when he . . .
came in. . . . I do not know on this evening what happened, but I
can guess. I don't want to guess or think about it but I have to.
My face is rubbed into it for the room is saturated with something
that hangs on from his being here. I do know positively that whatever did happen was not rewarding. I think it was not good. She
makes a remark as she types — her back is turned — about not
being good at making love. I forget what I say but she amends it
to say she can be very good when she puts her mind upon it. Obviously she isn't satisfied at whatever happened. I don't like to
think of going to bed with her considering the night before so I
tell myself there was no such night and what has upset her is that
nothing came off. Therefore desire which was in her hasn't been
resolved. So she is full of a sense of frustration, irritation, and a
kind of baffled feeling that includes me and even — though probably unconsciously —blames me. She has every right to blame me. I
do obtrude upon any feeling she may want to entertain for someone else. It is a real difficulty, an obstacle, if you like. What to do
about it? I do not, cannot, know. She will never be at rest —
never. Does not want to be. So I finally stay, feel I am weak to do
so. Turn back the bed and see the two pillowcases, including the
one I ironed only the night before. So he stayed. How not freeze? I
cannot help it, lie feeling totally impotent and absolutely gone.
This she resents. She would like me to bend to her bow. I cannot,
cannot. . . . She had said during the evening how thin he is as if I
did not know what knowledge of that thinness implied. Why treat
me like a dummy fool? I know too much. Now she has said he returned but "nothing happened." Isn't that pure conventionality?
The cursed American fetish of the "act". The act isn't that important. The deed is in the mind and intention. That he returned and
was allowed to is the all. . . . She told me she was fickle — I should
believe her.

Then came the rest of the day and my determination to work
out of it into some kind of clear air. She comes back — after we
had separated in the morning — she is again inclined to be a little
sulky. Why? We parted tenderly, now this new cloud has come
from where? . . . It is the dark obstruction in her that has again
gained control. I determine not to notice — a spoiled brat having
a tantrum — and get a taxi. The day turns out beautiful — the
wonderful animals — Zimba, the wise creature with the great eyes
looking so intelligent, so knowing — the five horned owls . . . the
screaming birds . . . the silky leopards . . . so beautiful — food in

° One of Jean's lovers, an artist and musician, also appearing variously as the "Universal
Genius" and the "Great Lover."

the cafeteria and the walk toward the Plaza where the little tower rooms look so wonderfully high, like eagles' nests — and she wanted to live in a tower in the zoo with fine narrow windows and never leave.... Then the movie — the river and the nightingale — the old man and his love for trees — I feel whole again. We come home and then it begins all over. The afternoon's striving to heal, to make whole, seems all in vain. I feel the resentment of me, of her feeling for me, goes deep, deep. She cannot help but think — if it were not for you, it would be easier for me. Something more might happen than happens. I am held back by you — she even said, you are here even when you are absent. One sometimes longs to be rid of the presence of love — it can seem a grievous burden.... Oh what am I to do? ... I burst last night and today it all seems so wicked.... Wanton play with feeling is evil. To leap from one feeling to the other arbitrarily is inhuman. To be sweet one moment and the next to freeze — she wants something other than I can give at this moment and something that she has forfeited the right to. I cannot answer her bell at the moment she chooses to press it. I too have feelings — it is not as if I were the chambermaid in a hotel. I told her after she said perhaps we should not see each other for a week, all right, we won't, but any time you want to see me, I am here. This enraged her really — she told me I was too complacent. I often so enrage her — it is not goodness she wants but something stormy — to keep her stirred up, churned up. Doubtless good for poetry but I have not got the health for it and it destroys *my* work — oh where is my work? I have done nothing and my days are chopped up by the wrong hours, the too definite pressure of someone else's needs. ... I too resent, and deeply ... I have worked at this — patiently — tried to love, really truly in more than a clamor for myself — I do not think she wants that kind of loving though she needs it. She now thinks that I am preventing something — and I doubtless am. I see no way out except OUT. Really OUT. If it were not so sweet and she so basically good, it would be easier.... How well I see her situation and sympathize with it — I ask myself, what would I do? I do not know. Probably just what she does. And if I expected this to work — didn't I expect it just because I hoped we might be able to tread delicately, with infinite care, for one another's work, feelings, living, this most difficult, delicate path?

All of the elements of their long relationship are present in this passage: the jealousy that obstructed all rational efforts at accommodation, the self-serving characterizations by which Josie was always the innocent and Jean the guilty, no matter what happened, the excessive verbal analysis bringing no catharsis and no relaxation, only alternations of mood, until the end. Why they maintained it in the presence of so much unhappiness is a fair question. Certainly they were not simply "compatible." About the whole radical experience which Josie somehow embodied Jean knew absolutely nothing, and Jean's kind of poetry Josie would, at least initially, have found airy or worse. Radical, c. 60, seeks bohemian, c. 40, for purposes of what — misunderstanding? Externally so different that many of their friends could never grasp their connection, nonetheless their affinities were profound. Involvement with their sisters, early female losses, a perpetual childishness in Jean that made its way right into the center of Josie's empty maternal heart and an appearance of authority in Josie that always made Jean feel somehow secure — these were some of its sources. Yet it was not only their emotional histories that bound them together as the years passed, it was always the present. If suffering followed joy, joy always followed suffering again, world on end. "The very air crackled with pleasure when they were together" is a typical comment made about them by a friend. "They were always on stage for one another" is another. On a tape I have heard, made fifteen years after the period in question, they are alternately funny and boorish, stimulating and challenging, tender and nasty, delicate and lewd, but always with a kind of animal interaction that cannot be denied. For better or worse, richer or poorer, in sickness and in health — at least until the last time — they loved unsatisfactorily, but they did love. As far as Josie is concerned what is important is this: from the time she met Jean she was no longer alone. Someone knew her features, knew her feelings, knew her gestures, knew even her sagging old body, and accepted them. Jean even read the journal's most heartrending passages and commented on them, defending herself here, attacking there, amending a word or two in her own characterization, until it was almost as much a mutual as a solitary lament. No despair was too painful to be examined. No need was too shameful to be confessed. If one was aggressive and the other remote, if one was seductive and the other was shy, if one was self-pitying and the other self-centered, it was all somehow included. Josie and Jean were realists as well as romantics and if they concealed their emotional truth from others they accepted it themselves. But there was one difference between them and it existed from the beginning. No one would ever again mean more to Josie than Jean did, but to Jean many other people would mean a lot.

The work in which Josie was involved during the early years of her relationship with Jean took several forms but common to it all was a growing inclination to use herself and her experience as the foundation of whatever she had to say. In one way or another she had always done this, so the impulse was nothing new, but now it was becoming more explicit. A series of novellas, a novel, and a study of modern American writing, all drawing on her own life, as well as an autobiography, were all either under contemplation or under way at about this time, and she was also writing a biography of two early American naturalists, John and William Bartram, in which her love of nature as well as her political ideas functioned with a sensitive hand. Behind all this effort was a conviction traceable in her letters as far back as the late 1930s that the relationship between twentieth-century literature and politics was frequently misinterpreted and that as a participant in many important developments of the century she herself could interpret it better. A steadily increasing awareness of the singularity of her position as a woman and a new psychological awareness, in part inspired by Jean, appear to have contributed, too. Yet the decision to work in an autobiographical mode left many important related issues undecided. To use fiction and risk the loss of history or nonfiction and risk exposure of self: that was the underlying question. In all of the work of this period she was experimenting with different approaches to this dilemma.

The first work of the new period to bear fruit was a novella about her friend, Nathanael West, "Hunter of Doves." Published in the distinguished international journal *Botteghe Oscure* in 1954, the piece won for Josie the kind of literary admiration she had always wanted, and in recent years too the handful of scholars who have studied her work have been full of praise for it. The immediate sources of the story lie in the legends that had been accumulating about West since his death in a car accident in California in 1940, and Josie's frustration with them. As early as 1947, the first of a long string of West interpreters had made his way to her door with the thesis that *A Cool Million* correctly predicted American fascism and that his surrealism was linked to the atomic bomb —"All balls," Josie had exploded to Katherine Anne. "I did write the guy to hope he wouldn't put the fool's cap of prophecy on Pep West's dead head. Let him stand on what he did, a valid ground. Dostoievsky was Pep's real influence, and the man himself was very different from his work; that should give Bright Boy a clue." Several years later came "Hunter of Doves" in which her own perception of West's work and character were exquisitely and gently unveiled.

"Hunter of Doves" is a brooding and subtle story about a dead writer, Joel Bartram, a middle-aged artist who was once his friend, Constance Heath, and a fervent but simple biographer intent on his literary resurrection, Timothy Comfort. Interviewed by the young man in pursuit of his intellectual hero, Constance Heath is reluctant to participate in his mechanical reconstructions, but despite herself, as their conversation continues, her memories begin to pour forth. Nor are they simple memories of Bartram alone, they involve herself as well, for her friendship with Bartram took place at a crucial time in her life, just before the end of her marriage to Lucas Heath, and there are parts of their common history she has never been able to look at without pain. In a series of flashbacks, both in Comfort's presence and out, she recreates for herself and her questioner all the important scenes of the past. How the Heaths had gone at the word of a mutual friend to the New York hotel where Bartram was working as a manager and struggling to finish a novel. How they admired each other from the beginning, the three. How they brought him back to the country, imploring him to finish what he began. How he settled nearby, first in a hotel, where he completed his book, then permanently, in a neighboring farmhouse, where enmeshed, still, in his own inner landscape he tried to make a place for himself among his neighbors with his unfamiliar hounds and the inept but triumphant hunts which give the story its title. So fused are all the aspects of the work that it is the story of the Heaths' marriage and of Bartram's work simultaneously, and not only the story of his work, but of his soul. His relationship to various intellectual influences, as well as to members of his own family, are roundly and knowingly explored. A rare combination of fact and understanding, criticism and comprehension, as an interpretation of West "Hunter of Doves" has never been bettered, and in Josie's own work it stands as an artistic and psychological treasure. Yet despite its biographical fidelity as far as West is concerned, something important about Josie is missing. Josie and John did go to the Hotel Sutton to meet West at the suggestion of William Carlos Williams, they did bring him back to Erwinna, a convert both to them and to their way of life, and they did install him across the river in Frenchtown in the hotel where with their daily encouragement he finally finished *Miss Lonelyhearts.* Their intense triangular friendship was almost exactly as she describes. But the triangle recalled in "Hunter" was not the only triangle of the moment for in precisely the period in question, the autumn of 1932, Josie was pursuing her relationship with Marion Greenwood. While John was knocking about with Pep in the comical yet gallant expedition she so well describes, Josie was up in bed with her sore kidneys scribbling to Marion the letter beginning "Dear little Crocodile." If Mrs. Heath "stuck to her painting grimly but there were days when she did not know whether to paint out or paint in" there was good reason. To convert the hidden fervor of her feeling for Marion into the mysterious underground atmosphere that so exactly illuminated the character of West was an artistic leap greater than Josie had ever taken before, and the story worked perfectly. Among all the later "Bright Boys" who turned to Josie and "Hunter" for an illumination of West there was no one who ever guessed. Surely that was a part of its triumph.

"Hunter of Doves" was the only completed section of a project Josie envisioned as five or six interrelated novellas unified by the presence of Mrs. Heath. Two others, "Bright Signal," about Hemingway, and "Outside Time," about Gustav Regler, exist in drafts, which, though fragmentary, share with "Hunter" an almost mythic power. The remainder, including "Southern Belle," about Katherine Anne, "No Hero to His Valet," about William Phillips, and another, about Mother Bloor, were little more than notes and ideas. Portions of another novel centered about an older woman character, *Watcher with the Horn*, linking the 1920s to the 1940s and containing elements of her relationships with Maxwell Anderson, Clair Laning, and Alfred Kazin were also substantially done. In addition there were preliminary musings for a book about writers of the twenties, stimulated in part by her quarrel about Gertrude Stein with Katherine Anne, and the earliest pages of an actual autobiography, stimulated by resentment at the patronizing discussion of her as "Mrs. John Herrmann" by William Carlos Williams in his autobiography, published in 1951.* Of all the projects that were begun in this period, the only one besides "Hunter" ever actually completed was the biography of the Bartrams, *New Green World*. Originally undertaken as much out of external as of internal necessity, for the publisher who commissioned it, Hastings House, offered a $1,500 advance, *New Green World* quickly transcended its origins and became in addition to one of Josie's literarily most successful efforts a book as close as any to her heart. The well-received American edition, which appeared in 1954, was followed by an equally well received edition in England which included an introduction by Victoria Sackville-West. Of all Josie's books it may be the best-remembered today.

John Bartram was a pre-Revolutionary Pennsylvania farmer with a fascination for the plants of the American wilderness and a devotion to contributing to their classification. William, his son, was an eccentric lover of nature who obstinately failed at every respectable opportunity that crossed his path until he was allowed to establish himself among the Indians of Florida, whom he later wrote about with love. In a narrative so seamless that it is difficult to convey its quality, *New Green World* is about the relation of the Bartrams to each other, about each of their relations to the wilderness, man, and God, about England and the colonies, about poetry and science, and about the relationship of the eighteenth to the twentieth century itself. Excitement is on every page: the awe and wonder of the Americans at the botanical splendor of the new continent and the fascination of their sponsors in England for every new leaf or seed the explorers are able to ship their way. Based on extensive research in original sources, the whole cast of characters involved in one way or another with the romance of the New World becomes wonderfully alive in it. The sly Linnaeus, naming a plant *Hillia parasitica*, after an obsequious English colleague, Sir John Hill, "more noted for toadying to the Earl of Bute than for scientific accuracy." Coleridge and Wordsworth,

* See Notes.

searching the Bartrams' studies for material for their romantic poems. Benjamin Franklin, Bartram's friend, the one a tinkerer, the other a seeker, for "Bartram placed his reliance on scientific knowledge as a tool that might help him pierce the darkness surrounding mysteries, [while] Franklin appears to toy with its practical manifestations and to foretell the gadget." What did he do with lightning drawn down from the clouds with his kite except to recoil?" Josie inquired. "To fall back upon the safe and solid, upon common sense, which he glorified, sacrificing sensibility. In his down-to-earth fashion, he did much toward chopping down the flowering wild thing in new world minds that tameness might grow," while Bartram was the true philosopher and scientist, "who wanted first to *see* and after that, to *say.*" In a confident free-flowing form and in rich and original language *New Green World* manages to be at the same time an epic biographical poem about the Bartrams and a deliberate political parable about free inquiry, for above all it is a portrait of men for whom freedom was a condition of the soul won by hard labor or not at all and neither granted by nor revocable by law. *"New Green World* was written as a kind of rescue work for myself, for it was during the McCarthy period, when I felt so sunk, that I decided to recall the intransigent Bartrams and their group of wonder-seekers," she wrote to an appreciative reader in 1965. Yet it was not simply a political impulse. By including the feeling for nature which had previously not been a presence in her writing except for letters, she enlarged herself as a writer. Apparently discontinuous with her other work, the Bartram book has links to both the past and the future because what she was doing in it was examining the philosophical ground, beyond immediate allegiances, on which she hoped to be able to stand. Whether she would find the figure to put in it: that was the question. If she had not been so often interrupted, if she had not been so poor, if she had not been so distracted, she might perhaps have succeeded in these years in joining figure and ground, character and history, in the one statement about the past she so wanted to make, for there is no doubt from the quality of the separate pieces she did finish that she was working at a depth and with an originality greater than ever before. Instead of that, the realities of the present pulled her back.

"Be sure to destroy this letter as soon as you read it, for I want to tell you that as I turned on the Delaware road off the bridge a car was moving very slowly ahead of me, and I didn't try to pass," Josie wrote Jean in March, 1952. "It went along clear to my house and stopped. I got out. Two gents got out. Who but the FBI again . . . Had pictures which they wanted me to identify and tell the works . . . I have to control myself [not] to tell them to go to hell; better to do what I do, simply be polite and a clam." From the number of entries in Josie's government file it is clear that in this period she suffered frequent intrusions. It is not that she was singularly important — she was never placed on the "Security Index," though she did make the "Communist Index," incorrectly, in 1951 — rather that in the multiplication of investigations that characterized the McCarthy era, anyone who was at the crossroads of the thirties was automatically at the crossroads of the fifties, regardless of current beliefs. When Chambers added another detail about John, Josie, and Hiss: when Louis Budenz, whom she had never met, called her a "concealed Communist": when someone in the course of some other investigation into something else mentioned her name: there was the FBI in Erwinna again, chatting with the postmaster, cross-examining the butcher, sitting in her driveway awaiting her, ready to proceed. The inevitable result of these visitations was unease. If they were there after she came home, why not before? If they were talking to her about people she had not seen or heard from in a dozen years who were they talking to elsewhere about her? If she was not endangered by any particular line of questioning, the chances were that someone she once cared about was. In the atmosphere of the moment you never knew when a stray word could hurt others. It was just such a word in an FBI interview with her that contributed to the difficulties of a Washington friend of hers, Robert Coe.

Robert Coe was a longtime government employee, a physicist currently working for the Atomic Energy Commission at Oak Ridge — or rather, not working, while his security clearance was under review. He was married to a journalist, Fleeta Springer Coe, whom Josie had known since the early thirties, and during both of her stays in Washington, in 1938 and 1942, she had seen them often. As far as she knew, he was not interested in politics. Exactly what precipitated his security problem he never knew, but it seems likely from the record that a case of mistaken identity was in part to blame, for there was another family of Coes active in the Communist movement for many years, one of whom, whose first name was Charles but who was usually called "Bob," had been involved in farm politics overlapping with Hal Ware and had figured in Chambers' early charges. It was probably this Coe that the FBI had in mind when they questioned Josie about him during the Hiss queries, but the other that she meant when she responded he was a "lifelong friend." Since the "lifelong friend" went into her file along with such crucial items as the 1942 denunciation of Josie by Katherine Anne, the Josephine Herbst whom Coe was accused of knowing during the AEC's sweeping review of its employees' "associations" was the creature of Katherine Anne's imagination, the-concealed-Communist-who-made-intermittent-trips-to-Moscow-and-rejected-Earl-Browder-as-too-timid-because-he-did-not-advocate-enough-force. When Josie learned from Coe of the charges against her, so thoroughly entangled with the charges against him, she was baffled. She wanted to help him, but what could she do?

"The charges against me are so fantastic that I feel 'they' will stop at nothing," she wrote Coe's attorney, Gerhard Van Arkel, in the summer of 1952. "When I am charged that I was or am a secret member of the communist party, I can only speak the truth and deny it, but how am I to be believed? How can it be proved? This is the question. One might perhaps charge Whittaker Chambers with being a secret member today and one who for dark reasons was continuing a member. Could anyone actually prove it was not so? . . . No one could possibly dig up a card that was never there or show dues were paid that had never been paid. I would have had to belong to some faction, attend meetings of that faction, and no one in the world unless a complete falsifier who was willing to perjure himself, could show that was the case. But this is all being conducted in such a state of darkness that I wonder how I am to prove I am what I am." In fact she was able to accomplish a lot. Under Van Arkel's guidance she prepared a kind of dossier documenting her attitude toward the Communist Party at various critical junctures by reference to both her private correspondence and her published writing between 1931 and 1948. She also went to Washington to testify before a government hearing board on Coe's behalf. Since Coe was cleared her effort was rewarded, but as far as her own work was concerned, the price of disruption was high. Merely to scour the attic for the *New Masses* containing her attack on Mike Gold's attitude toward literature in 1936 was a burdensome task. "The Washington thing was unavoidable but really tragic for me, interrupting me at the very season when I needed most to be undisturbed," she wrote to Jean.

A case in which she became involved the following year had to do with the defense of another friend, Harvey O'Connor. O'Connor was a longtime labor editor and writer, author, among other things, of biographies of Andrew Mellon, the Guggenheims, and the Astors, and an authority on the politics of oil and steel. He was part of a liberal circle which included his wife, Jessie, and his sister-in-law, Mary Lloyd — daughters of Henry Demarest Lloyd, the crusading author of the 1894 populist classic *Wealth against Commonwealth* — as well as Clair Laning, a circle from which, as the radicalism of the 1930s receded more and more into the liberalism of the 1950s, Josie drew increasing support. In the summer of 1953 O'Connor was subpoenaed by McCarthy as part of an investigation into U.S. libraries abroad and accused of having sent his books overseas. Opposed to the investigation of political belief by congressional committee, O'Connor decided not to cooperate. "H held himself ready for Washington, determined to stand on first — not fifth — amendment," Josie reported to Clair Laning. "Talked with me about it — ready to go to jail if need be. Very firm and good — perhaps had in mind chance to bring case to court and test validity of such proceedings — also he was indignant, and rightly, said he had never sent any of his books to overseas libraries and that was what they were charging him with, but I pointed out it was useless to challenge that — he had a right to send books, even if he hadn't — it was the right to write that he had to defend." As it turned out that was not all he had to defend for when he appeared before the committee and refused either to say whether he was or was not a Communist or to claim protection against self-incrimination, he was cited for contempt. After more than a year of litigation O'Connor lost his case, receiving a suspended sentence and a fine, but in the interim an effort was made to use his stand to help generate opposition to McCarthy. On behalf of the Emergency Civil Liberties Committee, of which O'Connor was one of the founders, Josie wrote a masterful pamphlet articulating the political and constitutional issues in the case, to which, in keeping with her convictions about the rights and principles involved, she willingly signed her name. The O'Connor defense pamphlet, "Mind of Your Own," was probably one of the strongest political statements to have been made in the early 1950s. From the opening picture of O'Connor working away at his desk interrupted by a telephone call from committee counsel Roy Cohn, to the scene in the committee room where O'Connor explains to McCarthy the reasons for his conviction that the committee is acting out of bounds, to the final moment when, returning home from Washington he responds to the question of a reporter who meets his train "Have you ever been a Communist?" with "I am not a Communist. I have never been a Communist. I am perfectly willing to tell anyone how I stand except on demand from such a legislative group," it renders the confrontation between O'Connor and McCarthy so vivid it is still compelling today. As glad for her own sake as for the O'Connors of the opportunity it presented to dramatize what they felt, the pamphlet nonetheless did not spring full-blown from Josie's typewriter into the U.S. mails: it involved considerable effort. Like her trips to Washington for the Coe case, it took its toll.

It was not only the presence of things that marked the McCarthy period for her — the FBI visits here, an individual case or two there — it was also the absence of things. Liberalism was necessary but it was hardly sufficient. "I am as much in sympathy with any oppressed, anywhere, as I ever was . . . and if I have not signed protests it is simply because I no longer know what to sign that would be effective," she wrote Van Arkel on one occasion. Compared to the visions of the 1920s and '30s the very agenda of the 1950s was nagging and narrow. Then even strangers had had much in common. Now old friends could not agree. Everyone had a different position about everything. The Blankenhorns, for example, criticized Josie's lack of caution in testifying for Coe, while from California another old friend, Philip Stevenson, wrote to criticize her for cooperating with the authorities at all. Another characteristic of the moment was the absence of opportunity. Invulnerable to the blacklist by reason of poverty and self-employment, Josie was nonetheless subject to an informal "graylist" in which the number of possibilities that came her way was mysteriously small. Under other circumstances the accretion of her past experience and past writing might perhaps have made her into a welcome commentator on a range of contemporary issues. Now, apart from an eccentric magazine called *Tomorrow* which took a number of her reviews and other pieces, there was no one eager to publish what she had to say. Her literary reputation was virtually obliterated. The biographical notes in *Tomorrow* were always as unspecific as possible and when *New Green World* was published in 1954 the photograph of Josie on the jacket was a particularly demure one taken around 1939, and not one of her previous writings was mentioned by name. Small as her income had always been she had always earned something, but now it was more difficult than ever. Had it not been for the O'Connors, who began sending money they labeled a "fellowship," for Clair Laning, who provided innumerable meals as well as a place to stay in New York, and for a handful of other friends who increasingly offered small loans, how she could have continued to survive and write simultaneously is not at all clear. With all these other discontinuities came the inevitable absence of an audience. When she met the younger literary generation — writers and poets who were friends of Jean's — they rarely knew who she was. The American political reaction of the early 1950s was a relatively mild one, as Josie well understood. It was not Nazi Germany: it was not the Soviet Union: she was neither beaten, tortured, nor jailed, nor even harassed beyond endurance: it was merely a change of cycle in a very fortunate country —: but as a background for bringing to fruition works drawing on a radical past it was certainly inhospitable. Both for romantic reasons and for the distance it would provide, what Josie wanted more than anything was to go to Europe with Jean, who had never gone there, and they spoke of it often, but in August, 1951, when Josie applied for a passport she was refused. Unhappy at the prospect of further political complications and lacking the money for a lawyer, she decided, for the moment, to let the matter drop. But it remained very much on her mind.

During its earliest years Josie's relationship with Jean fell into a regular pattern. Its location fluctuated from Erwinna to New York and elsewhere as Jean moved around, the cast of peripheral characters fluctuated as Jean repeatedly fell in love (there were even several abortions, some of which Josie helped arrange, to suggest Jean's insouciance about the sex of her lovers), the only thing that did not fluctuate was the fact of fluctuation, the constant emotional uproar which held them together. A great longing, plotting, and scheming to see each other when they were apart, an unsatisfactory visit filled with tension and misunderstanding, and endless recriminations — that was their usual course. So repetitive was the cycle that you would think they might have noticed it but they never commented about it in their letters. Every small event was a large, fresh trauma. Out of everything that happened in those years the only thing that stands out is one particular love affair between Jean and another poet. Because it involved other lives than their own it is a delicate story to tell here, yet such are the laws of biography that it must be done because for Jean it was a serious romance, for Josie it involved a descent into behavior as questionable as any in her emotional career, and for their relationship it was a critical moment. This particular lover was one of our leading poets and the affair included the possibility of marriage.

In 1951, when Jean and the poet met, the poet was in his forties, a writer, teacher, and editor already of considerable repute. Living in the country, not too far from New York, he had a wife, a child, a house, and a dog, none of which he had any intention of giving up, yet, commuting to New York as he did often, he was also well situated for an affair. For some time he was no more than one of Jean's casual conquests and Josie, if she knew, paid little attention. She was more concerned about a flirtation Jean was having with another woman about the same time. Josie's own relation to the poet was somewhat collegial — they were loosely associated in an educational project involving politics and the arts — and she appreciated him as a writer, no more and no less. By exactly what progression Jean and the poet became more intimately involved, there is little evidence in Josie's papers, but by the winter of 1952-1953 that was the situation, and Josie was very upset about it.

Josie's reaction to the threat to her relationship with Jean was a prolonged emotional eruption which she struggled to control but which nonetheless left their personal landscape littered with debris. From her letters she appears to have been of three minds about it. There was the generous Josie who understood that Jean should have a man and a life of her own even if that meant Josie's giving her up; there was the unconventional Josie who insisted that Jean could love a man and a woman simultaneously; and there was the pathetic Josie who conceded that all Jean's attention was properly elsewhere but beseeched her former lover for the merest crumb. Each of these Josies also had an opposite number less attractive than the first. The other side of the generous Josie was an imperious busybody who told Jean exactly how she should run her affair; the other side of the unconventional Josie was an ideological harridan thundering denunciations of the relative status of women and men which she knew would strike home; and the other side of the pathetic Josie was the manipulative victim who would not stop even at hints of dying to get her way. These characters were not so much sequential as they were interchangeable, succeeding each other in control of the emotional keyboard less in accordance with external events than with an inner need. So inconsistent are the letters Josie sent Jean day after day that they have no individual credibility. That each of the myriad Josies generally uttered some truth is undeniable but irrelevant. The real point of all her arguments was possession.

Why Jean permitted these constant intrusions — and how her relationship with the poet flourished for all its deceptions — are good questions, but by the middle of 1953 his marriage was over and he and Jean were discussing traveling together, if not settling down. For Josie it was a scenario of the utmost difficulty. Without money and without a passport there was no way she could anticipate getting to Europe herself, yet Jean was considering staying a year or longer, and, with the poet planning to join her, there loomed the possibility of a permanent loss. That Josie's anxieties had to be borne in silence only made matters worse. "—— can come with his liquor and his flowers — he may be jealous of what he does not know, but still it is not concrete. He can be himself . . . I cannot get any space for myself that is my own," she complained. About the same time, prying through Jean's drawers for evidence of . . . crime? . . . she came upon two poems, one titled with the poet's initials and one for herself, with the name left blank, and she burst out in fury that "I cannot be named." With the poet ignorant, Josie muzzled, and Jean unwilling to entertain the possibility that she might be doing anything wrong, they were more like the figurines for See No Evil — Speak No Evil — Hear No Evil than they were a conventional triangle. In an effort to allay Josie's rising tensions the two women took a summer vacation together at the O'Connors' in Rhode Island, but the experiment was a failure. "It is no pleasure to be with someone who is so absorbed in someone else," Josie wrote her afterward. "—— is part of a couple; you are the other part, and I have had my nose rubbed in the two of you long enough. When you can be yourself again, I will welcome you . . . and that you may become yourself will heal me . . . if only now and then I can feel together with you and not that the sword of —— lies always between us." As fall came, and Jean's departure drew closer, Josie grew more and more distraught. There were more hysterical letters than ever before. Unable to prevent the journey and troubled by even her wish to do so she surrounded it with words as if, like a storybook crone hurling imprecations after her old grudges, she believed that her witches' curses could keep Jean's other dreams from coming true. "I *will* have trips with thee, alone, I *will* have thee in a room alone and in a theatre . . . and walking in a park, and looking . . ." she wrote in one letter. "You will go — will go — but I do not think you will forget me," she said in the next. Shortly before Jean left Josie gave her a small black pearl to carry with her as a secret sign between them of the life to which Josie hoped she would return. It was not the only irritant she contrived.

When Jean left for Europe in the fall of 1953, the house in Erwinna was leased to a tenant and Josie moved into Jean's apartment in Greenwich Village for the duration. Also in the apartment were voluminous letters and journals belonging to both Josie and Jean revealing the extent of their intimacy. Jean's lover had a key. To say that Josie left out the papers on purpose would be to convict her of an act she always denied, but she did leave them out and the poet did read them, and if anyone stood to benefit from his discovery of the true situation, it was certainly herself. In the tortured, evasive, three-way correspondence that followed nothing was established except that among the three of them, somehow, lesbianism, sabotage, and spying were equal crimes. Each of them was guilty about something and righteous about something else. Josie, guilty, at the minimum, of indiscretion, was righteous about Jean's lack of trust. Jean, righteous about the discovery of the letters, was guilty of having concealed her involvement with Josie from her lover. Her lover, guilty for having read the letters, was righteous because he had been deceived. Between Jean and the lover the question of whether loss of privacy or loss of illusion was the greater agony was furiously and eloquently argued. As for Josie, whatever her role in bringing it about, she felt humiliated and exposed. The fact that it was all covered over when the sexual issue at the heart of it was so unresolved is perhaps less a tribute to the power of love than to the power of words, but in any case it flared only briefly, then receded, and the poet went to Europe as planned. The pictures of Jean and the poet from their European journey show a good-humored American couple very much at their ease. There are Jean and the poet feeding the pigeons in the piazza, Jean ringing a church bell in a village chapel, Jean and the poet reading a newspaper in a café. Yet despite their apparent compatibility beneath the surface something fundamental had changed. "Long ago I shuffled off the conventional notions and tried to see love as it emerged, whether for a bird or you, for what it was, not in the framework that society insists upon," Josie had once written Jean, in language very close to words she had once used with Marion Greenwood, and Jean tried to live that way too, but the poet had not "shuffled" them off, nor pretended to, and in his later reflections on the affair the episode of the letters and the reality they represented was decisive. Nor did Josie withdraw in contrition once the damage was done. On the contrary, she pursued her advantage. Wherever they traveled they were engulfed in instructions from Josie advising them where to go, what to read, whom to meet, and how to act in cafés. With the question of the relative degree of independence to be maintained always an issue between Jean and her lover, there was plenty of room for misgivings and misunderstandings in their relationship, and wherever Josie sensed a weak point in their connection, there she pounced. In her constant reminders to Jean of Jean's need for freedom, she was particularly disingenuous. The rise and fall of the love affair of Jean Garrigue and the poet had sources not under Josie's control, and the part she played in its demise is not really possible to weigh, but if she did not destroy the relationship singlehandedly — you would have to say she tried.

In the late spring of 1954, conscious of the progressive erosion of the feeling between Jean and her lover, Josie reapplied for her passport at last, hoping to go to Europe in the summer and — perhaps — edge him out. The outcome was predictable — she was refused. "It is the practice of the State Department to inform the applicant of the reasons for the disapproval of his request . . . insofar as the security regulations permit," read the letter from the director of the Passport Office, R. B. Shipley. "In your case it has been alleged that you were a Communist." Now she was in a quandary. Having decided to face the passport issue and been rejected, she felt she had no choice but to fight because the possibility of a permanent restriction on travel was genuinely distressing and she did not want to let the government's accusation stand, yet she was staying at the MacDowell Colony where her work was going particularly smoothly and if it had not been for her eagerness to see Jean, she would not have risked disruption at all. Wishing to know how to proceed, she contacted Gerhard Van Arkel, the Washington lawyer she had met during the Coe case, who was able to extract a bill of particulars from the Passport Office. The charges — never formally listed — were more or less a random sample of all the other charges that had been attached to her name for the last dozen years. That she had visited the Soviet Union, that John was a Communist, that she had been mentioned by Chambers, and that she had signed, written, or supported four particular but miscellaneous documents, articles, or causes in the 1930s: these seven items are what stood between Josie and Europe in 1954.

However familiar the charges, they were nonetheless difficult to fight. For one thing, there was the matter of a "position." "I have not . . . been a professional anti-communist, as I was never a professional communist. . . . If this country had ever made anything but reactionary moves I could have been more outspoken," she wrote to Van Arkel. Responding was expensive: she had to enlist the O'Connors to pay the fees. It was draining: she had to make a special trip to Erwinna to find documentary evidence corroborating the explanations she was required to make. And it was also demoralizing: for once it was turned over to a lawyer it was out of her own control. Under Van Arkel's guidance she prepared a long autobiographical affidavit in which major passages of life marked by much ambiguity and sadness such as the transformation of her attitude toward the Communist Party are given conventional timing and twists, to the effect that "after I returned from Spain I no longer thought that, I thought this." We met, we married, we disagreed, we divorced —

the whole course of her relationship to John is treated the same way. It was also necessary to submit affidavits from friends in which the sanitized version of the evolution both of her views and her marriage was supported and reinforced. "Nothing that she ever did or said would have led me, or now leads me, to believe that she was a member of the Communist Party," pronounced John Cheever. It was the perfect — it was perhaps the only — answer to the cut and dried "It is reporteds" on the other side and other than her profession of ignorance about the 1934 activities of John Herrmann, which were now plainly endangering not only him but herself, her affidavit contained no real lies, but it was a bloodless recounting of events and situations about which she cared very deeply, and as a statement about both the historical and the personal experiences involved, it reflected more Van Arkel's understanding than her own. The liberal Josie deposing by her ancestors that she was not and had never been a Communist was very much in evidence: the radical Josie affirming that it would not have been wrong to be a Communist even though she did not technically happen to have been one was not much in sight. In March, 1955, after about ten months of bureaucratic deliberation, Josie's right to travel was officially restored, but there was very little joy in it. As a political gesture capping years of public commitment, the act was too isolated and too ambiguous to be of value, and as far as any plans of her own were concerned, Jean had returned months before. "I should have felt exhilarated . . . but it took so long and so much out of me that I couldn't seem to take it . . . except as a long delayed right which cost too much," she wrote the O'Connors. Both politically and personally the victory was hollow.

While Josie was wrestling with her passport Jean was wrestling with her heart and conscience, and in the fall of 1954, when Josie's inability to join her became certain, she had decided to come home. Before the decision was made, and particularly as long as Josie's visit lay in the realm of imagination, everything had been sweetness between them but as soon as their actual reunion on the home ground was definite, their correspondence became as rancorous as before. Whether Jean was coming back at all, whether the poet was coming back with her, whether she wanted Josie to be in New York or Erwinna — all the kind of details which Josie planned her life around but which it suited Jean to leave vague were very much up in the air. Sometime earlier in the history of their involvement — before the deepening of Jean's affair with the poet, before Europe, before the passport — Josie had written Jean a strange and haunting letter about what she felt were the sources of their connection. It had to do with a dream of childhood, "a marvelous happy dream," about "music, concealed music, behind a maze of shrubs, and intricate small pagodas set up for refreshment along interminable walks. There were birds somewhere, one could hear them clearly," she wrote.

"There was human music, low talking voices that one did not even need to understand. . . ."

I lay awake with a throng of recollections . . . almost preternaturally bright. Oddly I found myself repeating fragments of a poem — Blow bugle blow, set the wild echoes flying, answer echoes, dying, dying . . . I tried to remember the rest, rediscovered many lines, remembered suddenly with extreme vividness when I had first heard it. It was in . . . high school and a girl in my class was asked to read it aloud. She was . . . a marvelous reader, with a beautiful voice, and the words sent shivers down my back. It was my first real encounter with the magic of poetry. . . . Perhaps I admired the girl; certainly her voice was beautiful and the words suddenly revealed a magic world. This all came back to me, I saw myself in the hard wooden seat, with my hair in a great braid down my back, thick bangs, and when I was called upon to read next, I remember how thrilling it was. I can [not] explain the dream or my happiness in any reasonable detail . . . but it was real; perhaps the inexplicable is closest of all to the reality of experience. I did know, with gratitude and love, but for you I should not have dreamed so sweetly and . . . I suspect that what I look for from you is exactly this inexplicable, magic world. And it is not possession, in any earthy, tedious, sense. But it is also true, that I cannot feel this magic . . . if I am convinced that I am dispossessed. . . . As an exile I was exiled from more than you, I was exiled from some strange world in which I have to breathe. If I came to define it, probably this has caused alienations in my life from other human kind . . . where the warm and human thing became too human, and broke off some chain of deep enchantment that was necessary for my survival. I do not know fully or ask to know. All I do know is that with you I am in that earlier, primitive, imaginative world, perhaps where I can be a child, perhaps where I can feel a primitive maternity, too. . . . It is something of many things; I only ask to feel it and not to have intruded upon it too many other things that do not concern me, or you, or we. . . .

But by the time Jean returned from Europe the enchantment was over.

# PART EIGHT

# YESTERDAY'S ROAD

## CHAPTER TWENTY-EIGHT

# Animal Hotel

SOMETIME AROUND the middle of the 1950s, Josie began saving obituaries of people she had known, and her collection grew steadily, year after year, as more and more of her contemporaries met their fates. So many of them were gone now. From the literary figures of her long-ago past such as Maxwell Anderson and Edna St. Vincent Millay to radicals such as Mary Vorse and Joe Freeman who had remained part of her life: from reporters such as Milly Bennett and Christopher Buckley with whom she had shared some of the experience of Spain to the young Warren Miller to whose writings on Cuba she had been strongly drawn: from the friends of all seasons such as writers Nathan Asch and Holger Cahill to the newer but no less faithful Clair Laning on whom recently she had so come to depend: there were far more departures than arrivals in her life now and it bothered her more and more. Another kind of loss recorded in her file was her sister Frances, dead in Iowa, leaving only Alice and Alice's daughter Betty Davis, besides herself, as the remaining female branches of Mary's family tree. There was also an obituary of John. These declarations of nonexistence of people with whom her life had mingled in a hundred ways must have given her pause, for what they had in common in addition to their finality was that they were short. Playwright, poet, and partisan alike, however great the figure they had seemed to make in the world, no matter how much they had meant to themselves or to others, they meant little or nothing to *The New York Times.* Who would remember her when she was gone? she must have wondered. Who remembered her even now? If her obituary appeared tomorrow, which could happen at any time now, what would it say? By the stringent requirements of posterity her achievements were meager and as for her true story, her real sorrows and joys, the knowledge she had garnered on her far too transient journey, the lessons she had learned, where would it find any voice? A browser at a book sale wondering "Who was Josephine Herbst?" would never be able to find the answer. She found this fate unbearable. Immortality she was hardly asking, but for the world not to know she had been here awhile? To have pressed her fingers in so many places and have left no mark? Why should she be expected to accept that? A lifetime cognoscente of the transfigurations of literature, she knew what had to happen to have it otherwise. Writing could bring recognition, but it was not the only form of recognition. In the end, her greatest creation would be herself.

By the middle of the 1950s, the beginning of the period in question, Josie was at one of her lowest emotional ebbs and it is not hard to see the reasons. There is little that can be said about the circumstances of her life that has not been said often before — she was desperately poor, her work was all but forgotten, and she lived in a world whose opinions had so far shifted that as a survivor of the 1920s and '30s she was bound to seem a relic or worse — but the older she got the more difficult it became. In the past she had often been able to pull herself out of depression by work or travel but at the moment even that was beyond her, for after the long period of troubles in every aspect of her life she was not only financially and emotionally but also intellectually drained. Her work was temporarily at a standstill, her efforts confined to a trying — but paying — ghostwriting job for her old friend Albert Rhys Williams who was trying to complete his memoir of the Russian revolution; between the struggle for her passport and her struggles with Jean she had for the time being lost the desire to go abroad; and as for Jean herself, after her return from Europe her comings and goings kept Josie in what might best be described as a state of permanent disappointment. Without money or family, without a reputation, without anything material to show for her years of commitment and work, by any conventional standards Josie was not only a failure but a fool, for she had followed to their conclusion all the radical dreams of the twentieth century and they had left her where she now was: trapped: and yet failure was not what she felt. There was another reality on which her heart had been fixed ever since she first left Sioux City and if ever she were to be vindicated, that other reality would have to play its part. At some indefinable moment like those long ago when she and John had looked at each other across the table and then gone off or the moment sometime later when she had sat at the table herself, then gone to Spain, there was a crucial turning, and it had to do with the deepest question of whether life was really worth living and on what terms. Would others define her existence or would she? Who could tell her what her life had been? Pulling herself up for another effort as surely as if she had been setting out once again, as she had once conquered adversity by action now conquering inactivity by will, she gathered herself up for a final journey of great subtlety and complexity, of which the destination was uncertain and for which the ultimate reason was her old imperative, *Because.*

When I think of Josie as she was in her later years — or, rather, as she appeared — I see a vital woman surrounded by a circle of eager admirers, somewhat after the manner of the classic fairy tale in which a maternal figure has taken shelter deep in the heart of an enchanted forest surrounded by swarms of little people on whom she is really dependent but who are also under her spell. In the story the unorthodox household is occasionally menaced — someone is wounded or lost or word drifts in on the lips of animals about trouble in neighboring territories or from remnants of the past — but on the whole it is a safe and sufficient unit, mysteriously enveloped in a kind of protective charm. There actually was such a fable written about Erwinna, by Jean, a prose novella, *Animal Hotel,* first published in the periodical *New World Writing* in 1956. The saga of a country lodging run by an amiable but elusive Bear whose "past was more complicated than anybody could guess" had its origin, more or less, in fact, for as the 1950s progressed, the house in Erwinna was becoming a stopping place for a group of young men and women just beginning to make their marks on the world, and Josie was very much their star. It happened naturally, in a trail of association beginning with Jean, one person bringing another, the second returning with a third, so there never was one moment at which it could be said to have started or stopped, but by the end of the decade there were a number of younger writers and intellectuals who liked to think of Erwinna as a kind of spiritual home. Among the "customers" as Josie herself called them were several who had been associated with the experimental college, Black Mountain, in North Carolina and who shared many of its progressive convictions about life and art. These included Jane Mayhall and Leslie Katz, New York writers who were involved as participants and supporters in many other artistic enterprises as well; Elizabeth Pollet, another writer, who was caught in a difficult marriage to the ailing and unstable poet Delmore Schwartz and who lived with him for a time on a farm in New Jersey not far away; and Neal and Mary Daniels, a young Philadelphia couple with something of a political bent of whom the husband, a child psychologist, was working at Philadelphia General Hospital and the wife, who later obtained a doctorate in child development, was devoting herself to raising a family along progressive lines. Another visitor was Hilton Kramer, then a youthful editor of *Arts,* whose sharp social as well as aesthetic criticism was gaining him the following which would soon take him into prominence as chief art critic for *The New York Times.* These young people were not Josie's only friends during the late 1950s and '60s. Leading contemporary writers such as Saul Bellow, Alfred Kazin, and John Cheever; radicals and former radicals including writers Stanley Burnshaw and Edward Dahlberg; her niece, Betty Davis, who lived in Washington, D.C.; and a number of her Erwinna neighbors, were all regular, if at times remote, parts of her life these days; nor between one group and another were there lines firmly drawn. But in a sense the younger people were the most important for month in, month out, through all kinds of seasons and transformations, and in any number of ways Josie gradually came to count on, they were really there. Through their eyes the idea of Erwinna as a place of fellowship and creativity not just aloof from but superior to the world's demands was magically reborn. Here the delicate spirits of an indifferent era would find acceptance; here too, a life of commitment and one of contemplation were not at odds. As in Hicks' "Peaceable Kingdom" which hung on the wall, creatures of many different persuasions would genially mingle. "The birds would sit on the prongs of the deer, the chipmunk would nestle beside the cat while the blind mole would softly sit by himself in a dream of tunnels." "None of these animals were married," Jean continued subtly. "Perhaps some had been. . . . Perhaps some wanted to be. It doesn't matter. They were, for our purposes, bachelors, living in single blessedness. And was it so single? Didn't they all meet and chat and share . . . in one anothers' lives? Yes they did. The bear saw to that. And saw to more. She hated a mooning self-consciousness, a broodiness that excluded society. . . . A sable repentance, like that of the raven, would have finished her off. So if there were broken hearts in her midst, unfulfilled ones, or yearnings for some neat doe, she didn't want to hear of it. . . . Hers was an inn or a hotel, if you will, it wasn't a retreat for the lorn and the lost."

The sources of the attraction between Josie and her followers are not hard to see. There they were, trapped in the 1950s, a group of idealists for whose longings a bourgeois society offered little but scorn, and there was Josie, like a treasure from an earlier period, the very incarnation of all they held dear. What could be a more vivid embodiment of a life lived according to principle than the life of Josephine Herbst? Her very house rose up out of the hillside, a tribute, simultaneously, to poverty and imagination, primitive in its appointments and yet a miracle of taste and simplicity, its landscape of wildflowers its own rebuttal of the artifices of man. Neglected and yet unvanquished, she was dedicated as much as ever to her solitary craft, and with her invocations of an older credo in which the life of a writer was its own reward, she strengthened their hearts. The essence of the relationship Josie cultivated with her visitors had to do with the necessity of joy. It was true she was lonely: it was true she was sometimes ailing: it was true her cupboards were so barren one could not approach without a bagful of groceries and expect a meal, but once the elements were provided, what a feast in all the senses it could be. It was with this group Josie's storytelling probably reached its finest; with them her sense of humor probably seemed the funniest; with them Erwinna was restored to a gaiety with an annual spring festival in which the price of admission was a creative act — and Josie enthralled them all, enthralled herself, with her millionth rendition of "Mama the Man Is Standing There," which they, perchance, were hearing for the first time; with them whatever was left of her natural exuberance most readily came into play. Life was serious, she suggested, life was intense, it was often tragic or frightening, but to see the buds bloom, to cook by an old recipe, to argue as if the world really rested on the outcome — these were sacred moments, as close as any to what experience really mattered. "She made one feel that life was a kind of involved continuity": Jane Mayhall. "Reassurances and advisos toward attention to immediate events. But (the actress she was) she did suggest that there were realities beyond the moment. I don't think that it was just the revolution. Maybe a religious feeling. But, no, it was that animal health she had, to always be in the position of transforming the trap one was in." The connection between living and writing, that the first fed the second and the second fed the first, the two bound together in an eternal cycle of being and doing rising simultaneously to a deeper and more exalted pitch was another of the tenets of her own faith with which Josie inspired a later day's young. "For Josie, literature was in the living, part of the destiny of man": John Cheever; and by her identification of the aspirations of the present apprentices with the achievements of the old masters she ennobled their labors as well as her own. And her letters *were* literature. "Incomparable": Alfred Kazin. "The kind of letters people never even think of writing any more"; so filled with passionate explorations of all the elements of life from the bearing and raising of children to the death of a parent or spouse — and so well timed — that to the friends and the friends-of-friends who received them sometimes during their blackest moments they became part of the phenomenon of Josephine Herbst that was welding them almost into a movement. Josie's visitors were far from unperceptive and as time passed the realities of her position increasingly made themselves felt. In the periods of desperation in the years before her dying, these friends were her main support. Yet however much they knew of another side to the story, it was the legend of her sufficiency that was their bond, for they wanted to believe in it and she wanted to be believed. That the difficulties she seemed to have transcended often brought her down: that her inner life was anything but serene: that the self out of which she offered consolations was itself a fleeting visitor these days, she did not want to reveal. If she often complained to Jean that her callers did not understand her, think of what she concealed.

# Yesterday's Road

WHATEVER ELSE Josie might have seemed to be doing in the years between the middle of the 1950s and the end of her life, perhaps the cornerstone of her existence, not only intellectually, but in other ways, had to do with the large and ambitious literary undertaking that gradually emerged as her memoirs. So numerous were her approaches to this project that it is impossible to say exactly when she began it, nor did it ever end, but for nearly fifteen years, from about the time of the passport case literally until her dying moments, it was never far from her thoughts. The story of Josie and her memoirs is so elusive that only Josie herself could do it justice, and then only the Josie of the memoirs, for it is so convoluted and serpentine, so filled with forebodings and recapitulations, so entangled with her life both as it was at the moment and as she wished it to have been before, that it is ultimately more as a condition of her life in the present than as a commentary on the past that it left its mark. The reason for the elusiveness lies in the discrepancy between the actual memoirs and their place in her life. On the one hand, the memoirs are scanty. They consist of three published sections, or parts of sections — one on the 1920s, one on the 1930s, and one on Spain — and one long unfinished section on her childhood and youth. Yet their role in her life was enormous. Small enough to carry in a suitcase, yet large enough to carry the burden of her entire dialogue with life, they were alternately an ordeal and a blessing, but they were always a companion. If she was not working on them she was talking about them and if she was neither working on them nor talking about them she was thinking about them because thinking about them was the same as thinking about the past and the past was an endless resource. All this reflection was far from passive. There were not only her own files to be considered, there was current opinion to be sampled in the form of books and reviews on related topics, there was correspondence with other authors on some of the intricate points of their mutual interest, there was a world of inquiry to be pursued on behalf of the memoirs, and all these avenues she regularly followed. Nor was it wholly fruitless. Boxes of discarded pages and sections in the files at Yale attest to her growing command not only of the substance of the material but of a powerful literary style. Yet so determined was she to present to the world only the most inspired portrait of the period she had lived through, she was never satisfied, and it was hard to let it go. It is easy to look defeated when the disparity between effort and outcome is great, and when her references to her memoirs dragged on into the second decade, as always, there were tongues that wagged. There was gossip that she was talking away her best stories, there was gossip that there were issues she could not deal with, there was gossip that whatever it was she had once had, almost certainly she did not have it anymore, and in a sense all that was true. Yet no matter what might be said of the things that beset her, the unfinished memoirs themselves resist a facile conclusion, for without any question they are the finest writing of her career. Among the many factors that affected their progress must be reckoned this: The conversion of all that life to art was a very difficult task.

What is most distinctive about the memoirs in a literary sense is that they are neither strictly autobiographical nor strictly analytical, but weave back and forth between the personal and the general so that the general comments are given more weight by their embodiment in real people and the people are given more importance by their connection to larger events. The section on the later twenties, for example, published in 1961 under the title "A Year of Disgrace," follows her actual life with John during the year 1927 and explores the period at the same time. The amplitude of the long winter in Connecticut where "with both stoves going and the falling snow blocking the windows inch by inch, we gave ourselves up to the splendors of isolation," writing by day and reading by night, "one's mind [growing] accustomed to work in a particularly ample environment," gives concreteness to a later assertion that "the young writer had a private life where he could grow, change, develop." The catholicity of their own reading, where *Henry V* was followed by the Song of Solomon, Turgenev and Goncharov by Stendhal and Dickens, the *Iliad* and the *Odyssey* by Carl Sternheim and Heinrich von Kleist — "everything fused, fleetingly, in a flux and ferment" — gives resonance to her description of the literary hospitality of an era when "literature had not yet been boxed off from life." "The little magazines . . . tempted, teased, provoked, and ridiculed. The editors of the *Little Review* might publicly disagree, one stating that Hart Crane had better drop dead, the other claiming him as the finest of the hour. Irresponsible in any academic sense, the little magazines steered wildly, invited hugely, and didn't care a rap if they printed a shapeless imitation of Joyce by a youngster from Davenport alongside a hunk of the actual Joyce. . . . Whether it was the more solid, dignified *Dial*, whether it was the little magazine, the stage was set for an international set of players; the era that gave the Model-T Ford to the farmers opened the world to its literary young on a scale never before ventured and not equaled since." The very robustness of their private attraction — "We had met one April evening at the Café du Dôme on a day I had come up from Italy and two weeks later we had gone to Le Pouldu, a little town on the coast of Brittany where Gauguin had once lived and paid for his room with a painting" — gives immediacy to the larger observation that "If a fine martial spirit existed between the sexes, it was a tonic and a splendor after so much sticky intermingling and backboneless worship of the family and domesticated bliss." With an elaborate alternation between her own particular history and her assessment of the times, with the characters both themselves and emblematic, and the events and movements of the era always presented with a subjective as well as objective cast, a great panorama of her life and times gradually comes alive.

The voice of the memoirs, with its characteristic blending of personality and history, was the product of much time, effort, and experimentation during which she wrestled with a great many issues, some of which she understood clearly and some of which she did not. What she was attempting to consolidate operated on several levels, and she worked on them all at once, for she was hoping at the same time to recreate the literary vitality of the 1920s, defend the political involvement of the 1930s, and carve out a lasting position for herself, and these three desires were far from being abstractions, detachable from one another by intellectual means, but a single unified purpose for which she felt a real passion. Among the approaches she tried and brought to various degrees of completion were the critical history of twentieth-century writers and writing she sometimes called "The Burning Bush" and sometimes "Their Glorious Intention"; an essay on literature and politics, some of which appeared in *The Nation* in 1956 under the title "The Ruins of Memory"; and a literal autobiography, *The Ground We Tread;* but although they all had some merits and the *Nation* essay in particular had real distinction, none of them was complete enough to be what she wanted, the first because it was too narrow, the second because it was too combative, and the third because, among other things, it answered too simply the infinitely enigmatic question "Who was Josephine Herbst?" To carry the weight of her passionate conviction that the story of her own generation, whatever its errors, had a kind of glory, that whatever had turned out wrong about it, much was right, and that, right or wrong, whatever might be said by the historians of record, she was really there, she needed a vehicle that by its own art would win the arguments. In the vivid historical presence so at ease with language and time that her opinions were not just stated but demonstrated with an authority of feeling that transcended thought, she finally found it.

Whatever might be the psychological implications of muting herself as the subject of her memoirs in a personal sense in order to highlight more fully her sense of the times, there is no doubt that it is very successful as literature. Whether she is writing about a speakeasy in the Village where the subject is Gertrude Stein, an assembly in the Soviet Union where the subject is serving the revolution, or an evening in Spain where the subject is life and death, the settings unroll with a novelistic fullness and the characters have more than humanity about them, they have a touch of mortality as well. The presentation of people in such a way that the whole range of their being is somehow in evidence at a single moment applies to far more than herself. Hemingway appears in the Spanish memoir, for example, not only as the man he is then and there, but as the better man he was in Key West a decade earlier and the lesser man he will be a decade hence. The major source of fullness is a proliferation of association by which memories, ideas, and experiences from diverse times and places are all brought to bear upon a single point. Everything is in relation to something else. The twenties memoir, for example, substantially set in Connecticut, actually begins in New York, and before Connecticut is even mentioned — two paragraphs into the story — we have the entire furnishings of their New York apartment, a visit from Josie's uncle whose presence on the stairs suggests they are not quite as free of their pasts as they think, a brief look at their library where the volumes in French and German tell us where they have most recently been, and even the little model of the Breton fishing boat, *Le Pouldu*, that John made, to give a clue to their romance. The Spanish memoir refers plentifully to Iowa. In the single section of the thirties memoir about her wartime interrogation in Washington, there are references, among other things, to her schooling in Iowa and Berkeley, her experiences in Berlin in the twenties, Dada and Surrealism, literary friendships, and the entire story of Henri Barbusse's funeral in Paris in 1935.

Although there are times reading the uncompleted portions when one feels one is trapped in a maze and cannot quite get out, generally speaking, in the parts of the manuscript that were polished for publication, the writing works. So luxuriant are the descriptions of what is given, in fact, that it takes some effort to identify what is missing. "A Year of

Disgrace" is not simply about the twenties: it is a paean to the good years with John. "The Starched Blue Sky of Spain" is about political idealism and courage. "Yesterday's Road" is about political principle and fervor. In a series of recollections of events which had actually caused her much anguish and confusion, everything is reconstructed without the difficulties. Surely she could have said more about the collapse of her marriage to the husband who inhabits the memoirs so vividly than the concluding passage of "A Year of Disgrace" in which, after recounting their dramatic voyage across Casco Bay and its tragic finale in the deaths of Sacco and Vanzetti, she writes only, "How could I have known that night in Portland that once we had beached the *Josy* at Cohasset I would never see her again? But I never did. Years later John went to look for her, alone, and found her bashed by a heavy tide, the planks rotted, her skeleton white as bone. He wrote me about it. For by that time we had parted, and I no longer saw him." In recreating her political commitments from the vantage point of the 1950s and '60s surely "Don't get me wrong. In those early years I went about as far left as you can go" left far too much unspecified. "Unite and fight seemed so terribly urgent that no one could believe the news," she says of the uprising in Barcelona put down by the Communists on which so much political understanding turned, but she never explains the news. "But where was Brecht?" and "Where was the dramatist Ernst Toller?" she asks of the Soviet Writers Congress she attended with John, but not what had happened to the rest of the participants since. Of course these were only installments. They were panels of a tapestry, parts of a whole. Again and again she returned to these issues in her reading or circled them in her drafts but they were not the parts that got done. To produce a portrait of her era that honestly reflected the complexity of her own experience she would have had to remove the veil over some very sorrowful private and political moments and this she could not bear to do. Against the bitterness and disappointments which she harbored in the present, the memoirs became an emotional enclosure in which nothing too terrible ever happened. "She made a little island of her past and climbed aboard with all her dead and gone," she had written about Anne Wendel in the trilogy. To the last her mother's daughter, she left the bad parts out.

All during the initial years of working on the memoirs — on both sides of her ghost work for Albert Rhys Williams in 1956; before and after an anticlimactic trip to Europe in 1957; and during a research fellowship at the Newberry Library in Chicago in 1958 — she kept them to herself, unwilling to risk her independence by too early a commitment to a publisher, but by the fall of 1959, with a large chunk of manuscript finally in hand, she was ready to seek an outlet. Her first thought was to turn to Scribner's, where her editor, Burroughs Mitchell, had become a friend, but though Mitchell respected Josie and admired the manuscript, there was a problem. Between the twenties and the thirties sections a great deal of attention was inevitably given to Hemingway — and Ernest Hemingway was nothing less than Scribner's favorite son. Concentrating on the inner qualities of the man in relation to his times, rather than on the external appearances that were the subject of so much Hemingway lore, Josie herself believed, as she wrote to Mitchell, that "Hem would [not] quibble a jot over anything in the piece," but between the joint possibilities of alienating Hemingway and inhibiting Josie, it did not seem wise to either Mitchell or Charles Scribner to take it on, and after considerable deliberation between themselves, they turned it down. Josie was not dismayed. Since several other publishers, including Doubleday, Harcourt, Brace, and Houghton Mifflin, had already expressed an interest in it, she was confident she could get a contract when she wanted, and she also felt that unless a publisher were either exceptionally enthusiastic or exceptionally generous, there was no particular reason for her to settle now. Why, then, almost immediately after the close of her discussions with Scribner's she suddenly signed an option with the Atlantic Monthly Press for only $350 — whether Seymour Lawrence, then the editorial director, was so convincing she believed he belonged in the enthusiastic category, or she was so sure the manuscript would soon be ready that she expected additional money almost at once — is not clear from the available evidence, but in any case that is what happened. When she signed the agreement that over the next decade brought her only $1,200, a few luncheons and books, and a lot of correspondence, she did so very casually.

If Josie was confident in 1959 that her memoirs would find not only a publisher but an audience, she was not relying on her own judgment alone. The few people to whom she had communicated anything of her real intentions for the book had been unanimously encouraging, and anyone who had seen, or heard her read, any part of the text was overwhelmingly so. Among the people who were important to her in the period when the memoirs began to take shape, none was more so than Saul Bellow, whom she had seen frequently during her stay in Chicago in 1958, and whose work she admired more than that of any other writer of the postwar period. So much a mainstay of her literary existence did Bellow become, in fact, that without his contribution it is not certain that any of the memoirs would have ever appeared. In his capacity as editor of the short-lived literary journal, *The Noble Savage*, he not only encouraged her to submit portions of the work in progress for publication, but helped her extricate from the tangled manuscript the most effective parts. His responses to the separate sections he eventually published so warmed her heart she was fond of quoting them in some of her letters to others. "I read your piece immediately and wouldn't put it down for any inducement. It's the sort of thing that gives the world a new spin" Bellow wrote her about the Spanish segment in September, 1959. "I see the ants running on the bark with different eyes as I read and I know I have fallen in with the real thing. Your piece goes along at first in a plain, truthful, fashion and suddenly, without effort or engineering, it becomes beautiful. . . . Everything is supported by feeling, and never in excess, and you're beautifully clear about Hemingway and Dos Passos and even lesser characters like Alberti. As for the self that comes through, it's the one I fell in love with in Yaddo's plutocratic dining room, coup de foudre." About a year later, reading what became "A Year of Disgrace," he was even richer in his praise. "The Jews have a formula called Daiyenu . . . 'It would have been enough,' " he told her. "It would have been enough, Lord, if you had only created the earth, but there is more. And the whole catalogue of gifts and miracles, which ends in Daiyenu — Had you done no more. Well, now, Josie, I'd love you whether you wrote or not. But there's more. The piece is wonderful — clear, full, pure, tranquil and generous, without an ounce of self-justification or self-advertisement. If you ever had any narcissism in your make-up, and I suppose you did, once, you've burned it off. . . ."

The rewards of her friendship with Bellow were far from limited to his literary accolades, for the whole effect of his attentions was to lessen her sense of isolation from the world. On one occasion in early 1961, while publication of the second installment was pending, he took her to dinner in New York and introduced her to another editor, Keith Botsford, whose awareness of her former reputation she found very gratifying. "Botsford in meeting me overwhelmed me, taking my hand and saying he could not begin to say how glad he was to meet me," she reported to Jean. "During the evening he turned to me and said that he had been reading everything I wrote, that it deserved to be reprinted, and that he hoped to do something about it." Later when the conversation turned to money and Josie remarked that she had never had any sense about it, "Botsford leaned toward me and said, but you got good books written. It is so long since anyone has spoken to me about those books that I could hardly believe my ears." Several years later, when no more of the memoirs had been published than appeared under Bellow's hand and she was in despair about the mess they had become, she wrote to Bellow thanking him for yet another service and reminding him how stimulating his role with *The Noble Savage* had been. "Let me tell you, the part you have actually played in recent years is not to be estimated by this or that," she told him. "If I had been with a publisher with an editor like you, this would now be out in hardback and maybe in paperback too. . . . If any publisher had ever said, look, here's three thousand dollars, now go ahead, it would have worked," and though the exact relation between money and writing was never simple, even for Josie, perhaps, it would have. However, that was not how it happened.

Throughout most of the period during and after the first emergence of her memoirs at the end of the 1950s, Josie's life continued in its usual fashion, and if there were no great positive excitements, there were also few negative surprises. From spring through autumn she generally stayed in Erwinna, sometimes with visitors, sometimes not; winters, when possible, she went to New York, either borrowing or sharing the apartments of friends. Money was a constant problem. Never "prudent," she had no social security, no medical insurance, no savings, and almost no income, and she lived in a private economy of hand-me-downs and handouts whose consequences to her self-respect and her relationships with others she did her best to ignore. The collection of sufficient funds to pay the taxes at Erwinna was an annual sleight-of-hand. Her relationship with Jean was also a kind of constant. It was real, it was special, it survived, beyond reason, both Josie's histrionics and Jean's affairs, but in the ordinary struggles of day-to-day existence, it did not count for much. "How simple it would have been if I had loved you alone and only you for all these years and, with no question of money on either side, or other bedevilments, we could have made the structured life together that people do in marriage. . . ." Jean reflected after nearly a decade of their involvement, but, compared to marriage, the proportion of vulnerability to security in their relationship was the reverse. More than friends, not really lovers, and with no expectation of change on either side, they continued in a state of wary irresolution in which no fulfillment seemed possible. They led widely separate lives, Jean, in the city, holding jobs, making conquests, publishing poems; Josie, in the country, maintaining her precarious lot as best she could, yet so strong was their emotional bond neither one of them was ever really free. Atop of this turmoil of both finances and passion, Josie's work nonetheless flourished as rarely before. Thanks in part to her friendship with Hilton Kramer, who, like Saul Bellow, had become one of her strongest supporters, she began writing critical essays for *Arts* and for smaller literary journals, and these pieces — some on major exhibits, such as a Van Gogh retrospective and another of paintings from the '20s which had originally appeared in *The Dial;* others on the work of various friends including Stanley Burnshaw and Edward Dahlberg, and another major essay on West — both stimulated her further work on the memoirs and strengthened her powers as a critic. Throughout the early 1960s she wrote periodically to Seymour Lawrence describing the advancing bulk of her manuscript and expressing optimism about the remainder, but since she was rejecting most of what she completed, the justification for it was wearing thin. When she first felt the fear that she would be able to go no further is a moment lost in her papers, but from that point on her confidence was largely bravado.

While Josie was struggling for the mellowness of language and spirit she wanted for her memoirs, a literary event occurred which aroused her as much as any in recent years, the triumphant publication in the spring of 1962, also by Seymour Lawrence, of Katherine Anne Porter's *Ship of Fools*. For more than twenty years it had been announced as "forthcoming," punctuated by rumors that a grand philosophical statement was in the making, and now, finally, all four hundred and ninety-seven pages of it, here it was. Speaking of consolidating one's literary position — the reviews were ecstatic. Whether it was truly a universal novel or merely a pretentious one was a debate that began after it had been out for some months, and still continues, but that it was a literary landmark, of a stature befitting serious moral inquiry, was accepted at once. Not only the critics, but the readers, took it to their hearts. Between sales which kept it on the best-seller lists for nearly a year and a movie version which reportedly brought the author half a million dollars, it was clearly a grand-scale American-style success. It was as if the public wanted The Word about the human condition to be revealed precisely by this elegant-seeming aristocratic ladylike character whose hair capped her face like a grandmother's bonnet either because if she was the one who was telling it, it could not be as bad as it seemed, or because if even she knew how bad it really was, it would confirm their darkest fears. Josie tried to like it, but as her own thoughts and feelings deepened, the phenomenon of public rejoicing over this particular novel was more than she could bear. For as Theodore Solotaroff put it in an analysis in *Commentary*, — "*Ship of Fools* and the Critics," — with which she strongly concurred, *Ship of Fools* was "the most sour and morbid indictment of humanity to appear in years."

If Josie was troubled by the general critical enthusiasm for *Ship of Fools* there was more than simple jealousy in her reaction. About the quality of Katherine Anne's writing, the magnitude of the effort, and the discipline required to devote herself to the task, Josie was always free in her praise. What bothered her was the same malevolence in Katherine Anne's spirit she had found in their correspondence about Germany at the end of the war, expanded and even elevated into a book. Indeed, as Josie saw it, the novel belonged to the very period in which many of the political issues which had furthered their later rupture were beginning to come to the fore. Into a novel set in 1931 Katherine Anne had inserted and somehow generalized the postwar sense of doom. Not only was it a novel in which, read either realistically or allegorically, everything was evil — it was also ahistorical. "I never saw a bunch of more unloving, irritable, touchy folks, either on ship or land," Josie wrote Alfred Kazin, to whom she often unburdened herself in these years.

There is not only no lovemaking but no fornication worthy of the name. Jenny, who represents KAP is traveling with a lover who sleeps in a separate cabin; she can't contrive even a single moonlight meeting with the poor guy, and is deeply offended when one night, slightly drunk, he tries to push her into her cabin. The moral emphasis is given to Jenny; Jenny is right, the man is a bruiser, at that point. Another woman, presented from perfume to painted toenails most lovingly, can't love, never has in spite of one marriage. On the big gala night she trips to her cabin, and longing to get out of herself and its prison, paints her face in imitation of the corrupt dancers who put on the gala. Then a drunken lout, Denny, in pursuit of his rightful game, one of the dancers, bounces against her door. When she opens it, he mistakes her painted face for the dancer's and clutches her. She beats the senseless man over the head with the heel of her sandal. . . . The moral is also given here in favor of this woman — the ship's doctor comments that it was an "act of justice." That is also the tone we are expected to take away. But it is the wrong accent. The guy had nothing to do with her frustrations — it was a case of mistaken identity, nothing more. She can only express herself through violence, not exactly a moral note. The activists on board are all evil. The others are collaborators or passive. This is not 1931. Everything has been abstracted in the way of a countervailant force . . . The 876 Spaniards in the steerage are rigged, as are the customers at the Captain's table. There is only one Jew aboard to play pariah, and he is a stereotyped version of "the Jew", he hates the Goyim and sells trinkets of a religious nature to Catholics whom he also hates. Hate is the big currency. The Spaniards below deck are actually made to get into a big brawl over a priest. This would have been utterly impossible for Spaniards of that class . . . at that date. . . . I am naturally not asking for "literal" rendering of anything. But where is the moral accent to come from, where the opacity of persons to be clarified if the empirical sources become so muddied? Even among Germans the big question in 1931 was not the Jewish question, fanatical as many were under cover. . . . Hitler had to push it across on the shoulders of more urgent issues, the "stab in the back", the shame of Versailles, the hideous unemployment, the chaos. These Germans never heard of the Weimar Republic, neither its glories nor its disgrace . . . In 1931, these Germans should have also been pretty nervous about the actual world, of unemployment and collapse, to which they were returning. The Americans too are abstracted from their meanings; never speak of the crisis here. . . . I am biased, of course . . . by having touched too closely the kinds of people she is describing. But isn't it sad that history has to be given to us, all the time . . . through someone's subjectivity which subtracts from the actual, rather than infiltrating it with light?

313

So opposed was Josie on so many grounds to Katherine Anne's version of history and its apotheosis that she wrote a five-thousand-word article for *Commentary* and when the piece was dropped in favor of the staff-written essay by Solotaroff, she arranged, through Elizabeth Pollet, to read it over the New York radio station WBAI. She also wrote to a number of friends about it, in terms of which the letter to Kazin is typical. Trying as she was in her own work, in the words of Rilke she frequently referred to around this period, "to let each impression and each germ of feeling come to completion in itself," to let each moment shimmer, she despised the contemptuous sameness with which Katherine Anne seemed to dismiss it all. In Josie's writing at least some of the Germans were Reglers, risking their health and lives in Spain. A Jew might be a Nathanael West for whom his Jewishness, far from being a grievance, could be a mystery, a vitality, a resource. Even the random characters in her memoirs, such as the old sea-captain in Maine, were given a specificity, a reflectiveness, and a decent human nature denied to all the passengers on *Ship of Fools*. As far as Josie was concerned, Katherine Anne's vision was false. There was not only destiny there was possibility and what mattered was not only how things actually turned out but how they had seemed at the time. If the reductionist view of history proposed by Katherine Anne was truly the mood of the hour, all was lost. "This has been a wonderful time for vaporizers like Porter; a hideous time for people like me," she wrote to Jean.

In the late spring of 1962, beset by problems she thought were largely external, Josie decided to go abroad, hoping that the change would restore her energy for work. Through various connections she was able to arrange for a lectureship on a Dutch student ship to pay her way. A previous trip, mainly to Italy, in 1957, had not been very rewarding — as old as she was, the satisfactions of traveling seemed fewer, the inconveniences greater than they had before — but she was so accustomed to "lighting out" at moments of difficulty, that when she felt herself flagging, she could think of no other response. As in 1957, she spent some of her time in Denmark, some by herself, and some with friends, and, as also on the earlier journey, she was joined somewhat later by Jean, and together they went to Amsterdam, Grenoble, and the French Alps. Although she originally intended to return in the fall, a chest ailment that worsened in the Alps made her wary of weathering the winter at home, and she headed instead for Ibiza, where she knew an inexpensive rental would be available, and where she hoped to be able to work; Jean went along. So certain was she that with distance both from her American subject and her own papers she would achieve the detachment necessary to finish up her memoirs that she wrote Seymour Lawrence it was practically accomplished, and he responded with another five hundred dollars of option money to help her remain abroad. For about two months, while Jean was there, they seem to have followed a peaceful, productive routine, but shortly after New Year's Jean grew restless and left. Again she was alone, in a primitive household, in a remote location. Except for the Mediterranean, she might almost have been at home.

The manuscript as it existed at that time seems to have consisted of a number of interrelated sections with some overlap and some repetition — Hemingway, for example, was discussed at length in a substantially developed section on the late '20s, "The Hour of Counterfeit Bliss," as well as in the section on Spain — and there were a number of floating incidents — such as the trip to Russia with John that became the basis for the second half of the last published installment, "Yesterday's Road" — not yet anchored to a home. Although piece by piece the sections are highly polished, they seem to have emerged haphazardly, in no particular order, and were not tied together by any overall plan. Some connective threads there undoubtedly were already, in the form of the personality of the narrator, the strong family and Iowa feeling, and the characteristically Proustian attitude toward time, but she wanted it to proceed from a center, from a framework, and that framework was to be nothing less than an entire interpretation of life. In an undated letter to Jane Mayhall, not written from Ibiza but reflecting her intentions during the period she was working there, she described much more frankly than usual what it was she was really trying to do. "I can only really fling out about myself in its uttermost by relating to others, and talking about someone not myself, and it is this exact thing, the mutations to which seem to me so really interesting and valid, that has become in a sense the central theme of this book," she explained.

> And, Jane, the central thing about this work is not the information I have, though I do have it, and it is important too in revealing certain aspects that I believe to have been smothered by other commentators, but a kind of creative core, which I call the burning bush. . . . And to get at this creative core, I had to get at Me, and this has made all the trouble. For there are then problems to solve and technical devices to invent which will allow me to use the material I have to use, some of which is so painful that I can't do it directly but have to find its metaphor. . . . For instance, I have to deal really and truly with love — and what I mean by it, and its relation to just plain sex, the volcano below. And I have to deal with the ruin it can make, and its dreadful craters and what can spring out from its ashes, as the grape vines do from the ashes of Etna. And I want to say some things that women don't ordinarily say, alas, and to do it objectifying myself — standing off, and seeing me, and being able to do it. . . .

And when I say that I have [wanted] to relate [it] all . . . to writing, and the choices one makes, and the kinds of experience one uses — the kinds that corrode and one merely gets beyond, burning the soles of one's feet, you can see what I have been involved with. I have been involved with heaven and hell and their relationships — and all the other business of memory about time and place, about people's literary output is only the exterior, necessary and objectifying the real core. . . . I can't even explain some things to myself — they are just there — and yet by relating them, by being able to see them in [a] concrete context . . . another dimension unfolds. . . . And what I was interested in was the mutations, and then to ask, what central core, what dynamo keeps the whole business *going* so that it can survive the destructions, the humiliations, the suffering? One snatches these from the very burning, and only so negates nothingness.

And if I had just been writing . . . anecdotes about other writers or myself or prattling even about events, as events, it would have been easy. But the event is more than itself, and that's the way I had to do it. Sometimes it is less than it seems. And beyond all else the true education is really sexual understanding and charity for others and they don't come at once. They are paid for, as any happiness is paid for, as anyone who has had any worth mentioning knows in his bones.

"Heaven and hell and their relationships." It was certainly a difficult order. To write about herself at the level she believed captured her deepest truths would mean recreating not only the sexual atmosphere of the twenties as a social force, as she had already done so brilliantly in "A Year of Disgrace," or the tentative small-town awakenings she was evoking so exquisitely now, but all those specific personal craters that belonged not so much to the landscape of her generation as to her own. Maxwell Anderson. Her abortion. Helen. John. Marion Greenwood. Even Jean. Memoirist yes, but woman as well, with a morality rooted in an earlier era and decades of tumultuous experience for which every day she was still paying a price — did she really want to tell all those stories? With or without metaphor, she would still find it perilous to do.

Shortly after Jean's departure there arrived in Josie's mailbox in Ibiza a book unlike any she — or anyone else — had ever encountered. It was Doris Lessing's *The Golden Notebook* and she read it with mounting awe. So different on the surface from her own serpentine narrative that their relationship is not at once apparent, the experience that gave rise to both efforts was nonetheless much the same. Two radical women leading free sexual lives in the shadow of the great twentieth-century political revolution — they were women shaped by the same circumstances. What Lessing was representing in her novel was the very life Josie had always lived and even written about in her letters, except for details. Yet how different were their literary responses. Where Josie was vague, Doris Lessing was blunt. "I no longer wrote for *The New Masses,* nor would, nor *could,"* Josie wrote in "Yesterday's Road," in one of her few references to the political developments that had led her away from the Communist Party. In *The Golden Notebook* there are lists of headlines — "11 COMMUNIST LEADERS HANGED IN PRAGUE" — Anna Wulf's refugee lover Michael describes "communists murdered by communists" abroad, and Anna herself leaves the Party, all in an atmosphere in which the very difficulty of facing the truth becomes itself part of the human evidence to be analyzed, rather than part of the secret to be concealed. The same contrast that characterizes their respective writing about politics also characterizes their respective writing about love and sex. While Lessing confronts the realities of relations between men and women through a series of half-mad affairs whose alternations between contempt and passion Josie well knew, in Josie's own writing these relations were either omitted, enveloped in sweetness, or obscured by inscrutable private allusions meant to falsify the essential fact that it was sometimes women and not men who were the lovers. Though it is true that in *The Golden Notebook* the connections between women are those of friendship and not love, even in the portrayal of the relationship of Anna and Molly, Lessing went beyond what Josie was writing about but, again, not beyond what, in her own friendships with women going perhaps as far back as her adolescence, she had actually felt. It is as if Lessing were writing about her own life more candidly than she could do it herself.

"You will have to see the Lessing book — I keep thinking of you as I read it. It's a very bold book — really good — . . . It's so jolting and provocative and I don't know anyone who has written so openly and frankly about women — she really puts it on the line," she wrote to Jean. Coming at a critical point in her own writing *The Golden Notebook* was the greatest literary challenge Josie ever had to face. Her male contemporaries she had long ago rejected as literary models, for as she had come to read their memoirs and papers she realized how little about women they knew, and as for politics, to anything smacking of conventional anti-Communism she was more or less naturally immune, but for a woman of her own kind to look at her experience so squarely and write so freely about both sex and politics was an example of courage she could not ignore. It was what she had wanted to do as long ago as the story of Victoria and Jonathan in the trilogy — only Lessing was doing so much more. Where Josie was writing with a kind of breathless wonder about the Bolshevik and sexual revolutions as if they were still in the forefront of history, to Doris Lessing they had already become part of the continuing cycle of human experience to be churned over and reflected on as it went along. Far from being a narrow aesthetic matter, what was involved were some of the highest questions of political and moral integrity, and Josie was well aware of their weight. It was the difference between being an anachronism and being an artist. The meaning of *The Golden Notebook* as far as Josie was concerned was not only that women *could* write more freely about their experience but that of course they *would.* Not only that the revolution had devoured its children but those whom it had not devoured would rise up to tell the story. From the singular and powerful pages of this towering novel of women Josie received with undeniable force the intelligence she had resisted in so many other ways: that history was moving on. Unless she could overcome the inhibitions and loyalties of a lifetime, she would be left behind.

# A Time of Exposure

In May, 1963, after nearly a year abroad, Josie decided to return. She carried with her a large chunk of manuscript which, she assured Seymour Lawrence, except for retyping and a final checking against her personal files, was as good as done. Reluctant to face Erwinna, where the task of restoring the house to the status quo ante tenant was a well-known distraction, she went instead to Saratoga, not to Yaddo but to a house owned by Jane Mayhall and Leslie Katz, which they were not using at the time. She was joined for much of the summer by Hilton Kramer. Although she was greatly eased by both his company and his appreciation of the manuscript, which he told her was even better than what had appeared in *The Noble Savage*, she thought herself that the different styles she had adopted at different points in her experimentation were not yet fully integrated, and she spent much of the time attempting to revise. She continued to brood about *The Golden Notebook*. At Erwinna in the autumn her expectation of rapid completion remained unabated — she was so persuasive she wrested another $350 from Seymour Lawrence — but though her excitement about the originality of what she had accomplished briefly reached one of its highest peaks, it was not long before her momentum began to falter. The difficulty was not with the manuscript as much as it was with her life. She resumed having visitors, she was often invited to go places and to do things, but whether because of her long stay abroad, the demands of the work itself, or even the fact that she was no longer hearing as well as she used to, she was feeling uncomfortably cut off. "You are the one person who could draw me into life more — the one I have loved — and I feel I am not drawn in . . . I have no one to tie my thoughts to," she lamented to Jean. A sense of diminution in her daily existence warred with the sense of importance necessary to finish the book. On one occasion, after feeling excluded from a general conversation of friends, some of which had to do with the literary past, she was full of doubt. "I wondered who I was or what my past had ever been. I often wonder that. And it is one of the major difficulties in writing this book. . . . Everybody can now read heaven knows how many books on 'the past' and there are authorities which are taken as gospel. One can take Matthew Josephson or Sylvia Beach — who needs another voice, especially when it is a different one. It's all set," she burst out to Jean. Another time, after failing to provoke a conversation on some topic she particularly wanted to discuss, she was even more disturbed. "It is odd how completely silent I have been on the very questions that deep down seem to me the most important. I presume this is what goes into a book but if it can only be recognized in a book — what of life itself?" she demanded of Jean. Not for the first time, but not yet for the last, it all seemed too much. "I have little luck in my life except my own spirit and my spirit is now failing me. It just is perched on a bare rock and that's not enough," she wrote to Jean.

Despite the combination of circumstances that might have kept her down, like the majority of Josie's moods this depression was not eternal, and what with one diversion and another she soon began to feel somewhat better. One source of her changing mood was a renewal of interest in politics — specifically the revived radical politics of the 1960s. "The Negroes have made this country about as interesting a place to be in as anywhere . . . I'm glad they turned militant — nothing ever got through for anybody without that," she wrote Stanley Burnshaw about the civil rights march on Washington in the summer of 1963, shortly after she got home. Five years later she was defending the Columbia sit-ins to Jean. The gratification provided by the resurgence of political action was both intellectual and personal. It had to do with the fulfillment of her sense of history. Having outlasted a period when, in the words of a Brecht poem she admired, "there was injustice only and no outcry," there was no question which she preferred. The injustice had not gone away during the forties and fifties, in her view, only the outcry had been silenced, and for it to be addressed again, by a generation seemingly free of the partisan bitterness of her own, she interpreted as evidence that she had not been wrong. Events had deprived the masses of the foothold they were struggling for in her day, but now they were stirring again, there was continuity in movement, and as she had in Cuba, the Guadarrama, and following the caisson of Henri Barbusse, she felt sure in her heart of their inevitable rise. Whether the issue involved black people or white people, the Vietnam war or the universities, America or Europe, no matter what, in particular, was happening, she was glad it was going on. When her young friends, the Danielses, who were involved in the draft resistance movement in Philadelphia, were concerned about a conflict between a date they had made with her and a demonstration, she assured them she knew which was more important. "Go to the demonstration — these things don't last forever — whenever the people are in the streets, join them," she told them. She wished to have been with Norman Mailer at the Pentagon. When friends sent her money to be used for herself she turned right around and sent some of it to the Free Speech Movement at Berkeley and to various civil rights groups — contributions all the more striking since she had almost nothing at hand.

So strongly did she identify herself with the young radicals that the gap in perception between the generations that was so much a part of the atmosphere of the 1960s simply did not occur in her case, and as dissent grew more generalized, the more fervent she became. "Just where do you think you stand in all this?" she railed at Jean who had expressed disquiet during the spring of 1968. "There is a bunch up at Columbia out to protect 'property' and according to a faculty member [have] been among the most violent of the provocateurs — throwing eggs and empty bottles at the striking students. I think it is very critical to decide where you are — this is something more fundamental than mere youth rebellions. It doesn't matter if they make mistakes. A new political force is emerging. . . . It may be true that they pulled up plane trees in Paris for barricades — other sources say they merely took the iron grills from around trees to make a barricade — but for god's sake — who are you for? You spend a lot of time inveighing against the bulldozers and those who pull down worthy old buildings in the name of Order and Progress. Who do you care about? I don't want trees pulled up but in comparison to trees, wildlife, landscape, people's dwellings simply ordered off the face of the earth by legal standards, what in hell are a few trees tossed in by students who — nameless, without power — are challenging massive and entrenched power. They probably won't win — now — or can't — but by god they are right and you better find out where your feelings lie. And not monkey around with gossip about outside agitators and all that crap." It was a thoroughly unsceptical reaction. Others of her generation might criticize or cavil — Josie would only rejoice. It was really a matter of the world being in motion again, as if when the underdog growled at its masters and the poor fought the rich, whatever the particulars, decades of cloud-cover suddenly dissipated and lo! the constellations were in their familiar places once more. Into Erwinna poured I. F. Stone's *Weekly, The New York Review of Books, Liberation,* and other literature associated with New Left, their columns soon crowded with marginal applause. Veteran that she was, to her last days a new slogan could make her exuberant. "Today [the Paris students] barged into the stock exchange shouting Temple of Gold, Temple of Gold — which exhilarates me," she wrote in the same letter to Jean.

Another factor that acted as a shield against depression as the long struggle with her memoirs wore on was her renewed recognition as a writer. Not only was she publishing articles on both literary and political subjects in journals ranging from *The Nation* to the *Georgia Review*, but beginning in the middle of the 1960s there were other forms of recognition as well. In 1965 there was a large cash grant from the Rockefeller Foundation, in 1966 there was an award from the National Institute of Arts and Letters which involved both cash and prestige, and in 1967 she was a member of the fiction advisory panel for the National Book Awards. All these emoluments were engineered by her friends as much out of awareness of her necessity as out of appreciation of her talent. The Rockefeller grant seems to have come about at the instigation of Saul Bellow. Her award from the National Institute of Arts and Letters has an intricate history, but it appears to have been the persistent efforts of Bellow, Cheever, and Robert Penn Warren that finally got her one.° Another invisible hand was Alfred Kazin's. Just what had happened all of a sudden to elevate her from obscurity to eminence Josie was ignorant and she seems to have taken the merit of it for granted, but she was cynical about it all the same. "You mention my 'happy possession of the Academy check' — but I don't know if it was that happy," she wrote to Alfred Kazin. "Glad though I was to get the dough, the moment was very much tinged with chagrin. The nicest thing said to me that day was said by the professor from Berkeley . . . who wrote the Sinclair Lewis biography and also wrote the absurd review of Ship of Fools for the N Y Times who said, drily, 'They should have given it to you long ago.' Which is of course true. It was just about too late, too damnably late. And do you think all that doesn't signify something to me? . . . I have seen those old Culture-Hands dish out awards year after year to people I barely respect. So they had finally come to the bottom of the barrel of my generation and scratched up me. Egged on too by the Rockefeller award — and not to be left in midstream without a paddle. Oh no, I'm never in such a plight as to be too everlastingly blind when I am touched on the shoulder and told it is my turn, at long last." Nonetheless, the money was a relief. "I have been damaged — whether temporarily or not — by a long monotonous poverty which I had to pretend was not there to live at all. I truly think I did it often with better elan than many people could manage, but it got too much for me at last and affected my thoughts and feelings in areas that may seem wide of the mark," she confessed to Jean. "It has

° See Notes.

been humiliating in a deep way to have to take money, even from dearest friends."

Just at a point where her energy and spirits were restored and she was working herself up to what she hoped would be her final attack on the memoirs, she learned as a result of a routine physical examination that she had cancer of the cervix. Since the doctors were optimistic from the beginning that the disease had been found early enough to be cured and she believed them, the sense of a confrontation with death was something she was largely spared, and she did recover, but the treatment itself — six weeks in the summer of 1966 in New York Hospital for radium and cobalt, some of which required immobilization — was a physical ordeal. She took it extremely well. The sense of the life of the hospital with its huge varied population of patients and staff, the complicated technology, even the view of the East River which she could see from her room, all seemed a reprieve from her usual isolation. "I can't say I didn't enjoy it, for to tell the truth I was so curious about everything and they were so good about telling me what was happening each step of the way that it was a genuine experience," she told Alfred Kazin. "Besides they were wonderful to me, the nurses came to my room to chat, the doctors chatted about more than disease and everyone was so tender and considerate that I found life outside, once I had got there, a bit difficult. In a way all that kind of time is a kind of exposure. You re-see everything and in a startling way. But I have been re-seeing so often in recent years that for that reason alone I have been so slow in my work. But I can't go into all that, it is too complex — in fact everything is, and my trouble always has been too much, too much — it pours in, that's all there is to it, and excites me very much. It will to the day I die."

For a brief period following her hospitalization, Josie knew what was important. It was what she had always thought. She would write steadily to complete the work in which she deeply believed: she would value her communication with her friends: she would treasure every moment of real experience from the sun rising to the dew falling of which she could possibly keep herself aware. It was difficult for her to sustain it. The illness had had its compensations, but soon the same problems were at hand. As she drew closer to the moment of reckoning when the sad facts of actuality were measured against the tests of eternity, her existence could appear very bare. "What's it all about? Do you know?" asks Uncle Daniel, her mother's brother, on a final visit to Josie and John in the distant past poignantly recaptured in a section of the memoirs that was on her table now. "And once more the arrogance of youth protected me; I thought to myself, when it's my time, I'd know more. I wouldn't be asking questions of someone forty years younger." But now here she was and her time was nearly on her and somehow the question of Uncle Daniel had become her own. "What's it all about? Do you know?" As much as she wanted to have it otherwise, she found it was hard to be sure.

Exactly what Josie was doing on the memoirs from the time they were "nearly finished" in the summer of 1963 until the time they were also "nearly finished" five years later is difficult to tell, for her references to them grew vaguer as time passed and the editorial record is obscure, but apart from a final section on the early twenties involving Helen and Maxwell, which she was always attempting but could never bring herself to write, it appears to have been a matter of making relatively small improvements not so much in the substance of the manuscript but in its tone. An atmosphere of serene contemplation, an appearance of profound acceptance not just in the interpretation of events but in the character of the narrator — this is what she was struggling to achieve. "I keep revising and I, too, am revising myself, for the better, I hope," she wrote in 1967 to Peter Davison, who had become the director of the Atlantic Monthly Press a few years before. What is remarkable about Josie's efforts is not that ultimately she was unable to complete them, but how close to fruition they came. "The first thing to say is that it is absolutely *beautiful* — not a word I use lightly," wrote Hilton Kramer who read the section on her childhood and youth in the summer of 1968. "The prose is so limpid and felt and evocative, all the family figures so vividly and lovingly drawn, and the period so delicately conveyed in so many homely particulars — I read most of it with such a huge lump of feeling in my throat that I could hardly swallow when I was finished . . . If the book included nothing else, these sections on your family and your early life in Iowa would constitute a classic in themselves . . . I've long felt that your book would be important, but I think I see some aspects of its importance now that I had not been so conscious of before. From the point of view of American literary history, this is the only book that attempts to sustain a sense of continuity between the materials and experience of the older writers . . . and . . . the world that is now our material and experience. And you are the only writer . . . who could even attempt it. No wonder it has been such a struggle — that it *is* such a struggle. It has the makings of a masterpiece, of great illumination, and in every detail and phrase — whether the episode of the Easter egg with your uncle or the scene with the American visitor in the Berlin restaurant — one feels some terrible personal pain being delicately transmuted into poetry." It was a response with which Alfred Kazin, who read it about the same time and sent a telegram pronouncing it "exquisite," obviously concurred. Out of memories that still tortured her in their nonliterary apparitions, transcending the ignominious present, she was creating a world of such pellucid splendor that Hilton Kramer's "transmute" — transmutation — is the only right word. So great was the gap between the quiet majesty of Josie's prose and the meager circumstances of its composition that it is almost enough in itself to explain her deferments, for to go from one to the other was a kind of spiritual crossing which could be accomplished only rarely and at great cost. For when she expelled the harshness from the Eden of her memoirs it accumulated elsewhere. And the place that it settled was her life.

Starting at about the time of her 1966 hospitalization, Josie's personality seems to have gone into a kind of decline. Certainly she had always been difficult and certainly too her character had not been improved by her years of living alone, but there is little doubt both from what people say about her and from the written record, that she had reached the point where in order to be appreciated she had first to be forgiven. Friends and strangers alike found her garrulous and inconsiderate. Stanley Burnshaw, whom she visited often during the 1960s at his homes in Martha's Vineyard and Florida, recalls a moment when, in the midst of a conversation he was having with Josie, his wife Leda came in carrying heavy packages and he rose to help her, Josie simply lit a cigarette and went right on talking. Justin Kaplan, who shared a platform with her on the occasion of the presentation of the 1968 National Book Awards, recalls that she talked through the entire ceremony. Other people found her inconsistent, contradictory, changing her stories about her past to fit not so much her history as her audience. The chief victim of this emotional attrition appears to have been her relationship with Jean. Certainly it too had always been difficult and it, too, had not been bettered by the replication of the same quarrels year after year, but as the aftermath of Josie's illness revealed ever more starkly the disparities between their ages and situations, the more tinged with final judgment did every passing quarrel between them appear.

The issues between Josie and Jean were so many and so murky that it was difficult even for them to separate them, but uppermost among the emotions that began to surface at this time seems to have been Josie's feeling of desertion. Jean had stayed close at hand for a time during Josie's hospitalization and afterward had joined her briefly during her recuperation at the home of Erwinna friends, but then she had drifted off to spend the summer elsewhere and Josie had been left — too soon in her opinion — to cope with her recovery alone. Another issue had to do with other relationships. Jean was involved with another woman, as she had often been before, Josie was becoming more and more dependent on the men who were her friends, and the opposing character of their rival attachments provided the impetus for highly insulting exchanges, meant to be taken personally, on the triviality and subjectivity of women and the fawning of intellectual men. In addition to these issues which were more or less late arrivals, there were a number of other grievances which had also been voiced in the past. Jean did not come often enough to Erwinna and when she did come she did not help with the housework . . . speaking of work, Jean did not care at all about Josie's accomplishments either past or present and was only exploiting the facilities, such as the chicken coop, to further advance her own . . . indeed Jean was not interested in Josie at all as a person but would far rather direct her energies elsewhere, as witness her behavior on such and such an occasion —: and all this in one letter alone. To all Josie's charges Jean responded as John had long ago, with denials that grew more tepid as their futility grew more apparent. With the furies engaged to the point where Jean's leaving a piece of wrapper on a butter plate became the occasion for an attack by Josie on her entire character, what could she do? But what really distinguished their relationship at this point from their relationship at any earlier period has less to do with any specific grievance than with their unremitting quality. Formerly there was alternation between transgression and forgiveness — for both parties. Increasingly, on Josie's side, there was only rage.

By the summer of 1968 Josie was poised on a brink. To the extent that the meaning is defined by the ending, her life still had different possible meanings. On the one hand she was engaged in activities that could bring her not just attention and security in the immediate present, but a purchase on the future. On the other she had very little strength. Not only was she determined to conquer the final section of the memoirs, involving Helen and Maxwell, at long last, but there were a number of other projects, large and small. Theodore Solotaroff had published a third installment of the memoirs in an early edition of his *New American Review* a few months before, and she was now attempting to isolate out other sections that would make up a new installment on Yaddo. She had agreed to write an introduction to *Journey into Revolution* by Albert Rhys Williams, the same account of his experiences in Russia in 1917 she had tried to help him write in the 1950s, now put together by Virginia Gardner Marberry and published posthumously, and she was involved with Virginia Marberry in a lively political correspondence as stimulating as any she had had in years. She was even planning to contribute an essay on another friend, the writer Bravig Imbs, to a collection of literary eulogies to be called *Obits*. Most important of all was the fact that, beginning at about the time of her illness, a number of university libraries had begun expressing an interest in acquiring her papers, and after a great deal of consideration of all the possibilities she had eventually settled on Yale.

The sale of her letters to a prestigious university archive was of great significance. Both practically and psychologically it was a complicated business and because it included preparation of the papers in the form of cataloguing and sorting, it was a lot of work, but it offered great rewards. Not only would she receive $25,000, a sum perhaps not much less than the total amount of money that had passed through her hands in her en-

tire lifetime, but the existence of the archive would substantially broaden
the claim on which her foothold in posterity was based. Without the archive she was a minor writer like so many others who had come to bloom
and faded. With it she was a major personage whose participation in and
perception of events had been unique. There was also another consideration. While it is true that what the library wanted were the first editions
of Joyce published in Paris by Robert McAlmon, the brilliant letters of
Katherine Anne Porter, the declamations of James Farrell, the short,
pungent communications from Hemingway and Dos Passos and West,
that is not all there were. In the ceaseless creation and dissolution of relationships that had characterized her lifetime, a lot of her own letters had
been returned. Ignoring her own commands on the files, nothing had
been "Destroyed." Paralleling the public record was the passionate private record of a life lived fundamentally on no other terms than its own.
The stories of Helen and Maxwell Anderson might not be in the memoirs,
but they were there in the papers. So the romance with Marion Greenwood. Between the exquisite reserve of the memoirs and the tumultuous
disclosures of the papers surely she would be leaving sufficient record to
justify her election to the pantheon of human history — if only she could
get it all done. Either things could go forward so she could keep her
commitments and reap the rewards of her accomplishments, or they
could fall apart. They fell apart. The summer was very hot. What she
was attempting might well have been too much for even a younger
woman. And she was feeling indefinably unwell. Longing to meet the
deadlines that were closing in on her from all directions she pleaded with
Jean to come to Erwinna for a visit and lend a hand, but Jean did not
choose to come. Nor was there help from other quarters, for her friends
had scattered as they often did in summers, and most of the people on
whom she usually counted to help her were not around. It was the perfect explanation — and not only for her inability to function. Her self-
pity mounted to Olympian heights. Beleaguered and bereft, without a
true friend in the universe, how could she possibly fulfill the tasks laid
upon her? In much of her correspondence she kept up appearances as
usual and on her smaller projects she even made some progress, but in a
series of bitter missives to Jean so identical with laments reaching far
back into her past that they are comic and tragic in equal measure even
at this juncture, she dissipated her energies in a burst of vituperation, and
the other work never got done. The underlying emotion of Josie's final
summer was frustration. She would never taste the fruits of her labors.
"Her hands still felt like stumps that were bound behind her back" and
she was doomed, as she had written of Victoria in her trilogy, "to wander
in a grove with the pears always too high for her mouth."

By the fall following the desperate summer Josie's situation had considerably worsened. Disturbed by her continued weakness and other

minor discomforts, she made an appointment with her doctor, who pronounced her well, but despite the verdict a feeling of illness remained. "I seemed to have pitched down following a visit to my wonderful New York doctor a couple of weeks ago who took all the tests and said nothing was wrong with me and I could live to be Ninety if I took more care of myself," she wrote in early November to Jessie O'Connor. "Probably the threat of longevity was too much of a shocker." She continued to attempt to complete all her business but was more and more haunted by intuitions of doom. Summoning her niece, Betty Davis, from Washington, D.C., she discussed with her for the first time in their lives the details of her material existence, including her decision to attempt to leave Betty the disputed house, she confirmed an agreement with Hilton Kramer that he would become executor of her papers, and she made plans to incorporate these arrangements in a will. This particular disposition of the things that meant most to her involved the total exclusion of Jean with whom her relationship was now deeply ruptured. When Jean finally visited Erwinna the third week in November she was shouted out of the house. Despairing at the accusations of indifference, which she did not think she deserved, Jean wrote plaintively from New York — "I know that you are in bad straits. It concerns me a great deal. There is hope coming, a ship coming in. But the Yale people are also a great demand on you. I am *aware* of your delicacy and the tasks out there and your night sweats & inability to eat and the rain falling. And the files. I know how bad it is for you. I know to the core how bad it is for you. This is also a part of my suffering" — and was temporarily forgiven, but shortly thereafter the malice resumed. Concerned about Josie's obviously perilous condition, her friends made elaborate plans for her rescue. Officials from Yale were scheduled to arrive on Monday November the twenty-fifth to take her to lunch and collect the first installment of her papers. Hilton Kramer and Leslie Katz would come two days later, help her close up the house, and drive her to New York, from which she would go by train with Hilton Kramer to Connecticut, where she would spend Thanksgiving with himself and his wife Esta in their new house. Then she would go to New York to a quiet hotel — an arrangement made by Stanley Burnshaw — and later in the winter she would go to Yaddo. It all seemed to be going according to plan — except for how badly she felt. At her luncheon at the famous Delaware Canal tavern with the men from Yale that was in a sense one of the highest tributes to her career, she was barely able to swallow. When she left for the last time the house that had harbored her for forty years, she cared very little about her property or her papers. All that she cared about was life.

# "Tell My Friends . . ."

FROM THE MOMENT she entered New York Hospital in the middle of December, 1968, until her death from cancer about six weeks later, Josie realized she must be dying, and she did not try to deny it. At the Kramers', at Thanksgiving, she was barely able to eat, and at the hotel in New York where she established herself afterward it was much the same. In the light of her doctor's recent reassurances about her health, she persisted in hoping that the problem was only exhaustion, but it was getting harder and harder to believe. Sick to her stomach even when she had eaten nothing, what she could bring herself to smell she could barely swallow and what she could bring herself to swallow she could not keep down. During the month of November alone she had lost a dozen pounds. On December 7 she made an emergency appointment with her doctor, who was shocked by the change in her appearance, and she was admitted to the hospital on December 14. What the hospital summary called a "very wild carcinoma of the lung" not visible in the autumn was now not only in her lungs but encircling her esophagus, with metastases into both the brain and liver, raging completely out of control. Except for some radiation therapy, delivered without conviction, there was nothing even in theory that could be done. Not long before, working over her memoirs, she had paused once again at the moment on the beaches of Oregon when life stretched out before her like the ocean, like the sand. "There was someone's beyond behind you, and a beyond to come to pass," she had written of the evenings around the fire listening to her mother's and uncle's stories of their own childhood and youth. But her "beyonds" had all come and gone.

When word went out among the people who had known her that Josephine Herbst was dying there was a great stirring of response and into the hospital room poured messages of love from her friends far and wide. Close at hand, too, there was a great swelling of concern, and in a blur of comings and goings there appeared at her bedside a constant stream of visitors from both her present and her past. The burden of her illness in a practical sense fell most heavily on her companions of later years, the "customers" of Erwinna and a few others, who came in shifts every day to nurse her with their own hands when a strike threatened her care and who paid out of their own pockets for the death she could not afford herself. There was also Jean. In desperation, in remorse, she hovered humbly about the sickroom, trying to perform in illness all the homely little functions she had loathed to perform in health, but Josie was unforgiving. As the coming of death made clearer that all that happened already was all that there ever was between them, or would be, Jean was overcome by a storm of conflicting emotions, partly grievance, partly grief, from which she never really recovered. She herself died of cancer, at fifty-nine, three years later. As for the others, they too were sick at heart. Later would come a distance as time unveiled conflicting visions of their star as well as themselves. But for now there was only sorrow.

In the center of this universe of devotion and love lay the patient herself, diminishing daily, barred by the condition of her suffering physical body from her usual consolations in the world outside herself. "It was a hard slow laborious work, like a dreadful birth," she had written about the death of her mother many years earlier, and her own was much the same. It had all been so "very strange and wonderful." Mary had kept "sinking and reviving," "sinking and reviving." "One moment we thought she was gone, the next she was sitting up and asking for ham & eggs & wanting to brush her teeth & actually *doing* it." "We all go," she had told her mother. "The leaves fall," but like her mother before her "she was so strong for life she couldn't die," and she hung on and on. The record of Josie's ending has a curiously vacant quality, for except for a few items dictated to others, from the time she came to the hospital she wrote no more letters. With the number and the character of the observers who were present there is far from being a shortage of description, but when the observers, the observed, and the very moments of observation all vary as they do, whose perception of her experience is it that is to be believed? If we seek to find the moment that captures the essence of her last days and hours, should we choose the time that she insisted that Jean and Jean alone could comb her hair for her or the moment she commanded her to leave the room? Would it be the moment she welcomed to her bedside the distinguished critic she had not seen for years or the moment she castigated him behind his back? To borrow a device from her forever-unfinished memoirs — Who can say?

Yet of all the information that exists about her dying, one source stands out above all the others, the notes made in the hospital by her doctor of many years, and from these it appears that though as much as possible she carried on as usual during the daytime, reading and talking, her fear and suffering were sometimes substantial, and, like every person who had ever died before her and everyone after, she experienced her darkest moments alone. " 'I am just slowly drowning,' " "Sitting up too long to converse with a friend felt pain," "Very rough — general panic," "Losing ground," are some of the entries. A note made in the last week is particularly revealing — "Patient reliving her life in tortuous fashion" — because it suggests that the struggle with her memories was not yet over. On January 25, 1969, with little consciousness left, she asked the doctor to take a final message to her friends. "Tell my friends I do not repent. That I love life unto eternity — love and life," she murmured, and the doctor wrote it down. So moved were those who heard of it that the words passed from friend to friend like a gift at parting, although no one quite knew what she meant. Repeated in the eulogy by Alfred Kazin, which appeared in *The New York Review of Books*, they became part of my own first instruction in the legend of Josephine Herbst. For a long time I was puzzled, as her friends were — Josie? "Repent?" Who among them would think that she would? — but gradually I felt I understood the answer, for as she departed more and more from the company of the living the generations unrolled before her in a bright white light and she was thinking of her unrepentant uncle "pouring liquor down his throat as long as he could swallow" and of her mother refusing Jesus and while it was hardly likely that anyone would expect repentance now, in this era, she had better make it clear she would not consider it just to be on the safe side. It was a matter of family honor. About the other part of Josie's message I am not as certain, but I believe it was a last performance. "Love life" she did and love as well regardless, but why did she make the effort to mention it? With her estate headed for permanent sanctuary, a youthful executor whose name would command respect, and a large group of eminent friends who would treasure her stories as her future biographer would come to treasure theirs, it was time for her to relax finally, for she had done all she could, but Josie was taking no chances. With the grand final statement that no doctor and no eulogizer and no biographer could ever resist, she was also writing her epitaph.

# Josephine Herbst's
# Major Published Works

*Fiction*

*Nothing Is Sacred*, Coward-McCann, New York, 1928.
*Money for Love*, Coward-McCann, New York, 1929.
*Pity Is Not Enough*, Harcourt, Brace, New York, 1933.
*The Executioner Waits*, Harcourt, Brace, New York, 1934.
*Rope of Gold*, Harcourt, Brace, New York, 1939.
*Satan's Sergeants*, Scribner's, New York, 1941.
*Somewhere the Tempest Fell*, Scribner's, New York, 1947.
"Hunter of Doves," *Botteghe Oscure*, Spring, 1954.

*Nonfiction*

*New Green World*, Hastings House, New York, 1954.
"The Starched Blue Sky of Spain," *The Noble Savage*, 1, 1960.
"A Year of Disgrace," *The Noble Savage*, 3, 1961.
"Yesterday's Road," *New American Review*, 3, 1968.

For additional citations both of published works and unpublished manuscripts see text and Notes, passim. A complete bibliography of Josephine Herbst's published work, in both fiction and nonfiction, was prepared by Martha Pickering in 1968 with her cooperation. It is available at the Beinecke Library, Yale.

# Notes

~~~~~~~~~~~~~~~~~~~~~~~~~~~~~~~~~~~~~~~~~~~~~~~~~~~~~~~~~~~~~~~~~~

JOSEPHINE HERBST was an inexhaustible chronicler of her own existence. For her relationship with Ernest Hemingway, to take one example, there exists an early version of a long unfinished manuscript largely about Key West; another unpublished memoir of her childhood and youth which incorporates much of the same material; an uncompleted novella about Hemingway which itself exists in several drafts; a published memoir of the Spanish Civil War in which Hemingway plays an important role; a great number of miscellaneous notes and jottings which formed the basis for all of the above, including a journal kept in Spain; and a substantial correspondence not only with Hemingway's primary biographer but with a number of other scholars, editors, and participants in the events she describes — and this is a case in which the communications between the principals themselves were uncharacteristically sparse. Her accounts of her mother's death, to take an example of a different kind, can be found in letters written to friends at the time it occurred; in two of her novels; in notes for her memoirs; and in the memoirs themselves. The catalogue of her correspondents itself consists of more than twenty-five pages and sometimes even in the case of relative strangers the volume of any individual correspondence could be immense. In her private writing even minor episodes were endlessly reiterated. By far the largest portion of this material, including letters, manuscripts, notebooks, notes, and assorted memorabilia, are in the Collection of American Literature, Beinecke Rare Book and Manuscript Library, Yale University, which is where everything not otherwise identified below is located. I wish to thank former curator Donald Gallup and the staff of the library, particularly Anne Whelpley and Patricia Howell, for their unfailing assistance in the archival stages of this work, and the present curator, David Schoonover, for his cooperation. In addition to the Yale archive, however, there are a number of other important categories of sources, particularly an additional collection of family papers inherited by Josephine Herbst from her mother and left to her niece Betty Hansen Davis, who generously loaned them to me. Material from these papers, which include the eighteenth- and nineteenth-century documents on which Josephine Herbst based her trilogy, is designated *TB*, for the family heirloom, a tin box, which originally housed it. Eventually it will be given to Yale. Other papers in

333

my personal possession are designated *EL*. Letters remaining in the possession of their recipients are designated by the repetition of the initials of the recipients after the citation. The citation for the "Letter from Josephine Herbst" at the beginning, for example, reads, "JH to Mary and Neal Daniels, Feb. 17, 1966, *M/ND.*" Most of the letters from Josephine Herbst to Katherine Anne Porter are in the Special Collections Division, University of Maryland Libraries, College Park, Maryland, and are designated *MD*. Letters from Josephine Herbst to Jean Garrigue at the Henry W. and Albert A. Berg Collection of the New York Public Library, and other letters there, are designated *BERG*. Letters of John Herrmann and other miscellaneous material at the Humanities Research Center, University of Texas at Austin, are designated *TEX*. Two other designations recurring in certain chapters are *AHF*, for the Alger Hiss Files, an archive currently maintained by the Harvard Law School Library, and *FOIA*, for material retrieved from the government under the Freedom of Information Act and now in my possession. The FOIA material will also eventually be given to Yale. Letters or other material in the collections of other libraries or institutions are specifically identified where they occur. In the case of copies: unless otherwise indicated, if the copy is in the Herbst archive and thus available there to scholars it is treated as an original; otherwise, all citations are to the originals, even though copies may exist. Where a citation is given as "JH notes" it refers to fragmentary jottings of Josephine Herbst, usually undated, that can be found among her papers at Yale. The citation "Notes" refers to the Notes section that follows. Spellings have been corrected except where otherwise indicated, and there have been occasional minor alterations in punctuation or capitalization for reasons of clarity. Because of the identity of the initials of Josephine Herbst and John Herrmann, the abbreviation *JH* has been used to refer to Josephine Herbst alone. No abbreviation has been employed for John Herrmann. The abbreviation of other names, e.g., *KAP* for Katherine Anne Porter, should be obvious. Such was the cast of memory characteristic of Josephine Herbst that a recollection of her childhood is apt to occur in the midst of an account of a journey to the Soviet Union and the journey to the Soviet Union is apt to be interwoven with an account of a trip made with her father in a horse-drawn wagon years before, and in addition to her letters, which are inclined to be specific and apply to limited periods or incidents, I have drawn plentifully on a number of unpublished manuscripts which tend to apply throughout. These have been abbreviated as follows. For *The Ground We Tread*, a literal autobiographical account of her childhood and youth — *GROUND;* for *Magicians and Their Apprentices*, a later, more poeticized version of the same material — *MAGICIANS;* and for an important preliminary memoir of the 1920s, *The Hour of Counterfeit Bliss* — *HOUR*. What is true of the cast of her unpublished manuscripts is equally true of both her published memoirs and her novels, which often cover the same material, and I have also drawn plentifully on these, particularly the novels which make up her trilogy, *Pity Is Not Enough* — *PITY; The Executioner Waits* — *EXECUTIONER;* and *Rope of Gold* — *ROPE;* and the three completed portions of her memoirs, *The Starched Blue Sky of Spain* — *STARCHED; A Year of Disgrace* — *DISGRACE;* and *Yesterday's Road* — *ROAD*. Josephine Herbst was always an autobiographical writer, she used fiction and nonfiction interchangeably, and whatever governed her choice of form in any given instance, it was not fidelity to fact. Except in cases where they genuinely had an impact on this work, are directly quoted, or involve specialized material not available elsewhere, I have not included secondary references. Josephine Herbst was not only an unremitting observer, she was also a reliable one and her papers constitute a primary archive which I believe speaks for itself.

PART I. INTRODUCTION

*Page*
ix–x    A Letter from Josephine Herbst. ". . . I went to see the Madrid movie . . .": JH to Mary and Neal Daniels, February 17, 1966, *N/MD.*

*Chapter 1. "If in Fact I Have Found a Heroine . . ."*

4    "I cannot pretend . . .": JH to Ben Wells, January 21, 1969, courtesy of Neal and Mary Daniels, *N/MD.*

*Page*

4     "three excellent titles . . .": "Writers in the Thirties," by Granville Hicks, in *As We Saw the Thirties*, Rita Simon, ed., University of Illinois Press, 1967, p. 93.

6–7     "JOSEPHINE HERBST, NOVELIST AND SOCIAL-POLITICAL RE-PORTER, DEAD" *The New York Times*, January 29, 1969. The obituary is factually unreliable and contains a lot of misinformation ultimately traceable to her own hand, including the dates of her birth and her marriage. Other points which are incorrect concern her coverage of the Scottsboro trial and her membership on the Dreiser commission. Contrary to many published reports, she did not actually go to either Alabama or Kentucky.

7     The eulogy by Alfred Kazin, "Josephine Herbst (1897–1969)" — again the birthdate is incorrect — appeared in *The New York Review of Books*, March 27, 1969, pp. 19–20. The phrase "desperate pedestrianism" appears in *On Native Grounds*, 1942; Harcourt, Brace paperback edition, 1970, p. 387.

9     "A number of editors . . .": Nina Finkelstein, for *Ms.*, to EL, March 7, 1973, *EL.*

9     "[Your article] leaves out a lot. . . .": Peter Davison, for *The Atlantic Monthly* to EL, March 27, 1973, *EL.*

10     "The present phase that tends . . .": JH, "The Ruins of Memory," *The Nation*, April 14, 1956, pp. 302–304.

11     "I found your account . . .": Hilton Kramer to EL, April 22, 1973, *EL.* "Without putting her work down . . .": Alfred Kazin to EL, March 3, 1973, *EL.*

13     "*There* became *here* . . .": *MAGICIANS*, p. 7.

13     "Your Fifth of March" or "Your little Fifth of March" was an often-repeated closing on Josie's birthday letters, e.g., her March 5, 1920 letter to her mother from New York.

PART II. THE LITTLE STRANDS AND TREES

## Chapter 2. *Magicians and Their Apprentices*

17–19     The Frey family history is documented in detail in original letters and papers which were passed on from generation to generation (Yale, *TB*); in an informal history, "The Stars at Home," by Jennie Fry Walsh (1953), (*EL*); in the memoirs *GROUND* and *MAGICIANS;* and in the first volume of the trilogy, *PITY*, which traces the stories of Mary Frey's brothers and sisters at some length. Much of the material in the trilogy is taken directly from the historical sources and used with only minor alterations. There appears to have been no comparable body of material from the Herbst side of the family.

19     "If anyone had been sent . . .": Mary Frey to Georgia Ripley, September 11, 1882, *TB.*

20     "I find that it is quite possible . . .": Mary Frey Herbst to Daniel Frey, October 28, 1884, *TB.*

20     "I'm greatly pleased . . .": Mary Frey Herbst to William Benton Herbst, August 30, 1886.

22     "Angel," "The more children Mary has. . . ," "How pretty — wouldn't it look sweet. . . ," etc. These incidents appear with small variations in several of the sources mentioned above. If no pages are cited, the version given here is a paraphrase or composite, rather than a direct quotation.

22     "Mother never called me . . .": JH, New York notebook, 1920, p. 8.

22     "You were like *one being* . . .": Mary Herbst to JH, November 13, 1920.

23     "she cannot help being born . . .": Mary Herbst to William Benton Herbst, August 30, 1886.

24     "Today Robert Fliegel . . .": According to one version of this tale, Frances' complete diary entry read: "Today Robert Fliegel took his books home from school never to return. His family is moving to Kansas City. I shall never for-

get this sad day and on every anniversary will make a pan of fudge to his memory." *GROUND*, p. 17.

24–25 The portrait of Josie's father that emerges from her writings — honored by the mother but largely isolated from the real life of the female household and strikingly unoriginal in relation to his imaginative wife — is supported by the recollections of Josie's brother-in-law Andrew Bernhard, Helen's husband, who confirmed that Mary Herbst was the family intellectual and Bent a nonreader whose only recreation was, indeed, the Royal Arcanum Lodge. Conversation, Andrew Bernhard, October, 1973. For many years editor of the Pittsburgh *Post Gazette*, Andy Bernhard was an extraordinary raconteur, and his perceptive recollections of the Herbst family, his own relationship with Helen, and Josie herself, greatly enriched my understanding. He died in 1982.

24 "That his own daughters . . .": *GROUND*, p. 35.

24 "whose honor was so much a habit . . .": ibid.

24 "passing the collection plate . . .": ibid., p. 36.

24 "unrepentant drunkard . . .": The first account of Jacob Frey's death was written by Josie's grandfather, Joshua Frey, to a relative, in 1843 (*TB*). It appears, nearly intact, in *PITY*, p. 11, and in the family history, "The Stars at Home," p. 3 (*EL*). This remained one of Josie's favorite stories and she referred to it in her own writing many times. The original letter reads:

> Talking was painful and difficult for him during the whole of his illness but toward the end it was still more so. He frequently lamented during the last month that he could not speak better. What he wished to say if he had been able to do so, Heaven only knows. He never expressed any regret or repentance at his former evil course, he never spoke of his wife or child while he was able to speak, yet what came to pass within his heart I will not undertake to say. Let no man judge. He is in the hands of the omnipotent. He died at the age of 48 years, 7 months, and five days. Never regret that you separated, he was an unreformed and unrepentant drunkard to the last, pouring the liquor down his throat as long as he could swallow. I hereby send a lock of his hair cut off a good while before his death.

Mary, too, loved the story of Jacob and would add her own embellishments. "There was an angel and a devil wrestling in Jacob my mother said, and when we children cried, 'Who won,' my mother did not answer at once but stared thoughtfully toward a distant country, and said slowly 'I don't know' ": *GROUND*, p. 8. A sugar bowl belonging to Jacob and containing a garnet-colored Easter egg dyed for him by his father in 1803 was one of Josie's favorite family possessions.

25 "The Elegant Mr. Gason": letter from Frances Herbst Wells to JH about John Herrmann and John Gason, "1927, Tuesday afternoon."

25 "Maybe you'll be a lawyer . . .": For a published version of this often-repeated encounter between mother and daughter, see *ROPE*, p. 47.

25 "Do you go *alone* . . .": Mary Herbst to JH, Dec. 8, 1912.

26 *"keeping the heart pure . . .":* Mary Herbst to Helen Herbst, Nov. 27, 1913.


*Chapter 3. Shakespeare Avenue*

27 There are numerous standard sources for the history of Iowa. Typical of the old style is the lengthy *History of Western Iowa*, published by the Western Publishing Company in 1882, with its extensive county-by-county analyses; no author listed. A comprehensive modern view is *A History of Iowa* by Leland Sage, Iowa State University Press, Ames, 1974. The WPA's Federal Writers' Project Guidebook *Iowa*, first published in 1938, contains valuable

historical material, as do a number of periodicals, particularly the *Iowa Journal of History and Politics* and the *Journal of Iowa History*. The past is very much alive in Iowa, and through institutions such as the State Historical Society in Iowa City and the Sioux City Public Museum it remains surprisingly accessible.

29     "She didn't snitch on Charles": *GROUND*, p. 37. Josie's other anecdotes about her early schooling appear in *GROUND*, pp. 19ff. and passim, as well as elsewhere.

30     "Resolved, that the Czarina's position . . .": and related high school items come from Josie's graduation book, "The Girl Graduate — Her Own Book,"1910, a kind of combined autograph and yearbook, which also contains many clippings.

30     "Today I fell in a mud puddle . . .": 1901 notebook. "Am ten years old . . .": 1902 notebook.

30     "Be a little careful . . .": This entire account of Josie's menstruation is taken from *MAGICIANS*, pp. 46–47.

31     "Mama has promised me . . .": This and entries immediately following, through "Did nothing, was sick," are from a single notebook, dated 1905–1907.

31–32     "The house was beautiful . . .": 1908 notebook, October 28. "How pretty the world is . . .": 1909 notebook, June 9. "How hard these days are . . .": 1910 notebook, June 16.

32–33     "What's the use": This and subsequent "Das" entries are from 1912; "Let the old year slip off . . ." is from 1911; *"Had to leave tea . . .":* 1912; and "My hope is that whatever happens . . .": 1912.

33     "rank highstepping idealism": JH notes, n.d.

33     "laudable and necessary": ibid.

33     "I feel a million years wiser . . .": JH to "Dearest Family," n.d.

34     "We're rambling . . .": JH to "Dear Helen," n.d. "Friday morning."

34     "I am very happy . . .": 1913 notebook, April 1.

34     "Bernie's birthday . . .": ibid., May 12.

34     "Left Bernie in bed . . .": ibid., June 8.

34     "No use writing . . .": ibid., June 24. The impact on the family of "Amos Wendel's" failure in business is dramatized in *EXECUTIONER*, passim.

34     "Isn't it strange . . .": JH to "Dear Folks," n.d.

35     "Why do people in little towns . . .": ibid.

35     "They aren't living, they are vegetating": ibid.

35     "The ignorance of my children . . .": JH to "Dear Mother," n.d.

35     "It is a sad shock . . .": JH to "Dear Papa," n.d.

35     "Bless you, I expect . . .": JH to "Dear Helen," n.d.

36     "I am wondering . . .": 1913–1914 Stratford journal.

## *Chapter 4. "I Fairly Writhe . . ."*

37     "I fairly writhe . . .": JH to "Dearest Mother," from Stratford, n.d.

37–38     One of Josie's most satisfactory evocations of life in Sioux City just before World War I is in *MAGICIANS*, passim.

38     "It all started with Ethel . . .": JH to "Dear Mother," n.d., "Wednesday night."

39     "Ethel had more done to her . . .": JH to "Dearest Mother," n.d., "Friday."

39     "I have learned so much about myself . . .": JH to "Dear Mother," n.d., "Wednesday night."

40     "I feel new bubbling life . . .": JH to "Dearest Folks," n.d., "Monday."

40     "It should not be deemed presumptuous . . .": "The Newer Gynecology," I. C. Rubin editorial, *American Journal of Surgery*, November, 1916, p. 6. Reprinted in *The Collected Papers of Dr. I. C. Rubin, 1910–1954*, privately printed. I am indebted to Dr. Ellen Bassuk for consultation on the matter of

Josie's surgery. According to Bassuk the reasoning employed by Josie's doctor in his treatment of both herself and Ethel is a classic instance of the Victorian theory of "reflex irritation" which held that unless the uterus were perfectly straight it became an irritant responsible for the production of a great many other symptoms, including nervous ones. Ellen Bassuk, M.D., to EL, private communication, spring, 1983, *EL.*

41 "I have no other idea for your future . . .": JH to "Dear Sister," January, 1916.

41 "We knew so little then . . .": Conversation, Jennie Fry Walsh, April, 1974. Jennie Walsh's recollections were strikingly consistent with Josie's on many points involving family matters, and I am grateful to her for conversation and correspondence, as well as for family materials.

41 "It repulsed me . . .": Jennie Fry to JH, October 16, 1916.

41 "It isn't perverted . . .": JH, on envelope, October 24, 1916.

41 "I've been haunted all week . . .": JH to Helen Herbst, September 25, 1917.

42 "You are in a tremendous hurry to live . . .": JH to "Dear Sister," January, 1916.

## Chapter 5. Preamble

43 "I guess I have seen . . .": JH to Helen Herbst, August 23, 1917.

44 "Do not look too hard . . .": Conversation, Andrew Bernhard, October, 1973.

44 "I always knew . . . ": JH to Mary Herbst, March 5, 1918.

45 "Don't show your brains . . .": JH notes. All subsequent quotes on these pages are from the same fragment.

45 "Poor Muddie . . .": JH to Mary Herbst, "Friday."

45 "erotic nature": Helen Herbst to Andrew Bernhard, n.d., *TB.*

46 "I'm going to wire him I'm coming . . .": JH, *EXECUTIONER,* p. 35.

46 "I truly feel you will be happier . . .": Mary Herbst to Helen Herbst, May 23, 1918.

47 "I wish you could have been here . . .": JH to Mary Herbst, November 13, 1918.

49 "The little strands and trees . . .": JH notes.

### PART III. UNMARRIED

## Chapter 6. Love — and Revolution

53-54 These descriptions of the life in the basement apartment of 12 St. Luke's and at the Gumbergs' are drawn in part from an informal memoir written by Josie for Genevieve Taggard's second husband, Kenneth Durant, in 1949.

54 "abominable," "[all] this uplift . . .": JH to Mary Herbst, November 3, 1919.

54 "They pay the girls so poorly . . .": JH to Mary Herbst, November 7, 1919.

54 "Thousands & hundreds of thousands . . .": JH to Mary Herbst, February 27, 1920.

55 "The more I see of the poor . . .": JH to Mary Herbst, November 3, 1919.

55-58 Josie's most complete portrait of her romance with Maxwell Anderson is in the unpublished autobiographical novel *Unmarried,* written in 1922-1923. Other JH sources on which this and the following chapter are based include a New York notebook, correspondence with both her parents and Helen during the course of the affair, and her letters to Genevieve Taggard. Anderson, on the other hand, seems largely to have covered his tracks, and both the episode and the poems it generated have been unknown to members of his family and students of his life and work until now. I am grateful to Mary Jane Simpson, of Washington, D.C., for conversation and correspondence about Anderson; to his biographer, Alfred S. Shivers, for further correspondence; and to his widow, Gilda Anderson, for permission to publish "Evening" and "Grief Castle." A special issue of the *North Dakota Quarterly*, Winter, 1970, devoted to Anderson, was also helpful. In addition to the poems quoted in the text, a small leather diary of poems to Josie in Anderson's handwriting, and other incidental communications among her papers at Yale provide persuasive documentation of the relationship. Much other correspondence was probably destroyed. See also my pp. 78–79, and related Notes.

56    "He knew one bed . . .": *Unmarried*, p. 65.

       "Aren't you afraid . . .": ibid., p. 67.

56    "We are all alone anyhow": JH to Helen Herbst, n.d., *TB*.

56    "blinding exquisite moment . . .": ibid.

57    "incorrigible gypsy": New York notebook, p. 43.

57    "[I had] happily fallen in love unhappily": JH to Kenneth Durant, 1949. See Note to pp. 53–54, above.

58    "It's not love but marriage . . .": *Unmarried*, p. 88.

## Chapter 7. *"Grief Castle"*

60    Josie described Anderson's attitude toward her pregnancy in a letter to Genevieve Taggard, September 15, 1921. A portion of the letter appears on p. 68.

61    "I hesitate to take any work . . .": Helen Herbst Bernhard to "Dear Sister," n.d.

62    "I keep thinking about you . . .": JH to Helen Herbst Bernhard, September 21, 1920.

62    "Hope you got the position with Mencken . . .": Helen Herbst Bernhard to "Dear Sister," n.d.

63    "It seems characteristic that Sioux City . . .": JH to Helen Herbst Bernhard, October 7, 1920.

64    "I've talked to more people . . .": JH to Helen Herbst Bernhard, October 13, 1920.

64    "I have been so distraught . . .": Helen Herbst Bernhard to JH, October 16, 1920.

64    "What hypocrites doctors are . . .": JH to Helen Herbst Bernhard, October 20, 1920. The handwritten original of "Grief Castle" from which Josie evidently typed her version to Helen is in the *TB*.

66    "It's my little sister . . .": *Unmarried*, p. 144. Josie described being interrupted in her sleep the night Helen died in a letter to Genevieve Taggard, October 24, 1920.

67    "It seems to me as if my sister's ashes . . .": JH to Genevieve Taggard, September 15, 1921.

67    "It hasn't been that I've consciously grieved . . .": JH to Mary Herbst, February 7, 1921. Genevieve Taggard's opinion that Josie was getting along "too brightly" is also reported by Josie to her mother in this letter. Josie's intimacy with Genevieve Taggard and Robert Wolf lasted through her stay in Europe, and when she returned, in 1924, it was to them that she most wanted to introduce John Herrmann; but shortly afterward, evidently because of some estrangement involving the four of them, it began to decline. Although Josie and John moved to Connecticut in 1925 partly to be near Jed and Bob, Jed and Bob separated at about the same time, and the intensity of the New York years was never rekindled. The exact nature of the incident that caused the estrangement is not clear from the available correspondence, but evidently it rankled, for when Josie encountered Jed at a support meeting for Vermont marble strikers in early 1936 she wrote William Phillips, "Genevieve Taggard was also there — she will never forgive me for something that happened ten years ago . . .": JH to William Phillips, "Sunday morning," n.d. Josie wrote about Jed in an informal memoir for Kenneth Durant, 1949, see Note to pp. 53–54, above.

NOTES

Page

Page

68    "too uncertain a child . . .": JH to Bob Wolf, December 13, 1921.

68    "he confuses me about writing . . .": JH to Bob Wolf, n.d., "Sunday." Josie's reference to Alan Gardner is in a letter to Genevieve Taggard, n.d., "Friday night."

68    "I agreed and added they were the only ones . . .": JH to Bob Wolf, December 13, 1921.

68    "Oh Jed — won't somebody help me . . .": JH to Genevieve Taggard, September 15, 1921. The letter to Josie from Margaret Anderson, dated September 10, 1921, is also in the JH files at Yale.

68    "I don't want to seem foolish . . .": JH to Genevieve Taggard, September 15, 1921, second letter. Considering that Josie felt so passionately about wanting a child in this period — or believed she did — it is surprising that it came up so infrequently in her life later. The recency of her abortion, and of the loss of Helen, were probably factors.

69    "Here, everyone I know . . .": JH to Mary Herbst, April 17, 1922. Recreating the same moment in the 1930s, Josie gave the impulse to go to Europe a more political cast: "Everyone she knew was making some kind of a new plan," she wrote of Victoria Wendel in *The Executioner Waits*. "Those who could were getting abroad as fast as possible. No one seemed to want to hang around in the States any more if they could help it. Tales of cheap living abroad and of music and art galleries and disturbances threatening every country made sitting at home, where troubles appeared to have been settled with a strong arm and an incipient dose of prosperity, very tame" (p. 274). Unlike Josie, however, Victoria does not actually get to Europe.

## Chapter 8. Following the Circle

70    "dollar princess": *STARCHED*, p. 78.

70    "mingled with the rich . . .": *ROAD*, p. 92.

71    "It seems as if all I get . . .": JH to Genevieve Taggard, July 8, 1923.

71    "There isn't any man . . .": JH to Genevieve Taggard, December 20, 1923.

72    "It seems as if it were my blood . . .": ibid.

72    "I never thought I would do": JH to Genevieve Taggard, April 22, 1924.

73    After Josie changed her birthdate, she never once recanted. It is given, incorrectly, as 1897, in Library of Congress notations, in all official records, even in a memorial poem written to her by a close friend. Her mother, too, had subtracted a little. " 'Why, she was only three years younger than I am after all,' my father crowed," when together they discovered Mary's baptismal certificate after she had died. " 'I thought she was ten years younger. You know, I sometimes wondered. Oh, she was a cute one!' ": JH, *MAGICIANS*, p. 53.

73    "I've known older men . . .": JH to Genevieve Taggard, April 22, 1924.

74    "your boy . . .": John's references to himself this way occur in several of his 1924 letters. Other sources for their early relationship include an annotated photo album, *TEX*, Josie's memoirs and notes for her memoirs, and their later correspondence. Conversations with Andrew Bernhard (October, 1973) and Ruth Allen (November, 1973) also contributed to this chapter.

## Chapter 9. An Even Race

76    "Somebody has got to support the family . . .": John Herrmann to JH, November 29, 1924.

77    "I am not serious . . .": John Herrmann to JH, n.d., "Monday afternoon."

77–78    This account of Mary's death draws principally on two sources, a letter from Josie to Genevieve Taggard and Robert Wolf, April 30, 1925, JH-GT/RW, and notes for her memoirs written many years later (JH/notes). The specific attributions are as follows: "sinking and reviving": JH-GT/RW; "One moment we thought . . .": ibid.; "Something beyond her will": JH/notes; "In

340

whose voice": ibid.; "You're my sunshine": ibid.; "ho to Jesus": ibid.; "It was hard slow laborious work . . . .": JH-GT/RW; "strange and wonderful": ibid. Josie also wrote about her mother's death in a number of published sources, particularly *SACRED*, of which it is the central event, pp. 229–237, and *EXECUTIONER*, pp. 333–337. The difference between Josie's relationships to her mother and her father was never more apparent than at the moment of her mother's death. "I'm prouder of her than anything. My father too, he's a wonderful old thing" was her only reference to Bent in her outpouring to Jed and Bob. Mary had cancer and diabetes, but Josie did not learn the diagnosis until afterward.

78–79 Josie's attempt to get money from Maxwell Anderson is documented in her letters to Genevieve Taggard, particularly January 16, 1925; to her sister Frances, June 18, 1925; and in her 1924 and 1925 correspondence with John, passim. "I'm going to tackle Maxwell Anderson for money. . . . I never had any money [from] the men whose wives were always so protected. . . . He must have made a good deal with that play. I want $5000. . . . I don't give a goddamned bit about pride or anything else. He hurt me, he nearly ruined my life, he stood off and patronized me, and he can pay for it. . . . He never even helped me pay my abortion bill, nothing, he sent me about $25 or $30 in 5 or 10 dollar bills or gave them to me in the spring of the year when I was out of a job. . . . If he had been different toward me I couldn't do this, but he was conceited and selfish and he can pay," reads the January 16, 1925, letter to Jed. By the time the event actually took place, however, about six months later, she must have considerably softened, for her letter to Frances on June 18, 1925, is not so much vindictive as depressed and a letter to Josie from John on June 19, 1925, says "It was nice of MA to be so prompt and pleasant." A fictionalized version of the incident appears in her novel *Money for Love*.

79 "I want to keep to myself . . .": JH to John Herrmann, January 17, 1925, *TEX*.

## PART IV. THE HOUR OF COUNTERFEIT BLISS

## *Chapter 10. Connecticut*

83 "And soon will your true love . . .": John Herrmann to JH, December 31, 1924.

83–87 *"Fall, 1925."* Two of Josie's fullest published accounts of her Connecticut adventures are *DISGRACE*, passim, and *EXECUTIONER*, pp. 299–324, where she tells the story of her marriage in an exaggerated style — "The Parents," "The Young Couple," and so forth — close to the one adopted here. According to several friends, she also told the story that way in person. Contemporary letters to her father — e.g., October 22, 1925 — as well as correspondence with Genevieve Taggard and Katherine Anne Porter, bear out her later accounts.

84 "Dry Sunday in Connecticut" appeared in *The American Mercury* in July, 1926. Still another JH story of Connecticut, focusing chiefly on Katherine Anne Porter and Ernest Stock, is "A Man of Steel," *The American Mercury*, January, 1934.

85–86 The full text of the July 18, 1926, letter from Henry Herrmann to John Herrmann is as follows:

Dear John

Since arriving home last Saturday evening and sending you the check we have learned of things which have shocked your mother and me very much. Your mother has had suspicions of your actions but has had no definite evidence until she found some letters which lead us to

believe that you have been living unmarried with a woman. This was
going on while you were abroad and has been going on since you left
Detroit and living at New Preston. We learned through an attorney
how you are living and other things concerning you and have evidence
to substantiate our information.

I immediately stopped payment on the check and will absolutely
not back you while you are living as you have been. It would be aid-
ing and condoning a moral and civil crime to do so and you know very
well you are liable to the law for your conduct. You will have to
either marry the woman or quit her immediately and while the
woman in this affair is no better or worse than the man, yet no one
would want to harbor such a person or have anything to do with her.
Get a job at honest work and quit or marry, and if you write any
smutty stories please have enough consideration for me not to sign
your name to them.

Any time you can show me that you have gotten to honest work and
decent living I shall be willing to back you to the best of my ability
but to think that your mother and I have worked hard these many
years and deprived ourselves of many things with the view of bringing
up our children to be decent, honorable and useful citizens, and then
have developments of this kind brought to our knowledge is extremely
distressing.

I hope you will let me hear from you soon and that you have
enough character to turn away from the path of vice and vagabondism
upon which you appear to have a considerable start.

Your Father.

P.S. I mailed you a thin summer suit recently.

A version only slightly altered appears in *EXECUTIONER*, pp. 306–307.

86  Henry Herrmann's letter requesting the marriage license, with John's note typed on the bottom, is dated August 4, 1926.

87  Josie's letter to John's parents, "Dear Mother," "Thursday," n.d., is also in the files.

## Chapter 11. New York

88  "I see you are carrying Gertie . . .": *DISGRACE*, p. 136.

89  "Mama the man is standing there": Josie quoted "Revolution in Revon" in both *EXECUTIONER*, p. 341, and *DISGRACE*, p. 143, as well as elsewhere, and when John was no longer around to do so, she often recited it for friends. It first appeared in *transition*, No. 8, 1927.

89  "A young man might phone his girl . . .": *DISGRACE*, p. 140.

89  "the two talkingest women . . .": Conversation, Malcolm Cowley, February, 1974. The account of the relationship between Josephine Herbst and Katherine Anne Porter given in this book is based principally on their own correspondence, to which I have had complete access thanks to the cooperation of Katherine Anne Porter before she died. I have also had the benefit of several years of close and generous cooperation with KAP's recent biographer, Joan Givner. The assistance of Dr. Robert Beare, curator of the KAP papers at the University of Maryland, and of her late literary agent Cyrilly Abels was invaluable. Isabel Bayley, KAP's literary trustee, kindly authorized quotation from her letters. Josie herself did a lot of miscellaneous writing about the friendship.

90  "Shouldn't I be writing . . .": JH notes. "November 12."

90  "misled," "misused," "lamentable," "disastrous": KAP to Joan Givner, July 6, 1976, *JG*.

91  "I was never a little lady . . .": JH notes.

94  "More seaworthy than the *Titanic*": In addition to *DISGRACE*, the sea

voyage was the subject of a contemporary story by Josie and two by John and in these there are several references to the *Titanic,* so it was evidently a sore point. Josie's "A Bad Blow" appeared in *Scribner's,* July, 1930; John's "The Gale of August Twentieth" in *Scribner's,* October, 1931, and his "A Last Look Back" in *Partisan Review and Anvil,* May, 1936. Two other stories by Josie about the Maine summer are "Summer Boarders," *Second American Caravan,* 1928, and "She Showed the Cloven Hoof," *The Magazine,* December, 1933.

95    Postcard from John Dos Passos, n.d., *TEX.* Josie and John's friendship with Dos Passos was never intimate but it was warm and companionable and he kept up his ties with both of them after they separated. See also Chapter 22, esp. pp. 219–223.

95–96    News accounts of the *What Happens* proceedings are in *The New York Times* for September 29, October 4, and October 5, 1927. I am grateful to Robert Penn Warren for his recollections of the atmosphere surrounding the case.

96    "Don't tell me that you love me": Conversation, Ruth Allen, November, 1973.

96    "4,000 days and nights": "Anne" to John Herrmann, January 23, 1937. *EL* (copy).

## Chapter 12. Erwinna

97–99    One of the best sources for descriptions of the house in Erwinna in Josie and John's early years there is an annotated photo album, *TEX.* The *TB* also contains many photographs.

99–100    "The Elegant Mr. Gason": *Smart Set,* July, 1923; "Happy Birthday!", *Smart Set,* November, 1923; "A Dreadful Night," *Pagany,* Winter, 1932; "Once a Year," *transition,* No. 16–17, 1929.

100    "I never dreamed you . . . thought so little of either John or I that you could publicly humiliate us so," Josie's sister Alice wrote her after reading *Nothing Is Sacred.* "I never even dreamed you could be so cruel. . . . If you had changed things just a little — the lodge, the exact am't of money, number of children, even good piano & car — even my poor teeth . . . — those could have had different names and not been so obvious and still made just as artistic a story." Alice Herbst Hansen to JH, "Tuesday the 8th," 1928. Josie and Alice were never particularly close and *Nothing Is Sacred* sealed a coolness between them they never overcame. This was unlike Josie's relationship with Frances, to whom she grew more attached over the years.

100    The story "A New Break" appeared in *Scribner's,* October, 1931; I am grateful to Clara Coffey for discussing it with me. Additional references: "had to write that . . .": JH to William Benton Herbst, "Saturday." "I just had to do it . . .": JH to KAP, "Around Feb. 1 or 2," *MD.*

100    "Ignorance Among the Living Dead" appeared in the *New Masses,* January, 1929.

100    "The misery of it was crushing me": JH to William Benton Herbst, "Saturday."

100    "I think myself I was too hard . . .": JH to John Herrmann, "74 Orange Street, Brooklyn," *TEX.*

101    Sinclair Lewis, "Is America a Paradise for Women?", *Pictorial Review,* June, 1929, p. 54.

101    "never liked the book . . .": Isidor Schneider's "The Fetish of Simplicity" appeared in *The Nation,* February 18, 1931, pp. 184–186; Josie's response, "Counterblast" appeared on March 11, 1931, pp. 275–276. In conversations in 1973 and 1974 respectively, Saul Bellow and John Cheever offered opinions about the relationship between Josie's talking and her writing almost identical to that of Schneider in 1931.

101    "I must say that we found . . .": JH to KAP, "Sat. a.m.," *MD.* The *transition* version, "The Phecanical Melonium," appeared in No. 16–17, 1929.

*Page*
102–103  John's novel, long titled *Woman of Promise* in his working drafts, was published by Covici, Friede as *Summer Is Ended* in 1933.
103  "Pennsylvania Idyl," *The American Mercury*, by Josephine Herbst and John Herrmann, January, 1929.
104  "Josephine Herbst will spend the summer . . .": in many papers, e.g., the *Atlanta Journal*, June 9, 1929.

## Chapter 13. Key West

106  "I was all wound up . . .": JH to KAP, n.d., "1425 Pearl Street."
107  "handcuffed together": *HOUR*, p. 11. Major sources for this chapter, in addition to *HOUR* and *MAGICIANS*, include several drafts of a novella, "Bright Signal," and related notes, as well as correspondence between Josie and Hemingway biographer Carlos Baker in 1963. There are no important distinctions between her fictional and her nonfictional versions. If direct quotations are used, the citation is given below; if not, assume an oft-told tale. The "sufficient evidence" for Hemingway's respect for Josie comes from a conversation with James Farrell, in October, 1977, in which Farrell told me that Hemingway had said as much, and from a letter from William Pike, M.D., physician of the Abraham Lincoln Battalion, February 25, 1980, *EL*. See also Chapter 22 and related Notes.
107  "like clear air": *HOUR*, p. 9.
108  "chatting about anything . . .": *HOUR*, p. 12.
108  "a tough fight," "boxing was nothing to it": *MAGICIANS*, p. 72. Similar phrasing appears in *HOUR*, p. 13.
108  "If the undertaker's assistant . . .": *BRIGHT SIGNAL*, p. 1.
108  "At present I am the only Herrmann . . .": JH to KAP, April 1, 1930, *MD*.
110  "He suffered, his whole look showed it": *BRIGHT SIGNAL*, notes.
110  "Give my regards to the Lord Mayor . . .": *BRIGHT SIGNAL*, p. 16A of one draft. The Asch episode also figures prominently in *HOUR* and *MAGICIANS*. "Nathan Asch, a tragic figure in retrospect, hated to be known as a son of the famous Yiddish novelist Sholem Asch. . . . He thought he was a better writer than his father, and indeed he wrote more lyrically, sometimes with deeper feeling, but he lacked the father's simple vigor and breadth of conception," wrote Malcolm Cowley in a note to — *And I Worked at the Writer's Trade*, Viking, 1978, pp. 64–65. Although Asch published a number of novels, short stories, and reviews in the 1920s and '30s, in addition to a well-received book of Depression reportage, *The Road* (1937), following World War II, according to Cowley, "he couldn't get his books published any longer, at a time when his father's books were selling more widely than ever." Particularly during the late 1930s, when they were often together at Yaddo and in Washington, D.C., Josie's friendship with Asch seems to have been close. There is a good deal of Asch in the character "Lester Tolman" in *EXECUTIONER* and *ROPE*, and he also appears in her memoirs. When Asch died in California in 1964, Josie was distressed. ". . . Alas, I have not heard from him for a long time. But he was a splendid letter writer and a very dear friend, and I feel very terrible to know so little about all this. . . ," she wrote to Cowley. "I know you kept in touch with him and if you can find time to drop me a few words, I would greatly appreciate it. . . . I can't bear just to let all this pass as if it were no more than a cocktail bar — but that's modern life, I guess. . . . Nathan's writing was far from negligible, but the damned circumstances of the literary drift snowballed around him and caught him, somehow." JH to Malcolm Cowley, January 16, 1965, *NEWBERRY LIBRARY*. See also Chapter 23 and Notes to p. 228.
111  "the liquor flows so freely . . .": John Herrmann to KAP, n.d., "Box 188 Key West," *MD*.
111  "rummy": *Ernest Hemingway, Selected Letters, 1917–1961*, ed. by Carlos Baker, Scribner's, 1981, passim.

Page
111     "the story of Hemingway and the Dry Tortugas . . .": *BRIGHT SIGNAL*,
        notes.
112     "If you don't stop talking that stuff . . .": *HOUR*, p. 29. Josie also described
        this incident to Carlos Baker in a letter dated August 19, 1963, and it appears
        in his *Ernest Hemingway: A Life Story*, Scribner's, 1969, p. 221.
112     "He had already destroyed something . . .": *BRIGHT SIGNAL*, notes.
112     "Josie, I'll never forgive you . . .": *STARCHED*, p. 81.


PART V THE LONG TENSION OF LIFE


*Chapter 14. "There'll Be No Distinctions . . ."*

115     "I would represent Kiwanis . . .": JH to KAP, September 23, 1930, *MD*. Josie's
        fullest account of her journey to the Soviet Union occurs in the late memoir,
        "Yesterday's Road." I am indebted to A. B. Magil, a member of the official
        American delegation elected by the John Reed Club, for clarification of the
        exact status of Josie and John at the Kharkov Conference. A. B. Magil to EL,
        April 19, 1977, *EL*.
116     Dos Passos' note is dated October 1, 1930, and attached to a letter to John
        Herrmann, n.d., *TEX*.
116     "You should have heard us . . .": JH to KAP, "Around Feb. 1 or 2," *MD*.
116     "Make no mistake . . .": JH, "Literature in the U.S.S.R.," *The New Republic*,
        April 29, 1931, p. 306.
116     "Some of their new cities . . .": JH to KAP, "Around Feb. 1 or 2," *MD*.
116     "they can listen to poetry . . .": ibid.
116     "suddenly the faces . . .": ibid.
116     "is just a dead city . . .": ibid.
116     "touristized . . .": JH to KAP, December 21, "On board the Bremen," *MD*.
117     "I tell you none of us live . . .": JH to KAP, "Around Feb. 1 or 2," *MD*.
118     "near beer": Dos Passos' famous comment that joining the Socialist Party
        would be like "drinking a bottle of near-beer" is quoted by his biographer,
        Townsend Ludington, in *John Dos Passos: A Twentieth Century Odyssey*,
        Dutton, 1980, p. 313, and by Malcolm Cowley, *The Dream of the Golden
        Mountains: Remembering the 1930s*, Viking, 1980, p. 112.
119     "John has developed . . .": JH to KAP, November 30, 1932, *EL*.
119     "exalted": Cowley, *Dream*, p. 83.
119     John's story, "The Big Short Trip," appeared in *Scribner's*, in August, 1932.
119     The date of John Herrmann's joining the Communist Party, or even whether
        he formally did so, is impossible to establish definitively but on the basis of a
        number of circumspect references in the correspondence between John and
        Josie during the summer of 1932, late 1931 seems most probable. When Josie
        wrote Katherine Anne from Yaddo that summer that there was "a new thing"
        in John's writing "that he feels very much," I think it was not only commu-
        nism in the abstract but the Communist Party in particular that she meant.
        JH to KAP, July 19, 1932, *MD*.
120     "Speaking of the latter . . .": JH to KAP, July 20, 1931, *MD*.
122     "Don't be stupid . . .": *PITY*, p. 95.
124     "I can't blame poor Josy . . .": John Herrmann to JH, "Friday." This account
        of Josie and John's domestic troubles is based on their 1931 and 1932 corre-
        spondence, Josie's unsent letters from Cuba in 1935 (see Chapter 18), and her
        endless subsequent rehashes over the years.


*Chapter 15. The Music Comes On Strong*

126–127 I am grateful to Sylvan Cole, Jr., director of the Associated American Artists
        Gallery, with which Marion Greenwood was affiliated, the late Jim Egleson,
        who knew her in Mexico, and Ruth Herrmann, who heard a good deal about
        her over the years, for discussing Marion Greenwood with me.

## Chapter 16. Feet in the Grass Roots

143    Josie's attitude toward publication was always curious and the idea for a book of short stories is a case in point. Although following the appearance of *Pity* she pursued it, seriously, briefly, she soon let the matter drop and she did not return to it following the appearance of *Executioner* despite the fact that the simultaneous or at least adjacent publication of the second volume of the trilogy and a collection of short stories is what Harcourt, Brace had in mind. Like a single edition of all three volumes of the trilogy, which never happened, the

publication of a collection of short stories could conceivably have made a difference to her reputation. Her personal relationships with her editors also appear to have been strangely sparse. Since a good deal of the relevant correspondence is not available this may in part be an artifact of the archives but the fact that it is missing seems itself significant and the editorial correspondence that does exist suggests an aloofness on her part not usually characteristic of her relationships. Her attitude did change with age. Starting about the time of publication of her final novel, in the late 1940s, through the long years of working on her memoirs, in the 1950s and '60s, she was much more concerned than earlier with the problem of establishing her place in American letters and her relationships with her various editors grew more intense. Her last two editors, Burroughs Mitchell at Scribner's, and Seymour Lawrence at the Atlantic Monthly Press, both became friends. See also Chapters 12, 23, 25, 27, 29, and 30, and related Notes.

143    "The only thing that will save me . . .": JH to MG, June 10, 1933.

143    "one of the few American important . . .": Horace Gregory, *Books*, May 28, 1933, p. 4.

144    "Ever since I can remember . . .": KAP to JH, May 24, 1933.

144    "success story in reverse": Bruce Catton's review appeared in the Huntington, West Virginia, *Advertiser*, June 25, 1933, signed; in the Lexington, Kentucky, *Leader*, June 5, 1933, unsigned; and elsewhere. For further discussion of the trilogy see Chapter 23 and related Notes.

145    "At least once . . .": *PITY*, p. 1.

145    "I believe that the state of caste and classes": *PITY*, p. 338.

145–146    "David Trexler": Josie seems not to have forgiven her Uncle Daniel either for his penuriousness or his pomposity, and her portrait of him in *Executioner* is her revenge. When I asked his daughter whether the representation of her father in the trilogy were not, perhaps, exaggerated, she replied no, if ever there was a perfect model for an American materialist, it was he; and Josie's nephew, Dr. Warren Wells, Frances' son, was also struck by the likeness between her portrayal, particularly of Daniel's household, and his own memories. Conversations, Jennie Fry Walsh, April, 1974, and Warren Wells, February, 1973. In two "David Trexler" stories, "The Top of the Stairs," *The American Mercury*, October, 1933, and "A Very Successful Man," *The American Mercury*, June, 1933, Josie's vision of Daniel is as harsh as it is in *Executioner*, but by the time she was writing *Magicians*, thirty years later, it had considerably softened.

146–151    The most important source for understanding the role of the Communist Party in the farm agitation of the 1930s is also the most recent — *Red Harvest: The Communist Party and American Farmers*, Lowell K. Dyson, University of Nebraska Press, 1982. Another invaluable source is an article, "The Communist Party and the Midwest Farm Crisis of 1933," by John L. Shover, *Journal of American History*, No. 51, September, 1964. Shover is also the author of a book on the farm crisis, *Cornbelt Rebellion*, University of Illinois Press, 1965. A pamphlet about Hal Ware by Lement Harris, *Harold M. Ware (1890–1935) Agricultural Pioneer, U.S.A. and U.S.S.R.*, American Institute for Marxist Studies, 1978, is also helpful, as is the autobiography of Mother Bloor, *We Are Many*, International Publishers, New York, 1940. None of these sources discusses what is generally referred to as the "Ware group" of employees of the Agriculture Department during the New Deal — presumably because, in the words of Dyson, "they seem to have had no connection with the Communist farm movement." Dyson, *Red Harvest*, p. 228, note 39. I have also had the benefit of conversation (November, 1974) and subsequent correspondence about Hal Ware with Jessica Smith, Hal Ware's third wife, who was married to him during the period in question. For further discussion, see Chapters 17 and 26 and related Notes.

147    "shy and retiring," "muted": Both Dyson, *Red Harvest*, p. 3, and Shover,

"Communist Party," p. 251, use the phrase "shy and retiring" in describing Hal Ware. The word "muted" comes from the Lement Harris pamphlet cited above, p. 69. The *Harper's* article, "Planning for Permanent Poverty: What Subsistence Farming Really Stands For," co-authored by Ware and Josie's subsequent traveling companion Webster Powell, appeared in April, 1935.

149     "the people at Appelbachsville . . .": JH to John Herrmann, October 8, no year, *TEX*.

149     "The trouble with us . . .": JH to KAP, October 3, 1933, *MD*.

150     "My head gets foggy . . .": JH to KAP, August 16, 1934, *MD*.

150     Josie's article for Mencken, "Iowa Takes to Literature," appeared in *The American Mercury*, April, 1926.

150     "The Farmers Form a United Front" and the Bliven correspondence, published under the title "The New Republic vs. the Farmer," appeared in the first weekly issue of *New Masses*, January 2, 1934.

151     "was failing miserably . . .": Dyson, *Red Harvest*, pp. 118–119.

## Chapter 17. *"The Most Unhappy Woman Alive"*

152–158     The reconstructions in this chapter are based on original materials in the Josephine Herbst archive at Yale or related materials collected by EL during the course of this work: e.g., FBI and other government records concerning Josephine Herbst obtained under the Freedom of Information Act (*FOIA*). Of these, the most important as far as the Communist underground is concerned are the 1934 letters from John Herrmann to Josephine Herbst. These are open to other scholars who may wish to make their own interpretations, and the related materials will eventually also be housed at Yale. Another important source is the archive concerning the Hiss case currently maintained by the Harvard Law School Library (Alger Hiss Files, or *AHF*), and I am grateful to both Allen Weinstein and George Eddy for sharing material from these files with me. Conversations with Ruth Herrmann in August 1974 and subsequent conversation and correspondence were invaluable. See also Chapters 16, 26, and related Notes.

153     Much later Josie and Marion Greenwood became almost friends, and Charles Fenn, a photographer to whom Marion was married for some years, took the jacket photo for Josie's 1941 novel, *Satan's Sergeants*.

153     Apropos her "longstanding suspicion": "Between us, probably the dive into the hotbed of radical communism not so good for the arts," Josie wrote KAP from Mexico. "I think I shall have to be a fellow traveler all my days so far as my work goes, no matter what my sympathies are, because I need to express so much more than they (the communists) would ever feel, at this moment anyhow, important." JH to KAP, February 27, 1933, *EL*.

154     "3:30 AM": JH to John Herrmann, n.d., *TEX*. There is a possibility that this note was written at a slightly earlier point in the decline of the marriage, but if it was, there was remarkable continuity of feeling.

155     "Neither an orator nor a glad-hander": Dyson, *Red Harvest*, p. 135.

155     "Was invited to the Soviet . . .": John Herrmann to JH, December 15, 1934.

156     "vainglorious": JH to William Reuben, November 6, 1968. On the question of the function of the Communist underground in 1934, Josie's impressions are supported by Whittaker Chambers who says in *Witness* (Random House, 1952) that "while the Ware group was not primarily a Marxist study group, neither was it an espionage group," p. 343. Its "historical importance," he maintains, is as "the root" from which later espionage activities sprang, p. 347. As far as the structure of authority is concerned, any organization that would place erratic newcomer Chambers over reliable old-timer Ware perhaps deserves the results, but that is what does appear to have been done. Considering the fact that their associations — particularly with the *New Masses* and with Maxim Lieber — overlapped, it is surprising that Josie had

Page

never met Whittaker Chambers before his incarnation as "Karl," but my years of investigation have not turned up the slightest suggestion in Josie's papers that she had. Her accounts, e.g., to Hiss' lawyers (Chapter 26) appear to be wholly truthful on this point.

158    "I told him . . .": John Herrmann to JH, September 19, 1934.
159–160  For Josie's criticisms of the Communist Party and John's defense, see their autumn, 1934, correspondence, passim. A *Scribner's* article, "The Farmer Looks Ahead," which appeared in February, 1935, was the major product of Josie's journey.
160    "instantly," etc.: Conversation, Ruth Herrmann, August, 1974. Not only on political, but also on personal matters, Ruth Herrmann's recollections have been invaluable and I am extremely grateful to her for her generous cooperation with this project.
160    "Chart of John": John Herrmann to JH, "Wednesday."
161    "one of the few major novelists": Horace Gregory, *Books*, October 28, 1934; "the best novel I have read in years . . .": William Carlos Williams to JH, "Thanksgiving morning, 1934." *The Nation* review, by Lionel Abel, appeared October 31, 1934, and Josie's reply, November 21, 1934.


## Chapter 18. Empty Mailbox

163–179  "Havana, 1935": In addition to Josie's own notes and articles, the basic sources for this chapter are *Cuba: The Making of a Revolution* by Ramon Eduardo Ruiz, Norton edition, 1970, and *Cuba 1933: Prologue to Revolution* by Luis E. Aguilar, Norton edition, 1974.
163    "Diplomacy, as I interpret it . . .": quoted in Aguilar, *Cuba 1933*, p. 223.
165    "O god": JH notes.
166–171  Letters from JH to John Herrmann, passim. Many of these particular letters were never mailed but were retained in Josie's own files. According to Ruth Herrmann they are no different from the ones she mailed. The political material is drawn from JH notes, passim.
173    "Sugarcane administrators . . .": JH draft article, "The Testimony of Cuba against the United States," p. 7.
173    "Coffee and bananas patchwork . . .": JH, "The Soviet in Cuba," *New Masses*, March 19, 1935, p. 9.
173    "electricity": ibid.
173    " 'Realengo 18' is a country . . .": ibid.
173    "In August 1934 . . .": ibid., p. 10.
174    "Talk is fine . . .": ibid., p. 11.
175    "chummy": ibid., p. 10.
175    "Two women showing each other . . .": ibid., p. 10.
176    The remaining articles in Josie's Cuba series were "Cuba — Sick for Freedom," *New Masses*, April 2, 1935, pp. 17–18; and "A Passport from Realengo 18," July 16, 1935, pp. 11–12. A short story, "The Enemy," juxtaposing the personal situation of a female journalist with the political situation, appeared in *Partisan Review* in October, 1936. The final novel of the trilogy, *Rope of Gold*, also contains a long section about Cuba.
177    "I just found one of the envelopes . . .": JH to John Herrmann, "From Josy on her birthday."
177    "My impression is that B is ready . . .": JH notes, March 8, 1935.
178    "A big bomb . . .": JH notes, passim.
178–179  Major sources for this discussion of John's later years are conversations with Ruth Herrmann, who always emphasized their common alcoholism; with Josie's niece Betty Hansen Davis, who also turned over to me a file of letters she herself had elicited from his friends in attempting to establish the ownership of the Erwinna house (*EL*); and a modest correspondence between JH and John himself over the years, usually arising from his various attempts to

get the house back. The amount of personal information contained in the government's political files about John is also substantial, *FOIA, EL.*

179   "She had not known . . .": *ROPE,* p. 202.

PART VI. TEARING PAST STATIONS

## Chapter 19. *Floating Feather*

183   "It's wrong to be a feather": JH to John Herrmann, n.d.
184–185 For this discussion of the American Writers' Congress, I have drawn on the indispensable *Writers on the Left,* by Daniel Aaron, Oxford ed., 1977, pp. 283–292; *The Dream of the Golden Mountain,* by Malcolm Cowley, pp. 269–275; and *James T. Farrell: The Revolutionary Socialist Years,* by Alan M. Wald, New York University Press, 1978, passim, as well as on Farrell's novel, *Yet Other Waters,* Vanguard, 1952, esp. pp. 93–131. Farrell's position at the time of the Congress is described by Wald, p. 31.
185   Tillie Olsen, Meridel Le Sueur, and Rebecca Pitts all shared with me their recollections of Josie at the Writers' Congress.
186   Willie Münzenberg is discussed by David Caute in *The Fellow Travelers: A Postscript to the Enlightenment,* Macmillan, 1973, passim. His visit to the U.S. in 1934 is described in Cowley, *Dream,* 232–240.
186   Josie described her contact with Hede Massing in an interview with Alger Hiss' lawyers, January 8, 1949, *AHF.*

## Chapter 20. *"The Italian Front Isn't the Hardest . . ."*

189   "Josephine Herbst arrived . . .": KAP to Caroline Gordon, July 12, 1935, *MD.*
190   "Dearest Katherine Anne . . .": JH to KAP, July 21, 1935, *MD.* The "gallantry under pressure" is Josie's misquotation — Hemingway said "grace."
191–193 All quotations are from "Behind the Swastika," passim, *New York Post,* 1935.
194   "precious": JH to James Farrell, n.d., 7 Rue Cels, Paris (XIV) France, *PENN.* The majority of Josie's letters to James T. Farrell are in the Rare Book Collection, Van Pelt Library, University of Pennsylvania, the location cited above, but in more than the usual number of cases, including this one, her own copies of these letters are at the Beinecke. I am grateful to Cleo Paturis, Neda Westlake, and particularly to Farrell's literary executor, Edgar Branch, for generous cooperation on many points involving the Farrell letters.
194   "My very voice changed": ibid.
194   "making me continually long": ibid. A fictional version of the garden party episode occurs in her 1947 novel, *Somewhere the Tempest Fell,* pp. 180–183.
194   "How *is* Italy?": JH notes.
194   "Giotto having been . . .": JH to James Farrell, n.d., 7 Rue Cels, Paris (XIV) France.
195   "with dead John's ghost": JH to John Herrmann, n.d.
196   Three of Josie's published accounts of Barbusse's funeral are "Farewell and a Promise to Barbusse," *New Masses,* October 1, 1935; an insert in *ROPE,* p. 357; and a section in *ROAD,* pp. 90–91; and she frequently recalled it to her friends.

## Chapter 21. *"Custer's Last Stand"*

198   "the kids": Malcolm Cowley, *Dream,* p. 281.
198   "Politics is about swamping literature . . .": JH to KAP, October 18, 1936, *MD.*

Page
198    Josie's files at Yale contain both sides of her correspondence with William Phillips, as well as notes for a story about Phillips, probably written in the 1940s, called "No Hero to His Valet."

199    "the only way the ring . . .": James T. Farrell to JH, January 28, 1936.

199    "Stumbling, Stumbling": James T. Farrell to JH, December 22, 1935.

199    "Lay Down and Die": Wald, *James T. Farrell: Revolutionary Socialist Years*, p. 34. Wald's book on Farrell is an extremely valuable contribution to understanding the 1930s.

199    "anti-intellectualism," "fascist": the phrase "anti-intellectualism" in reference to Gold appears in both Josie's original letter, supplied to me by Farrell, *EL*, and the March 10, 1936, *New Masses* version, but "fascist" appears only in the original.

199    "loved," "punch": James Farrell to JH, February 17, 1936.

199    "emasculated," "out-maneuvered . . .": James Farrell to JH, March 18, 1936. "Out-maneuvered" appears in quotes in Farrell's letter.

199    "Stalinism": Conversation with James Farrell, October, 1977. Wald, *James T. Farrell: Revolutionary Socialist Years*, follows Farrell's interpretation very closely on this point.

199    "amazed that you can think it possible": JH to James Farrell, March 15, 1936, *PENN*.

199    "outwitted": JH to James Farrell, March 19, 1936, *PENN*.

199    "I was persuaded . . .": JH to Edgar Branch, February 4, 1957.

200    "I am inclined to agree," "I have no business," "I don't know politics": JH to James Farrell, March 19, 1936, *PENN*.

200    "Came back from the marble strike": JH to William Phillips, n.d.

201    "Dear Miss (name of writer)": December 7, 1935, cover letter to JH, December 3, 1935.

202    "I am dead set against . . .": JH to Margaret Cowl, December 8, 1935.

204    "It seems to me altogether a wrong": ibid.

204    "I am trying to get out": JH to William Phillips, n.d.

204    "our work," "our movement": JH to Margaret Cowl, op. cit.

205    "to look the ogre in the face": JH to KAP, October 18, 1936, *MD*.

205    I am grateful to Eleanor Clark for sharing her recollections of the summer of 1936 in Erwinna with me (conversation, August, 1974) and to Betty Hansen Davis and John Cheever for other conversations about the period.

206    "Josie came back for Thanksgiving, and it was pleasant. It's true she has an awful voice, and its no good trying to deny it, she has a very underbred nature. . . ," reads Katherine Anne Porter's outburst to Gene. "Her road manners, the way she screams at other drivers, because she is a stupid driver herself, her real, immediate reactions of envy and hatred toward almost anyone who has the slightest good fortune or talent or beauty, her positive lack of any generosity. . . . I keep determinedly not noticing, but in the end one has the feeling of being with a servant girl who has managed by some freak of will and imagination, to lift herself to a plane above herself, but is not always able to stay there. This only to you, darling. It cannot be escaped. I have known her for years, and I never said this, or even let myself admit it, until now. If you had her in the kitchen, she would cheat and steal and break crockery to show you she was as good as you were, until you'd have to fire her and then would find the silver gone. . . . And she is not really of degenerate origin. It is that I can't understand. Dishonesty is entirely without caste, it takes various forms according to the opportunity, that is all, I believe. But her really *bad manners* — they are in her blood and bones, and *low* bad manners, not the high sort. There is a caste in manners, both in the good and bad kind. You can tell as much about the breeding of a person from his rudenesses, as from his courtesies." [. . .'s in the original]. KAP to Gene Pressly, November 28, 1936. *MD*.

## Chapter 22. Song of Spain

Page

210 "There were two . . .": Alvah Bessie, *Men in Battle,* quoted in Gabriel Jackson, *The Spanish Republic and the Civil War, 1931–1939,* Princeton, paperback edition, 1967, p. 337.

210 "about the Spain that is living": JH to Elizabeth Ames, March 13, 1937, *YADDO.*

210 "put iron into me": JH to Ilsa Barea, August 26, 1963.

210 "Don't expect an analysis": *STARCHED,* pp. 77–78.

211 "Ask Hem to explain . . .": JH, Spanish journal.

214 "Sometimes I wondered about Pauline . . .": *HOUR,* p. 39.

214–215 "Can't make it," "Hem good guy," "Is it sour grapes": JH, Spanish journal, passim.

215 "A man about to die . . .": JH unpublished ms. fragment, "Lost Image."

215 "The good Russia had arrived . . .": Gustav Regler, *The Owl of Minerva,* Farrar, Straus and Cudahy, 1959, p. 275.

217 "One night driving out . . .": *STARCHED,* pp. 106–108.

218 "The real Brüderschaft . . .": JH, Spanish journal.

219 "the women responded . . .": Dr. William Pike to EL, February 25, 1980. *EL.* In his letter Dr. Pike described many of the same incidents described by Josie in *STARCHED,* although he had never read it, and added others, e.g., this portrait of Josie and Hemingway at the Hotel Florida. "Herb Klein, a movie producer, and other writers who occupied [the] front rooms [most subjected to shelling] had decided to find other quieter quarters," he wrote. "Ernest Hemingway, whose rooms fronted on a quiet side street, led a movement to prevent such an exodus. It would be running away from the enemy, capitulating to the fascists! One day J, H., & I were descending from J's rooms. Klein entered the elevator on a lower floor. His entrance was like a red flag to H. who immediately began to insult him, called him a coward, refused to listen to his explanations, jostled him and finally 'I'd like to flatten your fat Jewish nose' . . . J. stepped between them. Quietly, tactfully, she calmed H. and the charged atmosphere dissipated. H. respected her for her honesty, integrity and calm, her lack of pretensions. A kind of dignity accompanied her, he told me. He, this generous man, could be cruelly critical even of his friends. Dos Passos, failing in health, was a 'Head-Twitcher,' Vincent Sheehan, 'a rummy' . . . Never did he criticize J. . . ."

219 "She risked her life . . .": Helen Seldes to EL, September 1, 1976, *EL.*

219 "One recollection . . .": John Tisa to EL, October 29, 1974, *EL.*

219 "Shall always remember how human . . .": John Dos Passos to JH, *The Fourteenth Chronicle: Letters of John Dos Passos,* ed. by Townsend Ludington, Gambit, 1973, p. 524.

219 "The men of the International Column . . .": JH to Harry Bloom, June 22, 1937.

219 "I imagine the Spaniards . . .": JH to Will Watson, August 2, 1967, *WW.* I am grateful to both Will Watson, whose unpublished ms., coauthored with Barton Whaley, "The Spanish Earth of Dos Passos and Hemingway," elicited an intense correspondence with Josie in 1967, and to Dos Passos' biographer, Townsend Ludington, two other aficionados of the Robles case, for sharing information and ideas with me, but with no evidence about what happened to Robles and conflicting evidence about what happened to Dos Passos, it appears that not only the principals but also their successors are doomed to make little headway with it. For Ludington's account, see *John Dos Passos: A Twentieth Century Odyssey,* pp. 371–372 and passim.

220 "The general impression . . .": John Dos Passos in *The New Republic,* July, 1939, *Fourteenth Chronicle,* ed. Ludington, p. 528.

221 "Dos Passos was worrying . . .": *STARCHED,* p. 93.

222 "with a little coffee cup": ibid., p. 99.

223 "When I heard his name . . .": ibid., p. 108.

223      *"Quotes.* Don't believe": JH, Spanish journal.

223      "pinpoint the decline . . .": "Spain's Agony: A Period of Exposure," *The Nation*, July 25, 1966, p. 91. Quite unlike her memoirs in tone, this article represents Josie's most concrete attempt to wrestle with the political issues generated by the war.

224      "a simple townsman . . .": *STARCHED*, pp. 116–117. The original incident appears also in the Spanish journal.

224      "I think we stayed three days . . .": George Orwell, *Homage to Catalonia*, 1952 Harvest ed., pp. 229–230.

225      "I am of the opinion . . .": JH to Will Watson, August 2, 1967, *WW*.

## Chapter 23. Tearing past Stations

226      The drawings are at Yale.

227      "I would like to be able to question . . .": JH to Granville Hicks, September 21, 1937. The Communists claimed that documents had been found linking the POUM to Franco. This letter to Hicks and her April 5, 1938, letter to KAP (pp. 232–233) are virtually the only references I have found in Josie's letters to the Soviet purges. In charting her withdrawal from active political involvement later she herself always gave more prominence to other factors. The absence of discussion of the purges in any of her published writing is another component of the presumption of "Stalinism" which was laid against her by Farrell and others in later years.

228      "I have — and for the last fifteen years I have had — more affection, tenderness, and respect for you than for anyone of our time, of our generation. Perhaps the dedication in my last book proves it," reads the letter from Nathan Asch. "But I am sorry — and in the company of all your friends I have to bear it — for the fact that you never can get back to work without sitting down at your machine and telling off somebody. Much love, Nathan." His 1937 book, *The Road*, published a few months earlier, was dedicated "To Josephine Herbst." See also Chapter 13, Notes to p. 110.

228      "[I] have been so terrified . . .": JH to KAP, August 10, 1937, *MD*.

228      "[It] is a bad society . . .": ibid.

228      "How little control . . .": JH to Elizabeth Ames, September 21, 1937, *YADDO*.

229      "Former Sioux City Girl . . .": Sioux City *Tribune*, April 4, 1938, *TB*.

229–230 Mangione's account of the "Spanish Road" episode is in *An Ethnic at Large*, Putnam's, pp. 231–234, passim. I am indebted to Mangione for further correspondence on this and other points. For an authoritative account of the Federal Writers' Project, see his *The Dream and the Deal: The Federal Writers' Project, 1935–1943*, Little, Brown, 1972.

231      "LEAGUE IN SUCCESSFUL . . .": "The Living Newspaper," March 22, 1938.

231      "Idiots!": ibid.

231      "I wish that we could keep from yelling . . .": JH to Granville Hicks, September 21, 1937.

232      "Maybe my morality is becoming sectarian . . ." and related phrases: William Phillips to JH, November 5, 1937. The issue of the "theft" of the *Partisan Review* was long-lasting. "From 1934 to 1936, PR was the literary magazine of the MOVEMENT, deliberately created to carry on the LITERARY tradition of the NM, which was now absorbed in politics because of the fight against fascism," Joe Freeman wrote Josie in 1958.

> The five editors of PR were Michael Gold, Granville Hicks and myself — plus Rahv and Phelps.* All of us were connected with the *New Masses*. I went off in 1934 to write *An American Testament;* . . . Mike

* A name sometimes used by Phillips during this period.

went off to Frisco, I think; Hicks was teaching up state or at Harvard or something; that left Rahv and Phillips to take care of the PR office and to edit the magazine actively as managing editors. . . .

In 1936, when I came back to NY to edit the NM, someone phoned and said that Rahv and Phillips had TAKEN the magazine and turned it over to the Trotzkyites.

"They can't do that", I said. "The magazine is not theirs to turn over to anybody".

How naive I was. The Balzacian era was beginning but I didn't know it. I called our lawyer and wanted to sue for PR. The lawyers advised me against it on the ground that a suit would entitle the lawyer for the other side to ask all sorts of questions which had nothing to do with the case but which we had to avoid — such as, Where and how was the Abraham Lincoln Battalion organised and how did you get the boys into Spain. So we let Rahv and Phelps keep the magazine they had literally stolen from our group and our movement.

For some years PR remained the organ of another group and another movement. Then it became only a literary magazine and the personal property of Rahv and Phillips. I never made an issue of this and, when I had been out of everything for years, I even tried to help them raise money — the cause this time being literature.

After a separation of 15 years, Rahv and I met, became reconciled; he invited me to dinner. There he said, "Bill and I are the only people in the whole history of the Comintern who had the courage to take a magazine away from Joe Stalin".

But this time I was not as naive as I used to be. I understood that R. had to mask his theft of the magazine, his *stalinist* usurpation of it, in lofty political terms.

"Don't boast", I told him. "You only took it away from Joe Freeman. . . ." — Joe Freeman to JH, August 4, 1958.

Josie was not particularly close to Freeman in either the '20s or the '30s but, during the 1950s, drawn together in part by mutual involvement in Albert Rhys Williams' attempt to write a memoir of the Russian revolution and in part by similarities in their political outlooks, they became close friends. Freeman was influential in helping Josie obtain a fellowship at the Newberry Library in 1958.

232    "I am up writing . . .": JH to KAP, April 5, 1938, *MD*.
233    "Yes you are right . . .": KAP to JH, April 8, 1938.
234    "I can't believe . . .": JH to KAP, June 15, 1938, *MD*.
234    "I think Partisan": JH to KAP, April 5, 1938, *MD*.
234    "Let us get the Partisan . . .": KAP to JH, April 8, 1938.
235    "I continue to think . . .": JH to KAP, June 15, 1938, *MD*.
236–237  All quotations are from *ROPE*, passim.
238    "I hardly get a single . . .": JH to KAP, August 6, 1938, *MD*.
238    "I would have made . . .": JH to KAP, December 6, 1938, *MD*.
239    "I have only two hands . . .": JH to KAP, August 6, 1938, *MD*.
239    "I got so sick . . .": JH to KAP, December 6, 1938, *MD*.
239    "You don't write . . .": JH to Will Watson, July 25, 1967, *WW*.
240    "rushing to and fro . . .": Philip Rahv, "A Variety of Fiction," *Partisan Review*, Spring, 1939, p. 110.
240    "I agree with you . . .": JH to Dwight Macdonald, June 6, 1939.
240    "sweeping," "ambitious": Harvey Swados, ed., *The American Writer and the Great Depression*, Bobbs-Merrill, 1966, p. 103. Another exception to the general neglect of the trilogy has been Walter Rideout. See his sympathetic remarks in *The Radical Novel in the United States*, Hill and Wang, 1956, passim, and his recent "Forgotten Images of the Thirties: Josephine Herbst" in *The Literary Review*, Fall, 1983. Rideout also supervised a perceptive dis-

sertation, "Josephine Herbst: A Critical Introduction," by Dion Kempthorne, University of Wisconsin, 1973. Two other recent dissertations are "The Evolution of Form in the Works of Josephine Herbst," by John Gourlie, New York University, 1975, and "The Novels of Josephine Herbst," by Winifred Farrant Bevilacqua, University of Iowa, 1977.

241     JH political correspondence, passim.

241     "We are not only . . .": JH, "The Ruins of Memory," *The Nation*, April 14, 1956, p. 303.

### PART VII. IT IS REPORTED

## Chapter 24. Measuring Sticks

245–246    "The War began . . .": JH wartime notes.

247     "Escaped fire there . . .": July 19, 1937, letter from Joe Pass to JH, note on bottom. There is no way of knowing on what date the note was actually written.

247     "The wilderness . . .": JH personal Bible, *EL*.

248     "She understands . . .": Ralph Thompson, "Books of the Times," *The New York Times*, May 6, 1941.

248     Josie's stay with Mary Heaton Vorse is memorialized in the fictionalized portrait "A Summer with Yorick," *Tomorrow*, June, 1949.

248     "migratory listening post": JH wartime notes, January 4, 1942.

248     "state of untotalitarian confusion": *New Republic* editorial, "A Job for Elmer Davis," June 22, 1942. For additional discussion of the politics of the information agencies during the war, see John Morton Blum, *V Was for Victory: Politics and American Culture During World War II*, Harvest/HBJ, 1977, passim.

249     "Feel every day . . .": JH wartime journal, March 9, 1942. The precise date on which Josie actually began work cannot be established, but it was between February 8 and March 9, 1942.

249     "There was a great deal of speculation . . .": Robert Sherwood testimony at Civil Service Commission hearing for Julia Older, July 22, 1942. I am indebted to Julia Older Bazer, the OCI employee fired with Josie in 1942, for sharing her recollections and her files with me. (Older was eventually reinstated.) In a note to J. Edgar Hoover, Colonel Donovan attributed the firing to "reasons which we feel are adequate" but did not specify what the reasons were. William Donovan to J. Edgar Hoover, May 20, 1942, *FOIA*. Donovan's note refers to the firing as already having taken place, but in fact it did not occur till the next day.

249     "As to the serious charge . . .": Robert Sherwood, ibid.

250     "national character," "a good writer . . . ," "Women's Club heartily. . . ," "the [Yaddo] Colony was very proud. . . ," "from her record. . . ," "if she ever belonged . . .": *FOIA*, passim. The report that Josie was a "national character in the Communist Party," taken from the field investigation, also appears in a May 23, 1942, memorandum from E. W. Timm to D. M. Ladd of the FBI.

251–254   The identification of Katherine Anne Porter as the author of the interview with the FBI is derived as follows. Item: FBI report 77-841 MM at Albany, New York, 5/12/42, states "At Saratoga Springs, New York: [excised] Yaddo Artists' Colony advised that KATHERINE ANNE PORTER was not presently residing at the Colony, but could be reached before the 15th of June at 303 Hill Street, Reno, Nevada." The reference on the interview printed on pp. 251–254 is to a report originating at Albany on the May 12, 1942, date. Item: In a letter to the Director of the FBI dated May 24, 1942, concerning the Herbst investigation Special Agent In Charge Jay C. Newman, of the Salt Lake City Bureau, writes, "The information obtained from [excised] was of a derogatory nature and she requested that her name not be mentioned in this

matter. She was, therefore, carried as a confidential informant in the report
. . . mentioned above." The date of the report "mentioned above" is given as
May 23, 1942, the date of the report of the interview, and Newman also cites
again the May 12, 1942, reference. Because of a typographical defect, the
"May 16" date on the report can be read as "May 10" but magnification es-
tablishes May 16 as the correct date. Item: the internal character of the interview supports the identification, resting as it does on many times and
places Josie and Katherine Anne were together, e.g., Connecticut and Paris,
and this is supported also by the list of amplifications referred to in the text
and printed below.

## CONFIDENTIAL INFORMANT

Confidential Informant #1 is [excised] better known as
[excised]. The letters referred to in the report written by
HERBST from 1930 to 1935 were written to [excised].

The statement of HERBST that BROWDER was too
timid . . . etc., was made by the former directly to [ex-
cised].

HERBST'S meeting with ARAGON in Paris is known by
[excised] since HERBST [excised] in Paris at that time.
HERBST originally made arrangements to meet ARAGON
at [excised]. This was the arrangement described by ARA-
GON as "indiscrete."

The nature of ARAGON'S rebuff was related by
HERBST directly to [EXCISED].

HERBST attempted to obtain entrance into America for
German Communists through [excised] in 1935. [Excised]
then was the [excised] the American Ambassador to
France.

HERBST'S statement concerning her interest in causing
bloodshed and prolonging strikes, etc. was made directly to
[excised] at the latter's home in New York immediately
prior to HERBST'S departure to Detroit.

[Excised] stated that HERBST had published a magazine
story containing the statement regarding voting the communist ticket as appears in the report.

Finally, Katherine Anne's presence in Reno during that period is confirmed in
the biography *Katherine Anne Porter: A Life*, by Joan Givner, Simon and
Schuster, 1982, pp. 325–326. Katherine Anne's charges against Josie remained
on file and one in particular surfaced in almost identical language at the time
of Josie's passport case twelve years later. See Notes to Chapter 27, for p. 294.
*FOIA*, passim.

255    "I remember too much . . .": JH to Rebecca Pitts, June 1, 1946, *RP.*

255    "Our feeling for each other . . .": JH notebook, 1941, "At Murray Hill Hotel,"
n.d.

256    "horrified": KAP to JH, December 28, 1943. "When I read about the Com-
munist-hunt in Washington, I remember that you were one of the early vic-
tims. You know I don't like Communists, the American brand. But I hate to
my bootsoles the Fascists who are doing so successfully just what Hitler did:
using the popular fear of Communism to cover the trail of his intentions, giving the people an enemy to distract their minds from the worse and real
enemy in their own country. . . ," reads another letter from Katherine Anne to
Josie, July 20, 1947 — the last letter from Katherine Anne Josie ever received.

257    "I am reported": "Josephine Herbst Tells Why She Was Fired from the
COI," *PM*, June 17, 1942.

257    "Interlocutors": *ROAD*, p. 91.

*Page*

257    "I have [done] little really . . .": "Notes from memory of interview with Mr. Cannon and Mr. Klein," p. 8. Josie dated her notes June 12 but the correct date was probably June 11.

257    "Somehow this has to be brought . . .": ibid., p. 7.

258    "The measuring stick": ibid.

258    "peremptory methods": COI protest, May 23, 1942. The *PM* article on Josie, one of a series, was headlined "Guards Ousted Liberal Writer" and carried a subheading "COI Worker Interrupted While Writing Boast That America Has No Gestapo," June 15, 1942. The *New Republic* article, a TRB column, was titled "America's Gestapo," June 15, 1942.

258    "extraordinary": Eleanor Roosevelt to Attorney General Biddle, June 17, 1942, *FOIA.*

259    "I am not interested in trying . . .": JH to Robert Sherwood, June 29, 1942. Her official letter of clearance was dated July 29, 1942.

259    For Josie's stay in Chicago I am indebted for conversations to Dorothy Farrell and to Alden Bland, who was then a student in her writing class and whose early novel, *Behold the Cry,* about black life in the north, she later helped persuade Maxwell Perkins at Scribner's to publish. The Chicago household which forms the backdrop for Josie's final novel, *Somewhere the Tempest Fell,* is Dorothy Farrell's.

260    "D-Day came early . . .": Wartime journal.

## Chapter 25. *"Somewhere the Tempest Fell . . ."*

262    "I am almost pathologically fearful . . .": JH to Rebecca Pitts, April 13, 1945. Josie's correspondence with Rebecca Pitts is a particularly valuable archive for the postwar period and I am indebted to Rebecca Pitts for making it available to me.

262    "When you say that all of us . . .": JH to RP, August 6, 1946, *EL.*

262    "why there are the autumn leaves . . .": JH to KAP, August 17, 1946, *MD.*

263    "If the dangling ends . . .": Diana Trilling, "Fiction in Review," *The Nation,* December 13, 1947, p. 653.

264    Josie reported Mitchell's account of Perkins' reaction to *Somewhere the Tempest Fell* in a letter to Clair Laning, n.d., "Wednesday, Erwinna," probably July 1947. From 1938 until his death in 1965 Clair Laning was one of Josie's principal confidants at least on relatively impersonal matters. He is discussed in Mangione's *The Dream and the Deal,* passim.

264    "The question is . . .": Richard Sullivan, "Three Novels Shadowed by Mars," *The New York Times, November* 23, 1947. The extensive discussion by Howard Mumford Jones, "The Fallacy of 'Advanced' Fiction," appeared in the *Saturday Review of Literature,* February 28, 1948.

264    "I ask you . . .": JH to Clair Laning, n.d.

264    "There is a mysterious silence . . .": JH to KAP, January 8, 1648 (misdated 1947), *MD.*

265    "I found a lot of your old letters . . .": KAP to JH, August 16, 1946.

265    "When I heard Berlin . . .": KAP to JH, April 29, 1945.

265    "national maledictions": JH to KAP, May 5, 1945, *MD.*

266    "It reads so persuasively . . .": JH to KAP, January 8, 1948, *MD.* Katherine Anne's article on Stein, "The Wooden Umbrella," first appeared in *Harper's* in late 1947, and is reprinted in *The Collected Essays and Occasional Writings of Katherine Anne Porter,* Delta ed., p. 256. Josie's "Miss Porter and Miss Stein" appeared in *Partisan Review,* May, 1948. In a note granting me permission to use her letters, Katherine Anne wrote, "Josie resented and dropped our friendship on account of my Wooden Umbrella piece about Gertrude Stein — I was never angry with Josie about anything. I know awful things about her life and her difficult nature," she said, but she did not wish to talk with me about them. "My days are more numbered than usual," was her explanation. KAP to EL, March, 1974, *EL.* Katherine Anne Porter died in 1980.

*Page*
267      "I told you so . . .": Gustav Regler to JH, "Saturday 21."
267      "I am no son . . .": Gustav Regler to JH, June, 1948. I am grateful to Peggy Regler for both correspondence and conversation.

## Chapter 26. Witness

268–269  Conversations with Ruth Herrmann, August, 1974, and conversations and correspondence subsequently, passim. Her impression that the Herbst papers had been "garnisheed," was, of course, mistaken. For further discussion of sources and acknowledgments see also Chapter 17 and related Notes.
269      "I did not know Herman . . .": Alger Hiss to EL, July 15, 1974, *EL.*
271      "So you knew Carl!!": Ann Blankenhorn to JH, "Labor Day," 1948.
271      "There was one rather ambiguous . . .": John Davis to Alger Hiss, November 22, 1948, *AHF.*
272      "I am very sympathetic . . .": "Paraphrase of Interview with Miss Josephine Herbst on Jan. 7, 1949." Hiss-Personal-2395, *AHF.* The date of the report itself is January 8, 1949.
272      "I do not recognize . . .": ibid.
272      "Miss Herbst can perhaps best . . .": ibid.
273      Chambers may have referred to John obliquely in *Witness.* In a very odd passage discussing the reluctance of any of the members of what he called the Ware group to support his testimony about it, he says, "I have reason to believe that there is still another witness with a first-hand knowledge of the Group. At least, like Hamlet, I see a cherub who sees one." John may be the cherub. Whittaker Chambers, *Witness,* Random House, 1952, p. 347. Chambers' discussions of John appear throughout his FBI interviews, *FOIA,* passim.
273–274  The first FBI report of its interview with Josie is dated February 8, 1949, *FOIA.*
274      Josie's letter to John is dated "Feb. 6." According to Ruth, when it reached them in Mexico, both she and John found it "transparent." (It is Josie's own copy of this letter that is at the Beinecke.)
274      The FBI's designation of Josie as "cooperative" in her first interview appears on a message from J. Edgar Hoover to field agents dated November 3, 1949, ordering that she be interviewed again, *FOIA.*
274      "My own impression . . .": "Interview with Josephine Herbst on April 10, 1949," dictated by Hiss attorney Harold Rosenwald, Hiss-Personal-2395, *AHF.*
274      "JOSEPHINE FREY HERBST . . .": FBI report of second interview with Josie, November 18, 1949, *FOIA.*
275      "John was the big person . . .": JH to Dorothy Teel, April 21, 1959.
275      "Anything you have stumbled on . . .": Conversation, Jessica Smith, New York, November, 1974.
276      "I think the Hiss case . . .": JH to Clair Laning, July 8, 1949.

## Chapter 27. Blow, Bugle, Blow

277      "In case of what is . . .": Will, October 17, 1950. Josie's friendship with John Cheever was not particularly intimate but it was comfortable and enduring and seems always to have had the kind of family feeling about it suggested by her bequest. Cheever went with Josie to the Washington wedding of her niece Betty Hansen to Hampton Davis in 1938 (along with Nathan Asch), and after Cheever himself married, in 1941, and had a family, Josie also became a friend of his wife, Mary, and was a frequent visitor to their Ossining home. Her letters to Cheever no longer exist.
278      " 'We are now men among men . . .' ": "In Memory," Jean Garrigue, *Studies for an Actress,* Collier, 1973.
278      "you wore that cap," "that dress," etc.: JH–Jean Garrigue, passim. The majority of Josie's letters to Jean are now in the Berg Collection of the New York

*Page*

Public Library. I am grateful to Jean Garrigue's executors, Leslie Katz and
Aileen Ward, for permission to study these papers prior to their deposit.

279    "Let us always be gay . . .": JH to JG, July 3, 1950, *BERG.*

279    "She told me I talked . . .": JH journal, 1951.

279–281    "The waxy flowers . . .": ibid.

282    "The very air . . .": Conversation, Leslie Katz, December, 1979.

282    "They were always on stage . . .": Conversation, Jane Mayhall, December,
1979.

283    "All balls": JH to KAP, March 10, 1947, *MD.*

284    "Dear little Crocodile . . .": JH to Marion Greenwood. See Chapter 15, pp.
136–137.

283–284    "stuck to her painting . . .": JH, "Hunter of Doves," *Botteghe Oscure*, Spring,
1954, p. 340. All Josie's writing about West has the same post facto quality as
"Hunter of Doves." The evidence remaining from the actual years of their
friendship — 1932–1940 — is very slim. John Cheever, who saw them together about 1936, thought that both literarily and temperamentally their affinities were profound — "Pep West is the one man Josie could have made it
with; she loved him," Cheever told me in 1974 — but apart from the indirect
testimony of Josie's continuing devotion to West's work, there is little conventional biographical support for Cheever's idea. In an interview with
West's biographer Jay Martin in 1966 Josie recalled her discomfort with
West's recurring fantasy of an island in the Pacific to which he would deport
all "misfits." "One of his major characters was a horrible great big lesbian —
he went into detail about her. Everytime he talked about lesbians or homosex-
uals I was scared," Josie said. I am grateful to Jay Martin for sharing his interview tapes with me. In addition to "Hunter," Josie wrote a critical essay on
West, "Nathanael West," which appeared in *Kenyon Review*, Fall, 1961.
Other than the fact that she was working on "Hunter" at the same time she
was writing the biography of the Bartrams, why Josie should have named
West "Bartram" in the novella is not really clear, but perhaps she was trying
to suggest — though largely to herself — that West, too, was an explorer of
sorts.

285    The record for the maximum number of inaccuracies about Josie and John
appearing in any one place goes to William Carlos Williams in his *Autobiography*, pp. 269–271. He attributes the story of John's "The Big Short Trip" to
*What Happens*, claims that Josie and John met at a dance hall in New York,
explains carefully that John met his next wife in New Orleans, and caps it all
off by saying quite untruly "I have never been able to praise as I should
like to, Jo's devoted work. But to Jo herself I constantly have my hat off."
See p. 161 for a brief quotation from a long, enthusiastic letter about *The
Executioner Waits* he wrote her in 1934. Despite her irritation over the *Autobiography*, their relations remained cordial. Williams quoted one of Josie's
letters in Book Five of *Paterson*, New Directions, 12th printing, pp. 209–210.
Josie was repeatedly surprised at the masculine prejudices of some of
her friends. "[Sherwood] Anderson's world and in fact the world of letters
seems so prevailing [sic] male that it is really astonishing to me," she wrote
Alfred Kazin in 1958 when she was reading the correspondence between Joe
Freeman and Floyd Dell at the Newberry Library. "It is so male that a man
like Edmund Wilson writing to Floyd Dell can be astonished to discover
how vivid Edna St. Vincent Millay's letters are, and to marvel that 'a contemporary woman writer' could write without cattiness and show such varied and profound interests in ideas and art." JH to Alfred Kazin, April 17,
1958. Josie's friendship with Alfred Kazin was among the most important of
her later years.

285    "more noted for toadying . . .": *New Green World*, p. 56.

286    "Bartram placed his reliance . . .": ibid., p. 93.

286    "who wanted first to *see* . . .": ibid.

286    "*New Green World* was written . . .": JH to reader, April 25, 1965.

286    "Be sure to destroy . . .": JH to JG, March 19, 1952, *BERG.*

*Page*
287     "lifelong friend": JH, FBI interview, February 8, 1949. I am grateful, once again, to Julia Older Bazer, for help in disentangling the two "Robert" Coes. Julia Bazer to EL, April 29 and May 7, 1980, *EL.*

288     "The charges against me . . .": JH to Gerhard Van Arkel, June 12, 1952. This was not the only case that Josie found "fantastic." "I think one thing that impressed me very much was Eleanor's [Clark] news that Lowell has actually been taken into custody in Chicago as an insane case," she wrote Elizabeth Ames of Yaddo about the political charges being made against Yaddo by Robert Lowell because of the long residence there of Agnes Smedley. "I don't wish ill of anyone, not even of a mortal enemy, but what impressed me about this final clue is that the world is so mad today that an insane person and his ravings are taken seriously and not even seen by disjointed individuals as the insanity they actually are." JH to Elizabeth Ames, April 10, 1949, *YADDO.* Despite the fact that they are often linked together as radical-women-writers, Josie does not seem ever to have met Agnes Smedley.

288     "The Washington thing . . .": JH to JG, June 10, 1952, *BERG.*

288     "H held himself ready . . .": JH to Clair Laning, July 22, 1953.

289     "Have you ever . . .": *Mind of Your Own,* pamphlet. I am grateful to Harvey and Jessie O'Connor and to a number of Jessie's recent assistants, particularly David Green, for providing me with a copy of this pamphlet as well as with copies of Josie's letters.

289     "I am as much . . .": JH to Gerhard Van Arkel, July 24, 1954.

290     Josie's passport refusal is dated August 14, 1951. The FOIA files also contain another uncontested refusal dated June 13, 1942 — after her government firing but before her clearance — suggesting that she had considered going abroad during the war, but had not pursued it. *FOIA* passim. See also Chapter 24 and related Notes.

290–294  I am extremely grateful to the poet in question for discussing these matters with me.

292     "—— can come . . .": JH to JG, March 31, 1953, *BERG.*

292     "I cannot be named . . .": ibid.

292     "It is no pleasure . . .": JH to JG, July 6, 1953.

292     "I *will* have trips . . .": JH to JG, September 8, 1953, *BERG.* The "thee" is an affectation that entered Josie's vocabulary with Jean, and there were others, but for the most part Jean's influence on Josie's writing was probably to the good. There is a good deal of continuity between Josie's earlier and her later writing, and what direction she might have taken simply by a process of natural maturing is impossible to know, but many people who knew them both think that Jean's contribution to the evolution of Josie's style was considerable. "It seems to me that the changes that occurred in Josie's literary style in her later writing, especially in the memoirs, probably had something to do with the influence — never acknowledged as far as I know — of Jean and *her* literary tastes," speculates Josie's literary executor, Hilton Kramer. "Rilke, for example, is not a writer Josie would be likely to have paid much attention to if not for Jean. Impatient and even intolerant as Josie often was of Jean's aestheticism, I think she nonetheless absorbed something from it — something she would have been incapable of absorbing in the thirties. I believe it made a difference in her work." Hilton Kramer to EL, July 25, 1983, *EL.* See Chapters 29 and 30 for a discussion of Josie's memoirs.

292     "You will go . . .": JH to JG, September 8, 1953, "Sunday night."

293     "Long ago I shuffled . . .": JH 1953 journal, a journal that was also intended as a letter to Jean.

294     "It is the practice . . .": R. B. Shipley to JH, June 28, 1954, *FOIA.* When Van Arkel did extract the charges from the Passport Office, one of them was "That you had written (time and place not specified) that 'With a group of Bucks County farmers, we went right down near where Washington crossed the Delaware and voted the straight Communist ticket' " — straight out of the FBI's 1942 interview with Katherine Anne Porter. The reference was to

Josie's contribution to an April 1936 *Partisan Review* symposium on "Marxism and the American Tradition" titled "What is Americanism?" but in the dozen years between Katherine Anne's interview and Josie's passport refusal, no one had taken the trouble to look it up. She supplied the citation herself — and explained her position — in her affidavit. Gerhard Van Arkel to JH, July 22, 1954.

294    "I have not been a professional ...": JH to Gerhard Van Arkel, July 24, 1954.

295    "Nothing that she ever did or said ...": John Cheever, affidavit, November 9, 1954, *FOIA*.

295    "I should have felt exhilarated ...": JH to Jessie O'Connor, March 8, 1955, *J.O'C.*

295–296    "a marvelous happy dream ...": JH to JG, January 19, 1953, *BERG*.

PART VIII. YESTERDAY'S ROAD

## *Chapter 28. Animal Hotel*

301    "past was more complicated ...": Jean Garrigue, *Animal Hotel*, Eakins Press, 1966, p. 9 — an edition dedicated to Josie and published by Leslie Katz. Parts of it had appeared ten years earlier in *New World Writing*, No. 10. Jean also wrote three memorial poems to Josie, published after she herself was dead in *Studies for an Actress*, Collier, 1973: "In Memory," "Requiem" and "For J."

302    "The birds would sit ...": Jean Garrigue, *Animal Hotel*, p. 8.

303    "She made one feel ...": Jane Mayhall to EL, February 1, 1980, *EL*.

303    "For Josie, literature ...": John Cheever, conversation, December, 1974.

303    "Incomparable ...": Alfred Kazin, "Josephine Herbst," memorial eulogy, *New York Review of Books*, March 27, 1969.

303    "I can't get anything out of merely social occasions and to have visitors come — pleasant, kind, good but just the same, in a deep sense, distant from any real me, and then to go — I don't know how to pull myself together — I am just so unstrung I cannot bear it" — a typical complaint from Josie to Jean, this one October 12, 1965, *BERG*.

## *Chapter 29. Yesterday's Road*

305–306    *DISGRACE*, passim. Josie's memoirs have received little scholarly attention, undoubtedly because few scholars are aware of them, but those who are have been unreservedly complimentary. See particularly Warren L. Susman, "The Thirties," in Stanley Coben and Lorman Ratner, eds., *The Development of an American Culture*, Prentice-Hall, 1970, who calls them "brilliant." "Miss Herbst's memoirs promise to be one of the classic accounts of the intellectual life of the 1920s and the 1930s," Susman said, p. 179.

308    "How could I have known ...": *DISGRACE*, p. 160.

308    "Don't get me wrong ...": *ROAD*, p. 103.

308    "Unite and fight ...": *STARCHED*, p. 115.

308    "But where was Brecht ...": *ROAD*, p. 101.

308    "She made a little island ...": *PITY*, p. 3.

309    "Hem would [not] quibble ...": JH to Burroughs Mitchell, October 2, 1959.

309    "I read your piece immediately ...": Saul Bellow to JH, September 5, 1959.

310    "The Jews have a formula ...": Saul Bellow to JH, n.d.

310    "Botsford in meeting me ...": JH to JG, January 13, 1961, *BERG*.

310    "Let me tell you ...": JH to Saul Bellow, May 28, 1965, Saul Bellow Papers, Department of Special Collections, University of Chicago Library.

*Page*

311    "How simple it would have been ...": JG to JH, January 24, 1958, *BERG*.

312    "the most sour ...": Theodore Solotaroff, "Ship of Fools and the Critics," in *Katherine Anne Porter: A Collection of Critical Essays*, ed. by Robert Penn Warren, Prentice-Hall, 1979, p. 142.

312    "I never saw a bunch ...": JH to Alfred Kazin, April 18, 1962, *BERG*. I am grateful to Alfred Kazin for lending me his entire collection of letters from Josie prior to their deposit at the New York Public Library.

314    "to let each impression ...": This and other phrases from Rilke appear in Josie's *Nation* essay, "The Ruins of Memory," April 14, 1956, p. 304.

314    "This has been a wonderful time ...": JH to JG, April 29, 1962, *BERG*.

315    "I can only really ...": JH to Jane Mayhall, n.d., *JM*.

317    "I no longer wrote ...": *ROAD*, p. 89.

317    "11 COMMUNIST LEADERS ...": Doris Lessing, *The Golden Notebook*, Ballantine ed., 1968, p. 247. Josie's omission of such issues from her memoirs was very striking to her friends such as Hilton Kramer, who heard her discuss them privately many times. It extended the issue of "Stalinism" from her own generation into another.

000    "You will have to see the Lessing ...": JH to JG, February 18, 1963, *BERG*. See Notes, Chapter 27, for p. 285, for Josie's attitude toward some of her male friends' memoirs.

## Chapter 30. A Time of Exposure

319    Josie reported Hilton Kramer's appreciation of her manuscript in the summer of 1963 in a letter to Seymour Lawrence, October 8, 1963. *AT. MONTHLY PRESS*.

320    "You are the one person ...": JH to JG, October 1, 1963, *BERG*.

320    "I wondered who I was ...": JH to JG, September 14, 1963, *BERG*.

320    "It is odd ...": JH to JG, September 21, 1963, *BERG*.

320    "I have little luck ...": JH to JG, October 1, 1963, *BERG*.

320    "The Negroes have made ...": JH to Stanley Burnshaw, August 29, 1963.

320    "there was injustice only ...": Berthold Brecht, "To Our Successors," Willet translation. I am indebted to Virginia Gardner Marberry for copies of Josie's late political correspondence and for calling my attention to Josie's attraction to this poem.

321    "Go to the demonstration ...": Conversation, Neal and Mary Daniels, September, 1975.

321    "Just where do you think ...": JH to JG, May 25, 1968, *BERG*.

322    "Today [the Paris students]": ibid.

322    "You mention my 'happy possession ...' ": JH to Alfred Kazin, September 11, 1966, *BERG*.

322    Josie's citation from the National Institute of Arts and Letters, May 25, 1966, reads "To JOSEPHINE HERBST, born in Sioux City, Iowa, in 1897, whose novels written in the 1930's speak to us now, in simple and rare veracity, beyond the fashions of that decade, or of ours, and whose later work, not in fiction, testifies to the same spirit and the same devoted skills." It was written by Robert Penn Warren. Josie was nominated for an award from the institute as early as 1949 and ten times thereafter. Lillian Hellman, Marianne Moore, and Conrad Aiken were some of her other supporters. In conversation in Boston in December 1974 John Cheever attributed most of the credit for the ultimate success of the campaign to Warren; his own view that Josie's conversation and influence on literature, as well as her books, qualified her for the award, Cheever said, had never been widely shared. According to the records of the American Academy and Institute of Arts and Letters, if Cheever had gotten a Rome fellowship in 1956, Josie would have gotten the regular award then, for she was chosen as an alternate recipient to Cheever in that year, but "Cheever did not go to Rome and he got the award, and Herbst had to wait

another ten years for her award." Nancy Johnson to EL, September 1, 1983, *EL.* I am grateful to Nancy Johnson of the American Academy and Institute of Arts and Letters for her research.

322     "I have been damaged . . .": JH to JG, June 30, 1965, *BERG.*

323     "I can't say I didn't enjoy . . .": JH to Alfred Kazin, September 11, 1966, *BERG.*

323     "What's it all about?": *MAGICIANS,* p. 10.

324     "I keep revising . . .": JH to Peter Davison, March 31, 1967, *AT. MONTHLY PRESS.*

324     "The first thing to say . . .": Hilton Kramer to JH, August 22, 1968.

324     "exquisite": Alfred Kazin's comment is reported by Josie in a letter to Peter Davison, August 26, 1968, *AT. MONTHLY PRESS.*

325     These observations about Josie were made to me in conversation by Stanley Burnshaw, summer, 1973, and Justin Kaplan, winter, 1983. I am especially grateful to Stanley Burnshaw for the complex view of Josie he insisted on from the beginning. The National Book Award jury of which Josie was a member awarded the fiction prize to that archenemy of Mike Gold in the 1930s, Thornton Wilder, for his *The Eighth Day.*

327     "Her hands still felt . . .": *ROPE,* p. 406.

328     "I seem to have pitched . . .": JH to Jessie O'Connor, November 13, 1968, *J.O'C.*

328     Conversations with Betty Davis form an important part of the backdrop for this section, as for many others.

328     "I . . . know that you are in bad straits . . .": JG to JH, November 18, 1968, *BERG.*

## Chapter 31. "Tell My Friends . . ."

329–331     I am grateful to very many of Josie's friends for sharing with me their memories of her days in the hospital, and particularly to her doctor, Constance Friess. A story by Jane Mayhall about Josie's death, "Hilda and Mildred," appeared in the *Colorado Quarterly,* Summer, 1977.

329     "very wild carcinoma . . .": JH records, New York Hospital, January, 1969, passim.

329     "There was someone's . . .": *MAGICIANS,* p. 6.

330     See Notes to Chapter 9, for pp. 77–78, for an account of Josie's description of her mother's death.

331     "I am just slowly drowning . . . ," and following notes: JH New York Hospital records, passim, "Patient reliving her life . . .": ibid., "Tell my friends. . . ," ibid., January 25, 1969. She died on January 28. Josie's memorial service was held on February 18, 1969. Her ashes are in a family plot at the Graceland Cemetery in Sioux City. In 1976 Betty Davis had a simple marker placed on her grave.

# Acknowledgments

~~~~~~~~~~~~~~~~~~~~~~~~~~~~~~~~~~~~~~~~~~~~~~~~~~~~~~~~~~~~~~~~

ONE OF MY happiest pastimes during the long years of preparation of this book has been imagining how to thank the very many people who have been involved in it. Having a drink with so and so I finally understood such and such, I would remember. Going over this subject with that person for the dozenth time, I finally understood that. Now that the moment has come I find that to truly acknowledge all the help I have been given is impossible, for to explain the precise role of any one person in contributing to the portrait of Josephine Herbst that finally materialized would require unraveling the whole. So I have left them all together: those who gave me their time and those who gave me material support; those in whose company I first understood an idea or an issue and those who, criticizing the manuscript later, tore my understanding apart; those who contributed to the resolution of innumerable scholarly fine points and those whose contributions were of the heart. In many cases there is further detail in the Notes. But there is a small group of people whose support for this effort has been so central right from the beginning that they simply will not go on a list: Josie's niece, Betty Davis; my editor, Peter Davison; Josie's friends Alfred Kazin, Jane Mayhall, and Leslie Katz; and above all, her friend and literary executor, Hilton Kramer. If there was anything any one of these people was ever unwilling to do for this project, I never found out what it was. In a place by himself is my husband, Martin Zwick, who shared with me the burden of the whole.

| | | |
|---|---|---|
| Daniel Aaron | Carlos Baker | Alden Bland |
| Cyrilly Abels | Ellen Bassuk, M.D. | Ralph Bogardus |
| Ruth Allen | Isabel Bayley | Georges Borchardt |
| American Academy and | Julia Older Bazer | Edgar Branch |
|   Institute of Arts and | Robert Beare | D. J. R. Bruckner |
|   Letters | Saul Bellow | Gordon Brumm |
| Gilda Anderson | Andrew Bernhard | Mary Ingraham Bunting |
| Nancy Andrews | Avery Bernhard |   Institute, Radcliffe |
| Atlantic Monthly Press | Winifred Bevilacqua |   College |

## ACKNOWLEDGMENTS

Leda Burnshaw
Stanley Burnshaw
John Cheever
Mary Cheever
Eleanor Clark
Grace Clark
Michelle Clark
Betty Anne Clarke
Clara Coffey
Sylvan Cole
Gardner Cowles
Malcolm Cowley
Mary Daniels
Neal Daniels
Hampton Davis
Kenneth Davis
George Eddy
Jim Egleson
David Farmer
Dorothy Farrell
James Farrell
Marge Frantz
Constance Friess, M.D.
Donald Gallup
John Giess
Todd Gitlin
Joan Givner
Bill Gordon
Linda Gordon
John Gourlie
David Green
Natalie Greenberg
John Simon Guggenheim
    Memorial Foundation
Philip Hamburger
Hexi Hamerstein
Harcourt, Brace
Curtis Harnack
Ruth Herrmann
Minnie Hickman
Granville Hicks

Nitza Hidalgo
Irving Howe
Patricia Howell
Elisabeth Humez
Estelle Jelinek
Nancy Johnson
Justin Kaplan
Dion Kempthorne
Esta Kramer
Stanley Kunitz
Ann Langer
Sydney Langer
Meridel LeSueur
Rick Levy
Maxim Lieber
Denver Lindley
Mary Lloyd
Mary Norris Lloyd
William Bross Lloyd
Lee Lowenfish
Townsend Ludington
MacDowell Colony
Jerre Mangione
Virginia Gardner Mar-
    berry
Jay Martin
Carey McWilliams
Dorothy Miller
Burroughs Mitchell
Jessica Mitford
National Endowment for
    the Arts
Helen North
Harvey O'Connor
Jessie O'Connor
Tillie Olsen
Oregon Arts Founda-
    tion
Cleo Paturis
William Phillips
William Pike, M.D.

Rebecca Pitts
Robert Plate
Elizabeth Pollet
Katherine Anne Porter
Rabinowitz Founda-
    tion
Renée Ralph
Ann Reeve
Peggy Regler
Walter Rideout
Deborah Robboy
Gretchen Rogovin
Howard Rogovin
Muriel Rukeyser
David Schoonover
George Seldes
Helen Seldes
Alfred S. Shivers
Mary Jane Simpson
Ben Sonnenberg
Jessica Smith
Wendy Speight
Janet Stevenson
Jean Strouse
Helen Gould Tierney
John Tisa
Loudon Wainwright
Jennie Fry Walsh
Alan Wald
Aileen Ward
Robert Penn Warren
Harriet Wasserman
Will Watson
Allen Weinstein
Jim Wells
Warren Wells
Neda Westlake
Anne Whelpley
Rhea Wilson
Yaddo
Arthur Zipser

365

# Index